Tom

Much Love at

Christmas 2017

Mum/x

THE PHILOSOPHY BOOK

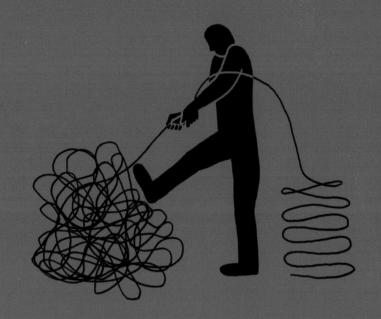

THE PHILOSOPHY BOOK

**LONDON, NEW YORK, MELBOURNE,
MUNICH, AND DELHI**

DK LONDON

PROJECT ART EDITOR
Anna Hall

SENIOR EDITOR
Sam Atkinson

EDITORS
Cecile Landau, Andrew Szudek,
Sarah Tomley

EDITORIAL ASSISTANT
Manisha Majithia

MANAGING ART EDITOR
Karen Self

MANAGING EDITOR
Camilla Hallinan

ART DIRECTOR
Philip Ormerod

ASSOCIATE PUBLISHER
Liz Wheeler

PUBLISHER
Jonathan Metcalf

ILLUSTRATIONS
James Graham

PICTURE RESEARCH
Ria Jones, Myriam Megharbi

PRODUCTION EDITOR
Luca Frassinetti

PRODUCTION CONTROLLER
Sophie Argyris

DK DELHI

PROJECT ART EDITOR
Neerja Rawat

ART EDITOR
Shriya Parameswaran

ASSISTANT ART EDITORS
Showmik Chakraborty, Devan Das,
Niyati Gosain, Akanksha Gupta,
Neha Sharma

MANAGING ART EDITOR
Arunesh Talapatra

HEAD OF PUBLISHING
OPERATIONS
Aparna Sharma

PRODUCTION MANAGER
Pankaj Sharma

DTP MANAGER/CTS
Balwant Singh

DTP DESIGNERS
Bimlesh Tiwary, Mohammad Usman

DTP OPERATOR
Neeraj Bhatia

styling by
STUDIO8 DESIGN

First published in Great Britain in
2011 by Dorling Kindersley Limited,
80 Strand, London, WC2R 0RL
A Penguin Random House company

20 21 22 23 24 25
086 - 176426 - Feb/2011

A CIP catalogue record for this
book is available from
the British Library.

ISBN: 978-1-4053-5329-8

Printed and bound in China

**Discover more at
www.dk.com**

CONTRIBUTORS

WILL BUCKINGHAM

A philosopher, novelist, and lecturer, Will Buckingham is particularly interested in the interplay of philosophy and narrative. He currently teaches at De Montfort University, Leicester, UK, and has written several books, including *Finding our Sea-Legs: Ethics, Experience and the Ocean of Stories*.

DOUGLAS BURNHAM

A professor of philosophy at Staffordshire University, UK, Douglas Burnham is the author of many books and articles on modern and European philosophy.

CLIVE HILL

A lecturer in political theory and British history, Clive Hill has a particular interest in the role of the intellectual in the modern world.

PETER J. KING

A doctor of philosophy who lectures at Pembroke College, University of Oxford, UK, Peter J. King is the author of the recent book *One Hundred Philosophers: A Guide to the World's Greatest Thinkers*.

JOHN MARENBON

A Fellow of Trinity College, Cambridge, UK, John Marenbon studies and writes on medieval philosophy. His books include *Early Medieval Philosophy 480–1150: An Introduction*.

MARCUS WEEKS

A writer and musician, Marcus Weeks studied philosophy and worked as a teacher before embarking on a career as an author. He has contributed to many books on the arts and popular sciences.

OTHER CONTRIBUTORS

The publishers would also like to thank Richard Osborne, lecturer of philosophy and critical theory at Camberwell College of Arts, UK, for his enthusiasm and assistance in planning this book, and Stephanie Chilman for her help putting the Directory together.

CONTENTS

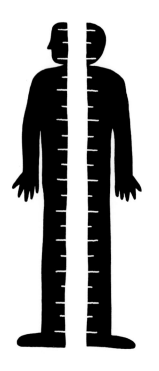

RENAISSANCE AND THE AGE OF REASON
1500–1750

THE AGE OF REVOLUTION
1750–1900

THE MODERN WORLD
1900–1950

CONTEMPORARY PHILOSOPHY
1950—PRESENT

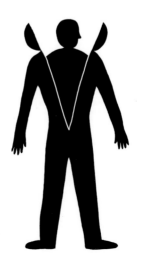

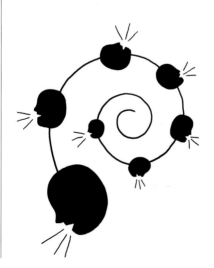

INTRODU

CTION

Philosophy is not just the preserve of brilliant but eccentric thinkers that it is popularly supposed to be. It is what everyone does when they're not busy dealing with their everyday business and get a chance simply to wonder what life and the universe are all about. We human beings are naturally inquisitive creatures, and can't help wondering about the world around us and our place in it. We're also equipped with a powerful intellectual capability, which allows us to reason as well as just wonder. Although we may not realize it, whenever we reason, we're thinking philosophically.

Philosophy is not so much about coming up with the answers to fundamental questions as it is about the process of trying to find these answers, using reasoning rather than accepting without question conventional views or traditional authority. The very first philosophers, in ancient Greece and China, were thinkers who were not satisfied with the established explanations provided by religion and custom, and sought answers which had rational justifications. And, just as we might share our views with friends and colleagues, they discussed their ideas with one another, and even set up

"schools" to teach not just the conclusions they had come to, but the way they had come to them. They encouraged their students to disagree and criticize ideas as a means of refining them and coming up with new and different ones. A popular misconception is that of the solitary philosopher arriving at his conclusions in isolation, but this is actually seldom the case. New ideas emerge through discussion and the examination, analysis, and criticism of other people's ideas.

Debate and dialogue
The archetypical philosopher in this respect was Socrates. He didn't leave any writings, or even

Wonder is very much the affection of a philosopher; for there is no other beginning of philosophy than this.
Plato

any big ideas as the conclusions of his thinking. Indeed, he prided himself on being the wisest of men because he knew he didn't know anything. His legacy lay in the tradition he established of debate and discussion, of questioning the assumptions of other people to gain deeper understanding and elicit fundamental truths. The writings of Socrates' pupil, Plato, are almost invariably in the form of dialogues, with Socrates as a major character. Many later philosophers also adopted the device of dialogues to present their ideas, giving arguments and counter-arguments rather than a simple statement of their reasoning and conclusions.

The philosopher who presents his ideas to the world is liable to be met with comments beginning "Yes, but ..." or "What if ..." rather than wholehearted acceptance. In fact, philosophers have fiercely disagreed with one another about almost every aspect of philosophy. Plato and his pupil Aristotle, for example, held diametrically opposed views on fundamental philosophical questions, and their different approaches have divided opinions among philosophers ever since. This has, in turn, provoked more discussion and prompted yet more fresh ideas.

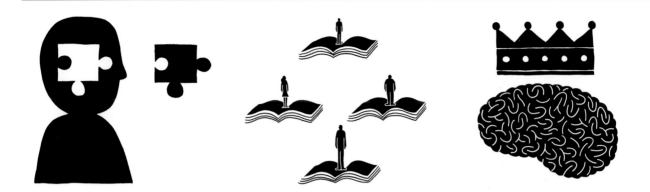

But how can it be that these philosophical questions are still being discussed and debated? Why haven't thinkers come up with definitive answers? What are these "fundamental questions" that philosophers through the ages have wrestled with?

Existence and knowledge

When the first true philosophers appeared in ancient Greece some 2,500 years ago, it was the world around them that inspired their sense of wonder. They saw the Earth and all the different forms of life inhabiting it; the sun, moon, planets, and stars; and natural phenomena such as the weather, earthquakes, and eclipses. They sought explanations for all these things – not the traditional myths and legends about the gods, but something that would satisfy their curiosity and their intellect. The first question that occupied these early philosophers was "What is the universe made of?", which was soon expanded to become the wider question of "What is the nature of whatever it is that exists?"

This is the branch of philosophy we now call metaphysics. Although much of the original question has since been explained by modern science, related questions of metaphysics such as "Why is there something rather than nothing?" are not so simply answered.

Because we, too, exist as a part of the universe, metaphysics also considers the nature of human existence and what it means to be a conscious being. How do we perceive the world around us, and do things exist independently of our perception? What is the relationship between our mind and body, and is there such a thing as an immortal soul? The area of metaphysics concerned with questions of existence, ontology, is a huge one and forms the basis for much of Western philosophy.

Once philosophers had started to put received wisdom to the test of rational examination, another fundamental question became obvious: "How can we know?" The study of the nature and limits of knowledge forms a second main branch of philosophy, epistemology.

At its heart is the question of how we acquire knowledge, how we come to know what we know; is some (or even all) knowledge innate, or do we learn everything from experience? Can we know something from reasoning alone? These questions are vital to philosophical thinking, as we need to be able to rely on our knowledge in order to reason correctly. We also need to determine the scope and limits of our knowledge. Otherwise we cannot be sure that we actually do know what we think we know, and haven't somehow been "tricked" into believing it by our senses.

Logic and language

Reasoning relies on establishing the truth of statements, which can then be used to build up a train of thought leading to a conclusion. This might seem obvious to us now, but the idea of constructing a rational argument distinguished philosophy from the superstitious and religious explanations that had existed before the first philosophers. These thinkers had to devise a way of ensuring their ideas had validity. »

Superstition sets the whole world in flames; philosophy quenches them.
Voltaire

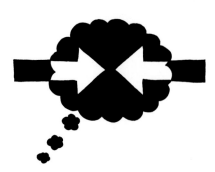

What emerged from their thinking was logic, a technique of reasoning that was gradually refined over time. At first simply a useful tool for analysing whether an argument held water, logic developed rules and conventions, and soon became a field of study in its own right, another branch of the expanding subject of philosophy.

Like so much of philosophy, logic has intimate connections with science, and mathematics in particular. The basic structure of a logical argument, starting from a premise and working through a series of steps to a conclusion, is the same as that of a mathematical proof. It's not surprising then that philosophers have often turned to mathematics for examples of self-evident, incontrovertible truths, nor that many of the greatest thinkers, from Pythagoras to René Descartes and Gottfried Leibniz, were also accomplished mathematicians.

Although logic might seem to be the most exact and "scientific" branch of philosophy, a field where things are either right or wrong, a closer look at the subject shows that it is not so simple. Advances in mathematics in the 19th century called into question the rules of logic that had been laid down by Aristotle, but even in ancient times

Zeno of Elea's famous paradoxes reached absurd conclusions from apparently faultless arguments.

A large part of the problem is that philosophical logic, unlike mathematics, is expressed in words rather than numbers or symbols, and is subject to all the ambiguities and subtleties inherent in language. Constructing a reasoned argument involves using language carefully and accurately, examining our statements and arguments to make sure they mean what we think they mean; and when we study other people's arguments, we have to analyse not only the logical steps they take, but also the language they use, to see if their conclusions hold water. Out of this process came yet another field of philosophy that flourished in the 20th century, the philosophy of language, which examined terms and their meanings.

Morality, art, and politics
Because our language is imprecise, philosophers have attempted to clarify meanings in their search for answers to philosophical questions. The sort of questions that Socrates asked the citizens of Athens tried to get to the bottom of what they actually believed certain concepts to be. He would ask seemingly simple questions such as "What is

justice?" or "What is beauty?" not only to elicit meanings, but also to explore the concepts themselves. In discussions of this sort, Socrates challenged assumptions about the way we live our lives and the things we consider to be important.

The examination of what it means to lead a "good" life, what concepts such as justice and happiness actually mean and how we can achieve them, and how we should behave, forms the basis for the branch of philosophy known as ethics (or moral philosophy); and the related branch stemming from the question of what constitutes beauty and art is known as aesthetics.

O philosophy, life's guide!
O searcher-out of virtue
and expeller of vices!
What could we and every
age of men have been
without thee?
Cicero

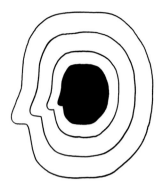

From considering ethical questions about our individual lives, it is a natural step to start thinking about the sort of society we would like to live in – how it should be governed, the rights and responsibilities of its citizens, and so on. Political philosophy, the last of the major branches of philosophy, deals with these ideas, and philosophers have come up with models of how they believe society should be organized, ranging from Plato's *Republic* to Karl Marx's *Communist Manifesto*.

Religion: East and West
The various branches of philosophy are not only interlinked, but overlap considerably, and it is sometimes difficult to say in which area a particular idea falls. Philosophy also encroaches on many completely different subjects, including the sciences, history, and the arts. With its beginnings in questioning the dogmas of religion and superstition, philosophy also examines religion itself, specifically asking questions such as "Does god exist?" and "Do we have an immortal soul?" These are questions that have their roots in metaphysics, but they have implications in ethics too. For example, some philosophers have asked whether our morality comes from god or whether it is a purely

human construct – and this in turn has raised the whole debate as to what extent humanity has free will.

In the Eastern philosophies that evolved in China and India (particularly Daoism and Buddhism) the lines between philosophy and religion are less clear, at least to Western ways of thinking. This marks one of the major differences between Western and Eastern philosophies. Although Eastern philosophies are not generally a result of divine revelation or religious dogma, they are often intricately linked with what we would consider matters of faith. Even though philosophical reasoning is frequently used to justify faith in the Judeo-Christian and Islamic world, faith and belief

There is nothing either good or bad, but thinking makes it so.
William Shakespeare

form an integral part of Eastern philosophy that has no parallel in the West. Eastern and Western philosophy also differ in their starting points. Where the ancient Greeks posed metaphysical questions, the first Chinese philosophers considered these adequately dealt with by religion, and instead concerned themselves with moral and political philosophy.

Following the reasoning
Philosophy has provided us with some of the most important and influential ideas in history. What this book presents is a collection of ideas from the best-known philosophers, encapsulated in well known quotes or pithy summaries of their ideas. Perhaps the best-known quotation in philosophy is Descartes' "cogito, ergo sum" (often translated from the Latin as "I think, therefore I am"). It ranks as one of the most important ideas in the history of philosophy, and is widely considered a turning point in thinking, leading us into the modern era. On its own however, the quotation doesn't mean much. It is the conclusion of a line of argument about the nature of certainty, and only when we examine the reasoning leading to it does the idea begin to make sense. And it's only »

when we see where Descartes took the idea – what the consequences of that conclusion are – that we see its importance.

Many of the ideas in this book may seem puzzling at first glance. Some may appear self-evident, others paradoxical or flying in the face of common sense. They might even appear to prove Bertrand Russell's flippant remark that "the point of philosophy is to start with something so simple as not to seem worth stating, and to end with something so paradoxical that no one will believe it". So why are these ideas important?

Systems of thought
Sometimes the theories presented in this book were the first of their kind to appear in the history of thought. While their conclusions may seem obvious to us now, in hindsight, they were startlingly new in their time, and despite their apparent simplicity, they may make us re-examine things that we take for granted. The theories presented here that seem to be paradoxes and counter-intuitive statements are the ideas that really call into question our assumptions about ourselves and the world – and they also make us think in new ways about how we see things. There are many

ideas here that raise issues that philosophers still puzzle over. Some ideas may relate to other thoughts and theories in different fields of the same philosopher's thinking, or have come from an analysis or criticism of another philosopher's work. These latter ideas form part of a line of reasoning that may extend over several generations or even centuries, or be the central idea of a particular "school" of philosophy.

Many of the great philosophers formed integrated "systems" of philosophy with interconnecting ideas. For example, their opinions about how we acquire knowledge led to a particular metaphysical view of the universe and man's soul. This in turn has implications for what kind of life the philosopher believes we should lead and what type of society would be ideal. And in turn, this entire system of ideas has been the starting point for subsequent philosophers.

We must remember too that these ideas never quite become outdated. They still have much to tell us, even when their conclusions have been proved wrong by subsequent philosophers and scientists. In fact, many ideas that had been dismissed for centuries were later to be proved startlingly

prescient – the theories of the ancient Greek atomists for example. More importantly, these thinkers established the processes of philosophy, ways of thinking and organizing our thoughts. We must remember that these ideas are only a small part of a philosopher's thinking – usually the conclusion to a longer line of reasoning.

Science and society
These ideas spread their influence beyond philosophy too. Some have spawned mainstream scientific, political, or artistic movements. Often the relationship between science and philosophy is a back-and-forth affair, with ideas from one informing the other. Indeed, there is a whole branch of philosophy that studies the thinking behind

Scepticism is the first step towards truth.
Denis Diderot

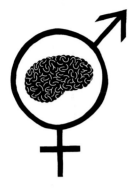

scientific methods and practices. The development of logical thinking affected how maths evolved and became the basis for the scientific method, which relies on systematic observation to explain the world. Ideas about the nature of the self and consciousness have developed into the science of psychology.

The same is true of philosophy's relationship with society. Ethics of all sorts found adherents in political leaders throughout history, shaping the societies we live in today, and even prompting revolutions. The ethical decisions made in all kinds of professions have moral dimensions that are informed by the ideas of the great thinkers of philosophy.

Behind the ideas

The ideas in this book have come from people living in societies and cultures which have shaped those ideas. As we examine the ideas, we get a picture of certain national and regional characteristics, as well as a flavour of the times they lived in.

The philosophers presented here emerge as distinct personalities – some thinkers are optimistic, others pessimistic; some are meticulous and painstaking, others think in broad sweeps; some express themselves in clear, precise language, others in a poetic way,

and still more in dense, abstract language that takes time to unpick. If you read these ideas in the original texts, you will not only agree or disagree with the what they say, and follow the reasoning by which they reached their conclusions, but also get a feeling of what kind of person is behind it. You might, for example, warm to the witty and charming Hume, appreciating his beautifully clear prose, while not altogether feeling at home with what he has to say; or find Schopenhauer both persuasive and a delight to read, while getting the distinct feeling that he was not a particularly likeable man.

Above all these thinkers were (and still are) interesting and stimulating. The best were also great writers too, and reading their original writings can be as rewarding as reading literature; we can appreciate not just their literary style, but also their philosophical style, the way they present their arguments. As well as being thought-provoking, it can be as uplifting as great art, as elegant as a mathematical proof, and as witty as an after-dinner speaker.

Philosophy is not simply about ideas – it's a way of thinking. There are frequently no right or wrong answers, and different philosophers

often come to radically different conclusions in their investigations into questions that science cannot – and religion does not – explain.

Enjoying philosophy

If wonder and curiosity are human attributes, so too are the thrill of exploration and the joy of discovery. We can gain the same sort of "buzz" from philosophy that we might get from physical activity, and the same pleasure that we enjoy from an appreciating the arts. Above all, we gain the satisfaction of arriving at beliefs and ideas that are not handed down or forced upon us by society, teachers, religion, or even philosophers, but through our own individual reasoning. ∎

The beginning of thought is in disagreement – not only with others but also with ourselves.
Eric Hoffer

THE ANC
WORLD
700 BCE—250 CE

ENT

Thales of Miletus, the first known Greek philosopher, seeks **rational answers** to questions about the world we live in.

Traditional date of birth of **Kong Fuzi (Confucius)**, whose philosophy is centred on **respect and tradition.**

Death of **Siddhartha Gautama, the Buddha,** founder of the religion and philosophy of **Buddhism.**

Empedocles proposes his theory of the **four Classical elements**; he is the last Greek philosopher to record his ideas in **verse.**

624–546 BCE   **551** BCE   **480** BCE   c.**460** BCE

569 BCE   **508** BCE   **469** BCE   **404** BCE

Birth of **Pythagoras,** the Greek thinker who combined philosophy and mathematics.

The powerful Greek city-state of Athens adopts a **democratic constitution.**

Birth of **Socrates,** whose **methods of questioning** in Athens formed the basis for much of later Western philosophy.

Defeat in the **Peloponnesian War** leads to the decline of Athens' political power.

From the beginning of human history, people have asked questions about the world and their place within it. For early societies, the answers to the most fundamental questions were found in religion: the actions of the gods explained the workings of the universe, and provided a framework for human civilizations.

Some people, however, found the traditional religious explanations inadequate, and they began to search for answers based on reason rather than convention or religion. This shift marked the birth of philosophy, and the first of the great thinkers that we know of was Thales of Miletus, a Greek settlement in modern-day Turkey. Thales used reason to inquire into the nature of the universe, and encouraged others to do likewise. What he passed on to his followers was not only his answers, but the whole process of thinking rationally, together with an idea of what kind of explanations could be considered satisfactory. For this reason Thales is generally regarded as the first philosopher.

The main concern of the early philosophers centred around Thales' basic question: "What is the world made of?" Their answers form the foundations of scientific thought, and forged a relationship between science and philosophy that still exists today. The work of Pythagoras marked a key turning point, as he sought to explain the world not in terms of some form of primal matter, but in terms of mathematics. He and his followers described the structure of the cosmos in numbers, ratios, and geometry. Although some of these mathematical relationships acquired mystical significance for Pythagoras and his followers, their numerical explanation of the cosmos had a profound influence on the beginnings of scientific thought.

Classical Greek philosophy
As the Greek city-states grew in stature, philosophy spread across the Greek world from Ionia, and in particular to Athens, which was rapidly becoming the cultural centre of Greece. It was here that philosophers broadened the scope of philosophy to include new questions, such as "How do we know what we know?" and "How should we live our lives?" It was an Athenian, Socrates, who ushered in the short but hugely influential period of Classical Greek philosophy. Although he left no writings, his ideas were so important that they steered the

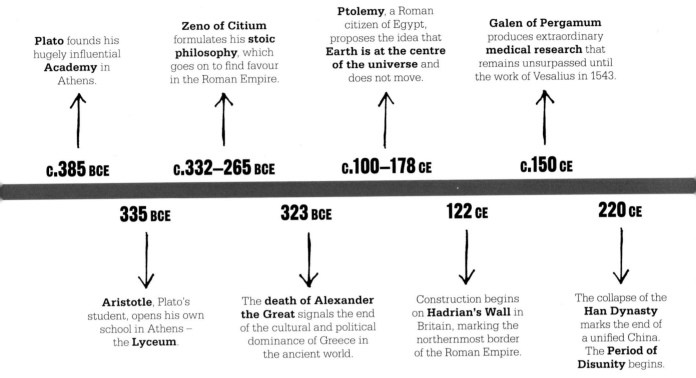

Plato founds his hugely influential **Academy** in Athens.

Zeno of Citium formulates his **stoic philosophy**, which goes on to find favour in the Roman Empire.

Ptolemy, a Roman citizen of Egypt, proposes the idea that **Earth is at the centre of the universe** and does not move.

Galen of Pergamum produces extraordinary **medical research** that remains unsurpassed until the work of Vesalius in 1543.

c.385 BCE

c.332–265 BCE

c.100–178 CE

c.150 CE

335 BCE

323 BCE

122 CE

220 CE

Aristotle, Plato's student, opens his own school in Athens – the **Lyceum**.

The **death of Alexander the Great** signals the end of the cultural and political dominance of Greece in the ancient world.

Construction begins on **Hadrian's Wall** in Britain, marking the northernmost border of the Roman Empire.

The collapse of the **Han Dynasty** marks the end of a unified China. The **Period of Disunity** begins.

future course of philosophy, and all philosophers before him became known as the pre-Socratics. His pupil Plato founded a philosophical school in Athens called the Academy (from which the word "academic" derives) where he taught and developed his master's ideas, passing them on to students such as Aristotle, who was a pupil and teacher there for 20 years. The contrasting ideas and methods of these great thinkers – Socrates, Plato, and Aristotle – form the basis of Western philosophy as we know it today, and their differences of opinion have continued to divide philosophers throughout history.

The Classical period of ancient Greece effectively came to an end with the death of Alexander the Great in 323 BCE. This great leader had unified Greece, and Greek city-states that had worked together

once again became rivals. Following the death of Aristotle in 322 BCE, philosophy also divided into very different schools of thought, as the cynics, sceptics, epicureans, and stoics argued their positions.

Over the next couple of centuries, Greek culture waned as the Roman Empire grew. The Romans had little time for Greek philosophy apart from stoicism, but Greek ideas persisted, mainly because they were preserved in the manuscripts and translations of the Arab world. They resurfaced later, during medieval times, with the rise of Christianity and Islam.

Eastern philosophies
Thinkers throughout Asia were also questioning conventional wisdom. Political upheaval in China from 771 to 481 BCE led to a collection of

philosophies that were less concerned with the nature of the universe than with how best to organize a just society and provide moral guidelines for the individuals within it; in the process examining what constitutes a "good" life. The so-called "Hundred Schools of Thought" flourished in this period, and the most significant of these were Confucianism and Daoism, both of which continued to dominate Chinese philosophy until the 20th century.

To the south of China an equally influential philosopher appeared: Siddhartha Gautama, later known as the Buddha. From his teaching in northern India around 500 BCE, his philosophy spread across the subcontinent and over most of southern Asia, where it is still widely practised. ∎

EVERYTHING IS MADE OF WATER

THALES OF MILETUS (c.624–546 BCE)

IN CONTEXT

BRANCH
Metaphysics

APPROACH
Monism

BEFORE
2500–900 BCE The Minoan civilization in Crete and the later Mycenaean civilization in Greece rely on religion to explain physical phenomena.

c.1100 BCE The Babylonian creation myth, *Enûma Eliš*, describes the primal state of the world as a watery mass.

c.700 BCE *Theogony* by the Greek poet Hesiod relates how the gods created the universe.

AFTER
Early 5th century BCE Empedocles proposes the four basic elements of the cosmos: earth, water, air, and fire.

c.400 BCE Leucippus and Democritus conclude that the cosmos is made up solely of atoms and empty space.

From observation, Thales deduced that specific weather conditions, not appeals to the gods, led to a good harvest. Predicting a high yield of olives one year, he is said to have bought up all the local olive presses, then profited by renting them out to meet increased demand.

During the Archaic period (mid-8th–6th century BCE), the peoples of the Greek peninsula gradually settled into a group of city-states. They developed an alphabetical system of writing, as well as the beginnings of what is now recognized as Western philosophy. Previous civilizations had relied on religion to explain phenomena in the world around them; now a new breed of thinkers emerged, who attempted to find natural, rational explanations.

The first of these new scientific thinkers that we are aware of was Thales of Miletus. Nothing survives of his writings, but we know that he had a good grasp of geometry and astronomy, and is reputed to have predicted the total eclipse of the sun in 585 BCE. This practical turn of mind led him to believe that events in the world were not due to supernatural intervention, but had natural causes that reason and observation would reveal.

Fundamental substance
Thales needed to establish a first principle from which to work, so he posed the question, "What is the basic material of the cosmos?" The idea that everything in the universe can be ultimately reduced to a single substance is the theory of monism, and Thales and his followers were the first to propose it within Western philosophy. Thales reasons that the fundamental

See also: Anaximander 330 ▪ Anaximenes of Miletus 330 ▪ Pythagoras 26–29 ▪ Empedocles 330 ▪ Democritus and Leucippus 45 ▪ Aristotle 56–63

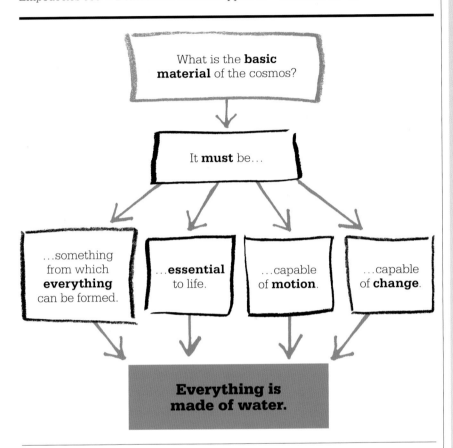

What is the **basic material** of the cosmos?

It **must** be…

…something from which **everything** can be formed.

…**essential** to life.

…capable of **motion**.

…capable of **change**.

Everything is made of water.

Thales of Miletus

Although we know that Thales was born and lived in Miletus, on the coast of what is now Turkey, we know very little about his life. None of his writings, if indeed he left any, have survived. However, his reputation as one of the key early Greek thinkers seems deserved, and he is referred to in some detail by both Aristotle and Diogenes Laertius, the 3rd-century biographer of the ancient Greek philosophers.

Anecdotal evidence suggests that as well as being a philosopher, Thales was actively involved in politics and was a very successful businessman. He is thought to have travelled widely around the eastern Mediterranean, and while visiting Egypt, to have learned the practical geometry that was to become the basis of his deductive reasoning.

However, Thales was above all a teacher, the first of the so-called Milesian School of philosophers. Anaximander, his pupil, expanded his scientific theories, and in turn became a mentor to Anaximenes, who is believed to have taught the young mathematician Pythagoras.

material of the universe had to be something out of which everything else could be formed, as well as being essential to life, and capable of motion and therefore of change. He observes that water is clearly necessary to sustain all forms of life, and that it moves and changes, assuming different forms – from liquid to solid ice and vaporous mist. So Thales concludes that all matter, regardless of its apparent properties, must be water in some stage of transformation.

Thales also notes that every landmass appears to come to an end at the water's edge. From this he deduces that the whole of the earth must be floating on a bed of water, from which it has emerged.

When anything occurs to cause ripples or tremors in this water, Thales states, we experience them as earthquakes.

However, as interesting as the details of Thales' theories are, they are not the main reason why he is considered a major figure in the history of philosophy. His true importance lies in the fact that he was the first known thinker to seek naturalistic, rational answers to fundamental questions, rather than to ascribe objects and events to the whims of capricious gods. By doing so, he and the later philosophers of the Milesian School laid the foundations for future scientific and philosophical thought across the Western world. ■

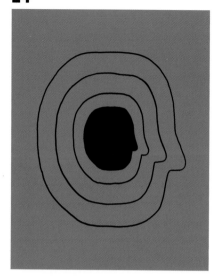

THE DAO THAT CAN BE TOLD IS NOT THE ETERNAL DAO
LAOZI (c.6TH CENTURY BCE)

IN CONTEXT

TRADITION
Chinese philosophy

APPROACH
Daoism

BEFORE
1600–1046 BCE During the Shang Dynasty, people believe fate is controlled by deities and practise ancestor worship.

1045–256 BCE Under the Zhou Dynasty, the Mandate of Heaven (god-given authority) justifies political decisions.

AFTER
5th century BCE Confucius (Kong Fuzi) sets out his rules for personal development and for ethical government.

4th century BCE Philosopher Zhuangzi moves the focus of Daoist teaching more towards the actions of the individual, rather than those of the state.

3rd century CE Scholars Wang Bi and Guo Xiang create a Neo-Daoist school.

In the 6th century BCE, China moved towards a state of internal warfare as the ruling Zhou Dynasty disintegrated. This change bred a new social class of administrators and magistrates within the courts, who occupied themselves with the business of devising strategies for ruling more effectively. The large body of ideas that was produced by these officials became known as the Hundred Schools of Thought.

All this coincided with the emergence of philosophy in Greece, and shared some of its concerns, such as seeking stability in a constantly changing world, and alternatives to what had previously been prescribed by religion. But

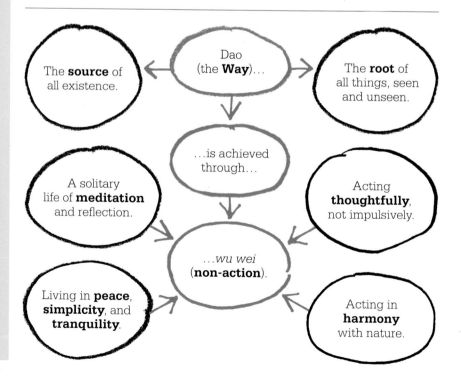

Dao (the **Way**)…

The **source** of all existence.

The **root** of all things, seen and unseen.

…is achieved through…

A solitary life of **meditation** and reflection.

Acting **thoughtfully**, not impulsively.

…*wu wei* (**non-action**).

Living in **peace**, **simplicity**, and **tranquility**.

Acting in **harmony** with nature.

See also: Siddhartha Gautama 30–33 ▪ Confucius 34–39 ▪ Mozi 44 ▪ Wang Bi 331 ▪ Hajime Tanabe 244–45

Chinese philosophy evolved from practical politics and was therefore concerned with morality and ethics rather than the nature of the cosmos.

One of the most important ideas to appear at this time came from the *Daode jing* (*The Way and its Power*), which has been attributed to Laozi (Lao Tzu). It was one of the first attempts to propose a theory of just rule, based on *de* (virtue),

Living in harmony with nature is one path the *Daode jing* prescribes for a well-balanced life. For this man that could mean respecting the ecological balance of the lake and not over-fishing.

which could be found by following *dao* (the Way), and forms the basis of the philosophy known as Daoism.

Cycles of change

In order to understand the concept of *dao*, it is necessary to know how the ancient Chinese viewed the ever-changing world. For them, the changes are cyclical, continually moving from one state to another, such as from night to day, summer to winter, and so on. They saw the different states not as opposites, but as related, one arising from the other. These states also possess complementary properties that together make up a whole. The process of change is seen as an expression of *dao,* and leads to the 10,000 manifestations that make up the world. Laozi, in the *Daode jing*, says that humans are merely one of these 10,000 manifestations and have no special status. But because of our desire and free will, we can stray from the *dao*, and disturb the world's harmonious balance. To live a virtuous life means acting in accordance with the *dao*.

> Knowing others is intelligence; knowing yourself is true wisdom.
> **Laozi**

Following the *dao*, however, is not a simple matter, as the *Daode jing* acknowledges. Philosophizing about *dao* is pointless, as it is beyond anything that humans can conceive of. It is characterized by *wu* ("not-being"), so we can only live according to the *dao* by *wu wei*, literally "non-action". By this Laozi does not mean "not doing", but acting in accordance with nature – spontaneously and intuitively. That in turn entails acting without desire, ambition, or recourse to social conventions. ▪

Laozi

So little is known for certain about the author of the *Daode jing*, who is traditionally assumed to be Laozi (Lao Tzu). He has become an almost mythical figure; it has even been suggested that the book was not by Laozi, but is in fact a compilation of sayings by a number of scholars. What we do know is that there was a scholar born in the state of Chu, with the name Li Er or Lao Tan, during the Zhou dynasty, who became known as Laozi (the Old Master). Several texts indicate that he was an archivist at the Zhou court, and that Confucius consulted him on

rituals and ceremonies. Legend states that Laozi left the court as the Zhou dynasty declined, and journeyed west in search of solitude. As he was about to cross the border, one of the guards recognized him and asked for a record of his wisdom. Laozi wrote the *Daode jing* for him, and then continued on his way, never to be seen again.

Key works

c.6th century BCE
Daode jing (also known as the *Laozi*)

NUMBER IS THE RULER OF FORMS AND IDEAS

PYTHAGORAS (c.570–495 BCE)

IN CONTEXT

BRANCH
Metaphysics

APPROACH
Pythagoreanism

BEFORE
6th century BCE Thales proposes a non-religious explanation of the cosmos.

AFTER
c.535–c.475 BCE Heraclitus dismisses Pythagoreanism and says that the cosmos is governed by change.

c.428 BCE Plato introduces his concept of perfect Forms, which are revealed to the intellect and not the senses.

c.300 BCE Euclid, a Greek mathematician, establishes the principles of geometry.

1619 German mathematician Johannes Kepler describes the relationship between geometry and physical phenomena.

Western philosophy was in its infancy when Pythagoras was born. In Miletus, Greece, a group of philosophers known collectively as the Milesian School had started to seek rational explanations for natural phenomena only a generation or so earlier, marking the beginning of the Western philosophical tradition. Pythagoras spent his childhood not far from Miletus, so it is very likely that he knew of them, and may even have studied in their academy. Like Thales, the founder of the Milesian School, Pythagoras is said to have learnt the rudiments of geometry during a trip to Egypt. With this background, it is not

See also: Thales of Miletus 22–23 ▪ Siddhartha Gautama 30–33 ▪ Heraclitus 40 ▪ Plato 50–55 ▪ René Descartes 116–23

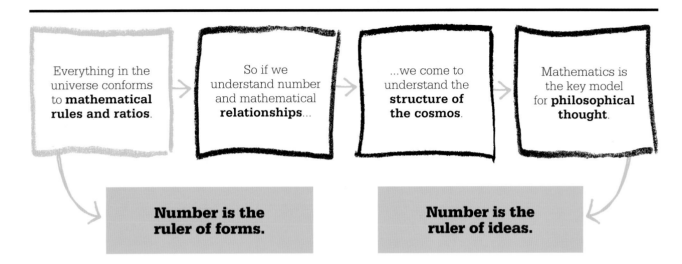

Everything in the universe conforms to **mathematical rules and ratios**.

So if we understand number and mathematical **relationships**...

...we come to understand the **structure of the cosmos**.

Mathematics is the key model for **philosophical thought**.

Number is the ruler of forms.

Number is the ruler of ideas.

surprising that he should approach philosophical thinking in a scientific and mathematical way.

The Pythagorean academy

Pythagoras was also, however, a deeply religious and superstitious man. He believed in reincarnation and the transmigration of souls, and he established a religious cult, with himself cast as a virtual messiah, in Croton, southern Italy. His disciples lived in a collective commune, following strict behavioural and dietary rules, while studying his religious and philosophical theories. The Pythagoreans, as his disciples were known, saw his ideas as mystical revelations, to the extent that some of the discoveries attributed to him as "revelations" may in fact have come from others in the community. His ideas were recorded by his students, who included his wife, Theano of Crotona, and daughters. The two sides of Pythagoras's beliefs – the mystical and the scientific – seem to be irreconcilable, but Pythagoras himself does not see them as contradictory. For him, the goal of life is freedom from the cycle of reincarnation, which can be gained by adhering to a strict set of behavioural rules, and by contemplation, or what we would call objective scientific thinking. In geometry and mathematics he found truths that he regarded »

Pythagoras

Little is known about Pythagoras's life. He left no writings himself, and unfortunately, as the Greek philosopher Porphyry noted in his *Vita Pythagorae*, "No one knows for certain what Pythagoras told his associates, since they observed an unusual silence." However, modern scholars believe that Pythagoras was probably born on the island of Samos, off the coast of modern-day Turkey. As a young man, he travelled widely, perhaps studying at the Milesian School, and probably visiting Egypt, which was a centre of learning. At the age of about 40, he set up a community of around 300 people in Croton, southern Italy. Its members studied a mixture of mystical and academic studies, and despite its collective nature, Pythagoras was clearly the community's leader. At the age of 60, he is said to have married a young girl, Theano of Crotona. Growing hostility towards the Pythagorean cult eventually forced him to leave Croton, and he fled to Metapontum, also in southern Italy, where he died soon after. His community had virtually disappeared by the end of the 4th century BCE.

Pythagoras's Theorem showed that shapes and ratios are governed by principles that can be discovered. This suggested that it might be possible, in time, to work out the structure of the entire cosmos.

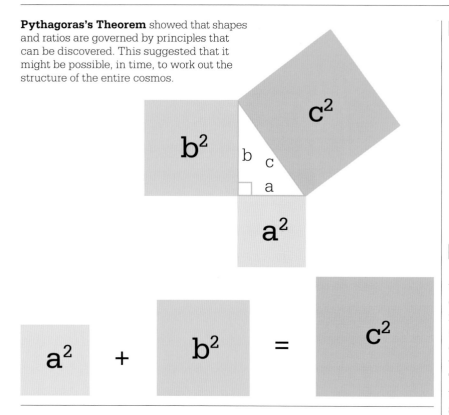

There is geometry in the humming of the strings, there is music in the spacing of the spheres.
Pythagoras

triangular shape made up of rows of dots) had a particular significance in Pythagorean ritual. Less contentiously, they saw the number one as a single point, a unity, from which other things could be derived. The number two, in this way of thinking, was a line, number three a surface or plane, and four a solid; the correspondence with our modern concept of dimensions is obvious.

The Pythagorean explanation of the creation of the universe followed a mathematical pattern: on the Unlimited (the infinite that existed before the universe), God imposed a Limit, so that all that exists came to have an actual size. In this way God created a *measurable* unity from which everything else was formed.

Numerical harmonies

Pythagoras's most important discovery was the relationships between numbers: the ratios and proportions. This was reinforced by his investigations into music, and in particular into the relationships between notes that sounded pleasant together. The story goes that he first stumbled onto this idea when listening to blacksmiths at work. One had an anvil half the size of the other, and the sounds they made when

as self-evident, as if god-given, and worked out mathematical proofs that had the impact of divine revelation.

Because these mathematical discoveries were a product of pure reasoning, Pythagoras believes they are more valuable than mere observations. For example, the Egyptians had discovered that a triangle whose sides have ratios of 3:4:5 always has a right angle, and this was useful in practice, such as in architecture. But Pythagoras uncovered the underlying principle behind all right-angled triangles (that the square of the hypotenuse equals the sum of the squares of the other two sides) and found it to be universally true. This discovery was so extraordinary, and held such potential, that the Pythagoreans took it to be divine revelation.

Pythagoras concludes that the whole cosmos must be governed by mathematical rules. He says

that number (numerical ratios and mathematical axioms) can be used to explain the very structure of the cosmos. He does not totally dismiss the Milesian idea that the universe is made up of one fundamental substance, but he shifts the enquiry from substance to form.

This was such a profound change in the way of looking at the world, that we should probably forgive Pythagoras and his disciples for getting somewhat carried away, and giving numbers a mystical significance. Through exploring the relationship between numbers and geometry, they discoved the square numbers and cube numbers that we speak of today, but they also attributed characteristics to them, such as "good" to the even numbers and "evil" to the odd ones, and even specifics such as "justice" to the number four, and so on. The number ten, in the form of the tetractys (a hit with a hammer were exactly an octave (eight notes) apart. While this may be true, it was probably by experimenting with a plucked string that Pythagoras determined the ratios of the consonant intervals (the number of notes between two notes that determines whether they will sound harmonious if struck together). What he discovered was that these intervals were harmonious because the relationship between them was a precise and simple mathematical ratio. This series, which we now know as the harmonic series, confirmed for him that the elegance of the mathematics he had found in abstract geometry also existed in the natural world.

The stars and elements

Pythagoras had now proved not only that the structure of the universe can be explained in mathemathical terms – "number is the ruler of forms" – but also that acoustics is an exact science, and number governs harmonious proportions. He then started to apply his theories to the whole cosmos, demonstrating the harmonic relationship of the stars, planets, and elements. His idea of harmonic relationships between the stars was eagerly taken up by medieval and Renaissance astronomers, who developed whole theories around the idea of the music of the spheres, and his suggestion that the elements were arranged harmoniously was revisited over 2,000 years after his death. In 1865 English chemist John Newlands discovered that when the chemical elements are arranged according to

Classical architecture follows Pythagorean mathematical ratios. Harmonious shapes and ratios are used throughout, scaled down in the smaller parts, and up for the overall structure.

atomic weight, those with similar properties occur at every eighth element, like notes of music. This discovery became known as the Law of Octaves, and it helped lead to the development of the Periodic Law of chemical elements still used today.

Pythagoras also established the principle of deductive reasoning, which is the step-by-step process of starting with self-evident axioms (such as "2 + 2 = 4") to build towards a new conclusion or fact. Deductive reasoning was later refined by Euclid, and it formed the basis of mathematical thinking into medieval times and beyond.

One of Pythagoras's most important contributions to the development of philosophy was the idea that abstract thinking is superior to the evidence of the senses. This was taken up by Plato in his theory of Forms, and resurfaced in the philosophical method of the rationalists in the 17th century. The Pythagorean attempt to combine the rational with the religious was the first

> Reason is immortal, all else mortal.
> **Pythagoras**

attempt to grapple with a problem that has dogged philosophy and religion in some ways ever since.

Almost everything we know about Pythagoras comes to us from others; even the bare facts of his life are largely conjecture. Yet he has achieved a near-legendary status (which he apparently encouraged) for the ideas attributed to him. Whether or not he was in fact the originator of these ideas does not really matter; what is important is their profound effect on philosophical thought. ■

HAPPY IS HE WHO HAS OVERCOME HIS EGO

SIDDHARTHA GAUTAMA (c.563–483 BCE)

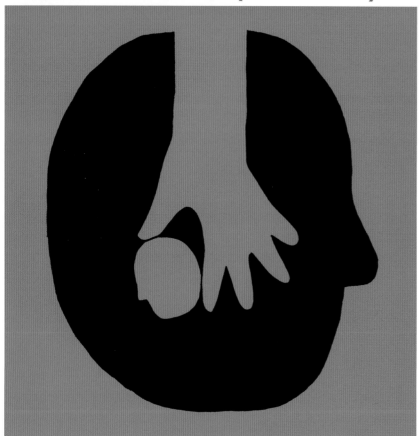

IN CONTEXT

TRADITION
Eastern philosophy

APPROACH
Buddhism

BEFORE
c.1500 BCE Vedism reaches
the Indian subcontinent.

c.10th–5th centuries BCE
Brahmanism replaces
Vedic beliefs.

AFTER
3rd century BCE Buddhism
spreads from the Ganges
valley westwards across India.

1st century BCE The
teachings of Siddhartha
Gautama are written down
for the first time.

1st century CE Buddhism
starts to spread to China
and Southeast Asia. Different
schools of Buddhism begin
to evolve in different areas.

Siddhartha Gautama, later known as the Buddha, "the enlightened one", lived in India during a period when religious and mythological accounts of the world were being questioned. In Greece, thinkers such as Pythagoras were examining the cosmos using reason, and in China, Laozi and Confucius were detaching ethics from religious dogma. Brahmanism, a religion that had evolved from Vedism – an ancient belief based on the sacred Veda texts – was the dominant faith in the Indian subcontinent in the 6th century BCE, and Siddhartha Gautama was the first to challenge its teachings with philosophical reasoning.

See also: Laozi 24–25 ▪ Pythagoras 26–29 ▪ Confucius 34–39 ▪
David Hume 148–53 ▪ Arthur Schopenhauer 186–188 ▪ Hajime Tanabe 244–45

The Four Noble Truths

Suffering is an **inherent part of existence** from birth, through sickness and old age, to death. → The truth of suffering **(Dukkha)**

The cause of suffering is **desire**: craving for sensual pleasures and attachment to worldly possessions and power. → The truth of the origin of suffering **(Samudaya)**

Suffering can be ended by **detaching oneself** from craving and attachment. → The truth of the ending of suffering **(Nirodha)**

The **Eightfold Path** is the means to eliminate desire and overcome the ego. → The truth of the path to the ending of suffering **(Magga)**

Siddhartha Gautama

Almost all we know of Siddhartha Gautama's life comes from biographies written by his followers centuries after his death, and which differ widely in many details. What is certain is that he was born in Lumbini, modern-day Nepal, some time around 560 BCE. His father was an official, possibly the leader of a clan, and Siddhartha led a privileged life of luxury and high status.

Dissatisfied with this, Siddhartha left his wife and son to find a spiritual path, and discovered the "middle way" between sensual indulgence and asceticism. He experienced enlightenment while thinking in the shade of a bodhi tree, and devoted the rest of his life to travelling throughout India, preaching. After his death, his teachings were passed down orally for some 400 years before being written down in the *Tipitaka (Three Baskets)*.

Key works

1st century CE
Tipitaka (recounted by his followers), comprising:
Vinaya-pitaka, Sutta-pitaka, Abhidhamma-pitaka

Gautama, although revered by Buddhists for his wisdom, was neither a messiah nor a prophet, and he did not act as a medium between God and Man. His ideas were arrived at through reasoning, not divine revelation, and it is this that marks Buddhism out as a philosophy as much as (perhaps even more than) a religion. His quest was a philosophical one – to discover truths – and he maintained that the truths he proposed are available to all of us through the power of reason. Like most Eastern philosophers, he was not interested in the unanswerable questions of metaphysics that preoccupied the Greeks. Dealing with entities beyond our experience, this kind of enquiry was senseless speculation. Instead, he concerned himself with the question of the goal of life, which in turn involved examining the concepts of happiness, virtue, and the "good" life.

The middle way

In his early life, Gautama enjoyed luxury and, we are told, all the sensual pleasures. However, he realized that these were not enough on their own to bring him true happiness. He was acutely aware of the suffering in the world, and saw that it was largely due to sickness, old age, and death, and the fact that people lack what »

The Buddha cut off his hair as part of his renunciation of the material world. According to Buddhist teaching, the temptations of the world are the source of all suffering, and must be resisted.

they need. He also recognized that the sensual pleasure we indulge in to relieve suffering is rarely satisfying, and that when it is, the effects are transitory. He found the experience of extreme asceticism (austerity and abstinence) equally dissatisfying, bringing him no nearer to an understanding of how to achieve happiness.

Gautama came to the conclusion that there must be a "middle way" between self-indulgence and self-mortification. This middle way, he believed, should lead to true happiness, or "enlightenment", and to find it he applied reason to his own experiences.

Suffering, he realized, is universal. It is an integral part of existence, and the root cause of our suffering is the frustration of our desires and expectations. These desires he calls "attachments", and they include not only our sensual desires and worldly ambitions, but our most basic instinct for self-preservation. Satisfying these attachments, he argues,

may bring short-term gratification, but not happiness in the sense of contentment and peace of mind.

The "not-self"

The next step in Gautama's reasoning is that the elimination of attachments will prevent any disappointment, and so avoid suffering. To achieve this, he suggests a root cause of our attachments – our selfishness, and by selfishness he means more than just our tendency to seek gratification. For Gautama, selfishness is self-centredness and self-attachment – the domain of what today we would call the "ego". So, to free ourselves from attachments that cause us pain, it is not enough merely to renounce the things we desire – we must overcome our attachment to that which desires – the "self".

But how can this be done? Desire, ambition, and expectation are part of our nature, and for most of us constitute our very reasons for living. The answer, for Gautama, is that the ego's world is illusory – as he shows, again, by a process of reasoning. He argues that nothing in the universe is self-caused, for everything is the result of some previous action, and each of us is only a transitory part of this eternal process – ultimately impermanent and without substance. So, in reality, there is no "self" that is not part of the greater whole – or the "not-self" – and suffering results from our failure to recognize this. This does not mean that we should deny our existence or personal identity, rather that we should understand them for what they are – transient and insubstantial. Grasping the concept of being a constituent part of an eternal "not-self", rather than clinging to the

Believe nothing, no matter where you read it, or who said it, unless it agrees with your own reason.
Siddhartha Gautama

notion of being a unique "self", is the key to losing that attachment, and finding a release from suffering.

The Eightfold Path

Gautama's reasoning from the causes of suffering to the way to achieve happiness is codified in Buddhist teachings in the Four Noble Truths: that suffering is universal; that desire is the cause of suffering; that suffering can be avoided by eliminating desire; that following the Eightfold Path will eliminate desire. This last Truth refers to what amounts to a practical guide to the "middle way" that Gautama laid out for his followers to achieve enlightenment.

Peace comes from within. Do not seek it without.
Siddhartha Gautama

The Eightfold Path (right action, right intention, right livelihood, right effort, right concentration, right speech, right understanding, and right mindfulness) is in effect a code of ethics – a prescription for a good life and the happiness that Gautama first set out to find.

Nirvana

Gautama sees the ultimate goal of life on Earth to be the ending of the cycle of suffering (birth, death, and rebirth) into which we are born. By following the Eightfold Path, a man can overcome his ego and live a life free from suffering, and through his enlightenment he can avoid the pain of rebirth into another life of suffering. He has realized his place in the "not-self", and become at one with the eternal. He has attained the state of Nirvana – which is variously translated as "non-attachment", "not-being", or literally "blowing out" (as of a candle).

In the Brahmanism of Gautama's time, and the Hindu religion that followed, Nirvana was seen as becoming one with god, but Gautama carefully avoids any mention of a deity or of an ultimate purpose to life. He merely describes Nirvana as "unborn, unoriginated, uncreated, and unformed", and transcending any sensory experience. It is an eternal and unchanging state of not-being, and so the ultimate freedom from the suffering of existence.

Gautama spent many years after his enlightenment travelling around India, preaching and teaching. During his lifetime, he gained a considerable following, and Buddhism became established as a major religion as well as a philosophy. His teachings were passed down orally from generation to generation by his followers, until the 1st century CE, when they were written down for the first time. Various schools began to appear as Buddhism spread across India, and later spread eastwards into China and Southeast Asia, where it rivalled Confucianism and Daoism in its popularity.

Gautama's teachings spread as far as the Greek empire by the 3rd century BCE, but had little influence on Western philosophy. However, there were similarities between Gautama's approach to philosophy and that of the Greeks, not least Gautama's emphasis on reasoning as a means of finding happiness, and his disciples' use of philosophical dialogues to elucidate his teachings. His thoughts also find echoes in the ideas of later Western philosophers, such as in Hume's concept of the self and Schopenhauer's view of the human condition. But it was not until the 20th century that Buddhism was to have any direct influence on Western thinking. Since then, more and more Westerners have turned to it for guidance on how to live. ∎

The mind is everything. What you think, you become.
Siddhartha Gautama

The dharma wheel, one of the oldest Buddhist symbols, represents the Eightfold Path to Nirvana. In Buddhism, the word "dharma" refers to the teachings of the Buddha.

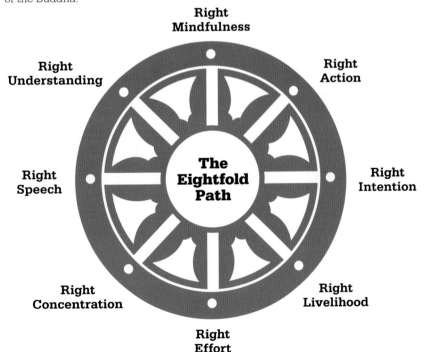

Right Mindfulness

Right Understanding

Right Action

Right Speech

The Eightfold Path

Right Intention

Right Concentration

Right Livelihood

Right Effort

HOLD
FAITHFULNESS
AND SINCERITY
AS FIRST PRINCIPLES

CONFUCIUS (551–479 BCE)

From 770 to 220 BCE, China enjoyed an era of great cultural development, and the philosophies that emerged at this time were known as the Hundred Schools of Thought. By the 6th century BCE, the Zhou Dynasty was in decline – moving from the stability of the Spring and Autumn Period to the aptly named Warring States Period – and it was during this time that Kong Fuzi, the Master Kong, or Confucius, was born. Like other philosophers of the age – such as Thales, Pythagoras, and Heraclitus of Greece – Confucius sought constants in a world of change, and for him this meant a search for moral values that could enable rulers to govern justly.

The Analects
Unlike many of the early Chinese philosophers, Confucius looked to the past for his inspiration. He was conservative by nature, and had a great respect for ritual and ancestor worship – both of which were maintained by the Zhou Dynasty, whose rulers received authority from the gods via the so-called Heavenly Mandate.

The superior man does what is proper to the station in which he is; he does not desire to go beyond this.
Confucius

A rigid social hierarchy existed in China, but Confucius was part of a new class of scholars who acted as advisors to the courts – in effect a class of civil servants – and they achieved their status not through inheritance, but by merit. It was Confucius's integration of the old ideals with the emerging meritocracy that produced his unique new moral philosophy.

The main source we have for the teachings of Confucius is the *Analects*, a collection of fragments of his writings and sayings compiled by his disciples. It is primarily a political treatise, made up of

Confucius

According to tradition, Confucius was born in 551 BCE in Qufu, in the state of Lu, China. His name was originally Kong Qiu, and only later did he earn the title Kong Fuzi, or "Master Kong". Little is known about his life, except that he was from a well-to-do family, and that as a young man he worked as a servant to support his family after his father died. He nevertheless managed to find time to study, and became an administrator in the Lu court, but when his suggestions to the rulers were ignored he left to concentrate on teaching.

As a teacher he travelled throughout the empire, and at the end of his life he returned to Qufu, where he died in 479 BCE. His teaching survives in fragments and sayings passed down orally to his disciples, and collected in the *Analects* and anthologies compiled by Confucian scholars.

Key works

5th century BCE
Analects
Doctrine of the Mean
Great Learning

See also: Thales of Miletus 22–23 ▪ Laozi 24–25 ▪ Pythagoras 26–29 ▪ Siddhartha Gautama 30–33 ▪ Heraclitus 40 ▪ Hajime Tanabe 244–45

aphorisms and anecdotes that together form a sort of rule book for good government – but his use of the word *junzi* (literally "gentleman") to denote a superior, virtuous man, indicates that his concerns were as much social as political. Indeed, many passages of the *Analects* read like a book of etiquette. But to see the *Analects* as merely a social or political treatise is to miss its central point. At its heart lies a comprehensive ethical system.

The virtuous life

Before the appearance of the Hundred Schools of Thought, the world had been explained by mythology and religion, and power and moral authority were generally accepted to be god-given. Confucius is pointedly silent about the gods, but he often refers to *tian*, or

Heaven, as the source of moral order. According to the *Analects*, we humans are the agents that Heaven has chosen to embody its will and to unite the world with the moral order – an idea that was in line with traditional Chinese thinking. What breaks with tradition, however, is Confucius's belief that *de* – virtue – is not something Heaven-sent for the ruling classes, but something that can be cultivated – and cultivated by anyone. Having himself risen to be a minister of the Zhou court, he believed that it was a duty of the middle classes, as well as the rulers, to strive to act with virtue and benevolence (*ren*) to achieve a just and stable society.

To reconcile the fact that society was a rigid class system with his belief that all men can receive the

blessing of the Heavenly Mandate, Confucius argues that the virtuous man is not simply one who stands at the top of the social hierarchy, but one who understands his place within that hierarchy and embraces it to the full. And to define the various means of acting in accordance with *de* – virtue – he turns to traditional Chinese values: *zhong*, loyalty; *xiao*, filial piety; *li*, ritual propriety; and *shu*, reciprocity. The person who sincerely observes these values Confucius called *junzi*, the gentleman or superior man, by which he means a man of virtue, learning, and good manners.

The values of *de* had evolved within the ruling classes but had become little more than empty gestures in the disintegrating world of the Zhou Dynasty. Confucius is attempting to »

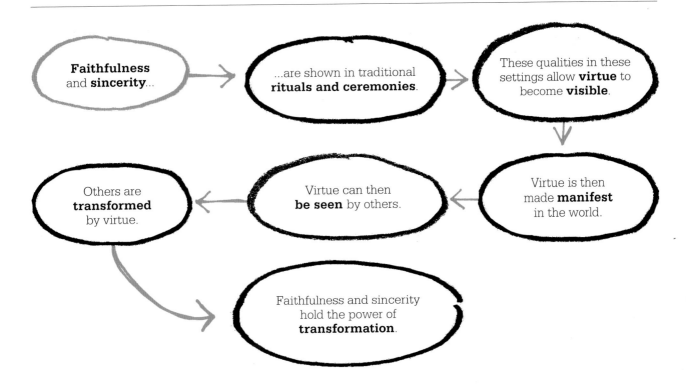

Faithfulness and **sincerity**… → …are shown in traditional **rituals and ceremonies**. → These qualities in these settings allow **virtue** to become **visible**. → Virtue is then made **manifest** in the world. → Virtue can then **be seen** by others. → Others are **transformed** by virtue. → Faithfulness and sincerity hold the power of **transformation**.

The Five Constant Relationships

Sovereign – Subject
Rulers should be benevolent, and subjects loyal.

Father – Son
A parent is to be loving, a child obedient.

Husband – Wife
Husbands are to be good and fair, and wives understanding.

Elder Brother – Younger Brother
An elder sibling is to be gentle, and younger siblings respectful.

Friend – Friend
Older friends are to be considerate, younger friends reverential.

persuade the rulers to return to these ideals and to restore a just government, but he also believes in the power of benevolence – arguing that ruling by example rather than by fear would inspire the people to follow a similarly virtuous life. The same principle, he believes, should govern personal relationships.

Loyalty and ritual

In his analysis of relationships, Confucius uses *zhong* – the virtue of loyalty – as a guiding principle. To begin with, he stresses the importance of the loyalty of a minister to his sovereign, then shows that a similar relation holds between father and son, husband and wife, elder brother and younger brother, and between friends. The order in which he arranges these is significant – political loyalty first, then family and clan loyalties, then loyalties to friends and strangers. For Confucius, this hierarchy reflects the fact that each person should know his station in society as a whole, as well his place in the family and the clan.

This aspect of "knowing one's station" is exemplified by *xiao* – filial piety – which for Confucius was much more than just respect for one's parents or elders. In fact, this is the closest he gets to religious ideas in the *Analects*, for *xiao* is connected to the traditional practice of ancestor worship. Above all, *xiao* reinforced the relationship of inferior to superior, which was central to his thinking.

It is in his insistence on *li* – ritual propriety – that Confucius is at his most conservative. *Li* did not simply refer to rituals such as ancestor worship, but also to the social norms that underpinned every aspect of contemporary Chinese life. These ranged from ceremonies such as marriages,

Ritual and tradition, for Confucius, are vital for binding an individual to his community. By knowing his place in society, the individual is free to become *junzi*, a man of virtue.

funerals, and sacrifices to the etiquette of receiving guests, presenting gifts, and the simple, everyday gestures of politeness, such as bowing and using the correct mode of address. These are, according to Confucius, the outward signs of an inner *de* – but only when they are performed with sincerity, which he considers to be the way of Heaven. Through the outward show of loyalty with inner sincerity, the superior man can transform society.

Sincerity

For Confucius, society can be changed by example. As he writes: "Sincerity becomes apparent. From being apparent, it becomes manifest. From being manifest, it becomes brilliant. Brilliant, it affects others. Affecting others, they are changed by it. Changed by it, they are transformed. Only he who is possessed of the most complete sincerity that can exist under Heaven, can transform."

Here, Confucius is at his least conservative, and he explains that the process of transformation can work both ways. The concept of *zhong* (faithfulness) also has an

> What you know,
> you know;
> what you don't know,
> you don't know.
> This is true wisdom.
> **Confucius**

implication of "regard for others". He took the view that one can learn to become a superior man by first recognizing what one does not know (an idea echoed a century later by the Greek philosopher Socrates, who claimed that his wisdom lay in accepting that he knew nothing), and then by watching other people: if they show virtue, try to become their equal; if they are inferior, be their guide.

Self-reflection

This notion of *zhong* as a regard for others is also tied to the last of the Confucian values of *de*: *shu*, reciprocity, or "self-reflection", which should govern our actions towards others. The so-called Golden Rule, "do as you would be done by", appears in Confucianism as a negative: "what you do not desire for yourself, do not do to others". The difference is subtle but crucial: Confucius does not prescribe what to do, only what not to do, emphasizing restraint rather than

Confucius's devotion to the idea of establishing a humane society led him to travel the Chinese empire for 12 years, teaching the virtues of faithfulness and sincerity.

action. This implies modesty and humility – values traditionally held in high regard in Chinese society, and which for Confucius express our true nature. Fostering these values is a form of loyalty to oneself, and another kind of sincerity.

Confucianism

Confucius had little success in persuading contemporary rulers to adopt his ideas in government, and turned his attention to teaching. His disciples, including Meng Zi (Mencius), continued to anthologize and expand on his writings, which survived the repressive Qin Dynasty, and inspired a revival of Confucianism in the Han Dynasty of the early Common Era. From then on, the impact of Confucius's ideas was profound, inspiring almost every aspect of Chinese society, from administration to politics and philosophy. The major religions of Daoism and Buddhism had also been flourishing in Confucius's time, replacing traditional beliefs, and although Confucius offered no opinion on

them, remaining silent about the gods, he nevertheless influenced aspects of both new faiths.

A Neo-Confucian school revitalized the movement in the 9th century, and reached its peak in the 12th century, when its influence was felt across Southeast Asia into Korea and Japan. Although Jesuit missionaries brought back Kong Fuzi's ideas to Europe (and Latinized his name to Confucius) in the 16th century, Confucianism was alien to European thought and had limited influence until translations of his work appeared in the late 17th century.

Despite the fall of imperial China in 1911, Confucian ideas continued to form the basis of many Chinese moral and social conventions, even if they were officially frowned upon. In recent years the People's Republic of China has shown a renewed interest in Confucius, integrating his ideas with both modern Chinese thought and Western philosophy, creating a hybrid philosophy known as "New Confucianism". ∎

EVERYTHING IS FLUX
HERACLITUS (c.535–475 BCE)

IN CONTEXT

BRANCH
Metaphysics

APPROACH
Monism

BEFORE
6th century BCE The Milesian philosophers claim that the cosmos is made up of a single specific substance.

6th century BCE Pythagoras states that the universe has an underlying structure that can be defined mathematically.

AFTER
Early 5th century BCE Parmenides uses logical deduction to prove change is impossible.

Late 4th century BCE Plato describes the world as being in a state of flux, but dismisses Heraclitus as contradictory.

Early 19th century Georg Hegel bases his dialectic system of philosophy on the integration of opposites.

Where other early Greek philosophers seek to uncover scientific explanations for the physical nature of the cosmos, Heraclitus sees it as being governed by a divine logos. Sometimes interpreted to mean "reason" or "argument", Heraclitus considers the logos to be a universal, cosmic law, according to which all things come into being, and by which all the material elements of the universe are held in balance.

It is the balancing of opposites, such as day and night and hot and cold, which Heraclitus believes

The road up and the road down are one and the same.
Heraclitus

leads to the unity of the universe, or the idea everything is part of a single fundamental process or substance – the central tenet of monism. But he also states that tension is constantly generated between these pairs of opposites, and he therefore concludes that everything must be in a permanent state of flux, or change. Day, for instance, changes into night, which in turn changes back again to day.

Heraclitus offers the example of a river to illustrate his theory: "You can never step into the same river twice." By this, he means that at the very moment you step into a river, fresh waters will immediately replace those into which you initially placed your foot, and yet the river itself is always described as one fixed and unchanging thing.

Heraclitus's belief that every object in the universe is in a state of constant flux runs counter to the thinking of the philosophers of the Milesian school, such as Thales and Anaximenes, who define all things by their quintessentially unchanging essence. ∎

See also: Thales of Miletus 22–23 ∎ Anaximenes of Miletus 330 ∎ Pythagoras 26–29 ∎ Parmenides 41 ∎ Plato 50–55 ∎ Georg Hegel 178–85

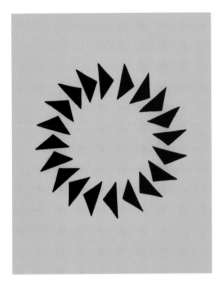

ALL IS ONE
PARMENIDES (c.515–445 BCE)

IN CONTEXT

BRANCH
Metaphysics

APPROACH
Monism

BEFORE
6th century BCE Pythagoras
sees mathematical structure,
rather than a substance, as
the foundation of the cosmos.

c.500 BCE Heraclitus says that
everything is in a state of flux.

AFTER
Late 5th century BCE Zeno
of Elea presents his paradoxes
to demonstrate the illusory
nature of our experience.

c.400 BCE Democritus and
Leucippus say the cosmos is
composed of atoms in a void.

Late 4th century BCE Plato
presents his theory of Forms,
claiming that abstract ideas
are the highest form of reality.

1927 Martin Heidegger writes
Being and Time, reviving the
question of the sense of being.

The ideas put forward by Parmenides mark a key turning point in Greek philosophy. Influenced by the logical, scientific thinking of Pythagoras, Parmenides employs deductive reasoning in an attempt to uncover the true physical nature of the world. His investigations lead him to take the opposite view to that of Heraclitus.

From the premise that something exists ("It is"), Parmenides deduces that it cannot also not exist ("It is not"), as this would involve a logical contradiction. It follows therefore that a state of nothing existing is impossible – there can be no void. Something cannot then come from nothing, and so must always have existed in some form. This permanent form cannot change, because something that is permanent cannot change into something else without it ceasing to be permanent. Fundamental change is therefore impossible.

Parmenides concludes from this pattern of thought that everything that is real must be eternal and

Understanding the cosmos is one of the oldest philosophical quests. In the 20th century, evidence from quantum physics emerged to support ideas that Parmenides reached by reason alone.

unchanging, and must have an indivisible unity – "all is one". More importantly for subsequent philosophers, Parmenides shows by his process of reasoning that our perception of the world is faulty and full of contradictions. We seem to experience change, and yet our reason tells us that change is impossible. The only conclusion we can come to is that we can never rely on the experience that is delivered to us by our senses. ∎

See also: Pythagoras 26–29 ▪ Heraclitus 40 ▪ Democritus and Leucippus 45 ▪ Zeno of Elea 331 ▪ Plato 50–55 ▪ Martin Heidegger 252–255

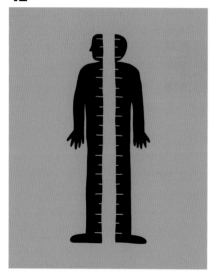

MAN IS THE MEASURE OF ALL THINGS
PROTAGORAS (c.490–420 BCE)

IN CONTEXT

BRANCH
Ethics

APPROACH
Relativism

BEFORE
Early 5th century BCE
Parmenides argues that we can rely more on reason than the evidence of our senses.

AFTER
Early 4th century BCE
Plato's theory of Forms states that there are "absolutes" or ideal forms of everything.

1580 French writer Michel de Montaigne espouses a form of relativism to describe human behaviour in his *Essays*.

1967–72 Jacques Derrida uses his technique of deconstruction to show that any text contains irreconcilable contradictions.

2005 Benedict XVI warns "we are moving towards a dictatorship of relativism" in his first public address as pope.

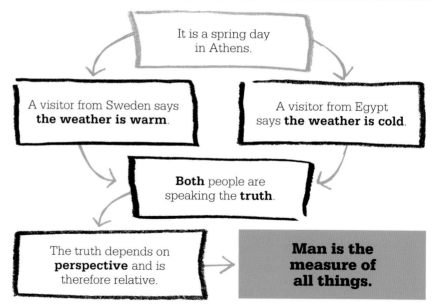

It is a spring day in Athens.

A visitor from Sweden says **the weather is warm**.

A visitor from Egypt says **the weather is cold**.

Both people are speaking the **truth**.

The truth depends on **perspective** and is therefore relative.

Man is the measure of all things.

During the 5th century BCE, Athens evolved into an important and prosperous city-state, and under the leadership of Pericles (445–429 BCE) it entered a "Golden Age" of scholarship and culture. This attracted people from all parts of Greece, and for those who knew and could interpret the law, there were rich pickings to be had. The city was run on broadly democratic principles, with an established legal system. Anyone taken to court was required to plead his own case; there were no advocates, but a recognized class of advisors soon evolved. Among this group was Protagoras.

Everything is relative
Protagoras lectured in law and rhetoric to anybody who could afford him. His teachings were essentially about practical matters, arguing to win a civil case rather than to prove a point, but he could

See also: Parmenides 41 ▪ Socrates 46–49 ▪ Plato 50–55 ▪ Michel de Montaigne 108–09 ▪ Jacques Derrida 308–13

Many things prevent
knowledge, including
the obscurity of
the subject and the
brevity of human life.
Protagoras

see the philosophical implications of what he taught. For Protagoras, every argument has two sides, and both may be equally valid. He claims that he can "make the worse case the better", proving not the worth of the argument, but the persuasiveness of its proponent. In this way, he recognizes that belief is subjective, and it is the man holding the view or opinion that is the measure of its worth. This style of reasoning, common in law and

politics at that time, was new to philosophy. By placing human beings at its centre, it continued a tradition of taking religion out of philosophical argument, and it also shifted the focus of philosophy away from an understanding of the nature of the universe to an examination of human behaviour. Protagoras is mainly interested in practical questions. Philosophical speculations on the substance of the cosmos or about the existence of the gods seem pointless to him, as he considers such things to be ultimately unknowable.

The main implication of "man is the measure of all things" is that belief is subjective and relative. This leads Protagoras to reject the existence of absolute definitions of truth, justice, or virtue. What is true for one person may be false for another, he claims. This relativism also applies to moral values, such as what is right and what is wrong. To Protagoras, nothing is inherently good in itself. Something is ethical, or right, only because a person or society judges it to be so.

Protagoras was the most influential of a group of itinerant teachers of law and rhetoric that became known as the Sophists (from the Greek *sophia*, meaning wisdom). Socrates and Plato derided the Sophists as mere rhetoricians, but with Protagoras there was a significant step in ethics towards the view that there are no absolutes and that all judgements, including moral judgements, are subjective. ▪

According to Protagoras, any "truth" uncovered by these two philosophers, depicted on a 5th-century BCE Greek drinking vessel, will depend on their use of rhetoric and their debating skill.

Protagoras

Protagoras was born in Abdera, in northeast Greece, but travelled widely as an itinerant teacher. At some stage, he moved to Athens, where he became advisor to the ruler of the city-state, Pericles, who commissioned him to write the constitution for the colony of Thurii in 444 BCE. Protagoras was a proponent of agnosticism, and legend has it that he was later tried for impiety, and that his books were publicly burned.

Only fragments of his writings survive, although Plato discusses the views of Protagoras at length in his dialogues.

Protagoras is believed to have lived to the age of 70, but his exact date and place of death are unknown.

Key works

5th century BCE
On the Gods
Truth
On Being
The Art of Controversy
On Mathematics
On the State
On Ambition
On Virtues
On the Original State of Things

WHEN ONE THROWS TO ME A PEACH, I RETURN TO HIM A PLUM
MOZI (c.470–391 BCE)

Born in about 470 BCE, shortly after the death of Confucius, Mozi had a traditional Chinese education based on the classic texts. Later, however, he came to dislike the emphasis on clan relationships that runs through Confucianism, and this led him to set up his own school of thought, advocating universal love or *jian ai*. By *jian ai*, Mozi means that we should care for all people equally, regardless of their status or their relationship to us. He regards this philosophy, which became known as Mohism and which "nourishes and sustains all life", as being fundamentally benevolent and in accordance with the way of heaven.

Mozi believes that there is always reciprocity in our actions. By treating others as we would wish to be treated ourselves, we will receive similar treatment in return. This is the meaning behind "when one throws to me a peach, I return to him a plum". When this principle of caring for everyone impartially is applied by rulers, Mozi states that it avoids conflict

Mao Zedong regarded Mozi as the true philosopher of the people, because of his humble origins. Mozi's view that everyone should be treated equally has been encouraged in modern China.

and war; when the same principle is practised by everyone, it leads to a more harmonious and therefore more productive society. This idea is similar in spirit to that of the Utilitarianism proposed by Western philosophers of the 19th century. ∎

See also: Laozi 24–25 ▪ Siddhartha Gautama 30–33 ▪ Confucius 34–39 ▪ Wang Bi 331 ▪ Jeremy Bentham 174 ▪ Hajime Tanabe 244–45

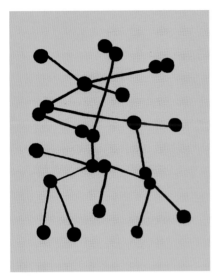

NOTHING EXISTS EXCEPT ATOMS AND EMPTY SPACE
DEMOCRITUS (c. 460–371 BCE) AND LEUCIPPUS (EARLY 5TH CENTURY BCE)

IN CONTEXT

BRANCH
Metaphysics

APPROACH
Atomism

BEFORE
Early 6th century BCE Thales says that the cosmos is made of one fundamental substance.

c.500 BCE Heraclitus declares that everything is in a state of constant flux, or change.

AFTER
c.300 BCE The Epicurians conclude that there is no afterlife, as the body's atoms disperse after death.

1805 British chemist John Dalton proposes that all pure substances contain atoms of a single type that combine to form compounds.

1897 The British physicist J.J. Thomson discovers that atoms can be divided into even smaller particles.

From the 6th century BCE onwards, philosophers began to consider whether the universe was made from a single fundamental substance. During the 5th century BCE, two philosophers from Abderra in Greece, named Democritus and Leucippus, suggested that everything was made up of tiny, indivisible and unchangeable particles, which they called atoms (*atomos* is Greek for uncuttable).

First atomic theory
Democritus and Leucippus also claim that a void or empty space separates atoms, allowing them to move around freely. As the atoms move, they may collide with each other to form new arrangements of atoms, so that objects in the world will appear to change. The two thinkers consider that there are an infinite number of these eternal atoms, but that the number of different combinations they can arrange themselves into is finite. This explains the apparent fixed number of different substances that

exist. The atoms that make up our bodies, for example, do not decay and disappear when we die, but are dispersed and can be reconstituted.

Known as atomism, the theory that Democritus and Leucippus devised offered the first complete mechanistic view of the universe, without any recourse to the notion of a god or gods. It also identified fundamental properties of matter that have proved critical to the development of the physical sciences, particularly from the 17th century onwards, right up to the atomic theories that revolutionized science in the 20th century.■

Man is a microcosm of the universe.
Democritus

See also: Thales of Miletus 22–23 ■ Heraclitus 40 ■ Epicurus 64–65

THE LIFE WHICH IS UNEXAMINED IS NOT WORTH LIVING

SOCRATES (469–399 BCE)

IN CONTEXT

BRANCH
Epistemology

APPROACH
Dialectical method

BEFORE
c.600–450 BCE Pre-Socratic philosophers in Ionia and Italy attempt to explain the nature of the cosmos.

Early 5th century BCE Parmenides states that we can only understand the universe through reasoning.

c.450 BCE Protagoras and the Sophists apply rhetoric to philosophical questions.

AFTER
c.399–355 BCE Plato portrays the character of Socrates in the *Apology* and numerous other dialogues.

4th century BCE Aristotle acknowledges his debt to Socrates' method.

Socrates is often referred to as one of the founders of Western philosophy, and yet he wrote nothing, established no school, and held no particular theories of his own. What he did do, however, was persistently ask the questions that interested him, and in doing so evolved a new way of thinking, or a new way of examining what we think. This has been called the Socratic, or dialectical, method ("dialectical" because it proceeds as a dialogue between opposing views), and it earned him many enemies in Athens, where he lived. He was vilified as a Sophist (someone who argues for the sake of deception), and was sentenced to

See also: Thales of Miletus 22–23 ▪ Pythagoras 26–29 ▪ Heraclitus 40 ▪ Parmenides 41 ▪ Protagoras 42–43 ▪ Plato 50–55 ▪ Aristotle 56–63

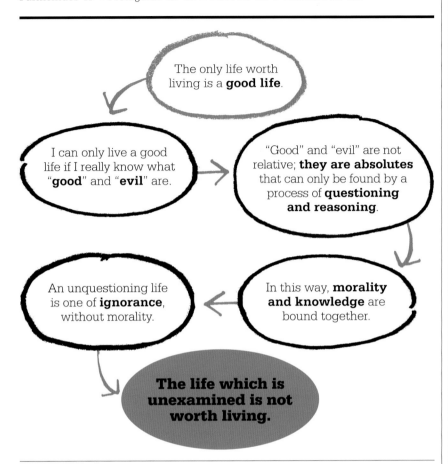

The only life worth living is a **good life**.

I can only live a good life if I really know what "**good**" and "**evil**" are.

"Good" and "evil" are not relative; **they are absolutes** that can only be found by a process of **questioning and reasoning**.

In this way, **morality and knowledge** are bound together.

An unquestioning life is one of **ignorance**, without morality.

The life which is unexamined is not worth living.

Socrates

Born in Athens in 469 BCE, Socrates was the son of a stonemason and a midwife. It is likely that he pursued his father's profession, and had the opportunity to study philosophy, before he was called up for military service. After distinguishing himself during the Peloponnesian War, he returned to Athens, and for a while involved himself in politics. However, when his father died he inherited enough money to live with his wife Xanthippe without having to work.

From then on, Socrates became a familiar sight around Athens, involving himself in philosophical discussions with fellow citizens and gaining a following of young students. He was eventually accused of corrupting the minds of young Athenians, and was sentenced to death. Although he was offered the choice of exile, he accepted the guilty verdict and was given a fatal dose of hemlock in 399 BCE.

Key works

4th–3rd century BCE
Plato's record of Socrates' life and philosophy in the *Apology* and numerous dialogues.

death on charges of corrupting the young with ideas that undermined tradition. But he also had many followers, and among them was Plato, who recorded Socrates' ideas in a series of written works, called dialogues, in which Socrates sets about examining various ideas. It is largely thanks to these dialogues – which include the *Apology*, *Phaedo,* and the *Symposium* – that Socrates' thought survived at all, and that it went on to guide the course of Western philosophy.

The purpose of life

Socrates lived in Athens in the second half of the 5th century BCE. As a young man he is believed to have studied natural philosophy, looking at the various explanations of the nature of the universe, but then became involved in the politics of the city-state and concerned with more down-to-earth ethical issues, such as the nature of justice. However, he was not interested in winning arguments, or arguing for the sake of making money – a charge that was leveled at many of his contemporaries. Nor was he seeking answers or explanations – he was simply examining the basis of the concepts we apply to ourselves (such as "good", "bad", and "just"), for he believed that understanding what we are is the first task of philosophy. »

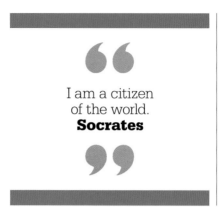

> I am a citizen
> of the world.
> **Socrates**

Socrates' central concern, then, was the examination of life, and it was his ruthless questioning of people's most cherished beliefs (largely about themselves) that earned him his enemies – but he remained committed to his task until the very end. According to the account of his defence at his trial, recorded by Plato, Socrates chose death rather than face a life of ignorance: "The life which is unexamined is not worth living."

But what exactly is involved in this examination of life? For Socrates it was a process of questioning the meaning of essential concepts that we use every day but have never really thought about, thereby revealing their real meaning and our own knowledge or ignorance. Socrates was one of the first philosophers to consider what it was that constituted a "good" life; for him it meant achieving peace of mind as a result of doing the right thing, rather than living according to the moral codes of society. And the "right thing" can only be determined through rigorous examination.

Socrates rejected the notion that concepts such as virtue were relative, insisting instead that they were absolutes, applicable not just to citizens of Athens, or Greece, but to all people in the world. He believed that virtue (areté in Greek, which at the time implied excellence and fulfilment) was "the most valuable of possessions", and that no-one actually desires to do evil. Anyone performing evil actions would be acting against their conscience and would therefore feel uncomfortable; and as we all strive for peace of mind it is not something we would do willingly. Evil, he thought, was done because of lack of wisdom and knowledge. From this he concluded that "there is only one good: knowledge; and one evil: ignorance". Knowledge is inextricably bound to morality – it is the "only one good" – and for this reason we must continually "examine" our lives.

Care of the soul
For Socrates, knowledge may also play a part in life after death. In the *Apology*, Plato's Socrates prefaces his famous quote about the unexamined life by saying: "I tell you that to let no day pass without discussing goodness and all the

Socrates' dialectical method was a simple method of questioning that brought to light the often false assumptions on which particular claims to knowledge are based.

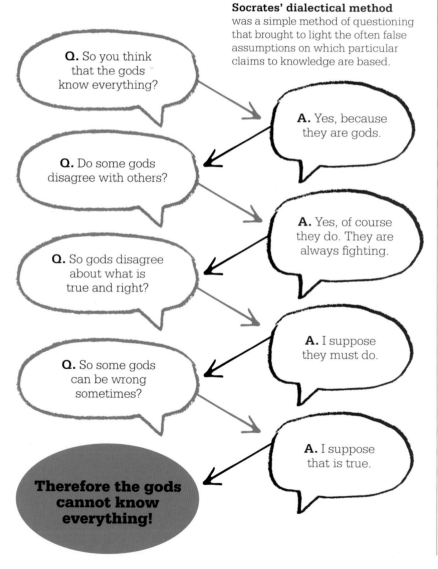

Q. So you think that the gods know everything?

A. Yes, because they are gods.

Q. Do some gods disagree with others?

A. Yes, of course they do. They are always fighting.

Q. So gods disagree about what is true and right?

A. I suppose they must do.

Q. So some gods can be wrong sometimes?

A. I suppose that is true.

Therefore the gods cannot know everything!

other subjects about which you hear me talking, and that examining both myself and others is really the very best thing a man can do." This gaining of knowledge, rather than wealth or high status, is the ultimate goal of life. It is not a matter of entertainment or curiosity – it is the reason why we exist. Moreover, all knowledge is ultimately self-knowledge, for it creates the person you are within this world, and fosters the care of the immortal soul. In *Phaedo*, Socrates says that an unexamined life leads the soul to be "confused and dizzy, as if it were drunk", while the wise soul achieves stability, its straying finally brought to an end.

Dialectical method

Socrates quickly became a well-known figure in Athens, with a reputation for an enquiring mind. A friend of his, so the story goes, asked the priestess of Apollo at Delphi who the wisest man in the world was: the oracular reply was that there was no-one wiser than Socrates. When Socrates heard about this, he was astounded, and went to the most knowledgeable people he could find to try to disprove it. What he discovered was that these people only thought they knew a great deal; under examination, their knowledge was proved to be either limited or false. What was more important, however, was the method he used to question their knowledge. He took the standpoint of someone who knew nothing, and merely asked questions, exposing contradictions in arguments and gaps in knowledge

to gradually elicit insights. He likened the process to his mother's profession of midwife, assisting in the birth of ideas.

Through these discussions, Socrates came to realize that the Delphic oracle had been right – he was the wisest man in Athens, not because of his knowledge but because he professed to know nothing. He also saw that the inscription on the entrance to the temple at Delphi, *gnothi seauton* ("know thyself"), was just as significant. To gain knowledge of the world and oneself it was necessary to realize the limits of one's own ignorance and to remove all preconceptions. Only then could one hope to determine the truth.

Socrates set about engaging the people of Athens in discussion on topics such as the nature of love, justice, and loyalty. His mission, misunderstood at the time as a dangerous form of Sophistry – or cleverness for the sake of it – was not to instruct the people, nor even simply to learn what they knew, but to explore the ideas that they had. It was the conversation itself, with Socrates guiding it, that provided him with insights. Through a series of questions, he revealed the ideas and assumptions his opponent held,

> I know nothing except the fact of my ignorance.
> **Socrates**

then exposed the contradictions within them and brought them to agree to a new set of conclusions.

This method of examining an argument by rational discussion from a position of ignorance marked a complete change in philosophical thinking. It was the first known use of inductive argument, in which a set of premises based on experience is first established to be true, and then shown to lead to a universal truth in conclusion. This powerful form of argument was developed by Aristotle, and later by Francis Bacon, who used it as the starting point of his scientific method. It became, therefore, the foundation not only of Western philosophy, but of all the empirical sciences. ∎

Socrates was put to death in 399 BCE, ultimately for questioning the basis of Athenian morality. Here he accepts the bowl of hemlock that will kill him, and gestures defiantly at the heavens.

EARTHLY
KNOWLEDGE IS BUT
SHADOW

PLATO (c.427–347 BCE)

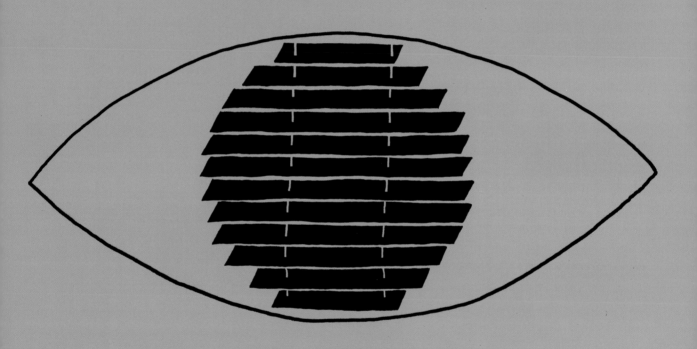

IN CONTEXT

BRANCH
Epistemology

APPROACH
Rationalism

BEFORE
6th century BCE The Milesian philosophers propose theories to explain the nature and substance of the cosmos.

c.500 BCE Heraclitus argues that everything is constantly in a state of flux or change.

c.450 BCE Protagoras says that truth is relative.

AFTER
c.335 BCE Aristotle teaches that we can find truth by observing the world around us.

c.250 CE Plotinus founds the Neo-Platonist school, a religious take on Plato's ideas.

386 St Augustine of Hippo integrates Plato's theories into Christian doctrine.

The real world is the **world of Ideas**, which contains the Ideal Forms of everything.

We are born with the concepts of these **Ideal Forms** in our minds.

The illusory world in which we live – the **world of the senses** – contains imperfect copies of the Ideal Forms.

We recognize **things in the world**, such as dogs, because we recognize they are **imperfect copies** of the concepts in our minds.

Everything in this world is a "shadow" of its Ideal Form in the world of Ideas.

I n 399 BCE, Plato's mentor Socrates was condemned to death. Socrates had left no writings, and Plato took it upon himself to preserve what he had learnt from his master for posterity – first in the *Apology,* his retelling of Socrates' defence at his trial, and later by using Socrates as a character in a series of dialogues. In these dialogues, it is sometimes difficult to untangle which are Socrates' thoughts and which are the original thoughts of Plato, but a picture emerges of Plato using the methods of his master to explore and explain his own ideas.

Initially Plato's concerns were very much those of his mentor: to search for definitions of abstract moral values such as "justice" and "virtue", and to refute Protagoras's notion that right and wrong are relative terms. In the *Republic*, Plato set out his vision of the ideal city-state and explored aspects of virtue. But in the process, he also tackled subjects outside moral philosophy. Like earlier Greek thinkers, he questioned the nature and substance of the cosmos, and explored how the immutable and eternal could exist in a seemingly changing world. However, unlike

his predecessors, Plato concluded that the "unchanging" in nature is the same as the "unchanging" in morals and society.

Seeking the Ideal
In the *Republic*, Plato describes Socrates posing questions about the virtues, or moral concepts, in order to establish clear and precise definitions of them. Socrates had famously said that "virtue is knowledge", and that to act justly, for example, you must first ask what justice is. Plato decides that before referring to any moral concept in our thinking or reasoning, we must

See also: Thales of Miletus 22–23 ∎ Heraclitus 40 ∎ Protagoras 42–43 ∎ Socrates 46–49 ∎ Aristotle 56–63 ∎ Plotinus 331 ∎ St Augustine of Hippo 72–73

first explore both what we mean by that concept and what makes it precisely the kind of thing that it is. He raises the question of how we would recognize the correct, or perfect, form of anything – a form that is true for all societies and for all time. By doing so, Plato is implying that he thinks some kind of ideal form of things in the world we inhabit – whether those things are moral concepts or physical objects – must actually exist, of which we are in some way aware.

Plato talks about objects in the world around us, such as beds. When we see a bed, he states, we know that it is a bed and we can recognize all beds, even though they may differ in numerous ways. Dogs in their many species are even more varied, yet all dogs share the characteristic of "dogginess", which is something we can recognize, and that allows us to say we know what a dog is. Plato argues that it is not just that a shared "dogginess" or "bedness" exists, but that we all have in our minds an idea of an ideal bed or dog, which we use to recognize any particular instance.

Taking a mathematical example to further his argument, Plato shows that true knowledge is reached by reasoning, rather than through our senses. He states that we can work out in logical steps that the square of the hypotenuse of a right-angled triangle is equal to the sum of the squares of the other two sides, or that the sum of the three interior

angles of any triangle is always 180 degrees. We know the truth of these statements, even though the perfect triangle does not exist anywhere in the natural world. Yet we are able to perceive the perfect triangle – or the perfect straight line or circle – in our minds, using our reason. Plato, therefore, asks whether such perfect forms can exist anywhere.

World of Ideas

Reasoning brings Plato to only one conclusion – that there must be a world of Ideas, or Forms, which is totally separate from the material world. It is there that the Idea of the perfect "triangle", along with the Idea of the perfect "bed" and "dog" exists. He concludes that human senses cannot perceive this place directly – it is only perceptible to us through reason. Plato even goes on to state that this realm of Ideas is "reality", and that the world around us is merely modelled upon it.

To illustrate his theory, Plato presents what has become known as the "Allegory of the Cave". He

If particulars are to have meaning, there must be universals.
Plato

asks us to imagine a cave in which people have been imprisoned since birth, tied up facing the back wall in the darkness. They can only face straight ahead. Behind the prisoners is a bright fire, which casts shadows onto the wall they are facing. There is also a rampart between the fire and the prisoners along which people walk and hold up various objects from time to time, so that the shadows of these objects are cast on the wall. These shadows are all the prisoners know of the »

The Allegory of the Cave, in which knowledge of the world is limited to mere shadows of reality and truth, is used by Plato to explain his idea of a world of perfect Forms, or Ideas.

According to Plato's theory of Forms, every horse that we encounter in the world around us is a lesser version of an "ideal", or perfect, horse that exists in a world of Forms or Ideas – a realm that humans can only access through their ability to reason.

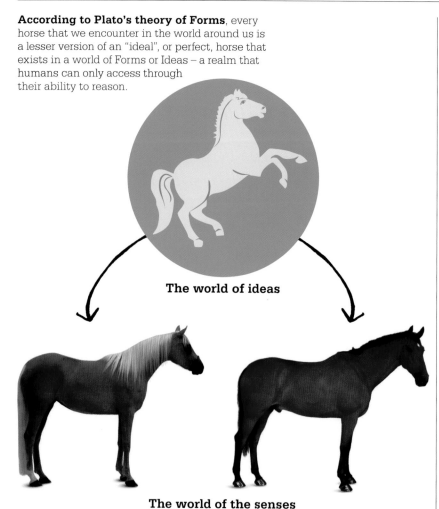

The world of ideas

The world of the senses

other of what Plato considers to be reality, also solves the problem of finding constants in an apparently changing world. The material world may be subject to change, but Plato's world of Ideas is eternal and immutable. Plato applies his theory not just to concrete things, such as beds and dogs, but also to abstract concepts. In Plato's world of Ideas, there is an Idea of justice, which is true justice, and all the instances of justice in the material world around us are models, or lesser variants, of it. The same is true of the concept of goodness, which Plato considers to be the ultimate Idea – and the goal of all philosophical enquiry.

Innate knowledge

The problem remains of how we can come to know these Ideas, so that we have the ability to recognize the imperfect instances of them in the world we inhabit. Plato argues that our conception of Ideal Forms must be innate, even if we are not aware of this. He believes that human beings are divided into two parts: the body and the soul. Our bodies possess the senses, through which we are able to perceive the material world, while the soul possesses the reason with which we can perceive the realm of Ideas. Plato concludes that our soul, which is immortal and eternal, must have

world; they have no concept of the actual objects themselves. If one of the prisoners manages to untie himself and turn around, he will see the objects themselves. But after a lifetime of entrapment, he is likely to be confused, as well as dazzled by the fire, and will most likely turn back towards the wall and the only reality he knows.

Plato believes that everything that our senses perceive in the material world is like the images on the cave wall, merely shadows of reality. This belief is the basis of his theory of Forms, which is that for every earthly thing that we have the power to perceive with our senses, there is a corresponding "Form" (or "Idea") – an eternal and perfect reality of that thing – in the world of Ideas. Because what we perceive via our senses is based on an experience of imperfect or incomplete "shadows" of reality, we can have no real knowledge of those things. At best, we may have opinions, but genuine knowledge can only come from study of the Ideas, and that can only ever be achieved through reason, rather than through our deceptive senses. This separation of two distinct worlds, one of appearance, the

The soul of man is immortal and imperishable.
Plato

Marcus Aurelius, Roman Emperor from 161 to 180 CE, was not just a powerful ruler, he was a noted scholar and thinker – a realization of Plato's idea that philosophers should lead society.

inhabited the world of Ideas before our birth, and still yearns to return to that realm after our death. So when we see variations of the Ideas in the world with our senses, we recognize them as a sort of recollection. Recalling the innate

memories of these Ideas requires reason – an attribute of the soul.

For Plato, the philosopher's job is to use reason to discover the Ideal Forms or Ideas. In the *Republic*, he also argues that it is philosophers, or rather those who are true to the philosopher's calling, who should be the ruling class. This is because only the true philosopher can understand the exact nature of the world and the truth of moral values. However, just like a prisoner in the "Allegory of the Cave" who sees the real objects rather than their shadows, many will just turn back to the only world they feel comfortable with. Plato often found it difficult to convince his fellow philosophers of the true nature of their calling.

Unsurpassed legacy

Plato himself was the embodiment of his ideal, or true, philosopher. He argued on questions of ethics that had been raised previously by the followers of Protagoras and Socrates, but in the process, he explored for the first time the path to knowledge itself. He was a profound influence on his pupil Aristotle – even if they fundamentally disagreed about the

What we call learning is only a process of recollection.
Plato

theory of Forms. Plato's ideas later found their way into the philosophy of medieval Islamic and Christian thinkers, including St Augustine of Hippo, who combined Plato's ideas with those of the Church.

By proposing that the use of reason, rather than observation, is the only way to acquire knowledge, Plato also laid the foundations of 17th-century rationalism. Plato's influence can still be felt today – the broad range of subjects he wrote about led the 20th-century British logician Alfred North Whitehead to say that subsequent Western philosophy "consists of a set of footnotes to Plato". ∎

Plato

Despite the large proportion of writings attributed to Plato that have survived, little is known about his life. He was born into a noble family in Athens in around 427 BCE and named Aristocles, but acquired the nickname "Plato" (meaning "broad"). Although probably destined for a life in politics, he became a pupil of Socrates. When Socrates was condemned to death, Plato is said to have become disillusioned with Athens, and left the city. He travelled widely, spending some time in southern Italy and Sicily, before returning to Athens around

385 BCE. Here he founded a school known as the Academy (from which the word "academic" comes), remaining its head until his death in 347 BCE.

Key works

c.399–387 BCE *Apology, Crito, Giorgias, Hippias Major, Meno, Protagoras* (early dialogues)
c.380–360 BCE *Phaedo, Phaedrus, Republic, Symposium* (middle dialogues)
c.360–355 BCE *Parmenides, Sophist, Theaetetus* (late dialogues)

TRUTH
RESIDES IN THE WORLD
AROUND US

ARISTOTLE (384–322 BCE)

IN CONTEXT

BRANCH
Epistemology

APPROACH
Empiricism

BEFORE
399 BCE Socrates argues that virtue is wisdom.

c.380 BCE Plato presents his theory of Forms in his Socratic dialogue, *The Republic*.

AFTER
9th century CE Aristotle's writings are translated into Arabic.

13th century Translations of Aristotle's works appear in Latin.

1690 John Locke establishes a school of British empiricism.

1735 Zoologist Carl Linnaeus lays the foundations of modern taxonomy in *Systema Naturae*, based on Aristotle's system of biological classification.

Aristotle was 17 years old when he arrived in Athens to study at the Academy under the great philosopher Plato. Plato himself was 60 at the time, and had already devised his theory of Forms. According to this theory, all earthly phenomena, such as justice and the colour green, are shadows of ideal counterparts, called Forms, which give their earthly models their particular identities.

Aristotle was a studious type, and no doubt learnt a great deal from his master, but he was also of a very different temperament. Where Plato was brilliant and intuitive, Aristotle was scholarly and methodical. Nevertheless, there was an obvious mutual respect, and Aristotle stayed at the Academy, both as a student and a teacher, until Plato died 20 years later. Surprisingly, he was not chosen as Plato's successor, and so he left Athens and took what would prove to be a fruitful trip to Ionia.

Plato's theory questioned

The break from teaching gave Aristotle the opportunity to indulge his passion for studying wildlife, which intensified his feeling that Plato's theory of Forms was wrong.

It is tempting to imagine that Aristotle's arguments had already had some influence on Plato, who in his later dialogues admitted some flaws in his earlier theories, but it is impossible to know for certain. We do know, though, that Plato was aware of the Third Man argument, which Aristotle used to refute his theory of Forms. This argument runs as follows: if there exists in a realm of Forms a perfect Form of Man on which earthly men are modelled, this Form, to have any conceivable content, would have to be based on a Form of the Form of Man – and this too would have to be based on a higher Form on which the Forms of the Forms are based, and so on *ad infinitum*.

Aristotle's later argument against the theory of Forms was more straightforward, and more directly related to his studies of the natural world. He realized that it was simply unnecessary to assume that there is a hypothetical realm of Forms, when the reality of things can already be seen here on Earth, inherent in everyday things.

Perhaps because his father had been a physician, Aristotle's scientific interests lay in what we

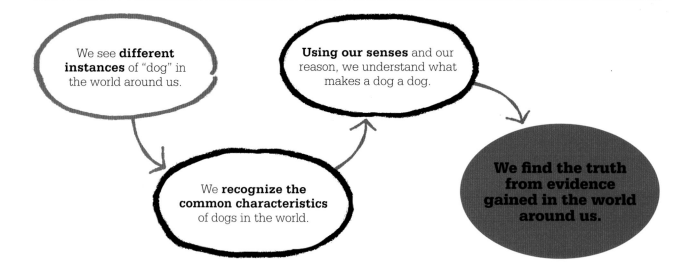

We see **different instances** of "dog" in the world around us.

We **recognize the common characteristics** of dogs in the world.

Using our senses and our reason, we understand what makes a dog a dog.

We find the truth from evidence gained in the world around us.

See also: Socrates 46–49 ▪ Plato 50–55 ▪ Avicenna 76–79 ▪ Averroes 82–83 ▪ René Descartes 116–123 ▪
John Locke 130–33 ▪ Gottfried Leibniz 134–37 ▪ George Berkeley 138–41 ▪ David Hume 148–53 ▪ Immanuel Kant 164–71

Plato and Aristotle differed in their opinion of the nature of universal qualities. For Plato, they reside in the higher realm of the Forms, but for Aristotle they reside here on Earth.

now call the biological sciences, whereas Plato's background had been firmly based in mathematics. This difference in background helps to explain the difference in approach between the two men. Mathematics, especially geometry, deals with abstract concepts that are far removed from the everyday world, whereas biology is very much about the world around us, and is based almost solely on observation. Plato sought confirmation of a realm of Forms from notions such as the perfect circle (which cannot exist in nature), but Aristotle found that certain constants can be discovered by examining the natural world.

Trusting the senses

What Aristotle proposed turned Plato's theory on its head. Far from mistrusting our senses, Aristotle relied on them for the evidence

to back up his theories. What he learnt from studying the natural world was that by observing the characteristics of every example of a particular plant or animal that he came across, he could build up a complete picture of what it was that distinguished it from other plants or animals, and deduce what makes it what it is. His own studies confirmed what he already believed – that we are not born with some innate ability to recognize Forms, as Plato maintained.

Each time a child comes across a dog, for example, it notes what it is about that animal that it has in common with other dogs, so that it can eventually recognize the things that make something a dog. The child now has an idea of "dogginess", or the "form", as Aristotle puts it, of a dog. In this way, we learn from our experience

of the world what the shared characteristics are that make things what they are – and the only way of experiencing the world is through our senses.

The essential form of things

Like Plato, then, Aristotle is concerned with finding some kind of immutable and eternal bedrock in a world characterized by change, but he concludes that there is no need to look for this anchor in a world of Forms that are only perceptible to the soul. The evidence is here in the world around us, perceptible through the senses. Aristotle believes that things in the material world are not imperfect copies of some ideal Form of themselves, but that the essential form of a thing is actually inherent in each instance of that thing. For example, "dogginess" is not just a shared characteristic of dogs – it is something that is inherent in each and every dog. »

Everything that depends on the action of nature is by nature as good as it can be.
Aristotle

> All men by nature
> desire to know.
> **Aristotle**

Aristotle classified many of the
different strands of knowledge and
learning that we have today, such
as physics, logic, metaphysics, poetics,
ethics, politics, and biology.

By studying particular things,
therefore, we can gain insight into
their universal, immutable nature.

What is true of examples in the
natural world, Aristotle reasons,
is also true of concepts relating
to human beings. Notions such
as "virtue", "justice", "beauty", and
"good" can be examined in exactly
the same way. As he sees it, when
we are born our minds are like
"unscribed tablets", and any ideas
that we gain can only be received
through our senses. At birth, we
have no innate ideas, so we can
have no idea of right or wrong. As
we encounter instances of justice
throughout our lives, however, we
learn to recognize the qualities that
these instances have in common,
and slowly build and refine our
understanding of what justice is.
In other words, the only way we
can come to know the eternal,
immutable idea of justice, is by
observing how it is manifested
in the world around us.

Aristotle departs from Plato,
then, not by denying that universal
qualities exist, but by questioning
both their nature and the means
by which we come to know them
(the latter being the fundamental
quesion of "epistemology", or the
theory of knowledge). And it was
this difference of opinion on how
we arrive at universal truths that
later divided philosophers into two
separate camps: the rationalists
(including René Descartes,
Immanuel Kant, and Gottfried
Leibniz), who believe in *a priori*,
or innate, knowledge; and the
empiricists (including John Locke,
George Berkeley, and David Hume),
who claim that all knowledge
comes from experience.

Biological classification

The manner in which Plato and
Aristotle arrive at their theories tells
us much about their temperaments.
Plato's theory of Forms is grand and
otherworldly, which is reflected in
the way he argues his case, using
highly imaginative fictionalized
dialogues between Socrates and
his contemporaries. By contrast,
Aristotle's theory is much more
down to earth, and is presented in
more prosaic, academic language.
Indeed, so convinced was Aristotle

that the truth of the world is to be
found here on Earth, and not in
some higher dimension, that he set
about collecting specimens of flora
and fauna, and classified them
according to their characteristics.

For this biological classification,
Aristotle devised a hierarchical
system – the first of its kind, and so
beautifully constructed that it forms
the basis of the taxonomy still in
use today. First, he divides the
natural world into living and non-
living things, then he turns his
attention to classifying the living
world. His next division is between
plants and animals, which involves
the same kind of thinking that
underpins his theory of universal
qualities: we may be able to
distinguish between a plant and
an animal almost without thinking,
but how do we know how to make
that distinction? The answer, for
Aristotle, is in the shared features
of either category. All plants share
the form "plant", and all animals
share the form "animal". And once
we understand the nature of those
forms, we can then recognize them
in each and every instance.

This fact becomes more apparent
the more Aristotle subdivides the
natural world. In order to classify a
specimen as a fish, for example, we
have to recognize what it is that
makes a fish a fish – which, again,
can be known through experience
and requires no innate knowledge
at all. As Aristotle builds up a
complete classification of all living
things, from the simplest organisms
to human beings, this fact is
confirmed again and again.

Teleological explanation

Another fact that became obvious
to Aristotle as he classified the
natural world is that the "form" of
a creature is not just a matter of its
physical characteristics, such as

its skin, fur, feather, or scales, but also a matter of what it does, and how it behaves – which, for Aristotle, has ethical implications.

To understand the link with ethics, we need first to appreciate that for Aristotle everything in the world is fully explained by four causes that fully account for a thing's existence. These four causes are: the material cause, or what a thing is made of; the formal cause, or the arrangement or shape of a

thing; the efficient cause, or how a thing is brought into being; and the final cause, or the function or purpose of a thing. And it is this last type of cause, the "final cause", that relates to ethics – a subject which, for Aristotle, is not separate from science, but rather a logical extension of biology.

An example that Aristotle gives is that of an eye: the final cause of an eye – its function – is to see. This function is the purpose, or

telos, of the eye – *telos* is a Greek word that gives us "teleology", or the study of purpose in nature. A teleological explanation of a thing is therefore an account of a thing's purpose, and to know the purpose of a thing is also to know what a "good" or a "bad" version of a thing is – a good eye for example, is one that sees well.

In the case of humans, a "good" life is therefore one in which we fulfill our purpose, or use all the characteristics that make us human to the full. A person can be considered "good" if he uses the characteristics he was born with, and can only be happy by using all his capabilities in the pursuit of virtue – the highest form of which, for Aristotle, is wisdom. Which brings us full circle back to the question of how we can recognize the thing that we call virtue – and for Aristotle, again, the answer is by observation. We understand the nature of the "good life" by seeing it in the people around us.

The syllogism
In the process of classification, Aristotle formulates a systematic form of logic which he applies to each specimen to determine »

Aristotle's classification of living things is the first detailed examination of the natural world. It proceeds from general observations about the characteristics shared by all animals, and then subdivides into ever more precise categories.

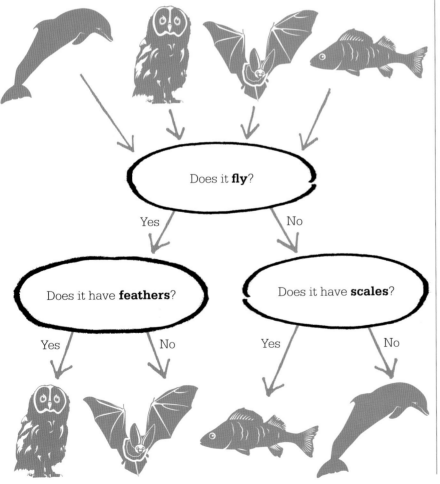

Linnaeus and Cuvier have been my two gods, though in very different ways, but they were mere schoolboys to old Aristotle.
Charles Darwin

"Socrates is mortal" is the undeniable conclusion to the most famous syllogism in history. Aristotle's syllogism – a simple deduction from two premises to a conclusion – was the first formal system of logic.

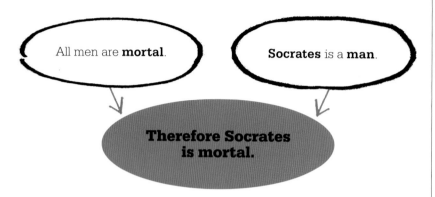

All men are **mortal**.

Socrates is a **man**.

Therefore Socrates is mortal.

Every action must be due to one or other of seven causes: chance, nature, compulsion, habit, reasoning, anger, or appetite.
Aristotle

whether it belongs to a certain category. For example, one of the characteristics common to all reptiles is that they are cold-blooded; so, if this particular specimen is warm-blooded, then it cannot be a reptile. Likewise, a characteristic common to all mammals is that they suckle their young; so, if this specimen is a mammal, it will suckle its young. Aristotle sees a pattern in this way of thinking – that of three propositions consisting of two premises and a conclusion, for example in the form: if As are Xs, and B is an A, then B is an X. The "syllogism", as this form of reasoning is known, is the first formal system of logic ever devised, and it remained the basic model for logic up until the 19th century.

But the syllogism was more than simply a by-product of Aristotle's systematic classification of the natural world. By using analytical reasoning in the form of logic, Aristotle realized that the power of reason was something that did not rely on the senses, and that it must therefore be an innate characteristic – part of what it is to be human. Although we have no innate ideas, we do possess this innate faculty, which is necessary for us to learn from experience. And as he applied this fact to his hierarchical system, he saw that the innate power of reason is what distinguishes us from all other living creatures, and placed us at the top of the hierarchy.

Decline of Classical Greece
The sheer scope of Aristotle's ideas, and the revolutionary way in which he overturns Plato's theory of Forms, should have ensured that his philosophy had a far greater impact than it did during his lifetime. That is not to say that his work was without fault – his geography and astronomy were flawed; his ethics supported the use of slaves and considered women to be inferior human beings; and his logic was incomplete by modern standards. However, what he got right amounted to a revolution both in philosophy and in science.

But Aristotle lived at the end of an era. Alexander the Great, whom he taught, died shortly before him, and so began the Hellenistic period of Greek history which saw a decline in Athens' influence. The Roman Empire was becoming the dominant power in the Mediterranean, and the philosophy it adopted from Greece was that of the Stoics. The rival schools of Plato and Aristotle – Plato's Academy and the Lyceum Aristotle founded in Athens – continued to operate, but they had lost their former eminence.

As a result of this neglect, many of Aristotle's writings were lost. It is believed that he wrote several hundred treatises and dialogues explaining his theories, but all that remain are fragments of his work, mainly in the form of lectures and teacher's notes. Luckily for posterity, these were preserved by his followers, and there is enough contained in them to give a picture of the full range of his work.

Aristotle's legacy
With the emergence of Islam in the 7th century CE, Aristotle's works were translated into Arabic and spread throughout the Islamic world, becoming essential reading for Middle Eastern scholars such as Avicenna and Averroes. In Western Europe, however, Boethius's Latin translation of Aristotle's treatise on logic (made in the 6th century CE) remained the only work of Aristotle's

The influence of Aristotle on the history of thought can be seen in the Great Chain of Being, a medieval Christian depiction of life as a hierarchy in which with God presides over all.

available until the 9th century CE, when all of Aristotle's works began to be translated from Arabic into Latin. It was also at this time that his ideas were collected into the the books we know today – such as *Physics, The Nicomachean Ethics,* and the *Organon.* In the 13th century, Thomas Aquinas braved a ban on Aristotle's work and integrated it into Christian philosophy, in the same way that St Augustine had adopted Plato, and Plato and Aristotle came to lock horns again.

Aristotle's notes on logic (laid out in the *Organon*) remained the standard text on logic until the emergence of mathematical logic in the 19th century. Likewise, his classification of living things dominated Western thinking throughout the Middle Ages, becoming the Christian *scala naturae* (the "ladder of nature"), or the Great Chain of Being. This depicted the whole of creation dominated by man, who stood second only to God. And during the Renaissance, Aristotle's empirical method of enquiry held sway.

In the 17th century, the debate between empiricists and rationalists reached its zenith after René Descartes published his *Discourse on the Method.* Descartes, and Leibniz and Kant after him, chose the rationalist route; in response, Locke, Berkeley, and Hume lined up as the empiricist opposition.

There is nothing in the mind except was first in the senses.
John Locke

Again, the differences between the philosophers were as much about temperament as they were about substance – the Continental versus the English, the poetic versus the academic, the Platonic versus the Aristotelian. Although the debate died down in the 19th century, there has been a revival of interest in Aristotle in recent times, and a reappraisal of his significance. His ethics in particular have been of great appeal to modern philosophers, who have seen in his functional definition of "good" a key to understanding the way we use ethical language. ∎

Aristotle

Born in Stagira, Chalcidice, in the northeast region of modern Greece, Aristotle was the son of a physician to the royal family of Macedon, and was educated as a member of the aristocracy. He was sent to Plato's Academy in Athens at the age of 17, and spent almost 20 years there both as a student and a teacher. When Plato died, Aristotle left Athens for Ionia, and spent several years studying the wildlife of the area. He was then appointed tutor at the Macedonian court, where he taught the young Alexander the Great and continued his studies.

In 335 BCE he returned to Athens, encouraged by Alexander, and set up the Lyceum, a school to rival Plato's. It was here that he did most of his writing, and formalized his ideas. After Alexander died in 323 BCE, anti-Macedonian feeling flared up in Athens, and Aristotle fled to Chalcis, on the island of Euboea, where he died the following year.

Key works

Organon, Physics (as compiled in book form in the 9th century).

DEATH IS NOTHING TO US
EPICURUS (341–270 BCE)

IN CONTEXT

BRANCH
Ethics

APPROACH
Epicureanism

BEFORE
Late 5th century BCE
Socrates states that seeking knowledge and truth is the key to a worthwhile life.

c.400 BCE Democritus and Leucippus conclude that the cosmos consists solely of atoms, moving in empty space.

AFTER
c.50 BCE Roman philosopher Lucretius writes *De rerum natura,* a poem exploring Epicurus's ideas.

1789 Jeremy Bentham advocates the utilitarian idea of "the greatest happiness for the greatest number".

1861 John Stuart Mill argues that intellectual and spiritual pleasures have more value than physical pleasures.

Epicurus grew up in a time when the philosophy of ancient Greece had already reached a pinnacle in the ideas of Plato and Aristotle. The main focus of philosophical thinking was shifting from metaphysics towards ethics – and also from political to personal ethics. Epicurus, however, found the seeds of a new school of thought in the quests of earlier philosophers, such as Socrates' examination of the truth of basic human concepts and values.

Terrifying images of the merciless god of death Thanatos were used to depict the pain and torment ancient Greeks might incur for their sins, both when they died and in the afterlife.

Central to the philosophy that Epicurus developed is the view that peace of mind, or tranquillity, is the goal of life. He argues that pleasure and pain are the roots of good and evil, and qualities such as virtue and justice derive from these roots, as "it is impossible to live a pleasant life without living wisely, honourably, and justly, and it is impossible to live wisely, honourably, and justly without living pleasantly". Epicurianism is often mistakenly interpreted as simply being about the pursuit of sensual pleasures. For Epicurus, the greatest pleasure is only attainable through knowledge and friendship, and a temperate life, with freedom from fear and pain.

Fear of death
One of the obstacles to enjoying the peace of a tranquil mind, Epicurus reasons, is the fear of death, and this fear is increased by the religious belief that if you incur the wrath of the gods, you will be severely punished in the afterlife. But rather than countering this fear by proposing an alternative state of immortality, Epicurus tries to explain the nature of death itself. He starts by proposing that when

See: Democritus and Leucippus 45 ▪ Socrates 46–49 ▪ Plato 50–55 ▪ Aristotle 56–63 ▪ Jeremy Bentham 174 ▪ John Stuart Mill 190–93

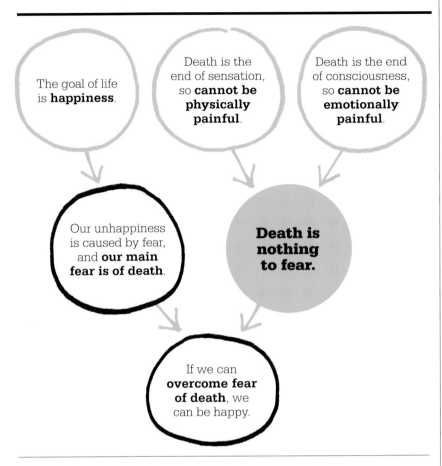

The goal of life is **happiness**.

Death is the end of sensation, so **cannot be physically painful**.

Death is the end of consciousness, so **cannot be emotionally painful**.

Our unhappiness is caused by fear, and **our main fear is of death**.

Death is nothing to fear.

If we can **overcome fear of death**, we can be happy.

Epicurus

Born to Athenian parents on the Aegean island of Samos, Epicurus was first taught philosophy by a disciple of Plato. In 323 BCE, Alexander the Great died and, in the political conflicts that followed, Epicurus and his family were forced to move to Colophon (now in Turkey). There he continued his studies with Nausiphanes, a follower of Democritus.

Epicurus taught briefly in Mytilene on the island of Lesbos, and in Lampsacus on the Greek mainland, before moving to Athens in 306 BCE. He founded a school, known as the The Garden, consisting of a community of friends and followers. There he set down in great detail the philosophy that was to become known as Epicureanism.

Despite frequent ill health, and often being in great pain, Epicurus lived to the age of 72. True to his beliefs, he described the last day of his life as a truly happy day.

Key works

Early 3rd century BCE
On Nature
Principal Doctrines,
Vatican Sayings

we die, we are unaware of our death, since our consciousness (our soul) ceases to exist at the point of death. To explain this, Epicurus takes the view that the entire universe consists of either atoms or empty space, as argued by the atomist philosophers Democritus and Leucippus. Epicurus then reasons that the soul could not be empty space, because it operates dynamically with the body, so it must be made up of atoms. He describes these atoms of the soul as being distributed around the body, but as being so fragile that they dissolve when we die, and so we are no longer capable of sensing anything. If you

are unable to feel anything, mentally or physically, when you die, it is foolish to let the fear of death cause you pain while you are still alive.

Epicurus attracted a small but devoted following in his lifetime, but he was perceived as being dismissive of religion, which made him unpopular. His thinking was largely ignored by mainstream philosophy for centuries, but it resurfaced in the 18th century, in the ideas of Jeremy Bentham and John Stuart Mill. In revolutionary politics, the tenets of Epicureanism are echoed in the words of the United States' Declaration of Independence: "life, liberty, and the pursuit of happiness". ▪

HE HAS THE MOST WHO IS MOST CONTENT WITH THE LEAST
DIOGENES OF SINOPE (c.404–323 BCE)

IN CONTEXT

BRANCH
Ethics

APPROACH
Cynicism

BEFORE
Late 5th century BCE
Socrates teaches that the ideal life is one spent in search of truth.

Early 4th century BCE
Socrates' pupil Antisthenes advocates an ascetic life, lived in harmony with nature.

AFTER
c.301 BCE Influenced by Diogenes, Zeno of Citium founds a school of Stoics.

4th century CE St Augustine of Hippo denounces the often shameless behaviour of the Cynics, although they become the model for several ascetic Christian orders.

1882 Friedrich Nietzsche refers to Diogenes and his ideas in *The Gay Science*.

Plato once described Diogenes as "a Socrates gone mad". Although this was meant as an insult, it is not far from the truth. Diogenes shares Socrates' passion for virtue and rejection of material comfort, but takes these ideas to the extreme. He argues that in order to lead a good life, or one that is worth living, it is necessary to free oneself from the external restrictions imposed by society, and from the internal discontentment that is caused by desire, emotion, and fear. This can be achieved, he states, by being content to live a simple life, governed by reason and natural impulses, rejecting conventions without shame, and renouncing the desire for property and comfort.

Diogenes was the first of a group of thinkers who became known as the Cynics, a term taken from the Greek *kunikos,* meaning "dog-like". It reflects the determination of the Cynics to spurn all forms of social custom and etiquette, and instead live in as natural a state as possible. They asserted that the more one

Rejecting worldly values, Diogenes chose to live on the streets. He flouted convention, by eating only discarded scraps and dressing – when he actually bothered to do so – in filthy rags.

can do this, as Diogenes himself did by living a life of poverty with only an abandoned tub for shelter, the nearer one will be to leading the ideal life.

The happiest person, who in Diogenes' phrase "has the most", is therefore someone who lives in accordance with the rhythms of the natural world, free from the conventions and values of civilized society, and is "content with the least". ∎

See also: Socrates 46–49 ▪ Plato 50–55 ▪ Zeno of Citium 67 ▪ St Augustine of Hippo 72–73 ▪ Friedrich Nietzsche 214–21

THE GOAL OF LIFE IS LIVING IN AGREEMENT WITH NATURE
ZENO OF CITIUM (c.332–265 BCE)

IN CONTEXT

BRANCH
Ethics

APPROACH
Stoicism

BEFORE
c.380 BCE Plato states his thoughts on ethics and the city-state in *The Republic.*

4th century BCE Diogenes of Sinope lives in extreme poverty to demonstrate his Cynic principles.

AFTER
c.40–45 CE Roman statesman and philosopher Seneca the Younger continues the Stoic tradition in his *Dialogues.*

c.150–180 Roman emperor Marcus Aurelius writes his 12-volume *Meditations* on Stoic philosophy.

1584 Flemish humanist Justus Lipsius writes *De Constantia*, combining Stoicism with Christianity to found a school of Neo-Stoicism.

Two main schools of philosophical thought emerged after Aristotle's death. These were the hedonistic, godless ethic of Epicurus, which had limited appeal, and the more popular and longer-lasting Stoicism of Zeno of Citium.

Zeno studied with a disciple of Diogenes of Sinope, the Cynic, and shared his no-nonsense approach to life. He had little patience with metaphysical speculation and came to believe that the cosmos was governed by natural laws that were ordained by a supreme lawgiver. Man, he declares, is completely powerless to change this reality, and in addition to enjoying its many benefits, man also has to accept its cruelty and injustice.

Free will
However, Zeno also declares that man has been given a rational soul with which to exercise free will. No one is forced to pursue a "good" life. It is up to the individual to choose whether to put aside the things over which he has little or no control, and be indifferent to pain and pleasure, poverty and riches. But if a person does so, Zeno is convinced that he will achieve a life that is in harmony with nature in all its aspects, good or bad, and live in accordance with the rulings of the supreme lawgiver.

Stoicism was to find favour across much of Hellenistic Greece. But it drew in even more followers in the expanding Roman empire, where it flourished as a basis for ethics – both personal and political – until it was supplanted by Christianity in the 6th century. ■

Happiness is a good flow of life.
Zeno of Citium

See also: Plato 50–55 ▪ Aristotle 56–63 ▪ Epicurus 64–65 ▪ Diogenes of Sinope 66

THE MED
WORLD
250–1500

EVAL

Plotinus founds **Neo-Platonism**, a school of mystical philosophy based on the writings of Plato.

↑

c.260

Crises brought on by both internal and external forces lead to the **division of the Roman Empire** into east and west. The western empire falls within a century.

↑

395

Boethius begins to translate Aristotle's work on logic.

↑

c.510

The prophet Muhammad performs the **Hejira**, his journey from Mecca to Medina, marking the beginning of the Muslim era.

↑

622

313

↓

Constantine I proclaims religious freedom within the Roman Empire in the **Edict of Milan**.

397–98

↓

St Augustine of Hippo writes his *Confessions*.

618

↓

The **Tang dynasty** is established in China, bringing a **Golden Age** of cultural development.

711

↓

Conquest of Christian Iberia (now Spain and Portugal) by Muslim invaders.

P hilosophy did not play a large part in Roman culture, other than Stoicism, which was admired by the Romans for its emphasis on virtuous conduct and doing one's duty. The broader philosophical tradition that had been established by the Classical Greeks was therefore effectively marginalized under the Roman Empire. Philosophy continued to be taught in Athens, but its influence dwindled, and no significant philosophers emerged until Plotinus in the 3rd century CE, who founded an important Neo-Platonist school.

During the first millennium of the Common Era, Roman influence also waned, both politically and culturally. Christianity became assimilated into the Roman culture, and after the fall of the empire in the 5th century, the Church

became the dominant authority in Western Europe, remaining so for almost 1,000 years. The Greek idea of philosophy as rational examination independent of religious doctrine sat uncomfortably with the rise of Christianity. Questions about the nature of the universe and what constitutes a virtuous life were held to be answered in the scriptures; they were not considered subjects for philosophical discussion.

Early Christian philosophers such as St Augustine of Hippo sought to integrate Greek philosophy into the Christian religion. This process was the main task of scholasticism, a philosophical approach that stemmed from the monastic schools and was renowned for its rigorous dialectical reasoning. The work of scholastic philosophers such as Augustine was not so much an

exploration of questions such as "Is there a God?" or "Does man have an immortal soul?" as a search for a rational justification for the belief in God and an immortal soul.

The Dark Ages
As the Roman Empire shrank and eventually fell, Europe sank into the "Dark Ages" and most of the culture it had inherited from Greece and Rome disappeared. The Church held the monopoly on learning, and the only true philosophy that survived was a form of Platonism deemed compatible with Christianity, and Boethius's translation of Aristotle's *Logic*.

Elsewhere, however, culture thrived. China and Japan in particular enjoyed a "Golden Age" of poetry and art, while traditional eastern philosophies co-existed

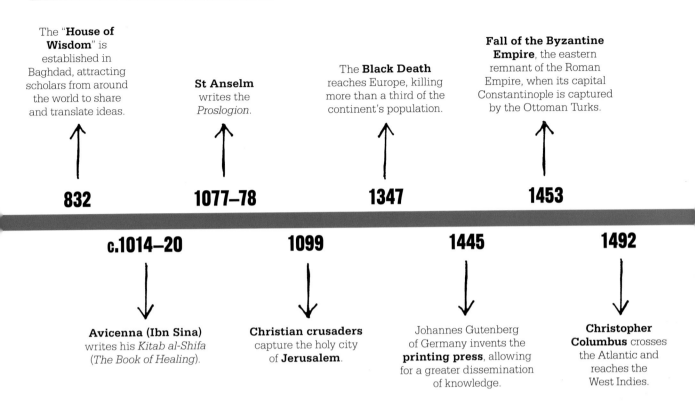

The "**House of Wisdom**" is established in Baghdad, attracting scholars from around the world to share and translate ideas.

St Anselm writes the *Proslogion*.

The **Black Death** reaches Europe, killing more than a third of the continent's population.

Fall of the Byzantine Empire, the eastern remnant of the Roman Empire, when its capital Constantinople is captured by the Ottoman Turks.

832   **1077–78**   **1347**   **1453**

c.1014–20   **1099**   **1445**   **1492**

Avicenna (Ibn Sina) writes his *Kitab al-Shifa* (*The Book of Healing*).

Christian crusaders capture the holy city of **Jerusalem**.

Johannes Gutenberg of Germany invents the **printing press**, allowing for a greater dissemination of knowledge.

Christopher Columbus crosses the Atlantic and reaches the West Indies.

happily with their religions. In the lands that had been part of Alexander the Great's empire, the Greek legacy commanded more respect than in Europe. Arabic and Persian scholars preserved and translated the works of the Classical Greek philosophers, incorporating their ideas into Islamic culture from the 6th century onwards.

As Islam spread eastwards into Asia and across north Africa and into Spain, its influence began to be felt in Europe. By the 12th century, news of ideas and inventions from the Islamic world were reaching as far north as Britain, and European scholars started to rediscover Greek mathematics and philosophy through Islamic sources. The works of Aristotle in particular came as something of a revelation, and they sparked a resurgence of philosophical thinking within the medieval Christian Church. But whereas Plato's philosophy had been comparatively easy to assimilate into Christian thought, because it provided rational justification for belief in God and the immortal human soul, Aristotle was treated with suspicion by the Church authorities. Nevertheless, Christian philosophers including Roger Bacon, Thomas Aquinas, Duns Scotus, and William of Ockham enthusiastically embraced the new Aristotelianism and eventually convinced the Church of its compatibility with Christian faith.

A new rationality

Along with the philosophy that revitalized the Church, the Islamic world also introduced a wealth of technological and scientific knowledge to medieval Europe. Aristotle's scientific methods had been refined to sophisticated levels in Persia, and advances in chemistry, physics, medicine, and particularly astronomy undermined the authority of the Church when they arrived in Europe.

The re-introduction of Greek thinking and the new ideas that led to Europe's Renaissance in the late 15th century sparked a change of mood as people began to look more towards reason rather than faith to provide them with answers. There was dissent even within the Church, as humanists such as Erasmus provoked the Reformation. Philosophers themselves turned their attention away from questions of God and the immortal soul towards the problems posed by science and the natural world. ∎

GOD IS NOT THE PARENT OF EVILS

ST AUGUSTINE OF HIPPO (354–430 CE)

IN CONTEXT

BRANCH
Ethics

APPROACH
Christian Platonism

BEFORE
c.400 BCE In *Gorgias*, Plato argues that evil is not a thing, but an absence of something.

3rd century CE Plotinus revives Plato's view of good and evil.

AFTER
c.520 Boethius uses an Augustinian theory of evil in *The Consolation of Philosophy*.

c.1130 Pierre Abélard rejects the idea that there are not evil things.

1525 Martin Luther, the German priest who inspired the Protestant reformation, publishes *On the Bondage of the Will*, arguing that the human will is not free.

Humans are **rational beings**.

In order to be rational, humans must have **free will**.

This means they must be able to **choose** between **good or evil.**

Humans can therefore act badly or well.

God is not the parent of evils.

Augustine was especially interested in the problem of evil. If God is entirely good and all-powerful, why is there evil in the world? For Christians such as Augustine, as well as for adherents of Judaism and Islam, this was, and remains, a central question. This is because it makes an obvious fact about the world – that it contains evil – into an argument against the existence of God.

Augustine is able to answer one aspect of the problem quite easily. He believes that although God created everything that exists, he did not create evil, because evil is not a thing, but a lack or deficiency of something. For example, the evil suffered by a blind man is that he is without sight; the evil in a thief is that he lacks honesty. Augustine borrowed this way of thinking from Plato and his followers.

An essential freedom
But Augustine still needs to explain why God should have created the world in such a way as to allow there to be these natural and moral evils, or deficiencies. His answer revolves around the idea that humans are rational beings. He argues that in order for God to

See also: Plato 50–55 ▪ Plotinus 331 ▪ Boethius 74–75 ▪ Pierre Abélard 333 ▪ David Hume 148–53

create rational creatures, such as human beings, he had to give them freedom of will. Having freedom of will means being able to choose, including choosing between good and evil. For this reason God had to leave open the possibility that the first man, Adam, would choose evil rather than good. According to the Bible this is exactly what happened, as Adam broke God's command not to eat fruit from the Tree of Knowledge.

In fact, Augustine's argument holds even without referring to the Bible. Rationality is the ability to evaluate choices through the process of reasoning. The process is only possible where there is freedom of choice, including the freedom to choose to do wrong.

Augustine also suggests a third solution to the problem, asking us to see the world as a thing of beauty. He says that although there is evil in the universe, it contributes to an overall good that is greater than it could be without evil – just as discords in music can make a harmony more lovely, or dark patches add to the beauty of a picture.

Explaining natural evils

Since Augustine's time, most Christian philosophers have tackled the problem of evil using one of his approaches, while their opponents, such as David Hume, have pointed to their weaknesses as arguments against Christianity. Calling sickness, for instance, an absence of health seems to be just playing with words: illness may be due to a deficiency of something, but the suffering of the sick person is real enough. And how are natural evils, such as earthquakes and plagues, explained?

Someone without a prior belief in God might still argue that the presence of evil in the world proves that there is no all-powerful and benevolent God. But for those who do already believe in God, Augustine's arguments might hold the answer. ▪

What made Adam capable of obeying God's commands also made him able to sin.
St Augustine of Hippo

A world without evil, Augustine says, would be a world without us – rational beings able to choose their actions. Just as for Adam and Eve, our moral choices allow for the possibility of evil.

St Augustine of Hippo

Aurelius Augustine was born in 354 CE in Thagaste, a small provincial town in North Africa, to a Christian mother and a pagan father. He was educated to be a rhetorician, and he went on to teach rhetoric in his home town, and at Carthage, Rome, and Milan, where he occupied a prestigious position.

For a while Augustine followed Manichaeism – a religion that sees good and evil as dual forces that rule the universe – but under the influence of Archbishop Ambrose of Milan, he became attracted to Christianity. In 386, he suffered a spiritual crisis and underwent a conversion. He abandoned his career and devoted himself to writing Christian works, many of a highly philosophical nature. In 395 he became Bishop of Hippo, in North Africa, and he held this post for the rest of his life. He died in Hippo, aged 75, when the town was beseiged and sacked by the Vandals.

Key works

c.388–95 *On Free Will*
c.397–401 *Confessions*
c.413–27 *On the City of God*

74

GOD FORESEES OUR FREE THOUGHTS AND ACTIONS
BOETHIUS (c.480–525 CE)

IN CONTEXT

BRANCH
Epistemology

APPROACH
Christian Platonism

BEFORE
c.350 BCE Aristotle outlines the problems of claiming as true any statement about the outcome of a future event.

c.300 BCE Syrian philosopher Iamblichus says that what can be known depends upon the knower's capacity.

AFTER
c.1250–70 Thomas Aquinas agrees with Boethius that God exists outside of time, and so is transcendent and beyond human understanding.

c.1300 John Duns Scotus says that human freedom rests on God's own freedom to act, and that God knows our future, free actions by knowing his own, unchanging – but free – will.

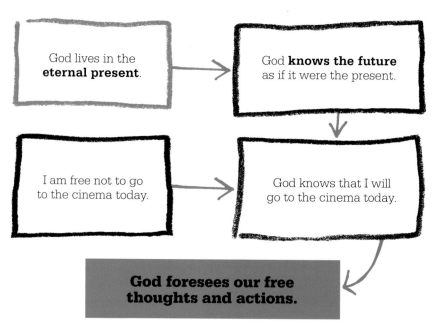

God lives in the **eternal present**.

God **knows the future** as if it were the present.

I am free not to go to the cinema today.

God knows that I will go to the cinema today.

God foresees our free thoughts and actions.

The Roman philosopher Boethius was trained in the Platonist tradition of philosophy, and was also a Christian. He is famous for his solution to a problem that predates Aristotle: if God already knows what we are going to do in the future, how can we be said to have free will?

The best way to understand the dilemma is to imagine a situation in everyday life. For instance, this afternoon I might go to the cinema, or I might spend time writing. As it turns out, I go to the cinema. That being the case, it is true now (before the event) that I will go the cinema this afternoon. But if it is true now, then it seems that I do not really have the choice of spending the afternoon writing. Aristotle was the first to define this problem, but his answer to it is not very clear; he seems to have thought that a sentence such

See also: Aristotle 56–63 ▪ Thomas Aquinas 88–95 ▪ John Duns Scotus 333 ▪ Benedictus Spinoza 126–29 ▪ Immanuel Kant 164–71

as "I shall go to the cinema this afternoon" is neither true nor false, or at least not in the same way as "I went to the cinema yesterday".

A God beyond time

Boethius faced a harder version of the same problem. He believed that God knows everything; not only the past and the present, but also the future. So if I am going to go to the cinema this afternoon, God knows it now. It seems, therefore, that I am not really free to choose to

> Everything is known, not according to itself, but according to the capacity of the knower.
> **Boethius**

spend the afternoon writing, since that would conflict with what God already knows.

Boethius solves the problem by arguing that the same thing can be known in different ways, depending on the nature of the knower. My dog, for instance, knows the sun only as something with qualities he can sense – by sight and touch. A person, however, can also reason about the category of thing the sun is, and may know which elements it is made of, its distance from Earth, and so on.

Boethius considers time in a similar kind of way. As we live in the flow of time, we can only know events as past (if they have occurred), present (if they are happening now), or future (if they will come to pass). We cannot know the outcome of uncertain future events. God, by contrast, is not in the flow of time. He lives in an eternal present, and knows what to us are past, present, and future in the same way that we know the present. And just as my knowledge that you are sitting now does not interfere with your freedom to stop, so too God's knowledge of

Lady Philosophy and Boethius discuss free will, determinism, and God's vision of the eternal present in his influential book, *The Consolation of Philosophy*.

our future actions, as if they were present, does not stop them from being free.

Some thinkers today argue that since I have not yet decided whether I shall go to the cinema this afternoon, there is simply nothing to be known about it, so even a God who is all-knowing does not, and cannot, know if I shall go or not. ▪

Anicius Boethius

Anicius Boethius was a Christian Roman aristocrat, born at a time when the Roman Empire was disintegrating and the Ostrogoths ruled Italy. He became an orphan at the age of seven and was brought up by an aristocratic family in Rome. He was extremely well educated, speaking fluent Greek and having an extensive knowledge of Latin and Greek literature and philosophy. He devoted his life to translating and commenting on Greek texts, especially Aristotle's works on logic, until he was made chief adviser to the Ostrogothic king

Theoderic. Some five years later he became a victim of court intrigue, was wrongly accused of treason, and sentenced to death. He wrote his most famous work, *The Consolation of Philosophy*, while in prison awaiting execution.

Key works

c.510 *Commentaries on Aristotle's "Categories"*
c.513–16 *Commentaries on Aristotle's "On Interpretation"*
c.523–26 *The Consolation of Philosophy*

THE SOUL IS DISTINCT FROM THE BODY

AVICENNA (980–1037)

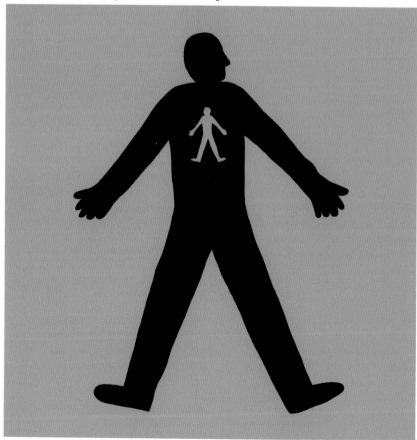

IN CONTEXT

BRANCH
Metaphysics

APPROACH
Arabic Aristotelianism

BEFORE
c.400 BCE Plato argues that mind and body are distinct substances.

4th century BCE Aristotle argues that mind is the "form" of the body.

c.800–950 CE Aristotle's works are translated into Arabic for the first time.

AFTER
1250s–60s Thomas Aquinas adapts Aristotle's account of the mind and body.

1640 René Descartes argues for dualism in his *Meditations*.

1949 Gilbert Ryle describes dualism as a "category mistake" in *The Concept of Mind*.

Avicenna, also known as Ibn Sînâ, is the most important philosopher in the Arabic tradition, and one of the world's greatest thinkers. Like his predecessors, al-Kindî and al-Fârâbî, and his successor, Averroes, Avicenna self-consciously marked himself out as a philosopher rather than an Islamic theologian, choosing to follow Greek wisdom and the path of reasoning and proof. In particular, he saw himself as a follower of Aristotle, and his main writings are encyclopaedias of Aristotelian philosophy.

However, these works explain Aristotle's philosophy as re-thought and synthesized by Avicenna. On

See also: Plato 50–55 ▪ Aristotle 56–63 ▪ Al-Kindî 332 ▪ Al-Fârâbî 332 ▪
Thomas Aquinas 88–95 ▪ René Descartes 116–23 ▪ Gilbert Ryle 337

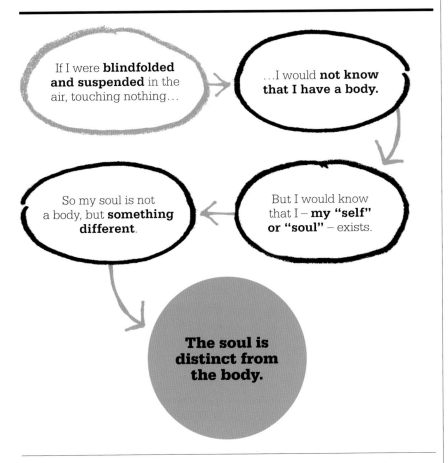

> If I were **blindfolded and suspended** in the air, touching nothing…

> …I would **not know that I have a body.**

> But I would know that I – **my "self" or "soul"** – exists.

> So my soul is not a body, but **something different**.

> **The soul is distinct from the body.**

Avicenna

Ibn Sînâ, or Avicenna as the Europeans called him, was born in 980 in a village near Bukhara, now in Uzbekhistan. Although he wrote mainly in Arabic, the language of learning throughout the Islamic world, he was a native Persian speaker. Avicenna was a child prodigy, rapidly surpassing his teachers not only in logic and philosophy, but also in medicine. While still in his teens, he became known to the Samanid ruler Nuh ibn Mansur as a brilliant physician, and was given the use of his magnificent library.

Avicenna's life was spent in the service of various princes, both as physician and political adviser. He started writing at the age of 21, and went on to write more than 200 texts, on subjects as diverse as metaphysics, animal physiology, mechanics of solids, and Arabic syntax. He died when his medications for colic were altered, possibly maliciously, while on campaign with his patron Alâ al-Dawla.

Key works

c.1014–20 *Book of Healing*
c.1015 *Canon of Medicine*
c.1030 *Pointers and Reminders*

some doctrines, such as the idea that the universe has always existed, Avicenna kept to the Aristotelian view despite the fact that it clashed with Islamic orthodoxy, but in other areas he felt free to depart radically from Aristotle. One striking example is his explanation of the relationship between mind (self or soul) and body.

Mind and body are distinct

Aristotle claims that the body and mind of humans (and other animals) are not two different things (or "substances"), but one unit, and that the mind is the "form" of the human body. As such, it is responsible for all the activities a human being can perform, including thinking. For this reason Aristotle does not seem to think it possible for anything to survive the death of the body.

By contrast, Avicenna is one of the most famous "dualists" in the history of philosophy – he thinks that the body and the mind are two distinct substances. His great predecessor in this view was Plato, who thought of the mind as a distinct thing that was imprisoned in the body. Plato believed that at the point of death, the mind would be released from its prison, to be later reincarnated in another body.

In seeking to prove the divided nature of mind and body, Avicenna devised a thought-experiment known as the "Flying Man". This » appears as a treatise, *On the Soul*, within his *Book of Healing*, and it aims to strip away any knowledge that can possibly be disproved, and leave us only with absolute truths. It remarkably anticipates the much later work of Descartes, the famous dualist of the 17th century, who also decided to believe nothing at all except that which he himself could know for certain. Both Avicenna and Descartes want to demonstrate that the mind or self exists because it knows it exists; and that it is distinct from the human body.

The Flying Man

In the Flying Man experiment, Avicenna wants to examine what we can know if we are effectively robbed of our senses, and cannot depend on them for information. He asks us each to imagine this: suppose I have just come into existence, but I have all my normal intelligence. Suppose, too, that I am blindfolded and that I am floating in the air, and my limbs are separated from each other, so I can touch nothing. Suppose I am entirely without any sensations. None the less, I will be sure that I myself exist. But what is this self, which is me? It cannot be any of the parts of my body, because I do not know that I have any. The self that I affirm as existing does not have length or breadth or depth. It has no extension, or physicality. And, if I were able to imagine, for instance, a hand, I would not think that it belonged to this self which I know exists.

It follows from this that the human self – what I am – is distinct from my body, or anything physical. The Flying Man experiment, says Avicenna, is a way of alerting and reminding oneself of the existence of the mind as something other than, and distinct from, the body.

Avicenna also has other ways to show that the mind cannot be something material. Most are based on the fact that the type of intellectual knowledge the mind can grasp cannot not be contained

> The secret conversation is a direct encounter between God and the soul, abstracted from all material constraints.
> **Avicenna**

by anything material. It is easy to see how the parts of physical, shaped things fit with the parts of a physical, shaped sense organ: the image of the wall that I see is stretched over the lens of my eye, each of its parts corresponding to a part of the lens. But the mind is not a sense organ; what it grasps are definitions, such as "Man is a rational, mortal animal". The parts of this phrase need to be grasped at once, together. The mind therefore cannot be in any way like or part of the body.

The immortal soul

Avicenna goes on to draw the conclusion that the mind is not destroyed when the body dies, and that it is immortal. This did not help to make his thinking more palatable to orthodox Muslims, who believe that the whole person, body and mind, is resurrected and enjoys the afterlife. Consequently, Avicenna was attacked in the 12th century by the great Islamic theologian al-Ghazâlî, who called him a heretic

Avicenna's medical knowledge was so vast that it won him royal patronage. His *Canon of Medicine* influenced European schools of medicine until the mid-17th century.

> But what is it
> that I am?
> A thinking thing.
> **René Descartes**

for abandoning the central Islamic tenet of the resurrection of the dead. But in the same century Avicenna's work was also translated into Latin, and his dualism became popular among Christian philosophers and theologians. They liked the way his interpretations of Aristotle's texts made them easily compatible with the idea of an immortal soul.

The indubitable self

Some 200 years later, in the 1250s, Thomas Aquinas championed a more faithful interpretation of Aristotle, in which the mind and body are much more closely tied together, and his views were widely accepted by the theologians of the 16th and 17th centuries. But in 1640 Descartes returned to a dualism that was nearer to Plato's than Aristotle's, and his argument for it was very like Avicenna's.

Descartes imagines that there is a demon who is trying to deceive him about everything on which he might possibly be deceived. The one

Philip Pullman's tale, *Northern Lights,* picks up on the ancient Greek idea of a person's soul, or *daimon*, being separate to the body, by presenting it as an entirely separate animal, such as a cat.

thing that he cannot be deceived about, he realizes, is that he exists. This self is exactly the self which Avicenna's Flying Man is sure of, when he has no other knowledge. Like Avicenna, Descartes can then conclude that the "I", or self, is completely distinct from the body, and that it must be immortal.

The ghost in the machine

One very strong objection to the dualism of Avicenna or Descartes is the argument used by Aquinas. He says that the self which thinks is the same as the self which feels sensations in the body. For instance, I do not just observe that there is a pain in my leg, in the way that a sailor might notice a hole in his ship. The pain belongs to me as much as my thoughts about philosophy, or what I might have for lunch.

Most contemporary philosophers reject mind-body dualism, largely because of the increasing scientific knowledge of the brain. Avicenna and Descartes were both very interested in physiology and they produced scientific accounts of activities such as movement and sensation. But the process of rational thinking was inexplicable with the scientific tools of their

times. We are now able to explain quite precisely how thinking goes on in different areas of the brain – though whether this means that we can explain thinking without reference to a self is not so clear. An influential 20th-century British philosopher, Gilbert Ryle, caricatured the dualists' self as "a ghost in the machine", and tried to show that we can explain how human beings perceive and function within the world without resorting to this "ghost" of a self.

Today philosophers are divided between a small number of dualists, a larger number of thinkers who say that the mind is simply a brain, and the majority, who agree that thinking is the result of the physical activity of the brain, but still insist there is a distinction between the physical states of the brain (the grey matter, the neurons, and so on), and the thinking which derives from them.

Many philosophers, especially continental European thinkers, still accept the results of Avicenna's thought experiment in one central way. It shows, they say, that we each have a self with a first-person view of the world (the "I") that is not accommodated by the objective view of scientific theories. ∎

JUST BY THINKING ABOUT GOD WE CAN KNOW HE EXISTS
ST ANSELM (1033–1109)

Although Christian thinkers believe as a matter of faith that God exists, in the Middle Ages they were keen to show that God's existence could also be proved by rational argument. The Ontological Argument invented by Anselm – an 11th-century Italian philosopher who worked on the basis of Aristotelian logic, Platonic thinking, and his own genius – is probably the most famous of all.

Anselm imagines himself arguing with a Fool, who denies that God exists (see opposite). The argument rests on an acceptance of two things: first, that God is "that than which nothing greater can be thought", and second, that existence is superior to non-existence. By the end of the argument the Fool is forced to either take up a self-contradictory position or admit that God exists.

The argument has been accepted by many great philosophers, such as René Descartes and Baruch Spinoza. But there have been many others who took up the Fool's side. One contemporary of Anselm's, Gaunilo of Marmoutiers, said that we could use the same argument to prove that there exists somewhere a marvellous island, greater than any island that can be thought. In the 18th century Immanuel Kant objected that the argument treats existence as if it were an attribute of things – as if I might describe my jacket like this: "it's green, made of tweed, and it exists". Existing is not like being green: if it did not exist, there would be no jacket to be green or tweed.

Kant holds that Anselm is also wrong to say that what exists in reality as well as in the mind is greater than what exists in the mind alone, but other philosophers disagree. Is there not a sense in which a real painting is greater than the mental concept the painter has before he starts work? ∎

We believe that
You [God] are that
than which nothing
greater can be thought.
St Anselm

See also: Plato 50–55 ▪ St Augustine of Hippo 72–73 ▪ Thomas Aquinas 88–95 ▪ René Descartes 116–23 ▪ Benedictus Spinoza 126–29

Anselm	**The Fool**

Anselm: Do you agree that if God existed he would be the greatest thing that there could be – "that than which nothing greater can be thought"?

The Fool: Yes.

Anselm: And do you agree that "that than which nothing greater can be thought" exists in your mind?

The Fool: Yes, in my mind – but not in reality.

Anselm: But would you agree that something that exists in reality as well as in the mind is greater than something that exists in the mind alone?

The Fool: Yes, I suppose so – an ice cream in my hand is better than one that's just in my imagination.

Anselm: So if "that than which nothing greater can be thought" exists only in the mind, it is less great than if it existed also in reality.

The Fool: That's true. The being that really exists would be greater.

Anselm: So now you are saying that there is something greater than "that than which nothing greater exists"?

The Fool: That doesn't even make sense.

Anselm: Exactly. And the only way around this contradiction is to admit that God ("that than which nothing greater exists") does exist – both in thought and reality.

Anselm's Ontological Argument was written in 1077–78, but acquired its title from the German philosopher Kant in 1781.

St Anselm

St Anselm of Canterbury was born in Aosta in Italy in 1033. He left home in his twenties to study at the monastery of Bec, in France, under an eminent logician, grammarian, and Biblical commentator named Lanfranc. Anselm became a monk of Bec in 1060, then prior, and eventually abbot in 1078. He travelled to England, and in 1093 was made Archbishop of Canterbury, despite his protestations of ill-health and lack of political skills. This position put him in conflict with the Anglo-Norman kings William II and Henry I, as he tried to uphold the Church against royal power. These disputes led to two periods of exile from England for Anselm, during which he visited the pope to plead the case for the English Church and his own removal from office. Ultimately reconciled with King Henry I, Anselm died in Canterbury aged 76.

Key works

1075–76 *Monologion*
1077–78 *Proslogion*
1095–98 *Why did God become Man?*
1080–86 *On the Fall of the Devil*

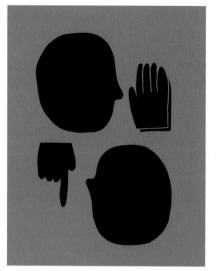

PHILOSOPHY AND RELIGION ARE NOT INCOMPATIBLE
AVERROES (1126–1198)

verroes worked in the legal profession; he was a *qâdî* (an Islamic judge) who worked under the Almohads, one of the strictest Islamic regimes in the Middle Ages. Yet he spent his nights writing commentaries on the work of an ancient pagan philosopher, Aristotle – and one of Averroes' avid readers was none other than the Almohad ruler, Abû Yacqûb Yûsuf.

Averroes reconciles religion and philosophy through a hierarchical theory of society. He thinks that only the educated elite are capable of thinking philosophically, and everyone else should be obliged to accept the teaching of the Qur'an literally. Averroes does not think that the Qur'an provides a completely accurate account of the universe if read in this literal way, but says that it is a poetic approximation of the truth, and this is the most that the uneducated can grasp.

However, Averroes believes that educated people have a religious obligation to use philosophical reasoning. Whenever reasoning shows the literal meaning of the Qur'an to be false, Averroes says that the text must be "interpreted";

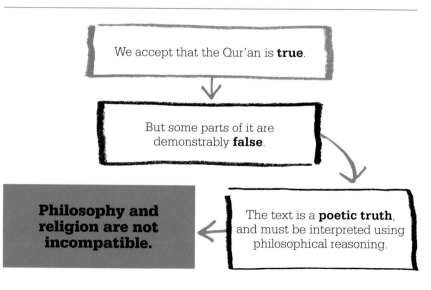

We accept that the Qur'an is **true**.

But some parts of it are demonstrably **false**.

The text is a **poetic truth**, and must be interpreted using philosophical reasoning.

Philosophy and religion are not incompatible.

See also: Plato 50–55 ▪ Aristotle 56–63 ▪ Al-Ghazâlî 332 ▪ Ibn Bâjja 333 ▪ Thomas Aquinas 88–95 ▪ Moses of Narbonne 334

> Philosophers believe that religious laws are necessary political arts.
> **Averroes**

that is to say the obvious meaning of the words should be disregarded and the scientific theory demonstrated by Aristotelian philosophy accepted in its place.

The immortal intellect

Averroes is willing to sacrifice some widely-held Islamic doctrines in order to maintain the compatibility of philosophy and religion. For instance, almost all Muslims believe that the universe has a beginning, but Averroes agrees with Aristotle that it has always existed, and says that there is nothing in the Qur'an

to contradict this view. However, the resurrection of the dead, a basic tenet of Islam, is harder to include within an Aristotelian universe. Averroes accepts that we must believe in personal immortality, and that anyone who denies this is a heretic who should be executed. But he takes a different position from his predecessors by saying that Aristotle's treatise *On the Soul* does not state that individual humans have immortal souls. According to Averroes' interpretation, Aristotle claims that humanity is immortal only through a shared intellect. Averroes seems to be saying that there are truths discoverable by humans that hold good for ever, but that you and I as individuals will perish when our bodies die.

Later Averroists

Averroes' advocacy of Aristotelian philosophy (if only for the elite) was shunned by his fellow Muslims. But his works, translated into Hebrew and Latin, had enormous influence in the 13th and 14th centuries. Scholars who supported the opinions

of Aristotle and Averroes became known as Averroists, and they included Jewish scholars such as Moses of Narbonne, and Latin scholars such as Boethius of Dacia and Siger of Brabant. The Latin Averroists acccepted Aristotle as interpreted by Averroes as the truth according to reason – despite also affirming an apparently conflicting set of Christian "truths". They have been described as advocating a "double truth" theory, but their view is rather that truth is relative to the context of enquiry. ▪

Some Muslims did not view philosophy as a legitimate subject for study in the 12th century, but Averroes argued that it was essential to engage with religion critically and philosophically.

Averroes

Ibn Rushd, known in Europe as Averroes, was born in 1126 in Cordoba, then part of Islamic Spain. He belonged to a family of distinguished lawyers and trained in law, science, and philosophy. His friendship with another doctor and philosopher, Ibn Tufayl, led to an introduction to the Caliph Abû Yacqûb Yûsuf, who appointed Averroes chief judge and later court physician. Abû Yacqûb also shared Averroes' interest in Aristotle, and commissioned him to write a series of paraphrases of all Aristotle's works, designed for non-specialists such as himself.

Despite the increasingly liberal views of the Almohads, the public disapproved of Averroes' unorthodox philosophy, and public pressure led to a banning of his books and personal exile in 1195. Reprieved two years later, Averroes returned to Cordoba but died the following year.

Key works

1179–80 *Decisive Treatise*
1179–80 *The Incoherence of the Incoherence*
c.1186 *Great Commentary on Aristotle's 'On the Soul'*

GOD HAS NO ATTRIBUTES
MOSES MAIMONIDES (1135–1204)

IN CONTEXT

BRANCH
Philosophy of religion

APPROACH
Jewish Aristotelian

BEFORE
c.400 CE The philosopher
Pseudo-Dionysius establishes
the tradition of Christian
negative theology, which
states that God is not being,
but more than being.

860s John Scotus Eriugena
suggests that God creates
the universe from the nothing
that is himself.

AFTER
1260s Thomas Aquinas
moderates Maimonides'
negative theology in his
Summa Theologiae.

Early 1300s Meister Eckhart
develops his negative theology.

1840–50s Søren Kierkegaard
claims that it is impossible
to provide any form of external
description of God.

Maimonides wrote on both Jewish law (in Hebrew) and Aristotelian thought (in Arabic). In both areas, one of his central concerns was to guard against anthropomorphizing God, which is the tendency to think about God in the same way as a human being. For Maimonides, the worst mistake of all is to take the Torah (the first part of the Hebrew Bible) as literal truth, and to think that God is a bodily thing. Anyone who thinks this, he says, should be excluded from the Jewish community. But in the *Guide of the Perplexed*, Maimonides pushes this idea to its farthest extent, developing a strand of thought known as "negative theology". This already existed in Christian theology, and it focuses on describing God only in terms of what God is not.

God, Maimonides says, has no attributes. We cannot rightly say that God is "good" or "powerful".

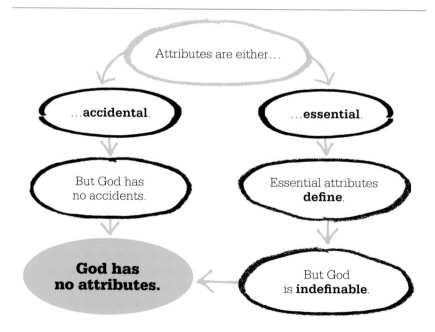

Attributes are either…

...accidental.

...essential.

But God has no accidents.

Essential attributes **define**.

God has no attributes.

But God is **indefinable**.

See also: Johannes Scotus Eriugena 332 ▪ Thomas Aquinas 88–95 ▪ Meister Eckhart 333 ▪ Søren Kierkegaard 194–95

This is because an attribute is either accidental (capable of change) or essential. One of my accidental attributes, for example, is that I am sitting; others are that I have grey hair and a long nose. But I would still be what I essentially am even if I were standing, red-haired, and had a snub-nose. Being human – that is, being a rational, mortal animal – is my essential attribute: it defines me. God, it is generally agreed, has no accidental attributes, because God is unchanging. In addition, says Maimonides, God cannot have any essential attributes either, because they would be defining, and God cannot be defined. So God has no attributes at all.

Speaking about God

Maimondes claims that we can say things about God, but they must be understood as telling us about God's actions, rather than God's being. Most discussions in the Torah should be understood in this way. So when

When the intellects contemplate God's essence, their apprehension turns into incapacity.
Maimonides

we are told that "God is a creator", we must understand this as stating what God does, rather than the sort of thing God is. If we were to consider the sentence "John is a writer", we might normally take it to mean that being a writer is John's profession. But Maimonides asks us to consider only what has been done: in this instance John has written words. The writing has been brought about by John but it does not tell us anything about him.

Maimonides also accepts that statements which seem to attribute qualities to God can be understood if they are taken as double negatives. "God is powerful": should be taken to mean that God is not powerless. Imagine a game in which I think of a thing and tell you what it is not (it is not large, it is not red...) until you guess what it is. The difference in the case of God is that we have only the negations to guide us: we cannot say what God is. ▪

The Mishneh Torah was a complete restatement of Jewish Oral Law, which Maimonides wrote in plain Hebrew so that "young and old" could know and understand all the Jewish observances.

Moses Maimonides

Moses Maimonides (also known as Rambam) was born in 1135 in Cordoba, Spain, into a Jewish family. His childhood was rich in cross-cultural influences: he was educated in both Hebrew and Arabic, and his father, a rabbinic judge, taught him Jewish law within the context of Islamic Spain. His family fled Spain when the Berber Almohad dynasty came to power in 1148, and lived nomadically for 10 years until they settled first in Fez (now in Morocco) and then Cairo. The family's financial problems led Maimonides to train as a physician, and his skill led to a royal appointment within only a few years. He also worked as a rabbinic judge, but this was an activity for which he thought it wrong to accept any payment. He was recognized as head of the Jewish community of Cairo in 1191, and after his death his tomb became a place of Jewish pilgrimage.

Key works

1168 *Commentary on the Mishna*
1168–78 *Mishneh Torah*
1190 *Guide of the Perplexed*

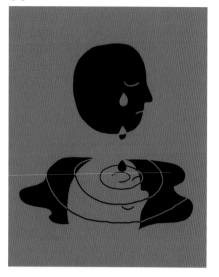

DON'T GRIEVE. ANYTHING YOU LOSE COMES ROUND IN ANOTHER FORM

JALAL AD-DIN MUHAMMAD RUMI (1207–1273)

IN CONTEXT

BRANCH
Islamic philosophy

APPROACH
Sufism

BEFORE
610 Islam is founded by the Prophet Mohammed.

644 Ali ibn Abi Talib, Mohammed's cousin and successor, becomes Caliph.

10th century Ali's mystical interpretation of the Qur'an becomes the basis for Sufism.

AFTER
1273 Rumi's followers found the Mawlawi Order of Sufism.

1925 After the founding of a secular Republic of Turkey, the Mawlawi Order is banned in Turkey. It remains illegal until 1954, when it receives the right to perform on certain occasions.

Today Rumi's works continue to be translated into many languages around the world.

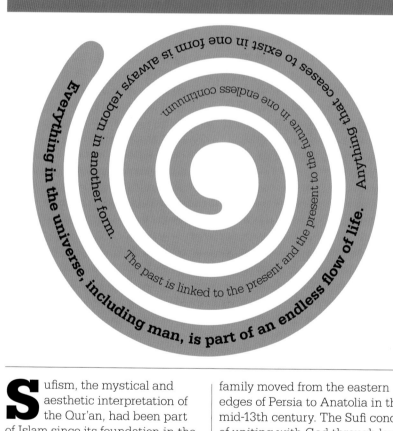

Everything in the universe, including man, is part of an endless flow of life.

Everything that ceases to exist in one form is always reborn in another form.

Anything that ceases to exist in one form is always reborn in the future to the present and the present to the future in one endless continuum.

The past is linked to the present and the present to the future in one endless continuum.

Sufism, the mystical and aesthetic interpretation of the Qur'an, had been part of Islam since its foundation in the 7th century, but had not always been accepted by mainstream Islamic scholars. Jalal ad-Din Muhammad Rumi, better known simply as Rumi, was brought up in orthodox Islam, and first came into contact with Sufism when his family moved from the eastern edges of Persia to Anatolia in the mid-13th century. The Sufi concept of uniting with God through love caught his imagination, and from this he developed a version of Sufism that sought to explain the relationship of man with the divine.

Rumi became a teacher in a Sufi order, and as such he believed he was a medium between God and

See also: Siddhartha Gautama 30–33 ▪ Avicenna 76–79 ▪ Averroes 82–83 ▪ Hajime Tanabe 244–45 ▪ Arne Naess 282–83

The Mawlawi Order, or Whirling Dervishes, dance as part of the Sufi Sema ceremony. The dance represents the spiritual journey of man from ignorance to perfection through love.

man. In contrast to general Islamic practice, he placed much emphasis on *dhikr* – ritual prayer or litany – rather than rational analysis of the Qur'an for divine guidance, and became known for his ecstatic revelations. He believed it was his task to communicate the visions he experienced, and so he wrote them down in the form of poetry. Central to his visionary philosophy is the idea that the universe and everything in it is an endless flow of life, in which God is an eternal presence. Man, as part of the universe, is also a part of this continuum, and Rumi seeks to explain our place within it.

Man, he believes, is a link between the past and future in a continual process of life, death, and rebirth – not as a cycle, but in a progression from one form to another stretching into eternity. Death and decay are inevitable and part of this endless flow of life, but as something ceases to exist in one form, it is reborn in another. Because of this, we should have no fear of death, and nor should we grieve a loss. In order to ensure our growth from one form to another, however, we should strive for spiritual growth and an understanding of the divine–human relationship. Rumi believes that this understanding comes from emotion rather than from reason – emotion enhanced by music, song, and dance.

Rumi's legacy

The mystical elements of Rumi's ideas were inspirational within Sufism, and influenced mainstream Islam too. They were also pivotal in converting much of Turkey from Orthodox Christianity to Islam. But this aspect of his thinking did not hold much sway in Europe, where rationalism was the order of the day. In the 20th century, however, his ideas became very popular in the West, mainly because his message of love chimed with the New Age values of the 1960s. Perhaps his greatest admirer in the 20th century was the poet and politician Muhammed Iqbal, advisor to Muhammad Ali Jinnah, who campaigned for an Islamic state of Pakistan in the 1930s. ▪

I died as a mineral and became a plant, I died as a plant and rose to animal, I died as animal and I was Man.
Jalal ad-Din Rumi

Jalal ad-Din Muhammad Rumi

Jalal ad-Din Muhammad Rumi, also known as Mawlana (Our Guide) or simply Rumi, was born in Balkh, in a province of Persia. When the Mongol invasions threatened the region, his family settled in Anatolia, Turkey, where Rumi met the Persian poets Attar and Shams al-Din Tabrizi. He decided to devote himself to Sufism, and went on to write thousands of verses of Persian and Arabic poetry.

In 1244 Rumi became the *shaykh* (Master) of a Sufi order, and taught his mystical-emotional interpretation of the Qur'an and the importance of music and dance in religious ceremony. After his death, his followers founded the Mawlawi Order of Sufism, which is famous for its Whirling Dervishes who perform a distinctive dance in the Sema ceremony – a form of *dhikr* unique to the sect.

Key works

Early–mid-13th century
Rhyming Couplets of Profound Spiritual Meaning
The Works of Shams of Tabriz
What is Within is Within
Seven Sessions

THE UNIVERSE HAS NOT ALWAYS EXISTED

THOMAS AQUINAS (c. 1225–1274)

IN CONTEXT

BRANCH
Metaphysics

APPROACH
Christian Aristotelian

BEFORE
c.340 BCE Aristotle says that
the universe is eternal.

c.540 CE John Philoponus
argues that the universe must
have a beginning.

1250s–60s French theologians
adopt Philoponus's argument.

AFTER
1290s French philosopher
Henry of Ghent criticizes
Aquinas, saying the universe
cannot have always existed.

1781 Immanuel Kant claims
he can show that the universe
has always existed, and that
it has not always existed.

1931 Belgian priest and
scientist Georges Lemaître
proposes the "Big Bang" theory
of the origins of the universe.

The opinions of people today
are still divided into those
that hold that the universe
had a beginning, and those that
hold that it has always existed.
Today we tend to look to physics
and astronomy for an answer, but
in the past this was a question for
philosophers and theologians. The
answer given by the Catholic priest
and philosopher Thomas Aquinas,
the most famous of all medieval
Christian philosophers, is especially
interesting. It is still a plausible
way of thinking about the problem,
and it also tells us a great deal about
how Aquinas combined his faith
with his philosophical reasoning,
despite their apparent contradictions.

Aristotle's influence
The central figure in Aquinas's
thinking is Aristotle, the ancient
Greek philosopher whose work was
intensively studied by medieval
thinkers. Aristotle was certain that
the universe has always existed,
and that it has always been home
to different things, from inanimate
objects like rocks, to living species,
such as humans, dogs, and horses.
He argued that the universe is
changing and moving, and this

can only be caused by change and
motion. So there could never have
been a first change or motion: the
universe must have been moving
and changing for ever.

The great Arabic philosophers,
Avicenna and Averroes, were
willing to accept Aristotle's view,
even though it put them at odds
with Islamic orthodoxy. Medieval
Jewish and Christian thinkers,
however, struggled to do so. They
held that, according to the Bible,
the universe has a beginning, so
Aristotle must be wrong: the
universe has not always existed.
But was this view something that
had to be accepted on faith, or
could it be refuted by reasoning?

John Philoponus, a Greek
Christian writer of the 6th century,
believed that he had found an
argument to show that Aristotle
must be wrong, and that the
universe had not always existed.
His reasoning was copied and
developed by a number of thinkers
in the 13th century, who needed to
find a flaw in Aristotle's reasoning
in order to protect the teachings of
the Church. Their line of argument
was especially clever, because it
took Aristotle's own ideas about

Thomas Aquinas

Thomas Aquinas was born in
1225 at Roccasecca in Italy. He
studied at the University of
Naples and then joined the
Dominican order (a new, highly
intellectual order of friars) against
the wishes of his family. As a
novitiate he studied in Paris and
then in Cologne under the German
Aristotelian theologian, Albert
the Great. Returning to Paris, he
became Master (professor) of
theology, before leaving to travel
around Italy teaching for 10 years.
Unusually, Aquinas was then
offered a second period of tenure
as Master at Paris. In 1273 he

experienced something that
has been considered both some
sort of vision and a possible
stroke; after it, he said that all
he had done was "mere straw",
and he never wrote again. He
died at the age of 49, and was
recognized as a saint by the
Catholic Church in 1323.

Key works

1256–59 *Disputed Questions on
Truth*
c.1265–74 *Summa Theologica*
1271 *On the Eternity of the
Universe*

See also: Aristotle 56–63 ▪ Avicenna 76–79 ▪ Averroes 82–83 ▪ John Philoponus 332 ▪ John Duns Scotus 333 ▪ Pierre Abélard 333 ▪ William of Ockham 334 ▪ Immanuel Kant 164–71

Aristotle says that the universe **has always existed**.

The Bible says that the universe **has not always existed**.

The world did have a beginning, but God could have created it in such a way that it **existed eternally**.

Aquinas is flanked by Aristotle and Plato in *The Triumph of Thomas Aquinas*. His understanding of ancient philosophy was considered greater than that of Averroes, who lies at his feet.

infinity as a point of departure, but turned them against his view of the universe as eternal.

An infinity of humans

According to Aristotle, the infinite is what has no limit. For instance, the sequence of numbers is infinite, because for each number, there is another higher number that follows. Similarly, the universe has existed for an infinite time, because for each day, there is a preceding day. In Aristotle's opinion, however, this is a "potential" infinity, as these days do not co-exist at the same time; an "actual" infinity – in which an infinite number of things all exist at the same time – is impossible.

Philoponus and his 13th-century followers, however, think that this argument presents problems that Aristotle had not noticed. They point to the fact that he believes that all

the types of living beings in the universe have always existed. If this were true, they say, it would mean that there were already an infinite number of human beings by the time Socrates was born – because if they have always existed, they existed then. But since Socrates' time, many more humans have been born, and so the number of humans born up until now must be greater than infinity. But no number can be greater than infinity.

In addition, these writers add, Christian thinkers believe that human souls are immortal. If this is so, and an infinite number of humans has already existed, there must be an infinite number of human souls in existence now. So there is an actual infinity of souls, not a potential infinity; and Aristotle has said actual infinity is impossible.

With these two arguments, using Aristotle's own principles as a starting point, Philoponus and his followers were confident they had demonstrated that the universe cannot always have existed.

Aristotle was therefore wrong; the universe is not eternal, and this fits perfectly with the Christian doctrine that God created the world.

Aquinas has little time for this line of reasoning. He points out that the universe could have existed for ever but that species such as humans and other animals might have had a beginning, and so the difficulties raised by Philoponus and his followers can be avoided. Despite his defence of Aristotle's reasoning, Aquinas does not »

There never was a time when there was not motion.
Aristotle

> 66
> God could have
> made the universe
> without humans and
> then made them.
> **Thomas Aquinas**
> 99

accept Aristotle's assertion that the universe is eternal, because the Christian faith says otherwise; but he doesn't think that Aristotle's position is illogical. Like Philoponus and his followers, Aquinas wants to show that the universe had a

beginning – but he also wants to show that there is no flaw in Aristotle's reasoning. He claims that his Christian contemporaries have confused two different points: the first is that God created the universe, and the second is that the universe had a beginning. Aquinas set out to prove that in fact Aristotle's position – that the universe has always existed – *could* be true, even if it is also true that God created the universe.

Creating the eternal

Aquinas steps away from Philoponus and his followers by insisting that although it is true, as the Bible says, that the universe had a beginning, this is not a necessary (undeniable) truth on logical grounds. As they all agree, God created the universe with a beginning, but he could just

as easily have created an eternal one. If something is created by God, then it owes its whole existence to God, but that does not mean that there must have been a time when it did not exist at all. It is therefore quite possible to believe in an eternal universe that had been created by God.

Aquinas gives an example of how this might work. Suppose there was a foot making a footprint in the sand and it had been there for ever. Although there would never have been a moment before the footprint was made, we would still recognize the foot as the cause of the footprint: if it were not for the foot, there would not be a footprint.

Aquinas and synthesis

Historians sometimes say that Aquinas "synthesized" Christianity and Aristotelian philosophy, as if he took the parts he wanted from each and made them into a smooth mixture. In fact, for Aquinas – as for most Christians – the teachings of the Church must all be accepted, without exception or compromise. Aquinas was unusual, however, because he thought that, properly understood, Aristotle did not contradict Christian teaching. The question of whether the universe always existed is the exception that proves the rule. In this particular case Aquinas thinks that Aristotle was wrong, but he was not wrong in principle, or in his reasoning. The universe really might have existed for ever, as far as the ancient philosophers knew. It was just that Aristotle, not having access to Christian revelation, had

Aquinas believed the creation story on faith, but claimed that some elements of Christian belief could be rationally demonstrated. For Aquinas, the Bible and reason need never conflict.

Aristotle believed that the universe was infinite, as each hour and day is succeed by another. Aquinas disagreed, believing that the universe had a beginning, but his respect for Aristotle's philosophy led him to argue that Aristotle could have been correct.

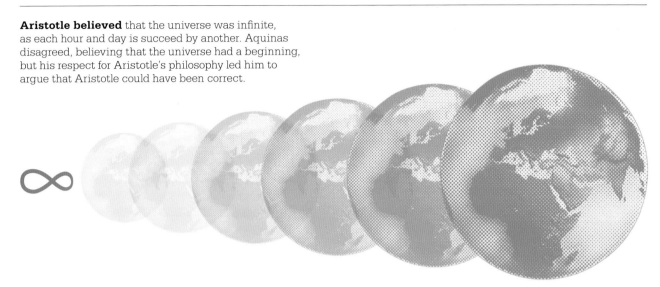

no way of knowing that it had not. Aquinas believes that there are a number of other doctrines central to Christianity that the ancient philosophers did not know and could not have known – such as the belief that God is a Trinity made up of three persons, and that one person of the Trinity, the Son, became a human. But in Aquinas's opinion, whenever humans reason correctly, they cannot come to any conclusion which contradicts Christian doctrine. This is because both human reason and Christian teaching come from the same source – God – and so they can never contradict each other.

Aquinas taught in convents and universities in France and Italy, and the idea that human reason could never conflict with Christian doctrine often placed him in fierce conflict with some of his academic contemporaries, especially those who specialized in the sciences, which at the time were derived from the work of Aristotle. Aquinas accused his fellow scholars of accepting certain positions on faith – for example, the position that we each have an immortal soul– but of saying at the same time that according to reason, these positions could be shown to be wrong.

How we gain knowledge

Aquinas keeps to these principles throughout his work, but they are particularly clear in two central areas of his thought: his account of how we gain knowledge and his treatment of the relation between mind and body. According to Aquinas, human beings acquire knowledge through using their senses: sight, hearing, smell, touch, and taste. These sense-impressions, however, only tell us what things are like superficially. For example, from where John sits, he has a visual impression of a tree-shaped object, which is green and brown. I, on the other hand, am standing next to the tree, and can feel the roughness of its bark and smell the scent of the forest. If John and I were dogs, our knowledge of the tree would be limited to these sense-impressions. But as human beings we are able to go beyond them and grasp what a tree is in a rational way, defining it and distinguishing it from other types of plants and of living things. Aquinas calls this "intellectual knowledge", because we gain it by using the innate power of our intellect to seize, on the basis of sense-impressions, the reality that lies behind them. Animals other than humans lack this inborn capacity, which is why their knowledge cannot stretch beyond the senses. All of our scientific understanding of the world is based on this intellectual knowledge. Aquinas's theory of knowledge owes much to Aristotle, although he clarifies and elaborates upon »

We should see whether there is a contradiction between something being created by God, and its existing forever.
Thomas Aquinas

the latter's thinking. For Aquinas, as a Christian thinker, human beings are only one type of the various sorts of beings that are capable of knowing things intellectually: souls separated from their bodies in the afterlife, angels, and God himself can also do this. These other knowing beings do not have to acquire knowledge through the senses. They can directly grasp the definitions of things. This aspect of Aquinas's theory has no parallel in Aristotle, but it is a coherent development of Aristotle's principles. Once again Aquinas is able to hold Christian beliefs without contradicting Aristotle, but going beyond him.

The human soul

According to Aristotle, the intellect is the life-principle or "soul" of a human being. All living things have a soul, he believes, which explains their capacity for different levels of what he calls "life-activity", such as growing and reproducing, for plants; moving, sensing, seeking, and avoiding, for animals; and thinking for humans.

Aristotle believes that "form" is what makes matter into the thing that it is. Within the human body, this form is the soul, which makes the body into the living thing that it is by giving it a particular set of life-activities. As such, the soul is tied to the body, and so Aristotle thinks that, even in the case of humans, the life-soul survives only so long as it animates a body, and at death it perishes.

Aquinas follows Aristotle's teaching about living things and their souls, and he insists that a human being has just one form: his or her intellect. Although other 13th- and 14th-century thinkers also adopted the main lines of Aristotle's view, they cut the connection Aristotle had made between the intellect and the body, so they could accommodate the Christian teaching that the human soul survives death. Aquinas, however, refuses to distort Aristotle's position. This made it far more difficult for him to argue – as he did – for the immortality of the human soul, in yet another example of his resolve to be a good Aristotelian, and philosopher, while remaining a faithful Christian.

After Aquinas

Since the Middle Ages, Aquinas has come to be regarded as the official orthodox philosopher of the Catholic Church. In his own time, when translations of Greek philosophy were being made from Arabic, complete with Arabic commentaries, he was one of the thinkers keenest to follow Aristotle's train of philosophical reasoning, even when it did not fit neatly with Christian doctrine. He always

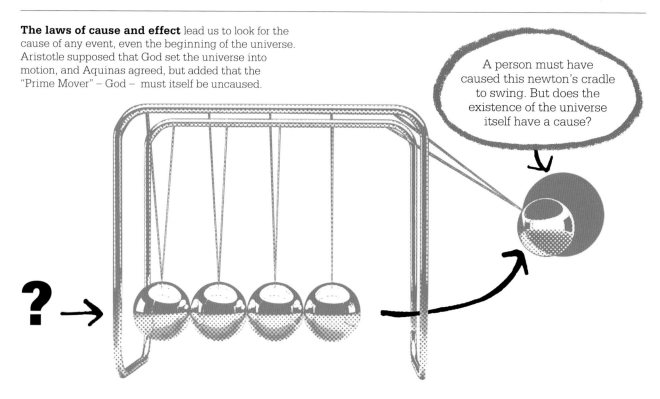

The laws of cause and effect lead us to look for the cause of any event, even the beginning of the universe. Aristotle supposed that God set the universe into motion, and Aquinas agreed, but added that the "Prime Mover" – God – must itself be uncaused.

A person must have caused this newton's cradle to swing. But does the existence of the universe itself have a cause?

? →

Cosmic background radiation
provides evidence of the "Big Bang" that started the universe, but we can still argue, like Aquinas, that this was not the only possible way for it to exist.

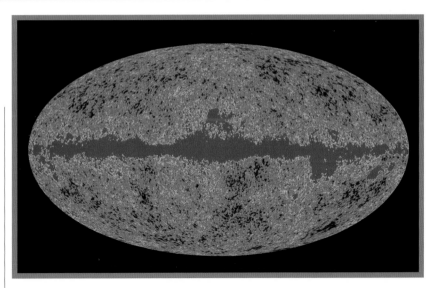

remained faithful to the Church's teachings, but this did not prevent his thought from almost being condemned as heretical shortly after his death. The great thinkers and teachers of the following century, such as the secular philosopher Henry of Ghent, and the Franciscans John Duns Scotus and William of Ockham, were all far more willing to say that purely philosophical reasoning, as best represented by Aristotle's arguments, is often mistaken.

Scotus thought that Aquinas's Aristotelian view of the soul was inadequate, and Ockham rejected Aristotle's account of knowledge almost entirely. Henry of Ghent explicitly criticized Aquinas's view that God could have created a universe that always exists. If it always existed, he argued, there would be no possibility of its not existing, and so God would not have been free to create or not create it. Aquinas's supreme confidence in the power of reason meant that he had more in common with the greatest philosopher of the previous century, the French philosopher and theologian Pierre Abélard, than he did with his contemporaries and successors.

Coherent belief
Both Aquinas's general view on the relation between philosophy and Christian doctrine, and his particular treatment of the eternity of the universe, remain relevant in the 21st century. Today few philosophers believe that religious positions, such as the existence of God or the immortality of the soul,

can be proved by philosophical reasoning. But what some claim for philosophy is that it can demonstrate that although religious believers hold certain doctrines as a matter of faith, their overall views are no less rational or coherent than those of agnostics or atheists. This view is an extension and development of Aquinas's constant endeavour to develop a philosophically coherent system of thought, while holding on to his Christian beliefs. Reading Aquinas's works is a lesson in tolerance, for Christians and non-Christians alike.

The role of philosophy
Today, we do not look to philosophy to tell us whether or not the universe has always existed, and most of us do not turn to the Bible, as Aquinas and other medieval philosophers did. Instead we look to physics, in particular to the theory of the "Big Bang" proposed by modern scientists, including the British physicist and cosmologist Stephen Hawking. This theory states that the universe expanded from a state of extremely high temperature and density at a particular point in time. Though most of us now turn to

science for an explanation of how the universe began, the arguments of Aquinas show that philosophy is still relevant to how we think about the subject. He demonstrates how philosophy can provide the tools for intelligent enquiry, allowing us to investigate not what happens to be the case, but what is possible and what is impossible, and what are intelligible questions to ask. Is it or is it not coherent to believe that the universe had a beginning? This is still a question for philosophers, and no amount of theoretical physics will be able to answer it. ∎

One may say that time had a beginning at the Big Bang, in the sense that earlier times simply would not be defined.
Stephen Hawking

GOD IS THE NOT-OTHER
NIKOLAUS VON KUES (1401–1464)

IN CONTEXT

BRANCH
Philosophy of religion

APPROACH
Christian Platonism

BEFORE
380–360 BCE Plato writes on "the Good" or "the One" as the ultimate source of reason, knowledge, and all existence.

Late 5th century CE
The Greek theologian and philosopher Dionysius the Areopagite describes God as "above being".

c.860 Johannes Scotus Eriugena promotes the ideas of Dionysius the Areopagite.

AFTER
1492 Giovanni Pico della Mirandola's *On Being and the One* marks a turning point in Renaissance thinking about God.

1991 French philosopher Jean-Luc Marion explores the theme of God as not a being.

Nikolaus von Kues belongs to a long tradition of medieval philosophers who attempt to describe the nature of God, stressing how God is unlike anything that the human mind is capable of grasping. Von Kues begins with the idea that we gain knowledge by using our reason to define things. So in order to know God, he deduces that we must try to define the basic nature of God.

Plato describes "the Good" or "the One" as the ultimate source of all other forms and knowledge, and some early Christian theologians talk of God as "above being". Von Kues, writing around 1440, goes further, stating that God is what comes before everything, even before the possibility of something existing. Yet reason tells us the possibility of any phenomenon existing must come before its actual existence. It is impossible for something to come into being before the possibility of it arises. The conclusion that von Kues comes to, therefore, is that something that is said to do this must be described as "Not-other".

Beyond apprehension
However, the use of the word "thing" in the line of reasoning that von Kues adopts is misleading, as the "Not-other" has no substance. It is, according to von Kues, "beyond apprehension", and is before all things in such a way that "they are not subsequent to it, but exist through it". For this reason too, von Kues thinks "Not-other" comes closer to a definition of God than any other term. ∎

Whatever-I-know is not God and whatever-I-conceive is not like God.
Nikolaus von Kues

See also: Plato 50–55 ▪ Johannes Scotus Eriugena 332 ▪ Meister Eckhart 333 ▪ Giovanni Pico della Mirandola 334

TO KNOW NOTHING IS THE HAPPIEST LIFE
DESIDERIUS ERASMUS (1466–1536)

IN CONTEXT

BRANCH
Philosophy of religion

APPROACH
Humanism

BEFORE
354–430 CE St Augustine
of Hippo integrates Platonism
into Christianity.

c.1265–1274 Thomas Aquinas
combines Aristotelian and
Christian philosophy in his
Summa Theologica.

AFTER
1517 Theologian Martin
Luther writes *The Ninety-Five
Theses*, protesting against
clerical abuses. It triggers the
start of the Reformation.

1637 René Descartes writes
Discourse on the Method,
putting human beings at
the centre of philosophy.

1689 John Locke argues
for separation of government
and religion in *A Letter
Concerning Toleration*.

The treatise *In Praise of Folly*, which Erasmus wrote in 1509, reflects the Humanist ideas that were beginning to flood across Europe during the early years of the Renaissance, and were to play a key role in the Reformation. It is a witty satire on the corruption and doctrinal wranglings of the Catholic Church. However, it also has a serious message, stating that folly – by which Erasmus meant naive ignorance – is an essential part of being human, and is what ultimately brings us the most happiness and contentment. He goes on to claim that knowledge, on the other hand, can be a burden and can lead to complications that may make for a troublesome life.

Faith and folly
Religion is a form of folly too, Erasmus states, in that true belief can only ever be based on faith, never on reason. He dismisses the mixing of ancient Greek rationalism with Christian theology by medieval philosophers, such as St Augustine of Hippo and Thomas Aquinas, as theological intellectualizing, claiming that it is the root cause of the corruption of religious faith. Instead, Erasmus advocates a return to simple heartfelt beliefs, with individuals forming a personal relationship with God, and not one prescribed by Catholic doctrine.

Erasmus advises us to embrace what he sees as the true spirit of the Scriptures – simplicity, naivety, and humility. These, he says, are the fundamental human traits that hold the key to a happy life. ∎

Happiness is
reached when a
person is ready to
be what he is.
Desiderius Erasmus

See also: St Augustine of Hippo 72–73 ∎ Thomas Aquinas 88–95 ∎ René Descartes 116–23 ∎ John Locke 130–33

RENAISS
AND THE
OF REAS
1500–1750

ANCE

AGE

ON

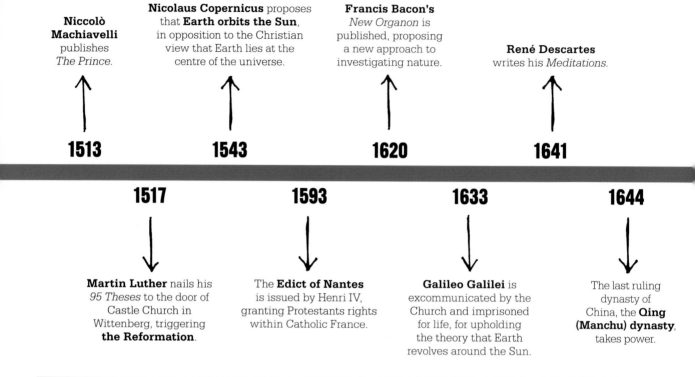

Niccolò Machiavelli publishes *The Prince*.

1513

Nicolaus Copernicus proposes that **Earth orbits the Sun**, in opposition to the Christian view that Earth lies at the centre of the universe.

1543

Francis Bacon's *New Organon* is published, proposing a new approach to investigating nature.

1620

René Descartes writes his *Meditations*.

1641

1517

Martin Luther nails his *95 Theses* to the door of Castle Church in Wittenberg, triggering **the Reformation**.

1593

The **Edict of Nantes** is issued by Henri IV, granting Protestants rights within Catholic France.

1633

Galileo Galilei is excommunicated by the Church and imprisoned for life, for upholding the theory that Earth revolves around the Sun.

1644

The last ruling dynasty of China, the **Qing (Manchu) dynasty**, takes power.

The Renaissance – a cultural "rebirth" of extraordinary creativity in Europe – began in 14th-century Florence. It was to spread across Europe, lasting until the 17th century, and it is now viewed as the bridge between the medieval and modern periods. Marked by a renewed interest in the whole of Greek and Latin Classical culture – not just the philosophical and mathematical texts assimilated by medieval Scholasticism – it was a movement that viewed humans, not God, at its centre. This new humanism was reflected in first the art and then the political and social structure of Italian society; republics such as Florence and Venice soon abandoned medieval feudalism in favour of plutocracies where commerce flourished alongside the new scientific discoveries.

By the end of the 15th century, Renaissance ideas had spread across Europe and virtually eclipsed the Church's monopoly of learning. Although Christian philosophers such as Erasmus and Thomas More had contributed to the arguments within the Church that had sparked the Reformation, a purely secular philosophy had yet to emerge. Unsurprisingly, the first truly Renaissance philosopher was a Florentine – Niccolò Machiavelli – and his philosophy marked a definitive movement from the theological to the political.

The Age of Reason

The final nail in the coffin of the Church's authority came from science. First Nicolaus Copernicus, then Johannes Kepler, and finally Galileo Galilei showed that the

Ptolemaic model of the universe with Earth at its centre was mistaken, and their demonstrations overturned centuries of Christian teaching. The Church fought back, ultimately imprisoning Galileo for heresy, but advances in all the sciences soon followed those in astronomy, providing alternative explanations for the workings of the universe, and a basis for a new kind of philosophy.

The victory of rational, scientific discovery over Christian dogma epitomized the thinking of the 17th century. British philosophers, notably Francis Bacon and Thomas Hobbes, took the lead in integrating scientific and philosophical reasoning. It was the beginning of a period that became known as the Age of Reason, which produced the first great "modern" philosophers

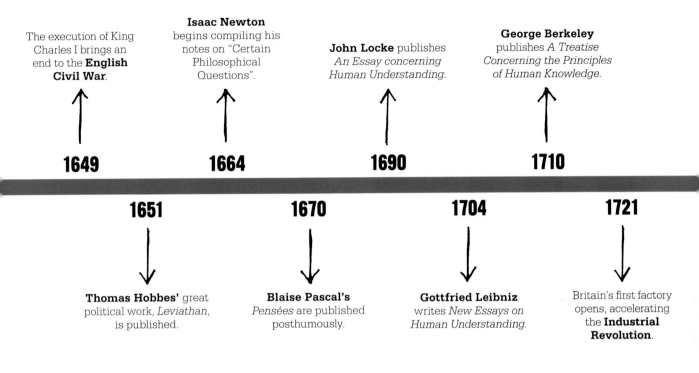

The execution of King Charles I brings an end to the **English Civil War**.

Isaac Newton begins compiling his notes on "Certain Philosophical Questions".

John Locke publishes *An Essay concerning Human Understanding*.

George Berkeley publishes *A Treatise Concerning the Principles of Human Knowledge*.

1649

1664

1690

1710

1651

1670

1704

1721

Thomas Hobbes' great political work, *Leviathan*, is published.

Blaise Pascal's *Pensées* are published posthumously.

Gottfried Leibniz writes *New Essays on Human Understanding*.

Britain's first factory opens, accelerating the **Industrial Revolution**.

and revived the connection between philosophy and science, especially mathematics, that dated back to pre-Socratic Greece.

The birth of rationalism

In the 17th century, many of the most significant philosophers in Europe were also accomplished mathematicians. In France, René Descartes and Blaise Pascal made major contributions to mathematics, as did Gottfried Leibniz in Germany. They believed that its reasoning process provided the best model for how to acquire all our knowledge of the world. Descartes's investigation of the question "What can I know?" led him to a position of rationalism – the belief that knowledge comes from reason alone – which was to become the predominant belief in continental Europe for the next

century. At the same time, a very different philosophical tradition was being established in Britain. Following the scientific reasoning espoused by Francis Bacon, John Locke came to the conclusion that our knowledge of the world comes not from reason, but experience. This view, known as empiricism, characterized British philosophy during the 17th and 18th centuries.

Despite the division between continental rationalism and British empiricism (the same division that had separated the philosophies of Plato and Aristotle), both had in common the placing of the human at their centres: it is this being whose reason or experience leads to knowledge. Philosophers on both sides of the Channel had moved from asking questions about the nature of the universe – which were

being answered by scientists such as Isaac Newton – to questioning how we can know what we know, and they now began to investigate the nature of the human mind and self. But these new philosophical strands had moral and political implications. Just as the Church's authority had been undermined by the ideas of the Renaissance, so the aristocracies and monarchies were threatened by the new ideas of the Enlightenment, as this period came to be known. If the old rulers were removed from power, what sort of society was to replace them?

In Britain, Hobbes and Locke had laid the foundations for democratic thinking during the turbulent 17th century, but it was another 100 years before a questioning of the status quo began in earnest elsewhere. ∎

THE END JUSTIFIES THE MEANS

NICCOLO MACHIAVELLI (1469–1527)

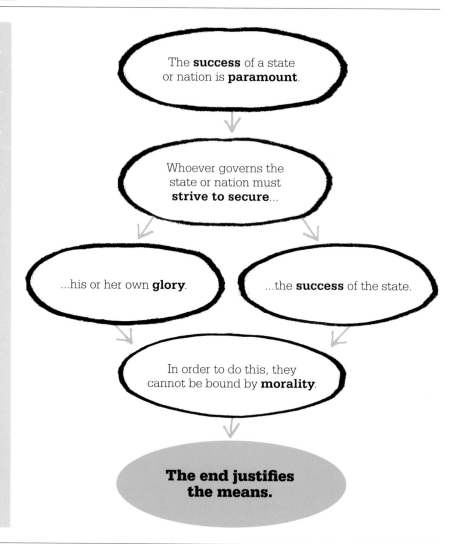

The **success** of a state or nation is **paramount**.

Whoever governs the state or nation must **strive to secure**...

...his or her own **glory**.

...the **success** of the state.

In order to do this, they cannot be bound by **morality**.

The end justifies the means.

I n order fully to understand Machiavelli's views on power, it is necessary to understand the background to his political concerns. Machiavelli was born in Florence, Italy, during a time of almost constant upheaval. The Medici family had been in open but unofficial control of the city-state for some 35 years, and the year of Machiavelli's birth saw Lorenzo de' Medici (Lorenzo the Magnificent) succeed his father as ruler, ushering in a period of great artistic activity in Florence. Lorenzo was succeeded in 1492 by his son Piero (known as Piero the Unfortunate), whose reign was short-lived. The French under Charles VIII invaded Italy in considerable force in 1494, and Piero was forced to surrender and then flee the city, as the citizens rebelled against him. Florence was declared a republic that same year.

The Dominican prior of the San Marco monastery, Girolamo Savonarola, then came to dominate Florentine political life. The city-state entered a democratic period under his guidance, but after accusing the pope of corruption Savonarola was eventually arrested and burnt as a heretic. This led to Machiavelli's first known involvement in Florentine politics, and he became Secretary to the second Chancery in 1498.

Career and influences

The invasion by Charles VIII in 1494 had sparked a turbulent period in the history of Italy, which at the time was divided into five powers: the papacy, Naples, Venice, Milan, and Florence. The country was fought over by various foreign powers, mainly France, Spain, and the Holy Roman Empire. Florence

See also: Plato 50–55 ▪ Francis Bacon 110–11 ▪ Jean-Jacques Rousseau 154–59 ▪ Karl Marx 196–203

Lorenzo the Magnificent (1449–1492) effectively ruled Florence from the death of his father in 1469 until his death. Though he ruled as a despot, the republic flourished under his guidance.

Machiavelli was released from prison within a month, but his chances of re-employment were slim, and his attempts to find a new political position came to nothing. He decided to present the head of the de' Medici family in Florence, Giuliano, with a book. By the time it was ready Giuliano had died, so Machiavelli changed the dedication to Giuliano's successor, Lorenzo. The book was of a type popular at the time: advice to a prince.

The Prince

Machiavelli's book *The Prince* was witty and cynical, and showed a great understanding of Italy in general and Florence in particular. In it, Machiavelli sets out his argument that the goals of a ruler justify the means used to obtain them. *The Prince* differed markedly from other books of its type in its resolute setting aside of Christian morality. Machiavelli wanted to »

was weak in the face of their armies, and Machiavelli spent 14 years travelling between various cities on diplomatic missions, trying to shore up the struggling republic.

In the course of his diplomatic activities, Machiavelli met Cesare Borgia, the illegitimate son of Pope Alexander VI. The pope was a powerful figure in northern Italy, and a significant threat to Florence. Although Cesare was Florence's enemy, Machiavelli – despite his republican views – was impressed by his vigour, intelligence, and ability. Here we see one of the sources for Machiavelli's famous work, *The Prince*.

Pope Alexander VI died in 1503, and his successor Pope Julius II was another strong and successful man who impressed Machiavelli with both his military ability and his cunning. But tension between France and the papacy led to Florence fighting with the French against the pope and his allies, the Spanish. The French lost, and Florence with them. In 1512 the Spanish dissolved the city-state's government, the Medicis returned, and what was in effect a tyranny under Cardinal de' Medici was installed. Machiavelli was sacked from his political office and exiled to his farm in Florence. His political career might have revived under the rule of the Medicis, but in February 1513 he was falsely implicated in a plot against the family, and he was tortured, fined, and imprisoned.

How difficult it is for a people accustomed to live under a prince to preserve their liberty!
Niccolò Machiavelli

give ruthlessly practical advice to a prince and, as his experience with extremely successful popes and cardinals had shown him, Christian values should be cast aside if they got in the way.

Machiavelli's approach centres on the notion of *virtù*, but this is not the modern notion of moral virtue. It shares more similarities with the medieval notion of virtues as the powers or functions of things, such as the healing powers of plants or minerals. Machiavelli is writing about the virtues of princes, and these were the powers and functions that concerned rule. The Latin root of *virtù* also relates it to manliness (as in "virile"), and this feeds into what Machiavelli has to say in its application both to the prince himself and to the state – where

sometimes *virtù* is used to mean "success", and describes a state that is to be admired and imitated.

Part of Machiavelli's point is that a ruler cannot be bound by morality, but must do what it takes to secure his own glory and the success of the state over which he rules – an approach that became known as realism. But Machiavelli does not argue that the end justifies the means in all cases. There are certain means that a wise prince must avoid, for though they might achieve the desired ends, they lay him open to future dangers.

The main means to be avoided consist of those that would make the people hate their prince. They may love him, they may fear him – preferably both, Machiavelli says, though it is more important for a

prince to be feared than to be loved. But the people must not hate him, for this is likely to lead to rebellion. Also, a prince who mistreats his people unnecessarily will be despised – a prince should have a reputation for compassion, not for cruelty. This might involve harsh punishment of a few in order to achieve general social order, which benefits more people in the long run.

In cases where Machiavelli does think that the end justifies the means, this rule applies only to princes. The proper conduct of citizens of the state is not at all the same as that of the prince. But even for ordinary citizens, Machiavelli generally disdains conventional Christian morality as being weak and unsuitable for a strong city.

Prince or republic

There are reasons to suspect that *The Prince* does not represent Machiavelli's own views. Perhaps the most important is the disparity between the ideas it contains and those expressed in his other main work, *Discourses on the Ten Books of Titus Livy*. In the *Discourses* Machiavelli argues that a republic is the ideal regime, and that it

A ruler needs to know how to act like a beast, Machiavelli says in *The Prince*, and must imitate the qualities of the fox as well as the lion.

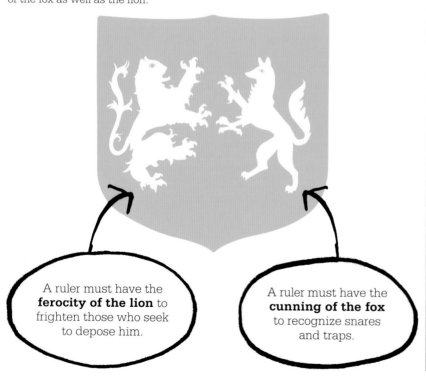

A ruler must have the **ferocity of the lion** to frighten those who seek to depose him.

A ruler must have the **cunning of the fox** to recognize snares and traps.

It must be understood that a prince cannot observe all those things which are considered good in men.
Niccolò Machiavelli

should be instituted whenever a reasonable degree of equality exists or can be established. A princedom is only suitable when equality does not exist in a state, and cannot be introduced. However, it can be argued that *The Prince* represents Machiavelli's genuine ideas about how the ruler should rule in such cases; if princedoms are sometimes a necessary evil, it is best that they be ruled as well as possible. Moreover, Machiavelli did believe that Florence was in such political turmoil that it needed a strong ruler to get it into shape.

Pleasing the readers

The fact that *The Prince* was written by Machiavelli in order to ingratiate himself with the Medicis is another reason to treat its contents with caution. However, he also dedicated the *Discourses* to members of Florence's republican government. Machiavelli, it could be argued, would have written what the dedicatee wanted to read.

The Prince, however, contains much that Machiavelli is thought to have genuinely believed, such as the need for a citizens' militia rather than reliance on mercenaries.

Ruthlessness has been a virtue of leadership throughout history. In the 20th century, the fascist dictator Benito Mussolini used a mixture of fear and love to hold on to power in Italy.

The world has become more like that of Machiavelli.
Bertrand Russell

The problem lies in discerning which parts are his actual beliefs and which are not. It is tempting to divide them according to how well they fit with the intended reader's own beliefs, but that is unlikely to give an accurate result.

It has also been suggested that Machiavelli was attempting satire, and his real intended audience was the republicans, not the ruling elite. This idea is supported by the fact that Machiavelli did not write it in

Latin, the language of the elite, but in Italian, the language of the people. Certainly, *The Prince* at times reads satirically, as though the audience is expected to conclude: "if that is how a good prince should behave, we should at all costs avoid being ruled by one!" If Machiavelli was also satirizing the idea that "the end justifies the means", then the purpose of this small, deceptively simple book is far more intriguing than one might originally assume. ∎

Niccolò Machiavelli

Machiavelli was born in Florence in 1469. Little is known of the first 28 years of his life; apart from a few inconclusive mentions in his father's diary, the first direct evidence is a business letter written in 1497. From his writings, though, it is clear that he received a good education, perhaps at the University of Florence.

By 1498, Machiavelli had become a politician and diplomat of the Florentine Republic. After his enforced retirement on the return of the Medicis to Florence in 1512, he devoted himself to various literary activities, as well as persistent attempts to return to the political arena. Eventually he regained the trust of the Medicis, and Cardinal Giulio de' Medici commissioned him to write a history of Florence. The book was finished in 1525, after the cardinal had become Pope Clement VII. Machiavelli died in 1527, without achieving his ambition to return to public life.

Key works

1513 *The Prince*
1517 *Discourses on the Ten Books of Titus Livy*

FAME AND TRANQUILLITY CAN NEVER BE BEDFELLOWS
MICHEL DE MONTAIGNE (1533–1592)

IN CONTEXT

BRANCH
Ethics

APPROACH
Humanism

BEFORE
4th century BCE Aristotle, in his *Nicomachean Ethics*, argues that to be virtuous, a person must be sociable and form close relationships with others; only a bestial man or a god can flourish alone.

AFTER
Late 18th century Anglican evangelical clergyman Richard Cecil states, "Solitude shows us what we should be; society shows us what we are."

Late 19th century Friedrich Nietzsche describes solitude as necessary to the task of self-examination, which he claims can alone free humans from the temptation just to thoughtlessly follow the mob.

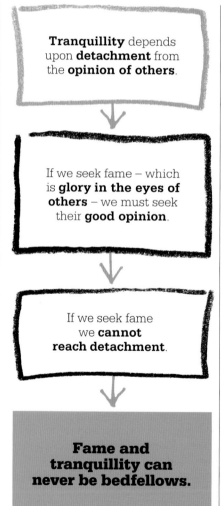

Tranquillity depends upon **detachment** from the **opinion of others**.

If we seek fame – which is **glory in the eyes of others** – we must seek their **good opinion**.

If we seek fame we **cannot reach detachment**.

Fame and tranquillity can never be bedfellows.

I n his essay "On Solitude" (from the first volume of his *Essays*), Montaigne takes up a theme that has been popular since ancient times: the intellectual and moral dangers of living among others, and the value of solitude. Montaigne is not stressing the importance of physical solitude, but rather of developing the ability to resist the temptation to mindlessly fall in with the opinion and actions of the mob. He compares our desire for the approval of our fellow humans to being overly attached to material wealth and possessions. Both passions diminish us, Montaigne claims, but he does not conclude that we should relinquish either, only that we should cultivate a detachment from them. By doing so, we may enjoy them – and even benefit from them – but we will not become emotionally enslaved to them, or devastated if we lose them.

"On Solitude" then considers how our desire for mass approval is linked to the pursuit of glory, or fame. Contrary to thinkers such as Niccolò Machiavelli, who see glory as a worthy goal, Montaigne believes that constant striving for fame is the greatest barrier to peace of mind, or tranquility. He

See also: Aristotle 56–63 ▪ Niccolò Machiavelli 102–07 ▪ Friedrich Nietzsche 214–21

says of those who present glory as a desirable goal that they "only have their arms and legs out of the crowd; their souls, their wills, are more engaged with it than ever".

Montaigne is not concerned with whether or not we achieve glory. His point is that we should shake off the desire for glory in the eyes of other people – that we should not always think of other people's approval and admiration as being valuable. He goes on to recommend that instead of looking for the approbation of those around us, we should imagine that some truly great and noble being is constantly with us, able to observe our most private thoughts, a being in whose presence even the mad would hide their failings. By doing this, we will learn to think clearly and objectively and behave in a more thoughtful and rational manner. Montaigne claims that caring too much about the opinion

of those around us will corrupt us, either because we end up imitating those who are evil, or become so consumed by hatred for them that we lose our reason.

Glory's pitfalls
Montaigne returns to his attack on the pursuit of glory in his later writings, pointing out that the acquisition of glory is often so much a matter of mere chance that it makes little sense to hold it in such reverence. "Many times I've seen [fortune] stepping out ahead of merit, and often a long way ahead," he writes. He also points out that encouraging statesmen and political leaders to value glory above all things, as Machiavelli does, merely teaches them never to attempt any endeavour unless an approving audience is on hand, ready and eager to bear witness to the remarkable nature of their powers and achievements. ■

Montaigne experienced the results of mindless mob violence during the French Wars of Religion (1562–98), including the atrocities of the St Bartholomew Day Massacre of 1572.

Contagion is very dangerous in crowds. You must either imitate the vicious or hate them.
Michel de Montaigne

Michel de Montaigne

Michel Eyquem de Montaigne was born and brought up in his wealthy family's chateau near Bordeaux. However, he was sent to live with a poor peasant family until the age of three, so that he would be familiar with the life led by the ordinary workers. He received all his education at home, and was allowed to speak only Latin until the age of six. French was effectively his second language.

From 1557, Montaigne spent 13 years as a member of his local parliament, but resigned in 1571, on inheriting the family estates.

Montaigne published his first volume of *Essays* in 1580, going on to write two more volumes before his death in 1592. In 1580, he also set out on an extensive tour of Europe, partly to seek a cure for kidney stones. He returned to politics in 1581, when he was elected Mayor of Bordeaux, an office he held until 1585.

Key works

1569 *In Defence of Raymond Sebond*
1580–1581 *Travel Journal*
1580, 1588, 1595 *Essays* (3 volumes)

KNOWLEDGE IS POWER

FRANCIS BACON (1561–1626)

IN CONTEXT

BRANCH
Philosophy of science

APPROACH
Empiricism

BEFORE
4th century BCE Aristotle sets observation and inductive reasoning at the centre of scientific thinking.

13th century English scholars Robert Grosseteste and Roger Bacon add experimentation to Aristotle's inductive approach to scientific knowledge.

AFTER
1739 David Hume's *Treatise of Human Nature* argues against the rationality of inductive thinking.

1843 John Stuart Mill's *System of Logic* outlines the five inductive principles that together regulate the sciences.

1934 Karl Popper states that falsification, not induction, defines the scientific method.

Bacon is often credited with being the first in a tradition of thought known as British empiricism, which is characterized by the view that all knowledge must come ultimately from sensory experience. He was born at a time when there was a shift from the Renaissance preoccupation with the rediscovered achievements of the ancient world towards a more scientific approach to knowledge. There had already been some innovative work by Renaissance scientists such as the astronomer Nicolaus Copernicus and the anatomist Andreas Vesalius, but this new period – sometimes called the Scientific Revolution – produced an astonishing number of scientific thinkers, including Galileo Galilei, William Harvey, Robert Boyle, Robert Hooke, and Isaac Newton.

Although the Church had been broadly welcoming to science for much of the medieval period, this was halted by the rise of opposition to the Vatican's authority during the Renaissance. Several religious reformers, such as Martin Luther, had complained that the Church had been too lax in countering scientific challenges to accounts of the world based on the Bible. In response, the Catholic Church, which had already lost adherents

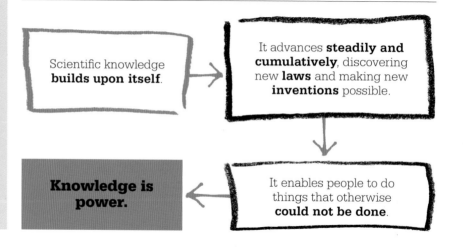

Scientific knowledge **builds upon itself**.

It advances **steadily and cumulatively**, discovering new **laws** and making new **inventions** possible.

It enables people to do things that otherwise **could not be done**.

Knowledge is power.

See also: Aristotle 56–63 ▪ Robert Grosseteste 333 ▪ David Hume 148–53 ▪ John Stuart Mill 190–93 ▪ Karl Popper 262–65

Science, not religion, was regarded increasingly as the key to knowledge from the 16th century onwards. This print depicts the observatory of Danish astronomer Tycho Brahe (1546–1601).

to Luther's new form of Christianity, changed its stance and turned against scientific endeavour. This opposition, from both sides of the religious divide, hampered the development of the sciences.

Bacon claims to accept the teachings of the Christian Church. But he also argues that science must be separated from religion, in order to make the acquisition of knowledge quicker and easier, so that it can be used to improve the quality of people's lives. Bacon stresses this transforming role for science. One of his complaints is that science's ability to enhance human existence had previously been ignored, in favour of a focus on academic and personal glory.

Bacon presents a list of the psychological barriers to pursuing scientific knowledge in terms that he calls collectively the "idols of the mind". These are the "idols of the tribe", the tendency of human beings as a species (or "tribe") to generalize; the "idols of the cave", the human tendency to impose

preconceptions on nature rather than to see what is really there; the "idols of the marketplace", our tendency to let social conventions distort our experience; and the "idols of the theatre", the distorting influence of prevailing philosophical and scientific dogma. The scientist, according to Bacon, must battle against all these handicaps to gain knowledge of the world.

Scientific method

Bacon goes on to argue that the advancement of science depends on formulating laws of ever-increasing generality. He proposes a scientific method that includes a variation of this approach. Instead of making a series of observations, such as instances of metals that expand when heated, and then concluding that heat must cause all metals to expand, he stresses the need to test a new theory by going on to look for negative instances – such as metals not expanding when they are heated.

Bacon's influence led to a focus on practical experimentation in science. He was, however, criticized for neglecting the importance of the imaginative leaps that drive all scientific progress. ▪

By far the best proof
is experience.
Francis Bacon

Francis Bacon

Born in London, Francis Bacon was educated privately, before being sent to Trinity College, Cambridge, at the age of 12. After graduation, he started training as a lawyer, but abandoned his studies to take up a diplomatic post in France. His father's death in 1579 left him impoverished, forcing him to return to the legal profession.

Bacon was elected to parliament in 1584, but his friendship with the treasonous Earl of Essex held back his political career until the accession of James I in 1603. In 1618, he was appointed Lord Chancellor, but was dismissed two years later, when he was convicted of accepting bribes.

Bacon spent the rest of his life writing and carrying out his scientific work. He died from bronchitis, contracted while stuffing a chicken with snow, as part of an experiment in food preservation.

Key works

1597 *Essays*
1605 *The Advancement of Learning*
1620 *Novum Organum*
1624 *Nova Atlantis*

MAN IS A MACHINE
THOMAS HOBBES (1588–1679)

IN CONTEXT

BRANCH
Metaphysics

APPROACH
Physicalism

BEFORE
4th century BCE Aristotle disagrees with Plato's theory of a distinct human soul and argues that the soul is a form or function of the body.

1641 René Descartes publishes his *Meditations on First Philosophy*, arguing that mind and body are completely different and distinct entities.

AFTER
1748 Julien Offray de la Mettrie's *The Man Machine* presents a mechanistic view of human beings.

1949 Gilbert Ryle states that Descartes' idea that mind and body are separate "substances" is a "category mistake".

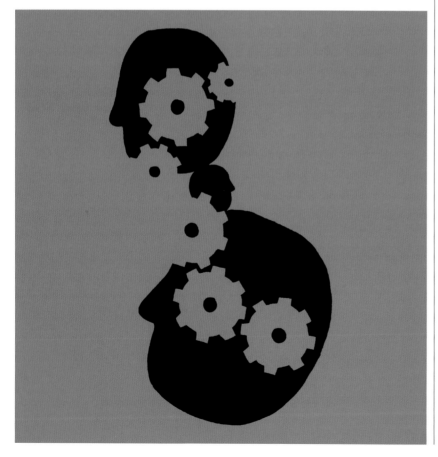

A lthough he is best known for his political philosophy, Thomas Hobbes wrote on a wide range of subjects. Many of his views are controversial, not least his defence of physicalism – the theory that everything in the world is exclusively physical in nature, allowing no room for the existence of other natural entities, such as the mind, or for supernatural beings. According to Hobbes, all animals, including humans, are nothing more than flesh-and-blood machines.

The kind of metaphysical theory that Hobbes favours was becoming increasingly popular at the time of his writing, in the mid-17th century. Knowledge in the physical sciences

See also: Aristotle 56–63 ▪ Francis Bacon 110–11 ▪ René Descartes 116–23 ▪ Julien Offray de la Mettrie 335 ▪ Gilbert Ryle 337

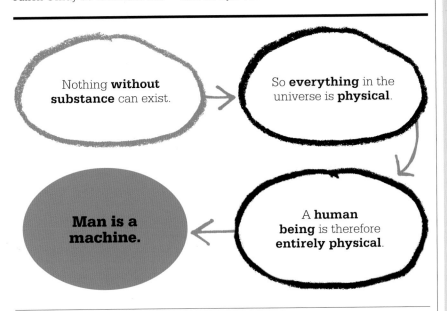

Nothing **without substance** can exist.

So **everything** in the universe is **physical**.

A **human being** is therefore **entirely physical**.

Man is a machine.

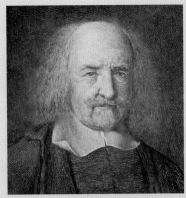

Thomas Hobbes

Orphaned in infancy, Thomas Hobbes was fortunately taken in by a wealthy uncle, who offered him a good education. A degree from the University of Oxford earned him the post of tutor to the sons of the Earl of Devonshire. This job gave Hobbes the opportunity to travel widely throughout Europe, where he met noted scientists and thinkers, such as the Italian astronomer Galileo Galilei as well as the French philosophers Marin Mersenne, Pierre Gassendi, and René Descartes.

In 1640, Hobbes fled to France to escape the English Civil War, staying there for 11 years. His first book, *De Cive*, was published in Paris in 1642. But it was his ideas on morality, politics, and the functions of society and the state, set out in *Leviathan*, that made him famous.

Also respected as a skilled translator and mathematician, Hobbes continued to write until his death at the age of 91.

Key works

1642 *De Cive*
1651 *Leviathan*
1656 *De Corpore*
1658 *De Homine*

was growing rapidly, bringing clearer explanations of phenomena that had long been obscure or misunderstood. Hobbes had met the Italian astronomer Galileo, frequently regarded as the "father of modern science", and had been closely associated with Francis Bacon, whose thinking had helped to revolutionize scientific practice.

In science and mathematics, Hobbes saw the perfect counter to the medieval Scholastic philosophy that had sought to reconcile the apparent contradictions between reason and faith. In common with many thinkers of his time, he believed there was no limit to what science could achieve, taking it as a matter of fact that any question about the nature of the world could be answered with a scientifically formulated explanation.

Hobbes' theory

In *Leviathan*, his major political work, Hobbes proclaims: "The universe – that is, the whole mass of things that are – is corporeal,

that is to say, body." He goes on to say that each of these bodies has "length, breadth, and depth", and "that which is not body is no part of the universe". Although Hobbes is stating that the nature of everything is purely physical, he is not claiming that because of this physicality everything can be perceived by us. Some bodies or objects, Hobbes declares, are imperceptible, even though they occupy physical space and have physical dimensions. These, he calls "spirits". Some of them, »

Life is but
a motion of limbs.
Thomas Hobbes

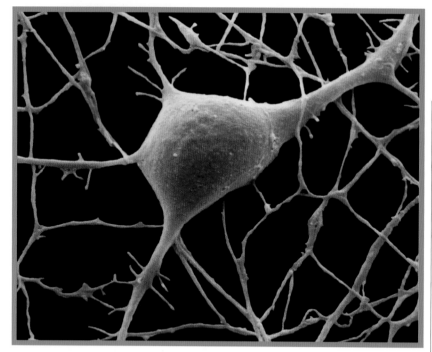

labelled "animal spirits" (in line with a common view at the time) are responsible for most animal, and especially human, activity. These animal spirits move around the body, carrying with them and passing on information, in much the same way as we now think of the nervous system doing.

Sometimes, Hobbes seems to apply his concept of physical spirits to God and other entities found in religion, such as angels. However, he does state that God himself, but not other physical spirits, should be described as "incorporeal". For Hobbes, the divine nature of God's attributes is not something that the human mind is capable of fully understanding, therefore the term "incorporeal" is the only one that recognizes and also honours the unknowable substance of God. Hobbes does make clear, however, that he believes the existence and nature of all religious entities are matters for faith, not science, and that God, in particular, will remain beyond our comprehension. All it is possible for human beings to know about God is that he exists, and that he is the first cause, or creator, of everything in the universe.

What is consciousness?

Because Hobbes considers that human beings are purely physical, and are therefore no more than biological machines, he is then faced with the problem of how to account for our mental nature. He makes no attempt to give an account of how the mind can be explained. He simply offers a general and rather sketchy account of what he thought science would eventually reveal to be the case. Even then, he only covers the mental activities such as voluntary motion, appetite, and aversion – all phenomena that can be studied and explained from a mechanistic point of view. Hobbes has nothing to say about what the modern-day Australian philosopher David Chalmers calls "the hard problem of consciousness". Chalmers points out that certain functions of consciousness – such as the use of language and the processing of information – can be explained relatively easily in terms of the mechanisms that perform those functions, and that physicalist philosophers have been offering variants of this approach for centuries. However, the harder problem of explaining the nature of subjective, first-person experience of consciousness remains unsolved by them. There seems to be a built-in mismatch between the objects of the physical sciences on the one hand and the subjects of conscious experience on the other – something that Hobbes does not seem to be aware of.

Hobbes' account of his belief offers very little argument for his conviction that everything in the world, including human beings, is wholly physical. He appears not to notice that his grounds for the

For what is the heart, but a spring; and the nerves, but so many strings; and the joints, but so many wheels, giving motion to the whole body.
Thomas Hobbes

existence of imperceptible material spirits could equally be grounds for a belief in non-material substances. To most people, something being imperceptible is more consistent with a mental than with a physical concept. In addition, because Hobbes' material spirits can only ever possess the same properties as other types of physical thing, they fail to offer any assistance towards an explanation of the mental nature of human beings.

Descartes' dualism

Hobbes also had to contend with the very different thinking about mind and body that Descartes set out in his *Meditations* of 1641. Descartes argues for the "Real Distinction" between mind and body – the notion that they are utterly distinct sorts of substance. In objections to Descartes' ideas that he expressed at the time, Hobbes makes no comment on this distinction. However, 14 years later, he addressed the problem again in a passage in his book *De Corpore*, presenting and criticizing what seems to be a muddled form of part of Descartes' argument. Here he rejects the conclusion Descartes came to – that mind and body are two distinct substances – on the basis that Descartes' use of the phrase "incorporeal substance" is an example of insignificant or empty language. Hobbes takes it to mean "a body without body", which appears to be nonsense. However, this definition must be based upon his own view that all substances are bodies; so what Hobbes appears to present as an

While Hobbes was formulating his mechanistic ideas, scientists such as the physician William Harvey were using empirical techniques to explore the workings of the human body.

argument for his position that there can be no incorporeal minds, in fact depends upon his inaccurate assumption that the only form of substance is body, and that there is no possibility of incorporeal things existing at all.

A simple prejudice

As Hobbes' definition of physical spirits indicates, it is ultimately unclear exactly what he took "physical" or "corporeal" to mean. If it was meant to be simply anything that had three spatial dimensions, then he would be excluding much of what we, at the beginning of the 21st century, might regard as being "physical". For example, his theories about the nature of the world would rule out the science of sub-atomic physics.

In the absence of any truly clear notion of what his key term means, Hobbes' insistence that everything in the world can be explained in physical terms begins to look less and less like a statement of scientific principle. Instead, it starts to appear to be merely an unscientific – and

Besides sense, and thoughts, and the train of thoughts, the mind of man has no other motion.
Thomas Hobbes

unphilosophical – prejudice against the mental. But his mechanistic theories about the nature of our world were very much in keeping with the spirit of an age that was to radically challenge most of the prevailing views on human nature and social order, as well as those concerned with the substance and workings of the universe that we inhabit. It was this revolution in thinking that laid the foundations of our modern world. ∎

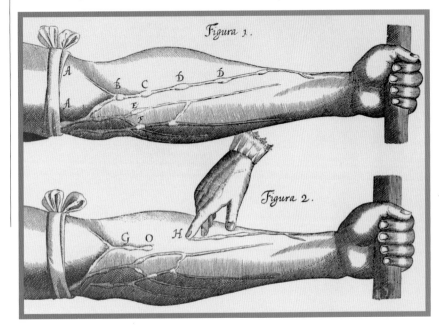

I THINK THEREFORE I AM

RENE DESCARTES (1596–1650)

IN CONTEXT

BRANCH
Epistemology

APPROACH
Rationalism

BEFORE
4th century BCE Aristotle argues that whenever we perform any action, including thinking, we are conscious that we perform it, and in this way we are conscious that we exist.

c.420 CE St Augustine writes in *The City of God* that he is certain he exists, because if he is mistaken, this itself proves his existence – in order to be mistaken, one must exist.

AFTER
1781 In his *Critique of Pure Reason*, Immanuel Kant argues against Descartes, but adopts the First Certainty – "I think therefore I exist" – as the heart and starting point of his idealist philosophy.

René Descartes lived in the early 17th century, during a period sometimes called the Scientific Revolution, an era of rapid advances in the sciences. The British scientist and philosopher Francis Bacon had established a new method for conducting scientific experiments, based on detailed observations and deductive reasoning, and his methodologies had provided a new framework for investigating the world. Descartes shared his excitement and optimism, but for different reasons. Bacon considered the practical applications of scientific discoveries to be their whole purpose and point, whereas Descartes was more fascinated by the project of extending knowledge and understanding of the world.

During the Renaissance – the preceding historical era – people had become more sceptical about science and the possibility of genuine knowledge in general, and this view continued to exert an influence in Descartes' time. So a major motivation of his "project of pure enquiry", as his work has become known, was the desire to rid the sciences of the annoyance of scepticism once and for all.

In the *Meditations on First Philosophy*, Descartes' most accomplished and rigorous work on metaphysics (the study of being and reality) and epistemology (the study of the nature and limits of knowledge), he seeks to demonstrate the possibility of knowledge even from the most sceptical of positions, and from this, to establish a firm foundation for the sciences. The

Descartes' book *De Homine Figuris* takes a biological look at the causes of knowledge. In it, he suggests that the pineal gland is the link between vision and conscious action.

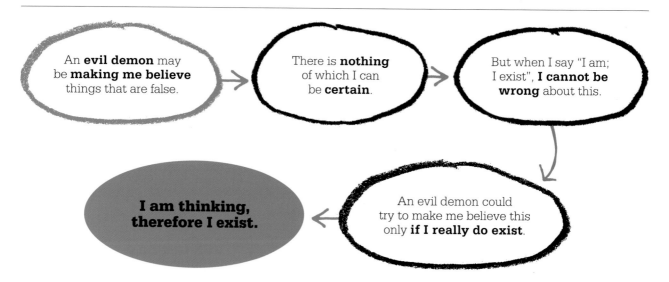

An **evil demon** may be **making me believe** things that are false.

There is **nothing** of which I can be **certain**.

But when I say "I am; I exist", **I cannot be wrong** about this.

An evil demon could try to make me believe this only **if I really do exist**.

I am thinking, therefore I exist.

Meditations is written in the first-person form – "I think…" – because he is not presenting arguments in order to prove or disprove certain statements, but instead wishes to lead the reader along the path that he himself has taken. In this way the reader is forced to adopt the standpoint of the meditator, thinking things through and discovering the truth just as Descartes had done. This approach is reminiscent of the Socratic method, in which the philosopher gradually draws out a person's understanding rather than presenting it already packaged and ready to take away.

The illusory world

In order to establish that his beliefs have stability and endurance, which Descartes takes to be two important marks of knowledge, he uses what is known as "the method of doubt". This starts with the meditator setting aside any belief whose truth can be doubted, whether slightly or completely. Descartes' aim is to show that, even if we start from the strongest possible sceptical position, doubting everything, we can still reach knowledge. The doubt is "hyperbolic" (exaggerated), and used only as a philosophical tool; as Descartes points out: "no sane person has ever seriously doubted these things".

Descartes starts by subjecting his beliefs to a series of increasingly rigorous sceptical arguments, questioning how we can be sure of the existence of anything at all. Could it be that the world we know is just an illusion? We cannot trust our senses, as we have all been "deceived" by them at one time or another, and so we cannot rely on them as a sure footing for

knowledge. Perhaps, he says, we are dreaming, and the apparently real world is no more than a dream world. He notes that this is possible, as there are no sure signs between being awake or asleep. But even so, this situation would leave open the possibility that some truths, such as mathematical axioms, could be known, though not through the senses. But even these "truths" might not in fact be true, because God, who is all-powerful, could deceive us even at this level. Even though we believe that God is good, it is possible that he made »

> It is necessary that at least once in your life you doubt, as far as possible, all things.
> **René Descartes**

An optical illusion of parallel lines that are made to look bent can fool our senses. Descartes thinks we must accept nothing as true or given, but must instead strip away all preconceptions before we can proceed to a position of knowledge.

An evil demon capable of deceiving humankind about everything cannot make me doubt my existence; if he tries, and I am forced to question my own existence, this only confirms it.

I shall suppose that some malicious demon of the utmost power and cunning has employed all his energies in order to deceive me.
René Descartes

us in such a way that we are prone to errors in our reasoning. Or perhaps there is no God – in which case we are even more likely to be imperfect beings (having arisen only by chance) that are capable of being deceived all the time.

Having reached a position in which there seems to be nothing at all of which he can be certain, Descartes then devises a vivid tool to help him to avoid slipping back into preconceived opinion: he supposes that there is a powerful and evil demon who can deceive him about anything. When he finds himself considering a belief,

he can ask: "could the demon be making me believe this even though it was false?" and if the answer is "yes" he must set aside the belief as open to doubt.

At this point, it seems as though Descartes has put himself into an impossible position – nothing seems beyond doubt, so he has no solid ground on which to stand. He describes himself as feeling helplessly tumbled around by a whirlpool of universal doubt, unable to find his footing. Scepticism seems to have made it impossible for him even to begin his journey back to knowledge and truth.

The First Certainty

It is at this point that Descartes realizes that there is one belief that he surely cannot doubt: his belief in his own existence. Each of us can

think or say: "I am, I exist", and while we are thinking or saying it we cannot be wrong about it. When Descartes tries to apply the evil demon test to this belief, he realizes that the demon could only make him believe that he exists if he does in fact exist; how can he doubt his existence unless he exists in order to do the doubting?

This axiom – "I am, I exist" – forms Descartes' First Certainty. In his earlier work, the *Discourse on the Method*, he presented it as: "I think therefore I am", but he abandoned this wording when he wrote the *Meditations*, as the inclusion of "therefore" makes the statement read like a premise and conclusion. Descartes wants the reader – the meditating "I" – to realize that as soon as I consider the fact that I exist, I know it to be true. This truth is instantly grasped. The realization that I exist is a direct intuition, not the conclusion of an argument.

Despite Descartes' move to a clearer expression of his position, the earlier formulation was so catchy that it stuck in people's minds, and to this day the First Certainty is generally known as "the cogito", from the Latin *cogito*

> This proposition, I am,
> I exist, is necessarily true
> whenever it is put forward
> by me or conceived
> in my mind.
> **René Descartes**

ergo sum, meaning "I think therefore I am". St Augustine of Hippo had used a very similar argument in *The City of God*, when he said: "for if I am mistaken, I exist"; meaning that if he did not exist, he could not be mistaken. Augustine, however, made little use of this in his thinking, and certainly did not reach it in the way that Descartes did.

What use, though, is a single belief? The simplest logical argument is a syllogism, which has two premises and a conclusion – such as: all birds have wings; a robin is a bird; therefore all robins have wings. We surely cannot get anywhere from the starting point of just one true belief. But Descartes was not looking to reach these kinds of conclusions from his First Certainty. As he explained: "Archimedes used to demand just one firm and immovable point in order to shift the entire Earth." For Descartes, the certainty of his own existence gives him the equivalent; it saves him from that whirlpool of doubt, gives him a firm foothold, and so allows him to start on the journey back from scepticism to knowledge. It is crucial to his project of enquiry, but it is not the foundation of his epistemology.

What is this "I"?

Despite the fact that the First Certainty's main function is to provide a firm footing for knowledge,

Descartes realizes that we might also be able to gain knowledge from the certainty itself. This is because the knowledge that I am thinking is bound up with the knowledge of my existence. So "thinking" is also something that I cannot rationally doubt, for doubting is a kind of thinking, so to doubt that I am thinking is to be thinking. As Descartes now knows that he exists and that he is thinking, then he – and every other meditator – also knows that he is a thinking thing.

Descartes makes clear, though, that this is as far as he can reason from the First Certainty. He is certainly not entitled to say that he is only a thinking thing – a mind – as he has no way of knowing what more he might be. He might be a physical thing that also has the ability to think, or he might be something else, something that he has not even conceived yet. The point is that at this stage of his meditations he knows only that »

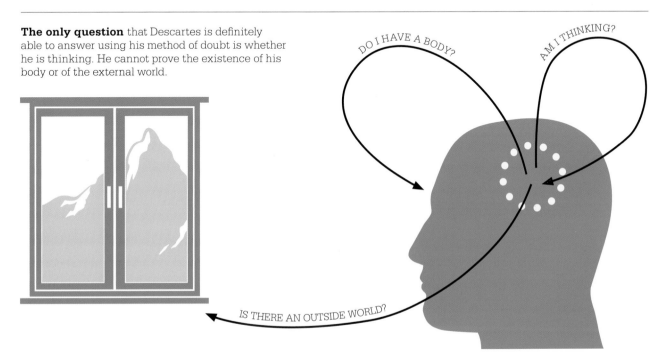

The only question that Descartes is definitely able to answer using his method of doubt is whether he is thinking. He cannot prove the existence of his body or of the external world.

DO I HAVE A BODY?

AM I THINKING?

IS THERE AN OUTSIDE WORLD?

> When someone says
> 'I am thinking, therefore
> I am', he recognizes
> it as something self-evident
> by a simple intuition
> of the mind.
> **René Descartes**

he is a thinking thing; as he puts it, he knows only that he is, "in the strict sense only" a thinking thing. Later, in the sixth book of the *Meditations*, Descartes presents an argument that mind and body are different sorts of thing – that they are distinct substances – but he is not yet in a position to do so.

Doubting Descartes

This First Certainty has been the target of criticism from many writers who hold that Descartes' approach to scepticism is doomed from the start. One of the main arguments against it takes issue with the very use of the term "I" in "I am, I exist". Although Descartes cannot be wrong in saying that thinking is occurring, how does he know that there is "a thinker" – a single, unified consciousness doing that thinking? What gives him the right to assert the existence of anything beyond the thoughts? On the other hand, can we make sense of the notion of thoughts floating around without a thinker?

It is difficult to imagine detached, coherent thoughts, and Descartes argues that it is impossible to conceive of such a state of affairs. However, if one were to disagree, and believe that a world of thoughts with no thinkers is genuinely possible, Descartes would not be entitled to the belief that he exists, and would thus fail to reach his First Certainty. The existence of thoughts would not give him the solid ground he needed.

The problem with this notion of thoughts floating around with no thinker is that reasoning would be impossible. In order to reason, it is necessary to relate ideas in a particular way. For example, if Patrick has the thought "all men are mortal" and Patricia has the thought "Socrates is a man", neither can conclude anything. But if Paula has both thoughts, she can conclude that "Socrates is mortal". Merely having the thoughts "all men are mortal" and "Socrates is a man" floating around is like two separate people having them; in order for reason to be possible we need to make these thoughts relative to one another, to link them in the right way. It turns out that making thoughts relative to anything other than a thinker (for example, to a place or to a time) fails to do the job. And since reasoning is possible, Descartes can conclude that there is a thinker.

Some modern philosophers have denied that Descartes' certainty of his own existence can do the job he requires of it; they argue that "I exist" has no content, as it merely refers to its subject but says nothing meaningful or important about it; it is simply pointing at the subject. For this reason nothing can follow from it, and Descartes' project fails at the beginning. This seems to miss Descartes' point; as we have seen, he does not use the First

---

René Descartes

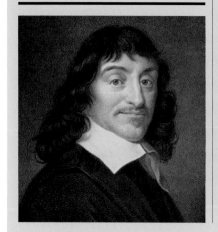

René Descartes was born near Tours, France, and was educated at the Jesuit Collège Royale, in La Flèche. Due to ill-health, he was allowed to stay in bed until late in the mornings, and he formed the habit of meditating. From the age of 16 he concentrated on studying mathematics, breaking off his studies for four years to volunteer as a soldier in Europe's Thirty Years War. During this time he found his philosophical calling, and after leaving the army, he settled first in Paris and then in the Netherlands, where he spent most of the rest of his life. In 1649 he was invited to Sweden by Queen Christina to discuss philosophy; he was expected to get up very early, much against his normal practice. He believed that this new regime – and the Swedish climate – caused him to contract pneumonia, of which he died a year later.

Key works

1637 *Discourse on the Method*
1641 *Meditations on First Philosophy*
1644 *Principles of Philosophy*
1662 *De Homine Fuguris*

Certainty as a premise from which to derive further knowledge – all he needs is that there be a self for him to point to. So even if "I exist" only succeeds in pointing to the meditator, then he has an escape from the whirlpool of doubt.

An unreal thinker

For those who have misunderstood Descartes to have been offering an argument from the fact of his thinking to the fact of his existence, we can point out that the First Certainty is a direct intuition, not a logical argument. Why, though, would it be a problem if Descartes had been offering an argument?

As it stands, the apparent inference "I am thinking, therefore I exist" is missing a major premise; that is, in order for the argument to work it needs another premise, such as "anything that is thinking exists". Sometimes an obvious premise is not actually stated in an argument, in which case it is known as a suppressed premise. But some of Descartes' critics complain that this suppressed premise is not at all obvious. For example, Hamlet, in Shakespeare's play, thought a great deal, but it is

also clearly true that he did not exist; so it is not true that anything that thinks exists.

We might say that in so far as Hamlet thought, he thought in the fictional world of a play, but he also existed in that fictional world; in so far as he did not exist, he did not exist in the real world. His "reality" and thinking are linked to the same world. But Descartes' critics might respond that that is precisely the point: knowing that someone called Hamlet was thinking – and no more than this – does not assure us that this person exists in the real world; for that, we should have to know that he was thinking in the real world. Knowing that something or someone – like Descartes – is thinking, is not enough to prove their reality in this world.

The answer to this dilemma lies in the first-person nature of the *Meditations*, and the reasons for Descartes' use of the "I" throughout now becomes clear. Because while I might be unsure whether Hamlet was thinking, and therefore existed, in a fictional world or the real world, I cannot be unsure about myself.

Modern philosophy

In the "Preface to the Reader" of the *Meditations*, Descartes accurately predicted that many readers would approach his work in such a way that most would "not bother to grasp the proper order of my arguments and the connection between them, but merely try to carp at individual sentences, as is the fashion". On the other hand, he also wrote that "I do not expect any popular approval, or indeed any wide audience", and in this he was much mistaken. He is often described as the father of modern philosophy. He sought to give philosophy the certainty of mathematics without recourse to any kind of dogma or authority,

and to establish a firm, rational foundation for knowledge. He is also well known for proposing that the mind and the body are two distinct substances – one material (the body) and the other immaterial (the mind) – which are nonetheless capable of interaction. This famous distinction, which he explains in the *Sixth Meditation*, became known as Cartesian dualism.

However, it is the rigour of Descartes' thought and his rejection of any reliance on authority that are perhaps his most important legacy. The centuries after his death were dominated by philosophers who either developed his ideas or those who took as their main task the refutation of his thoughts, such as Thomas Hobbes, Benedictus Spinoza, and Gottfried Leibniz. ∎

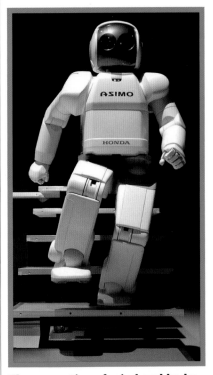

The separation of mind and body theorized by Descartes leaves open the following question: since all we can see of ourselves is our bodies, how could we prove that a robot is not conscious?

We ought to enquire as to what sort of knowledge human reason is capable of attaining, before we set about acquiring knowledge of things in particular.
René Descartes

IMAGINATION DECIDES EVERYTHING
BLAISE PASCAL (1623–1662)

IN CONTEXT

BRANCH
Philosophy of mind

APPROACH
Voluntarism

BEFORE
c.350 BCE Aristotle says that "imagination is the process by which we say that an image is presented to us," and that "the soul never thinks without a mental image."

1641 René Descartes claims that the philosopher must train his imagination for the sake of gaining knowledge.

AFTER
1740 In his *Treatise of Human Nature*, David Hume argues that "nothing we imagine is absolutely impossible".

1787 Immanuel Kant claims that we synthesize the incoherent messages from our senses into images, and then into concepts, using the imagination.

Imagination is a **powerful force** in human beings.

↓

It can **override our reason**.

↓

But it can lead either to **truths or falsehoods**.

↓

We may see beauty, justice, or happiness where it **does not really exist**.

↓

Imagination leads us astray.

Pascal's best-known book, *Pensées*, is not primarily a philosophical work. Rather, it is a compilation of fragments from his notes for a projected book on Christian theology. His ideas were aimed primarily at what he called *libertins* – ex-Catholics who had left religion as a result of the sort of free thinking encouraged by sceptical writers such as Montaigne. In one of the longer fragments, Pascal discusses imagination. He offers little or no argument for his claims, being concerned merely to set down his thoughts on the matter.

Pascal's point is that imagination is the most powerful force in human beings, and one of our chief sources of error. Imagination, he says, causes us to trust people despite what reason tells us. For example, because lawyers and doctors dress up in special clothes, we tend to trust them more. Conversely, we pay less attention to someone who looks shabby or odd, even if he is talking good sense.

What makes things worse is that, though it usually leads to falsehood, imagination occasionally leads to truth; if it were always false, then we could use it as a source of certainty by simply accepting its negation.

See also: Aristotle 56–63 ▪ Michel de Montaigne 108–09 ▪ René Descartes 116–23 ▪ David Hume 148–53 ▪
Immanuel Kant 164–71

After presenting the case against imagination in some detail, Pascal suddenly ends his discussion of it by writing: "Imagination decides everything: it produces beauty, justice, and happiness, which is the greatest thing in the world." Out of context, it might seem that he is praising imagination, but we can see from what preceded this passage that his intention is very different. As imagination usually leads to error, then the beauty, justice, and happiness that it produces will usually be false.

> Man is but a reed,
> the weakest nature;
> yet he is a thinking reed.
> **Blaise Pascal**

In the wider context of a work of Christian theology, and especially in light of Pascal's emphasis on the use of reason to bring people to religious belief, we can see that his aim is to show the *libertins* that the life of pleasure that they have chosen is not what they think it is. Although they believe that they have chosen the path of reason, they have in fact been misled by the power of the imagination.

Pascal's Wager

This view is relevant to one of the most complete notes in the *Pensées*, the famous argument known as Pascal's Wager. The wager was designed to give the *libertins* a reason to return to the Church, and it is a good example of "voluntarism", the idea that belief is a matter of decision. Pascal accepts that it is not possible to give good rational grounds for religious belief, but tries to offer good rational grounds for wanting to have such beliefs. These consist of weighing up the possible profit and loss of making a bet on the existence of God.

According to Pascal, we are constantly tricked by the imagination into making the wrong judgments – including judgements about people based on how they are dressed.

Pascal argues that betting that God does not exist risks losing a great deal (infinite happiness in Heaven), while only gaining a little (a finite sense of independence in this world) – but betting that God exists risks losing little while gaining a great deal. It is more rational, on this basis, to believe in God. ▪

Blaise Pascal

Blaise Pascal was born in Clermont-Ferrand, France. He was the son of a government functionary who had a keen interest in science and mathematics and who educated Pascal and his two sisters. Pascal published his first mathematical paper at the age of 16, and had invented the first digital calculator by the time he was 18. He also corresponded with the famous mathematician Pierre Fermat, with whom he laid the foundations of probability theory.

Pascal underwent two religious conversions, first to Jansenism (an approach to Christian teaching that was later declared heretical), and then to Christianity proper. This led him to abandon his mathematical and scientific work in favour of religious writings, including the *Pensées*. In 1660–62 he instituted the world's first public transport service, giving all profits to the poor, despite suffering from severe ill health from the 1650s until his death in 1662.

Key works

1657 *Lettres Provinciales*
1670 *Pensées*

GOD IS THE CAUSE OF ALL THINGS, WHICH ARE IN HIM

BENEDICTUS SPINOZA (1632–1677)

IN CONTEXT

BRANCH
Metaphysics

APPROACH
Substance monism

BEFORE
c.1190 Jewish philosopher Moses Maimonides invents a demythologised version of religion which later inspires Spinoza.

16th century Italian scientist Giordano Bruno develops a form of pantheism.

1641 René Descartes publishes his *Meditations*, another of Spinoza's influences.

AFTER
Late 20th century Philosophers Stuart Hampshire, Donald Davidson, and Thomas Nagel all develop approaches to the philosophy of mind that have similarities to Spinoza's monist thought.

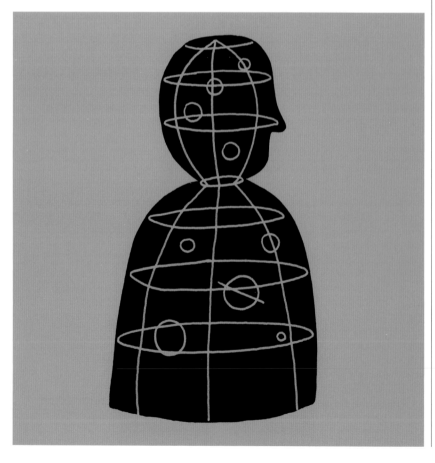

L ike most philosophies of the 17th century, Spinoza's philosophical system has the notion of "substance" at its heart. This concept can be traced back to Aristotle, who asked "What is it about an object that stays the same when it undergoes change?" Wax, for example, can melt and change its shape, size, colour, smell, and texture, and yet still remain "wax", prompting the question: what are we referring to when we speak of "the wax"? Since it can change in every way that we can perceive, the wax must also be something beyond its perceptible properties, and for Aristotle this unchanging thing is the wax's "substance". More

See also: Aristotle 56–63 ▪ Moses Maimonides 84–85 ▪ René Descartes 116–23 ▪ Donald Davidson 338

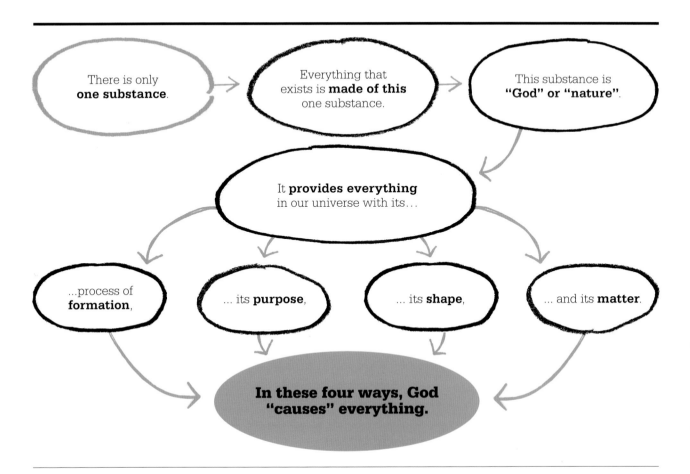

There is only **one substance**.

Everything that exists is **made of this** one substance.

This substance is **"God"** or **"nature"**.

It **provides everything** in our universe with its…

…process of **formation**,

… its **purpose**,

… its **shape**,

… and its **matter**.

In these four ways, God "causes" everything.

generally, substance is anything that has properties – or that which underlies the world of appearance.

Spinoza employs "substance" in a similar way, defining it as that which is self-explanatory – or that which can be understood by knowing its nature alone, as opposed to all other things that can be known only by their relationships with other things. For example, the concept "cart" can only be understood with reference to other concepts, such as "motion", "transport", and so on. Moreover, for Spinoza, there can only be one such substance, for if there were two, understanding one would entail understanding its relationship with the other, which contradicts the definition of substance. Furthermore, he argues, since there is only one such substance, there can, in fact, be nothing *but* that substance, and everything else is in some sense a part of it. Spinoza's position is known as "substance monism", which claims that all things are ultimately aspects of a single thing, as opposed to "substance dualism", which claims that there are ultimately two kinds of things in the universe, most commonly defined as "mind" and "matter".

Substance as God or nature

For Spinoza, then, substance underlies our experience, but it can also be known by its various attributes. He does not specify how many attributes substance has, but he says that human beings, at least, can conceive of two – namely, the attribute of extension (physicality) and the attribute of thought (mentality). For this reason, Spinoza is also known as an "attribute dualist", and he claims that these two attributes cannot be explained by each other, and so must be included in any complete account of the world. As for substance itself, Spinoza says that we are right to call it "God" or "nature" (*Deus sive natura*) – that self-explaining thing which, in human form, sees itself under the attributes of body and mind. »

All changes, from a change of mood to a change in a candle's shape, are, for Spinoza, alterations that occur to a single substance that has both mental and physical attributes.

At the level of individual things, including human beings, Spinoza's attribute dualism is intended in part to deal with the question of how minds and bodies interact. The things that we experience as individual bodies or minds are in fact modifications of the single substance as conceived under one of the attributes. Each modification is both a physical thing (in so far as it is conceived under the attribute of extension)

and a mental thing (in so far as it is conceived under the attribute of thought). In particular, a human mind is a modification of substance conceived under the attribute of thought, and the human brain is the same modification of substance conceived under the attribute of extension. In this way, Spinoza avoids any question about the interaction between mind and body: there is no interaction, only a one-to-one correspondence.

However, Spinoza's theory commits him to the view that it is not only human beings that are minds as well as bodies, but everything else too. Tables, rocks, trees – all of these are modifications of the one substance under the attributes of thought and extension. So, they are all both physical and mental things, although their mentality is very simple and they are not what we should call minds. This aspect of Spinoza's theory is difficult for many people either to accept or to understand.

The world is God
Spinoza's theory, which he explains fully in *Ethics*, is often referred to as a form of pantheism – the belief

Mind and body
are one.
Benedictus Spinoza

that God is the world, and that the world is God. Pantheism is often criticized by theists (people who believe in God), who argue that it is little more than atheism by another name. However, Spinoza's theory is in fact much closer to panentheism – the view that the world is God, but that God is more than the world. For in Spinoza's system, the world is not a mass of material and mental stuff – rather, the world of material things is a form of God as conceived under the attribute of extension, and the world of mental things is that same form of God as conceived under the attribute of thought. Therefore the

Benedictus Spinoza

Benedictus (or Baruch) Spinoza was born in Amsterdam, the Netherlands, in 1632. At the age of 23 he was excommunicated by the synagogue of Portuguese Jews in Amsterdam, who probably wished to distance themselves from Spinoza's teachings. Spinoza's *Theological-Political Treatise* was later attacked by Christian theologians and banned in 1674 – a fate that had already befallen the work of the French philosopher René Descartes. The furore caused him to withhold publication of his greatest work, the *Ethics*, until after his death.

Spinoza was a modest, intensely moral man who turned down numerous lucrative teaching positions for the sake of his intellectual freedom. Instead he lived a frugal life in various places in the Netherlands, making a living by private philosophy teaching and as a lens grinder. He died from tuberculosis in 1677.

Key works

1670 *Theological-Political Treatise*
1677 *Ethics*

> The human mind
> is part of the infinite
> intellect of God.
> **Benedictus Spinoza**

According to Spinoza, all objects, whether animal, vegetable, or mineral, have a mentality. Both their bodies and their mentalities are a part of God, who is greater than all the world's physical and mental attributes. God, for Spinoza, is the "substance" that underlies reality.

Every object in the universe, even a rock, has a **body and a mind**.

Body and mind are attributes of **substance**.

Substance is God, in whom all is explained.

one substance or God is more than the world, but the world itself is entirely substance or God.

However, Spinoza's God is clearly different from the God of standard Judaeo-Christian theology. Not only is it not a person, it cannot be regarded as being the creator of the world in the sense found in the Book of Genesis. Spinoza's God does not exist alone before creation, and then bring it into existence.

God as the cause

What can Spinoza mean, then, when he says that God is the cause of everything? The one substance is "God or nature" – so even if there is more to God than those modifications of substance that make up our world, how can the relationship between God and nature be causal?

First, we should note that Spinoza, in common with most philosophers before him, uses the word "cause" in a much richer sense than we do now – a sense that originates in Aristotle's definition of four types of cause. These are (using a statue as an example): a formal cause, or the relationship between a thing's parts (its shape or form); a material cause, or the matter a thing is made of (the bronze, marble, and so on);

an efficient cause, or that which brings a thing into being (the sculpting process); and a final cause, or the purpose for which a thing exists (the creation of a work of art, the desire for money, and so on).

For Aristotle and Spinoza, these together define "cause", and provide a complete explanation of a thing – unlike today's usage, which tends to relate to the "efficient" or "final" causes only. Therefore, when Spinoza speaks of God or substance being "self-caused" he means that it is self-explanatory, rather than that it is simply self-generating. When he talks of God

being the cause of all things, he means that all things find their explanation in God.

God, therefore, is not what Spinoza calls a "transitive" cause of the world – something external that brings the world into being. Rather, God is the "immanent" cause of the world. This means that God is in the world, that the world is in God, and that the existence and essence of the world are explained by God's existence and essence. For Spinoza, to fully appreciate this fact is to attain the highest state of freedom and salvation possible – a state he calls "blessedness". ∎

NO MAN'S KNOWLEDGE HERE CAN GO BEYOND HIS EXPERIENCE
JOHN LOCKE (1632–1704)

IN CONTEXT

BRANCH
Epistemology

APPROACH
Empiricism

BEFORE
c.380 BCE In his dialogue, *Meno*, Plato argues that we remember knowledge from previous lives.

Mid-13th century Thomas Aquinas puts forward the principle that "whatever is in our intellect must have previously been in the senses".

AFTER
Late 17th century Gottfried Leibniz argues that the mind may seem to be a tabula rasa at birth, but contains innate, underlying knowledge, which experience gradually uncovers.

1966 Noam Chomsky, in *Cartesian Linguistics*, sets out his theory of innate grammar.

John Locke is traditionally included in the group of philosophers known as the British Empiricists, together with two later philosophers, George Berkeley and David Hume. The empiricists are generally thought to hold the view that all human knowledge must come directly or indirectly from the experience of the world that we acquire through the use of our senses alone. This contrasts with the thinking of the rationalist philosophers, such as René Descartes, Benedictus Spinoza, and Gottfried Leibniz, who hold that in principle, at least, it is possible to acquire knowledge solely through the use of reason.

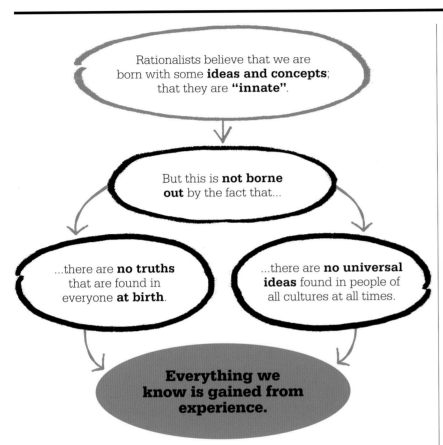

Rationalists believe that we are born with some **ideas and concepts**; that they are **"innate"**.

But this is **not borne out** by the fact that...

...there are **no truths** that are found in everyone **at birth**.

...there are **no universal ideas** found in people of all cultures at all times.

Everything we know is gained from experience.

If we attentively consider newborn children, we shall have little reason to think that they bring many ideas into the world with them.
John Locke

Understanding, against the theory proposed by the rationalists to explain how knowledge could be accessed without experience. This is the theory of innate ideas.

The concept that human beings are born with innate ideas, and that these can give us knowledge about the nature of the world around us, independently of anything we may experience, dates back to the dawn of philosophy. Plato had developed a concept, according to which all genuine knowledge is essentially located within us, but that when we die our souls are reincarnated into new bodies and the shock of birth causes us to forget it all. Education is therefore not about learning new facts, but about "un-forgetting", and the educator is not a teacher but a midwife.

However, many later thinkers countered Plato's theory, proposing that all knowledge cannot be innate and that only a limited number of concepts can be. These include the concept of God and also that of a perfect geometric structure, such as an equilateral triangle. This »

In fact, the division between these two groups is not as clear-cut as is often assumed. The rationalists all accept that in practice our knowledge of the world ultimately stems from our experience, and most notably from scientific enquiry. Locke reaches his distinctive views concerning the nature of the world by applying a process of reasoning later known as abduction (inference to the best explanation from the available evidence) to the facts of sensory experience. For example, Locke sets out to demonstrate that the best explanation of the world as we experience it is corpuscular theory. This is the theory that everything in the world is made up of sub-microscopic particles, or corpuscles, which we can have no direct knowledge of, but which, by their very existence, make sense of phenomena that would otherwise be difficult or impossible to explain. Corpuscular theory was becoming popular in 17th-century scientific thinking and is fundamental to Locke's view of the physical world.

Innate ideas

The claim that man's knowledge cannot go beyond his experience may therefore seem inappropriate, or at least an exaggeration, when attributed to Locke. However, Locke does argue at some length, in his *Essay Concerning Human*

type of knowledge, in their view, can be gained without any direct sensory experience, in the way that it is possible to devise a mathematical formula by using nothing more than the powers of reason and logic. René Descartes, for example, declares that although he believes that we all have an idea of God imprinted in us – like the mark that a craftsman makes in the clay of a pot – this knowledge of God's existence can only be brought into our conscious mind through a process of reasoning.

Locke's objections

Locke was against the idea that human beings possess any kind of innate knowledge. He takes the view that the mind at birth is a tabula rasa – a blank tablet or a new sheet of paper upon which experience writes, in the same way that light can create images on photographic film. According to Locke, we bring nothing to the process except the basic human ability to apply reason to the information that we gather through our senses. He argues that there is not the slightest empirical evidence to suggest that the minds of infants are other than blank at birth, and adds that this is also true of the minds of the mentally deficient, stating that "they have not the least apprehension or thought of them". Locke, therefore, declares that any doctrine supporting the existence of innate ideas must be false.

Locke also goes on to attack the very notion of innate ideas by arguing that it is incoherent. In order for something to be an idea at all, he states that it has to have been present at some point in somebody's mind. But, as Locke points out, any idea that claims to be truly innate must also be claiming to precede any form of human experience. Locke accepts that it is true, as Gottfried Leibniz states, that an idea may exist so deep in a person's memory that for a time it is difficult or even impossible to recall, and so is not accessible to the conscious mind. Innate ideas, on the other hand, are believed to somehow exist

> It seems to me a near contradiction to say that there are truths imprinted on the soul, which it perceives or understands not.
> **John Locke**

somewhere, before the presence of any sort of mechanism that is capable of conceiving them and bringing them into consciousness.

The supporters of the existence of innate ideas often also argue that as such ideas are present in all human beings at birth, they must be by nature universal, which means that they are found in all human societies at all points in history. Plato, for example, claims that everyone potentially has access to the same basic body of knowledge, denying any difference in that respect between men and women, or between slaves and freemen. Similarly, in Locke's time, the theory was frequently put forward that because innate ideas can only be placed in us by God, they must be universal, as God is not capable of being so unfair as to hand them out only to a select group of people. Locke counters the argument for universal ideas by once again bringing to our attention that a simple examination of the world around us will readily show that they do no exist. Even if there were concepts, or ideas, which absolutely every human being in

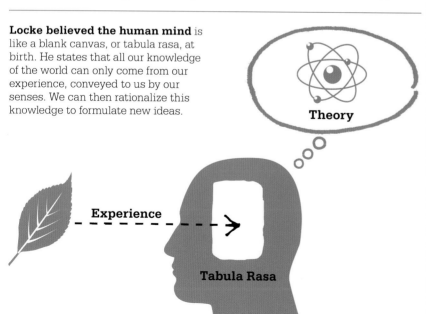

Locke believed the human mind is like a blank canvas, or tabula rasa, at birth. He states that all our knowledge of the world can only come from our experience, conveyed to us by our senses. We can then rationalize this knowledge to formulate new ideas.

Theory

Experience

Tabula Rasa

> Let us then suppose the mind to be white paper, void of all characters, without any ideas; how comes it to be furnished?
> **John Locke**

the world held in common, Locke argues that we would have no firm grounds for concluding that they were also innate. He declares that it would always be possible to discover other explanations for their universality, such as the fact that they stem from the most basic ways in which a human being experiences the world around him, which is something that we all must share.

In 1704, Gottfried Leibniz wrote a rebuttal of Locke's empiricist arguments in his *New Essays on the Human Understanding*. Leibniz declares that innate ideas are the one clear way that we can gain knowledge that is not based upon sensory experience, and that Locke is wrong to deny their possibility. The debate about whether human beings can know anything beyond what they perceive through their five basic senses continues.

Language as innate

Although Locke may reject the doctrine of innate ideas, he does not reject the concept that human beings have innate capacities. Indeed, the possession of capacities such as perception and reasoning are central to his accounts of the mechanism of human knowledge and understanding. In the late 20th century, the American philosophy Noam Chomsky took this idea further when he put forward his theory that there is an innate process of thinking in every human mind, which is capable of generating a universal "deep structure" of language. Chomsky believes that regardless of their apparent structural differences, all human languages have been generated from this common basis.

As the mind is a blank canvas, or tabula rasa, at birth, Locke believes that anybody can be transformed by a good education, one that encourages rational thought and individual talents.

Locke played an important role in questioning how human beings acquire knowledge, at a time when man's understanding of the world was expanding at an unprecedented rate. Earlier philosophers – notably the medieval Scholastic thinkers such as Thomas Aquinas – had concluded that some aspects of reality were beyond the grasp of the human mind. But Locke took this a stage further. By detailed analysis of man's mental faculties, he sought to set down the exact limits of what is knowable. ∎

John Locke

John Locke was born in 1632, the son of an English country lawyer. Thanks to wealthy patrons, he received a good education, first at Westminster School in London, then at Oxford. He was impressed with the empirical approach to science adopted by the pioneering chemist Robert Boyle, and he both promoted Boyle's ideas and assisted in his experimental work.

Though Locke's empiricist ideas are important, it was his political writing that made him famous. He proposed a social-contract theory of the legitimacy of government and the idea of natural rights to private property. Locke fled England twice, as a political exile, but returned in 1688, after the accession to the throne of William and Mary. He remained in England, writing as well as holding various government positions, until his death in 1704.

Key works

1689 *A Letter Concerning Toleration*
1690 *An Essay Concerning Human Understanding*
1690 *Two Treatises of Government*

THERE ARE TWO KINDS OF TRUTHS: TRUTHS OF REASONING AND TRUTHS OF FACT

GOTTFRIED LEIBNIZ (1646–1716)

E arly modern philosophy is often presented as being divided into two schools – that of the rationalists (including René Descartes, Benedictus Spinoza, and Immanuel Kant) and that of the empiricists (including John Locke, George Berkeley, and David Hume). In fact, the various philosophers did not easily fall into two clear groups, each being like and unlike each of the others in complex and overlapping ways. The essential difference between the two schools, however, was epistemological – that is, they differed in their opinions about what we can know, and how we know what we know. Put simply,

See also: Nicolaus of Autrecourt 334 ▪ René Descartes 116–23 ▪ David Hume 148–53 ▪ Immanuel Kant 164–71 ▪ Alfred North Whitehead 336

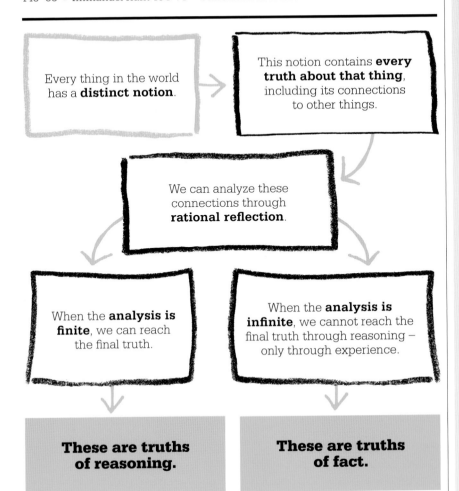

Every thing in the world has a **distinct notion**.

This notion contains **every truth about that thing**, including its connections to other things.

We can analyze these connections through **rational reflection**.

When the **analysis is finite**, we can reach the final truth.

When the **analysis is infinite**, we cannot reach the final truth through reasoning – only through experience.

These are truths of reasoning.

These are truths of fact.

Gottfried Leibniz

Gottfried Leibniz was a German philosopher and mathematician. He was born in Leipzig, and after university he took public service with the Elector of Mainz for five years, during which time he concentrated mainly on political writings. After a period spent travelling, he took up the post of librarian to the Duke of Brunswick, in Hanover, and remained there until his death. It was during this last period of his life that he did most of the work on the development of his unique philosophical system.

Leibniz is famous in mathematics for his invention of the so-called "infinitesimal calculus" and the row that followed this, as both Leibniz and Newton claimed the discovery as their own. It seems clear that they had in fact reached it independently, but Leibniz developed a much more usable notation which is still used today.

Key works

1673 *A Philosopher's Creed*
1685 *Discourse on Metaphysics*
1695 *The New System*
1710 *Theodicy*
1714 *Monadology*

the empiricists held that knowledge is derived from experience, while the rationalists claimed that knowledge can be gained through rational reflection alone.

Leibniz was a rationalist, and his distinction between truths of reasoning and truths of fact marks an interesting twist in the debate between rationalism and empiricism. His claim, which he makes in most famous work, the *Monadology*, is that in principle all knowledge can be accessed by rational reflection. However, due to shortcomings in our rational »

We know hardly anything adequately, few things *a priori*, and most things through experience.
Gottfried Wilhelm Leibniz

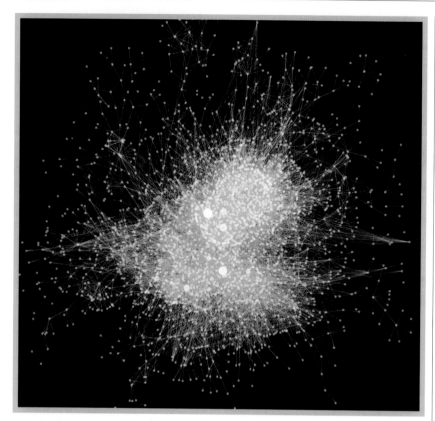

A map of the internet shows the innumerable connections between internet users. Leibniz's theory of monads suggests that all our minds are similarly connected.

According to Leibniz, this is how God created things – in a state of "pre-established harmony".

Leibniz claims that every human mind is a monad, and so contains a complete representation of the universe. It is therefore possible in principle for us to learn everything that there is to know about our world and beyond simply by exploring our own minds. Simply by analysing my notion of the star Betelgeuse, for example, I will eventually be able to determine the temperature on the surface of the actual star Betelgeuse. However, in practice, the analysis that is required for me reach this information is impossibly complex – Leibniz calls it "infinite" – and because I cannot complete it, the only way that I can discover the temperature of Betelgeuse is by measuring it empirically using astronomical equipment.

Is the temperature of the surface of Betelgeuse a truth of reasoning or a truth of fact? It may be true that I had to resort to empirical

faculties, human beings must also rely on experience as a means of acquiring knowledge.

A universe in our minds

To see how Leibniz arrives at this conclusion, we need to understand a little of his metaphysics – his view of how the universe is constructed. He holds that every part of the world, every individual thing, has a distinct concept or "notion" associated with it, and that every such notion contains within it everything that is true about itself, including its relations to other things. Because everything in the universe is connected, he argues, it follows that every notion is connected to every other notion, and so it is possible – at least in principle – to follow these connections and to discover truths about the entire universe through

rational reflection alone. Such reflection leads to Leibniz's "truths of reasoning". However, the human mind can grasp only a small number of such truths (such as those of mathematics), and so it has to rely on experience, which yields "truths of fact".

So how is it possible to progress from knowing that it is snowing, for example, to knowing what will happen tomorrow somewhere on the other side of the world? For Leibniz, the answer lies in the fact that the universe is composed of individual, simple substances called "monads". Each monad is isolated from other monads, and each contains a complete representation of the whole universe in its past, present, and future states. This representation is synchronized between all the monads, so that each one has the same content.

> Each singular substance expresses the whole universe in its own way.
> **Gottfried Wilhelm Leibniz**

methods to discover the answer, but had my rational faculties been better I could also have discovered it through rational reflection. Whether it is a truth of reasoning or a truth of fact, therefore, seems to depend on how I arrive at the answer – but is this what Leibniz is claiming?

Necessary truths

The trouble for Leibniz is that he holds that truths of reasoning are "necessary", meaning that it is impossible to contradict them, while truths of fact are "contingent"; they can be denied without logical contradiction. A mathematical truth is a necessary truth, because denying its conclusions contradicts the meanings of its own terms. But the proposition "it is raining in Spain" is contingent, because denying it does not involve a contradiction in terms – although it may still be factually incorrect.

Leibniz's distinction between truths of reasoning and truths of fact is not simply an epistemological one (about the limits of knowledge), but also a metaphysical one (about the nature of the world), and it is not clear that his arguments support his metaphysical claim. Leibniz's theory of monads seems to suggest that all truths are truths

God understands everything through eternal truth, since he does not need experience.
Gottfried Wilhelm Leibniz

of reasoning, which we would have access to if we could finish our rational analysis. But as a truth of reasoning is a necessary truth, in what way is it impossible for the temperature on Betelgeuse to be 2,401 Kelvin rather than 2,400 Kelvin? Certainly not impossible in the sense that the proposition $2 + 2 = 5$ is impossible, for the latter is simply a logical contradiction.

Likewise, if we follow Leibniz and separate neccesary and contingent truths, we end up with the following problem: I can discover Pythagoras's theorem simply by reflecting on the idea of triangles, so Pythagoras's theorem must be a truth of reasoning. But Betelgeuse's temperature and Pythagoras's theorem are both just as true, and just as much part of the monad that is my mind – so why should one be considered contingent and the other necessary?

Moreover, Leibniz tells us that whereas no-one can reach the end of an infinite analysis, God can grasp the whole universe at once, and so for him all truths are neccesary truths. The difference between a truth of reasoning and a truth of fact, therefore, does seem to be a matter of how one comes to know it – and in that case it is difficult to see why the former should always be seen to be necessarily true, while the latter may or may not be true.

An uncertain future

In setting out a scheme in which an omnipotent, omniscient God creates the universe, Leibniz inevitably faces the problem of accounting for the notion of freedom of will. How can I choose to act in a certain way if God already knows how I am going to act? But the problem runs deeper – there seems to be no room for genuine contingency at all. Leibniz's theory only allows for a

The mechanical calculator was one of Leibniz's many inventions. Its creation is a testament to his interest in mathematics and logic – fields in which he was a great innovator.

distinction between truths whose necessity we can discover, and truths whose necessity only God can see. We know (if we accept Leibniz's theory) that the future of the world is set by an omniscient and benevolent god, who therefore has created the best of all possible worlds. But we call the future contingent, or undetermined, because as limited human beings we cannot see its content.

Leibniz's legacy

In spite of the difficulties inherent in Leibniz's theory, his ideas went on to shape the work of numerous philosophers, including David Hume and Immanuel Kant. Kant refined Leibniz's truths of reasoning and truths of fact into the distinction between "analytic" and "synthetic" statements – a division that has remained central to European philosophy ever since.

Liebniz's theory of monads fared less well, and was criticized for its metaphysical extravagance. In the 20th century, however, the idea was rediscovered by scientists who were intrigued by Leibniz's description of space and time as a system of relationships, rather than the absolutes of traditional Newtonian physics. ∎

TO BE IS TO BE PERCEIVED

GEORGE BERKELEY (1685–1753)

IN CONTEXT

BRANCH
Metaphysics

APPROACH
Idealism

BEFORE
c.380 BCE In *The Republic*, Plato presents his theory of Forms, which states that the world of our experience is an imperfect shadow of reality.

AFTER
1781 Immanuel Kant develops Berkeley's theory into "transcendental idealism", according to which the world that we experience is only appearance.

1807 Georg Hegel replaces Kant's idealism with "absolute idealism" – the theory that absolute reality is Spirit.

1982 In his book *The Case for Idealism*, the British philosopher John Foster argues for a version of Berkeley's idealism.

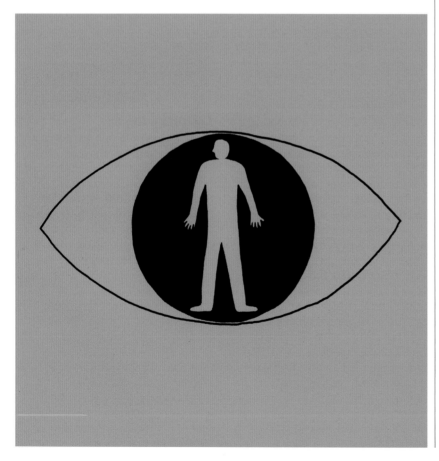

ike John Locke before him, George Berkeley was an empiricist, meaning that he saw experience as the primary source of knowledge. This view, which can be traced back to Aristotle, stands in contrast to the rationalist view that, in principle, all knowledge can be gained through rational reflection alone. Berkeley shared the same assumptions as Locke, but reached very different conclusions. According to Berkeley, Locke's empiricism was moderate; it still allowed for the existence of a world independent of the senses, and followed René Descartes in

See also: Plato 50–55 ▪ Aristotle 56–63 ▪ René Descartes 116–23 ▪
John Locke 130–33 ▪ Immanuel Kant 164–71 ▪ Georg Hegel 178–85

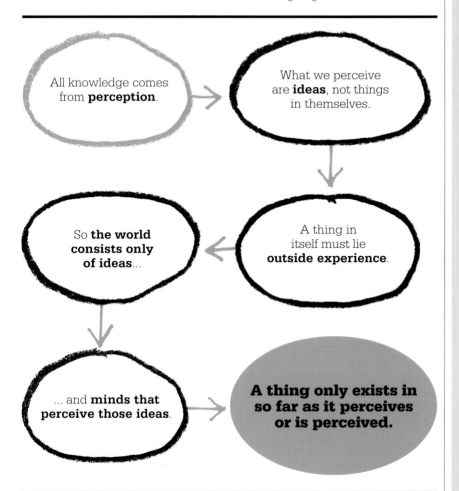

All knowledge comes from **perception**.

What we perceive are **ideas**, not things in themselves.

A thing in itself must lie **outside experience**.

So **the world consists only of ideas**...

... and **minds that perceive those ideas**.

A thing only exists in so far as it perceives or is perceived.

George Berkeley

George Berkeley was born and brought up at Dysart Castle, near the town of Kilkenny, Ireland. He was educated first at Kilkenny College, then at Trinity College, Dublin. In 1707 he was elected a Fellow of Trinity, and was ordained an Anglican priest. In 1714, having written all his major philosophical works, he left Ireland to travel around Europe, spending most of his time in London.

When he returned to Ireland he became Dean of Derry. His main concern, however, had become a project to found a seminary college in Bermuda. In 1728 he sailed to Newport, Rhode Island, with his wife, Anne Foster, and spent three years trying to raise money for the seminary. In 1731, when it became clear that funds were not forthcoming, he returned to London. Three years later he became Bishop of Cloyne, Dublin, where he lived for the rest of his life.

Key works

1710 *Treatise Concerning the Principles of Human Knowledge*
1713 *Three Dialogues Between Hylas and Philonous*

seeing humans as being made up of two distinct substances, namely mind and body.

Berkeley's empiricism, on the other hand, was far more extreme, and led him to a position known as "immaterialist idealism". This means that he was a monist, believing that there is only one kind of substance in the universe, and an idealist, believing that this single substance is mind, or thought, rather than matter.

Berkeley's position is often summarized by the Latin phrase *esse est percipi* ("to be is to be perceived"), but it is perhaps »

There is no such thing as what philosophers call material substance.
George Berkeley

> If there were external bodies, it is impossible we should ever come to know it.
> **George Berkeley**

> An idea can be like nothing but an idea; a colour or figure can be like nothing but another colour or figure.
> **George Berkeley**

better represented by *esse est aut perciperi aut percipi* ("to be is to perceive or to be perceived"). For according to Berkeley, the world consists only of perceiving minds and their ideas. This is not to say that he denies the existence of the external world, or claims that it is in any way different from what we perceive. His claim is rather that all knowledge must come from experience, and that all we ever have access to are our perceptions. And since these perceptions are simply "ideas" (or mental representations), we have no grounds for believing that anything exists other than ideas and the perceivers of ideas.

Causation and volition

Berkeley's target was Descartes' view of the world as elaborated by Locke and the scientist Robert Boyle. In this view, the physical world is made up of a vast number of physical particles, or "corpuscles", whose nature and interactions give rise to the world as we understand it. More controversially, for Berkeley, this view also maintains that the world causes the perceptual ideas we have of it by the way it interacts with our senses.

Berkeley has two main objections to this view. First, he argues that our understanding of causality (the fact that certain events cause other events) is based entirely on our experience of our own volitions (the way we cause events to happen through the action of our wills). His point is not simply that it is wrong for us to project our own experience of volitional action onto the world – which we do when we say that the world causes us to have ideas about the world. His point is that there is in fact no such thing as a "physical cause", because there is no such thing as a physical world beyond the world of ideas that could possibly be the cause of our ideas. The only type of cause that there is in the world, according to Berkeley, is precisely the volitional kind of cause that is the exercise of the will.

Berkeley's second objection is that because ideas are mental entities, they cannot resemble physical entities, because the two types of thing have completely different properties. A painting or a photograph can resemble a physical object because it is itself a physical thing, but to think of an idea as resembling a physical object is to mistake it for a physical thing itself. Ideas, then, can only resemble other ideas. And as our only experience of the world comes through our ideas, any claim that we can even understand the notion of "physical things" is mistaken. What we are really understanding are mental things. The world is constructed purely of thought, and whatever is not itself perceiving, exists only as one of our perceptions.

The cause of perception

If things that are not perceivers only exist in so far as they are perceived, however, this seems to mean that when I leave the room, my desk, computer, books, and so on all cease to exist, for they are no longer being perceived. Berkeley's response to this is that nothing is ever unperceived, for when I am not in my room, it is still perceived by God. His theory, therefore, not only depends on the existence of God, but of a particular type of God – one who is constantly involved in the world.

For Berkeley, God's involvement in the world runs deeper than this. As we have seen, he claims that there are no physical causes, but

Optical illusions are impossible, for Berkeley, since an object is always as it appears to be. A straw submerged in water, for example, really is bent, and a magnified object really is larger.

only "volitions", or acts of will, and it follows that only an act of will can produce the ideas that we have about the world. However, I am not in control of my experience of the world, and cannot choose what I experience – the world simply presents itself to me the way it does, whether I like it or not. Therefore, the volitions that cause my ideas about the world are not mine; they are God's. So for Berkeley, God not only creates us as perceivers, he is the cause and constant generator of all our perceptions. This raises a number of questions, the most urgent being: how is it that we sometimes perceive things incorrectly? Why would God want to deceive us?

Berkeley tries to answer this question by claiming that our perceptions are never, in fact, in error, and that where we go wrong is in the judgements we make about what we perceive. For example, if an oar half-submerged in water looks bent to me, then it really is bent – where I go wrong is thinking that it only appears to be bent.

However, what happens if I reach into the water and feel the oar? It certainly feels straight. And since

All the choir of heaven and furniture of earth – in a word, all those bodies which compose the frame of the world – have not any subsistence without a mind.
George Berkeley

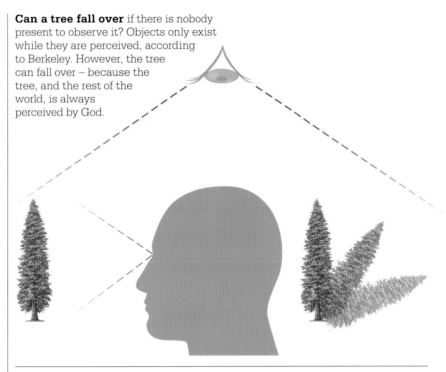

Can a tree fall over if there is nobody present to observe it? Objects only exist while they are perceived, according to Berkeley. However, the tree can fall over – because the tree, and the rest of the world, is always perceived by God.

the oar cannot be both straight and bent at the same time, there must in fact be two oars – one that I see and one that I feel. Even more problematic for Berkeley, however, is the fact that two different people seeing the same oar must in fact be seeing two different oars, for there is no single, "real" oar "out there" that their perceptions converge on.

The problem of solipsism

An inescapable fact of Berkeley's system, therefore, seems to be that we never perceive the same things. Each of us is locked in his own world, cut off from the worlds of other people. The fact that God has an idea of an oar cannot help us here, for that is a third idea, and therefore a third oar. God caused my idea and your idea, but unless we share a single mind with each other and with God, there are still three different ideas, so there are three different oars. This leads us to the problem of solipsism – the

possibility that the only thing I can be certain of existing – or that may in fact exist – is myself.

One possible solution to solipsism runs as follows: since I can cause changes in the world, such as raising my own hand, and since I notice similar changes in the bodies of other people, I can infer that those bodies are also changed by a "consciousness" inside them. The problem for Berkeley, though, is that there is no "real" hand being lifted – the most a person can do is be the cause of the idea of his own hand rising – and only their idea, not another person's. I, in other words, must still rely on God to supply me with my idea of another person's hand rising. Far from supplying us with empirical certainty, therefore, Berkeley leaves us depending for our knowledge of the world, and of the existence of other minds, upon our faith in a God that would never deceive us. ∎

THE AGE
REVOLU
1750–1900

OF
TION

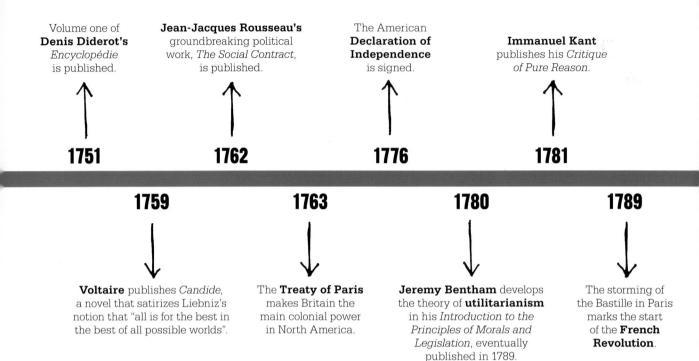

Volume one of **Denis Diderot's** *Encyclopédie* is published.

Jean-Jacques Rousseau's groundbreaking political work, *The Social Contract*, is published.

The American **Declaration of Independence** is signed.

Immanuel Kant publishes his *Critique of Pure Reason*.

1751

1762

1776

1781

1759

1763

1780

1789

Voltaire publishes *Candide,* a novel that satirizes Liebniz's notion that "all is for the best in the best of all possible worlds".

The **Treaty of Paris** makes Britain the main colonial power in North America.

Jeremy Bentham develops the theory of **utilitarianism** in his *Introduction to the Principles of Morals and Legislation*, eventually published in 1789.

The storming of the Bastille in Paris marks the start of the **French Revolution**.

During the Renaissance, Europe had evolved into a collection of separate nation states, having previously been a continent unified under the control of the Church. As power devolved to separate countries, distinctive national cultures formed, which were most obvious in arts and literature, but could also be seen in the philosophical styles that emerged during the 17th century.

During the Age of Reason there was a very clear difference between the rationalism of continental Europe and the empiricism of British philosophers, and in the 18th century philosophy continued to centre on France and Britain, as the Enlightenment period unfolded. Old values and feudal systems crumbled as the new nations founded on trade gave rise to a growing urban middle-class with unprecedented prosperity. The richest nations, such as Britain, France, Spain, Portugal, and the Netherlands, established colonies and empires around the world.

France and Britain

Philosophy increasingly focused on social and political issues, also along national lines. In Britain, where a revolution had already come and gone, empiricism reached a peak in the works of David Hume, while the new utilitarianism dominated political philosophy. This evolved alongside the Industrial Revolution that had started in the 1730s, as thinkers such as John Stuart Mill refined the utilitarianism of Jeremy Bentham and helped to establish both a liberal democracy and a framework for modern civil rights.

The situation in France, however, was less stable. The rationalism of René Descartes gave way to a generation of *philosophes*, radical political philosophers who were to popularize the new scientific way of thinking. They included the literary satirist Voltaire and the encyclopedist Denis Diderot, but the most revolutionary was Jean-Jacques Rousseau. His vision of a society governed on the principles of *liberté*, *egalité,* and *fraternité* (liberty, equality, and fraternity) provided the battle cry of the French Revolution in 1789, and has inspired radical thinkers ever since. Rousseau believed that civilization was a corrupting influence on people, who are instinctively good, and it was this part of his thinking set the tone for Romanticism, the movement that followed.

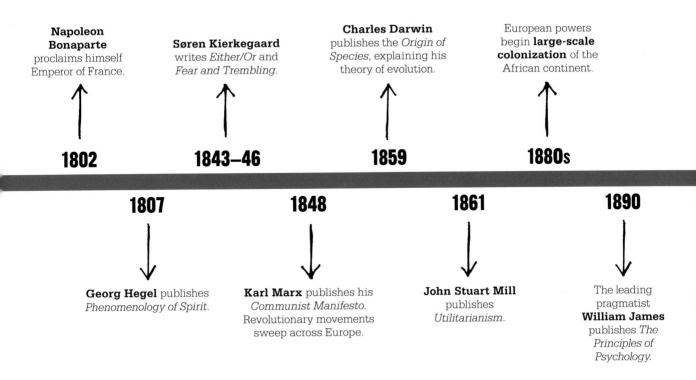

Napoleon Bonaparte proclaims himself Emperor of France.

1802

Søren Kierkegaard writes *Either/Or* and *Fear and Trembling*.

1843–46

Charles Darwin publishes the *Origin of Species*, explaining his theory of evolution.

1859

European powers begin **large-scale colonization** of the African continent.

1880s

1807

Georg Hegel publishes *Phenomenology of Spirit*.

1848

Karl Marx publishes his *Communist Manifesto*. Revolutionary movements sweep across Europe.

1861

John Stuart Mill publishes *Utilitarianism*.

1890

The leading pragmatist **William James** publishes *The Principles of Psychology*.

In the Romantic period, European literature, painting, and music became preoccupied with an idealized view of nature, in marked contrast to the sophisticated urban elegance of the Enlightenment. Perhaps the key difference was the way in which the Romantics valued feeling and intuition above reason. The movement took hold throughout Europe, continuing until the end of the 19th century.

German Idealism

German philosophy came to dominate the 19th century, largely due to the work of Immanuel Kant. His idealist philosophy, which claimed that we can never know anything about things that exist beyond our selves, radically altered the course of philosophical thought. Although only a few years younger than Hume and Rousseau, Kant belonged to the next generation: his major philosophical works were written after their deaths, and his new explanation of the universe and our knowledge of it managed to integrate the approaches of rationalism and empiricism in a way more suited both to Romanticism and to Germanic culture.

Kant's followers included Fichte, Schelling, and Hegel, who together became known as the German Idealists, but also Schopenhauer, whose idiosyncratic interpretation of Kant's philosophy incorporated ideas from Eastern philosophy.

Among the followers of Hegel's rigid Idealism was Karl Marx, who brilliantly brought together German philosophical methods, French revolutionary political philosophy, and British economic theory. After writing the *Communist Manifesto* with Friedrich Engels, he wrote *Das Kapital*, arguably one of the most influential philosophical works of all time. Within decades of his death, countries across the world had set up revolutionary states on the principles that he had proposed.

Meanwhile in the US, which had overthrown British colonial rule and established a republic based on Enlightenment values, an American culture independent of its European roots began to develop. At first Romantic, by the end of the 19th century it had produced a home-grown strand of philosophy, pragmatism, which examines the nature of truth. This was in keeping with the country's democratic roots and well suited to the culture of the new century. ∎

DOUBT IS NOT A PLEASANT CONDITION, BUT CERTAINTY IS ABSURD
VOLTAIRE (1694–1778)

IN CONTEXT

BRANCH
Epistemology

APPROACH
Scepticism

BEFORE
350 BCE Aristotle makes the first reference to a child's mind as a "blank slate", which later became known as a *tabula rasa*.

1690s John Locke argues that sense experience allows both children and adults to acquire reliable knowledge about the external world.

AFTER
1859 John Stuart Mill argues against assuming our own infallibility in *On Liberty*.

1900s Hans-Georg Gadamer and the postmodernists apply sceptical reasoning to all forms of knowledge, even that gained through empirical (sense-based) information.

Voltaire was a French intellectual who lived in the Age of Enlightenment. This period was characterized by an intense questioning of the world and how people live in it. European philosophers and writers turned their attention to the acknowledged authorities – such as the Church and state – to question their validity and their ideas, while also searching for new perspectives. Until the 17th century, Europeans had largely accepted the Church's explanations of what, why, and how things existed, but both scientists and philosophers had begun to demonstrate different approaches to establishing the truth. In 1690 the philosopher John Locke had argued that no ideas were innate (known at birth), and that all ideas arise from experience alone. His argument was given further weight by scientist Isaac Newton whose experiments provided new ways of discovering truths about the world. It was against this background of

Every fact and theory in history has been **revised** at some point.

We are not born with ideas and concepts **already in our heads**.

Every idea and theory can be **challenged**.

Doubt is not a pleasant condition, but certainty is absurd.

See also: Aristotle 56–63 ▪ John Locke 130–33 ▪ David Hume 148–53 ▪ John Stuart Mill 190–93 ▪ Hans-Georg Gadamer 260–61 ▪ Karl Popper 262–65

Scientific experiments during the Age of Enlightenment seemed to Voltaire to lead the way towards a better world, based on empirical evidence and unabashed curiosity.

rebellion against the accepted traditions that Voltaire pronounced that certainty is absurd.

Voltaire refutes the idea of certainty in two ways. First, he points out that apart from a few necessary truths of mathematics and logic, nearly every fact and theory in history has been revised at some point in time. So what appears to be "fact" is actually little more than a working hypothesis. Second, he agrees with Locke that there is no such thing as an innate idea, and points out that ideas we seem to know as true from birth may be only cultural, as these change from country to country.

Revolutionary doubt

Voltaire does not assert that there are no absolute truths, but he sees no means of reaching them. For this reason he thinks doubt is the only logical standpoint. Given that endless disagreement is therefore inevitable, Voltaire says that it is important to develop a system, such as science, to establish agreement.

In claiming that certainty is more pleasant than doubt, Voltaire hints at how much easier it is simply to accept authoritative statements – such as those issued by the monarchy or Church – than it is to challenge them and think for yourself. But Voltaire believes it is vitally important to doubt every "fact" and to challenge all authority. He holds that government should be limited but speech uncensored, and that science and education lead to material and moral progress. These were fundamental ideals of both the Enlightenment and the French Revolution, which took place 11 years after Voltaire's death. ▪

Voltaire

Voltaire was the pseudonym of the French writer and thinker, François Marie Arouet. He was born into a middle-class family in Paris, and was the youngest of three children. He studied law at university, but always preferred writing, and by 1715 was famous as a great literary wit. His satirical writing often landed him in trouble: he was imprisoned several times for insulting nobility, and was once exiled from France. This led to a stay in England, where he fell under the influence of English philosophy and science. After returning to France he became wealthy through speculation, and was thereafter able to devote himself to writing. He had several long and scandalous affairs, and travelled widely throughout Europe. In later life Voltaire campaigned vigorously for legal reform and against religious intolerance, in France and further afield.

Key works

1733 *Philosophical Letters*
1734 *Treatise on Metaphysics*
1759 *Candide*
1764 *Philosophical Dictionary*

CUSTOM
IS THE GREAT GUIDE OF HUMAN
LIFE
DAVID HUME (1711–1776)

IN CONTEXT

BRANCH
Epistemology

APPROACH
Empiricism

BEFORE
1637 René Descartes espouses rationalism in his *Discourse on the Method*.

1690 John Locke sets out the case for empiricism in *An Essay Concerning Human Understanding*.

AFTER
1781 Immanuel Kant is inspired by Hume to write his *Critique of Pure Reason*.

1844 Arthur Schopenhauer acknowledges his debt to Hume in *The World as Will and Representation*.

1934 Karl Popper proposes falsification as the basis for the scientific method, as opposed to observation and induction.

David Hume was born at a time when European philosophy was dominated by a debate about the nature of knowledge. René Descartes had in effect set the stage for modern philosophy in his *Discourse on the Method*, instigating a movement of rationalism in Europe, which claimed that knowledge can be arrived at by rational reflection alone. In Britain, John Locke had countered this with his empiricist argument that knowledge can only be derived from experience. George Berkeley had followed, formulating his own version of empiricism, according to which the world only exists in so far as it is perceived. But it was Hume, the third of the major British empiricists, who dealt the biggest blow to rationalism in an argument presented in his *Treatise of Human Nature*.

Hume's fork

With a remarkable clarity of language, Hume turns a sceptical eye to the problem of knowledge, and argues forcibly against the notion that we are born with "innate ideas" (a central tenet of rationalism). He does so by first dividing the contents of our minds into two kinds of phenomena, and then asking how these relate to each other. The two phenomena are "impressions" – or direct perceptions, which Hume calls the "sensations, passions, and emotions" – and "ideas", which are faint copies of our impressions, such as thoughts, reflections, and imaginings. And it is while analysing this distinction that Hume draws an unsettling conclusion – one that calls into question our most cherished

> In our reasonings concerning fact, there are all imaginable degrees of assurance. A wise man therefore proportions his belief to the evidence.
> **David Hume**

David Hume

Born in Edinburgh, Scotland, in 1711, Hume was a precocious child who entered the University of Edinburgh at the age of 12. Around 1729 he devoted his time to finding "some medium by which truth might be established", and after working himself into a nervous breakdown he moved to La Flèche in Anjou, France. Here he wrote *A Treatise of Human Nature*, setting out virtually all his philosophical ideas before returning to Edinburgh.

In 1763 he was appointed to the Embassy in Paris, where he befriended the philosopher Jean-Jacques Rousseau and became more widely known as a philosopher. The controversial *Dialogues Concerning Natural Religion* occupied Hume's final years and, because of what he called his "abundant caution", were only published after his death in Edinburgh in 1776.

Key works

1739 *A Treatise of Human Nature*
1748 *An Enquiry Concerning Human Understanding*
1779 *Dialogues Concerning Natural Religion*

See also: Plato 50–55 ▪ Aristotle 56–63 ▪ René Descartes 116–23 ▪ John Locke 130–33 ▪ George Berkeley 138–41 ▪ Immanuel Kant 164–71 ▪ Ludwig Wittgenstein 246–51 ▪ Karl Popper 262–65

beliefs, not only about logic and science, but about the nature of the world around us.

The problem, for Hume, is that very often we have ideas that cannot be supported by our impressions, and Hume concerns himself with finding the extent to which this is the case. To understand what he means, we need to note that for Hume there are only two kinds of statement – namely "demonstrative" and "probable" statements – and he claims that in everyday experience we somehow confuse the two types of knowledge that these express.

A demonstrative statement is one whose truth or falsity is self-evident. Take, for example, the statement 2 + 2 = 4. Denying this statement involves a logical contradiction – in other words, to claim that 2 + 2 does not equal 4 is to fail to grasp the meanings of the terms "2" or "4" (or "+" or "="). Demonstrative statements in logic, mathematics, and deductive reasoning are known to be true or false *a priori*, meaning "prior to experience". The truth of a »

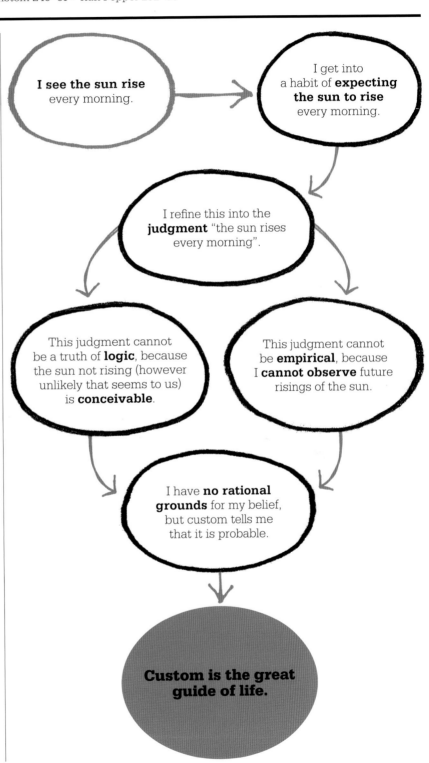

Mathematics and logic yield what Hume calls "demonstrative" truths, which cannot be denied without contradiction. These are the only certainties in Hume's philosophy.

probable statement, however, is not self-evident, for it is concerned with matters of empirical fact. For example, any statement about the world such as "Jim is upstairs", is a probable statement because it requires empirical evidence for it to be known to be true or false. In other words, its truth or falsity can only be known through some kind of experiment – such as by going upstairs to see if Jim is there.

In light of this, we can ask of any statement whether it is probable or demonstrative. If it is neither of these, then we cannot know it to be true or false, and so, for Hume, it is a meaningless statement. This division of all statements into two possible kinds, as if forming the horns of a dilemma, is often referred to as "Hume's fork".

Inductive reasoning

There are no surprises in Hume's reasoning so far, but things take a strange turn when he applies this line of argument to inductive inference – our ability to infer things from past evidence. We observe an unchanging pattern, and infer that it will continue in the future, tacitly assuming that nature will continue to behave in a uniform way. For example, we see the sun rise every morning, and infer that it will rise again tomorrow. But is our claim that nature follows this uniform pattern really justifiable? Claiming that the sun will rise tomorrow is not a demonstrative statement, as claiming the opposite involves no logical contradiction. Nor is it a probable statement, as we cannot experience the sun's future risings.

The same problem occurs if we apply Hume's fork to the evidence for causality. The statement "event A causes event B" seems on the face of it to be one that we can verify, but again, this does not stand up to scrutiny. There is no logical contradiction involved in denying that A causes B (as there would be in denying that 2 + 2 = 4), so it cannot be a demonstrative statement. Nor can it be proved empirically, since we cannot observe every event A to see if it is followed by B, so it is not a probable statement either. The fact that, in our limited experience, B invariably follows A is no rational ground for believing that A will always be followed by B, or that A causes B.

If there is never any rational basis for inferring cause and effect, then what justification do we have for making that connection? Hume explains this simply as "human nature" – a mental habit that reads uniformity into regular repetition, and a causal connection into what

The grounds for our belief that the sun will rise tomorrow, or that water rather than fruit will flow from a tap, are not logical, according to Hume. They are simply the result of our conditioning, which teaches us that tomorrow the world will be the same as it is today.

> Nature, by an absolute and uncontrollable necessity, has determined us to judge as well as to breathe and feel.
> **David Hume**

Science supplies us with ever more detailed information about the world. However, according to Hume, science deals with theories only, and can never yield a "law of nature".

he calls the "constant conjunction" of events. Indeed, it is this kind of inductive reasoning that is the basis of science, and tempts us to interpret our inferences as "laws" of nature – but despite what we may think, this practice cannot be justified by rational argument.

In saying this, Hume makes his strongest case against rationalism, for he is saying that it is belief (which he defines as "a lively idea related to or associated with a present impression"), guided by custom, that lies at the heart of our claims to knowledge rather than reason.

Custom as our guide

Hume goes on to acknowledge that although inductive inferences are not provable, this does not mean that they are not useful. After all, we still have a reasonable claim to expect something to happen, judging from past observation and experience. In the absence of a rational justification for inductive inference, custom is a good guide.

Hume adds, however, that this "mental habit" should be applied with caution. Before inferring cause and effect between two events, we should have evidence both that this succession of events has been invariable in the past, and that there is a necessary connection between them. We can reasonably predict that when we let go of an object it will fall to the ground, because this is what has always happened in the past, and there is an obvious connection between letting go of the object and its falling. On the other hand, two clocks set a few seconds apart will chime one after

another – but since there is no obvious connection between them, we should not infer that one clock's chiming is the cause of the other's.

Hume's treatment of the "problem of induction", as this became known, both undermines the claims of rationalism and elevates the role of belief and custom in our lives. As he says, the conclusions drawn by our beliefs are "as satisfactory to the mind... as the demonstrative kind."

A revolutionary idea

The brilliantly argued and innovative ideas in the *Treatise of Human Nature* were virtually ignored when they were published in 1739, despite being the high-point of British empiricism. Hume was better known in his own country for being the author of a *History of Great Britain* than for his philosophy; in Germany, however, the significance of his epistemology had more impact. Immanuel Kant admitted to being woken from his "dogmatic slumbers" by reading Hume, who

remained a significant influence on German philosophers of the 19th century and the logical positivists of the 20th century, who believed that only meaningful statements could be verifiable. Hume's account of the problem of induction remained unchallenged throughout this period, and resurfaced in the work of Karl Popper, who used it to back up his claim that a theory can only be deemed scientific if it is falsifiable. ■

Hume was perfectly right in pointing out that induction cannot be logically justified.
Karl Popper

MAN WAS BORN FREE YET EVERYWHERE HE IS IN CHAINS

JEAN-JACQUES ROUSSEAU (1712–1778)

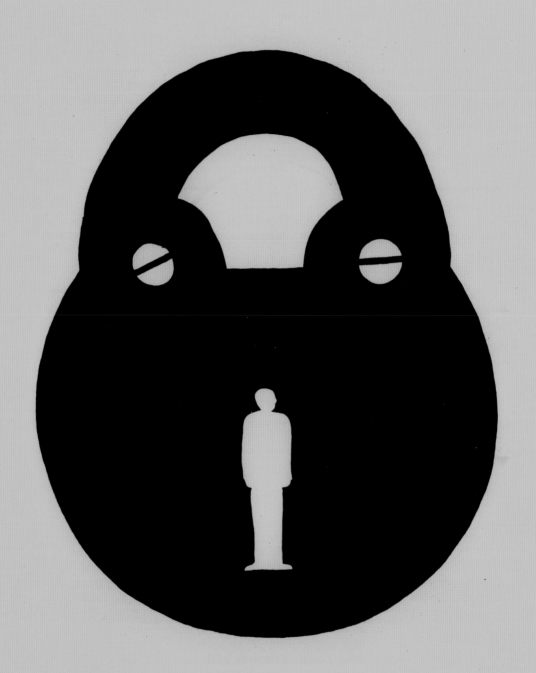

IN CONTEXT

BRANCH
Political philosophy

APPROACH
Social contract theory

BEFORE
1651 Thomas Hobbes puts forward the idea of a social contract in his book *Leviathan*.

1689 John Locke's *Two Treatises of Government* asserts a human's natural right to defend "life, health, liberty, or possessions".

AFTER
1791 Thomas Paine's *Rights of Man* argues that government's only purpose is to safeguard the rights of the individual.

1848 Karl Marx and Friedrich Engels publish *The Communist Manifesto*.

1971 John Rawls develops the idea of "Justice as Fairness" in his book *A Theory of Justice*.

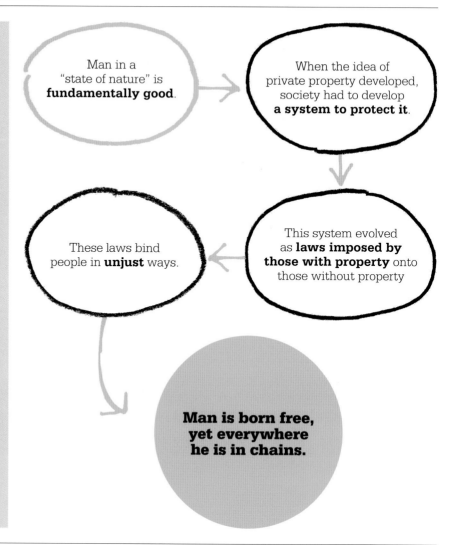

Man in a "state of nature" is **fundamentally good**.

When the idea of private property developed, society had to develop **a system to protect it**.

This system evolved as **laws imposed by those with property** onto those without property

These laws bind people in **unjust** ways.

Man is born free, yet everywhere he is in chains.

Rousseau was very much a product of the mid- to late-18th-century period known as the Enlightenment, and an embodiment of the continental European philosophy of the time. As a young man he tried to make his name as both a musician and composer, but in 1740 he met Denis Diderot and Jean d'Alembert, the philosopher compilers of the new *Encyclopédie*, and became interested in philosophy. The political mood in France at this time was uneasy. Enlightenment thinkers in France and England had begun to question the status quo, undermining the authority of both the Church and the aristocracy, and advocates of social reform such as Voltaire continually fell foul of the overbearing censorship of the establishment. Unsurprisingly in this context, Rousseau's main area of interest became political philosophy. His thinking was influenced not only by his French contemporaries, but also by the work of English philosophers – and in particular the idea of a social contract as proposed by Thomas Hobbes and refined by John Locke.

Like them, Rousseau compared an idea of humanity in a hypothetical "natural state" with how people actually live in a civil society. But he took such a radically different view of this natural state and the way it is affected by society, that it could be considered a form of "counter-Enlightenment" thinking. It held within it the seeds of the next great movement, Romanticism.

Science and art corrupt
Hobbes had envisaged life in the natural state as "solitary, poor,

See also: Thomas Hobbes 112–15 ▪ John Locke 130–33 ▪ Edmund Burke 172–73 ▪ John Stuart Mill 190–93 ▪ Karl Marx 196–203 ▪ John Rawls 294–95

nasty, brutish, and short". In his view humanity is instinctively self-interested and self-serving, and that civilization is necessary to place restrictions on these instincts. Rousseau, however, looks more kindly on human nature, and sees civil society as a much less benevolent force.

The idea that society might be a harmful influence first occurred to Rousseau when he wrote an essay for a competition organized by the Academy of Dijon, answering the question: "Has the restoration of the sciences and the arts contributed to refining moral practices?" The expected answer from thinkers of the time, and especially from a musician such as Rousseau, was an enthusiastic affirmative, but in fact Rousseau argued the opposite case. His *Discourse on the Sciences and Arts*, which won him first prize, controversially puts forward the idea that the arts and sciences corrupt and erode morals. He argues that far from improving minds and lives, the arts and sciences decrease human virtue and happiness.

The inequality of laws

Having broken with established thinking in his prize-winning and publicly acclaimed essay, Rousseau took the idea a stage further in a second essay, the *Discourse on the Origin and Foundations of Inequality among Men*. The subject matter chimed with the mood of the time, echoing the calls for social reform from writers such as Voltaire, but »

The Romantic movement in art and literature that dominated the late 18th and early 19th centuries reflected Rousseau's vision of the state of nature as one of beauty, innocence, and virtue.

Jean-Jacques Rousseau

Jean-Jacques Rousseau was born to a Calvinist family in Geneva. His mother died only a few days after his birth, and his father fled home following a duel a few years later, leaving him in the care of an uncle.

Aged 16, he left for France and converted to Catholicism. While trying to make his name as a composer, he worked as a civil servant and was posted to Venice for two years, but on his return he began to write philosophy. His controversial views led to his books being banned in Switzerland and France, and warrants being issued for his arrest. He was forced to accept David Hume's invitation to live in England for a short time, but after they quarrelled he returned to France under a false name. He was later allowed to return to Paris, where he lived until his death at the age of 66.

Key works

1750 *Discourse on the Sciences and Arts*
1755 *Discourse on the Origin and Foundations of Inequality among Men*
1755 *Discourse on Political Economy*
1762 *The Social Contract*

once again Rousseau contradicted conventional thinking with his analysis. The selfish, savage, and unjust state of nature depicted by Hobbes is, for Rousseau, a description not of "natural man", but of "civilized man". In fact he claims that it is civil society that induces this savage state. Humanity's natural state, he argues, is innocent, happy, and independent: man is born free.

Society corrupts

The state of nature that Rousseau describes is a pastoral idyll, where people in their natural state are fundamentally good. (The English wrongly interpreted Rousseau's idea of natural man as a "noble savage", but this was due to a mistranslation of the French *sauvage*, which means simply "natural", not brutish.) People are endowed with innate virtue and, more importantly, the attributes of compassion and empathy. But

Adam and Eve represent the kind of perfect "natural" humans that Rousseau thought predated society. He said that we, like them, are corrupted by knowledge, becoming ever more selfish and unhappy.

once this state of innocence is disrupted, and the power of reason begins to separate humankind from the rest of nature, people become detached from their natural virtues. The imposition of civil society on the state of nature therefore entails a move away from virtue towards vice, and from idyllic happiness towards misery.

Rousseau sees the fall from a state of nature and the establishment of civil society as regrettable but inevitable, because it resulted from the human capacity for reason. The process began, he thought, the first time that a man enclosed a piece of land for himself, so introducing the notion of property. As groups of people began to live side by side like this, they formed societies, which could only be maintained though a system of laws. But Rousseau claims that every society loses touch with humanity's natural virtues, including empathy, and so imposes laws that are not just, but selfish. They are designed to protect property, and they are inflicted on the poor by the rich. The move from a natural to a civilized state therefore brought about a move not only from virtue to vice, Rousseau points out, but also from innocence and freedom to injustice and enslavement. Although humanity is naturally virtuous, it is corrupted by society; and although man is born free, the laws imposed by society condemn him to a life "in chains".

The Social Contract

Rousseau's second *Discourse* ruffled even more feathers than his first, but it gained him a reputation and quite a following. His portrayal of the state of nature as desirable and not brutal formed a vital part of the emerging Romantic movement in literature. Rousseau's rallying cry of

Tranquility is found also in dungeons; but is that enough to make them desirable places to live in?
Jean-Jacques Rousseau

"back to nature!" and his pessimistic analysis of modern society as full of inequalities and injustices sat well with the growing social unrest of the 1750s, especially in France. Not content with merely stating the problem, Rousseau went on to offer a solution, in what is seen as perhaps his most influential work, *The Social Contract*.

Rousseau opens his book with the challenging declaration "Man is born free, yet everywhere he is in chains", which was considered such a call for radical change that it was adopted as a slogan during the French Revolution 27 years later. Having issued his challenge, Rousseau then sets out his vision of an alternative civil society, run not by aristocrats, the monarchy, and the Church, but by all citizens, who participate in the business of legislation. Modelled on Classical republican ideas of democracy, Rousseau imagines the citizen body operating as a unit, prescribing laws according to the *volonté générale*, or general will. The laws would arise from all and apply to all – everyone would be considered equal. In contrast with the social contract envisaged by Locke, which was designed to

The general will
should come from all
to apply to all.
**Jean-Jacques
Rousseau**

protect the rights and property of individuals, Rousseau advocates giving legislative power to the people as a whole, for the benefit of all, administered by the general will. He believes that the freedom to take part in the legislative process would lead to an elimination of inequality and injustice, and that it would promote a feeling of belonging to society – that it would inevitably lead to the *liberté, égalité, fraternité* (liberty, equality, fraternity) that became the motto of the new French Republic.

The evils of education
In another book written in the same year, entitled *Emile, or On Education*, Rousseau expanded on his theme, explaining that education was responsible for corrupting the state of nature and perpetuating the evils of modern society. In other books and essays he concentrated on the adverse effects of both conventional religion and atheism. At the centre of all his works lay the idea that

The French Revolution, which began 11 years after Rousseau's death, was inspired by his claim that it was unjust for the rich few to rule over the effectively voiceless, powerless poor.

reason threatens human innocence and, in turn, freedom and happiness. Instead of the education of the intellect, he proposes an education of the senses, and he suggests that our religious faith should be guided by the heart, not the head.

Political influence
Most of Rousseau's writings were immediately banned in France, gaining him both notoriety and a large following. By the time of his death in 1778, revolution in France and elsewhere was imminent, and his idea of a social contract in which the general will of the citizen body controlled the legislative process offered the revolutionaries a viable alternative to the corrupt system as it stood. But his philosophy was at odds with contemporary thinking, and his insistence that a state of nature was superior to civilization led him to fall out with fellow reformers such as Voltaire and Hume.

Rousseau's political influence was felt most strongly during the period of revolution immediately after his death, but his influence on philosophy, and political philosophy in particular, emerged to a greater extent in the 19th century. Georg Hegel integrated Rousseau's ideas of social contract into his own philosophical system. Later and more importantly, Karl Marx was particularly struck by some of Rousseau's work on inequality and injustice. Unlike Robespierre, one of the leaders of the French Revolution, who had appropriated Rousseau's philosophy for his own ends during the Reign of Terror, Marx fully understood and developed Rousseau's analysis of capitalist society and the revolutionary means of replacing it. Marx's *Communist Manifesto* ends with a nod to Rousseau, encouraging the proletarians (workers) have "nothing to lose but their chains". ∎

MAN IS AN ANIMAL THAT MAKES BARGAINS

ADAM SMITH (1723–1790)

IN CONTEXT

BRANCH
Political philosophy

APPROACH
Classical economics

BEFORE
c.350 BCE Aristotle emphasizes the importance of domestic production ("economy") and explains the role of money.

Early 1700s Dutch thinker Bernard Mandeville argues that selfish actions can lead indirectly to socially desirable consequences.

AFTER
1850s British writer John Ruskin argues that Smith's views are too materialistic and therefore anti-Christian.

1940s onwards Philosophers apply the idea of bargaining throughout the social sciences as a model for explaining human behaviour.

Scottish writer Adam Smith is often considered the most important economist the world has ever known. The concepts of bargaining and self-interest that he explored, and the possibility of different types of agreements and interests – such as "the common interest" – are of recurring appeal to philosophers. His writings are also important because they give a more general and abstract form to the idea of the "commercial" society that was developed by his friend David Hume.

Like his Swiss contemporary, Jean-Jacques Rousseau, Smith assumes that the motives of human beings are partly benevolent and

See also: David Hume 148–53 ▪ Jean-Jacques Rousseau 154–59 ▪ Edmund Burke 172–73 ▪ Karl Marx 196–203 ▪ Noam Chomsky 304–05

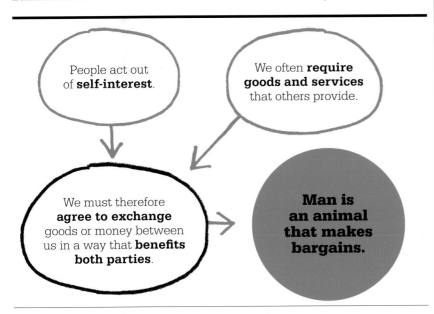

People act out of **self-interest**.

We often **require goods and services** that others provide.

We must therefore **agree to exchange** goods or money between us in a way that **benefits both parties**.

Man is an animal that makes bargains.

Adam Smith

The "father of modern economics" was born in Kirkcaldy, Fife, in 1723. An academic prodigy, Smith became a lecturer first at Edinburgh University, then at Glasgow University where he became a professor in 1750. In the 1760s, he took a lucrative job as a personal tutor to a young Scottish aristocrat, Henry Scott, with whom he visited France and Switzerland.

Already acquainted with David Hume and other Scottish Enlightenment thinkers, he seized the chance to meet leading figures of the European Enlightenment as well. On his return to Scotland, he spent a decade writing *The Wealth of Nations*, before returning to public service as Commissioner of Customs, a position that allowed him to advise the British government on various economic policies. In 1787, he rejoined Glasgow University, and spent the last three years of his life as its rector.

Key works

1759 *The Theory of Moral Sentiments*
1776 *The Wealth of Nations*
1795 *Essays on Philosophical Subjects*

partly self-interested, but that self-interest is the stronger trait and so is a better guide to human behaviour. He believes that this can be confirmed by social observation, and so, broadly speaking, his approach is an empirical one. In one of his most famous discussions of the psychology of bargaining, he contends that the most frequent opening gambit in a bargain is for one party to urge the other – "the best way for you to get what *you* want is for you to give me what *I* want". In other words, "we address ourselves, not to [another's] humanity, but to their self-love."

Smith goes on to claim that the exchange of useful objects is a distinctively human characteristic. He notes that dogs are never observed exchanging bones, and that should an animal wish to obtain something, the only way it can do so is to "gain the favour of those whose service it requires". Humans may also depend on this sort of "fawning or servile attention", but they cannot resort to it whenever they need help, because life requires "the cooperation and assistance of great multitudes". For example, to stay comfortably at an inn for a night we require the input of many people – to cook and serve the food, to prepare the room and so on – none of whose services can be depended on through good will alone. For this reason, "man is an animal that makes bargains" – and the bargain is struck by proposing a deal that appears to be in the self-interest of both parties.

The division of labour
In his account of the emergence of market economies, Smith argues that our ability to make bargains put an end to the once universal requirement that every person, or at least every family, be economically self-sufficient. Thanks to bargaining, it became possible for us to concentrate on producing fewer and fewer goods, and ultimately to produce just a single good, or offer a single service, and to exchange this for everything »

else we required. This process was revolutionized by the invention of money, which abolished the need to barter. From then on, in Smith's view, only those who were unable to work had to depend on charity. Everyone else could come to the marketplace to exchange their labour – or the money they earned through labour – for the products of other people's labour.

This elimination of the need to provide everything for ourselves led to the emergence of people with particular sets of skills (such as the baker and the carpenter), and then to what Smith calls a "division of labour" among workers. This is Smith's phrase for specialization, whereby an individual not only pursues a single type of work, but performs only a single task in a job that is shared by several people.

The market is the key to establishing an equitable society, in Smith's view. With the freedom provided by the buying and selling of goods, individuals can enjoy lives of "natural liberty".

The greatest improvement in the productive powers of labour seem to have been the effects of the division of labour.
Adam Smith

Civilized society stands at all times in need of the co-operation and assistance of great multitudes.
Adam Smith

Smith illustrates the importance of specialization at the beginning of his masterpiece, *The Wealth of Nations*, by showing how the making of a humble metal pin is radically improved by adopting the factory system. Where one man working alone would find it hard to produce 20 perfect pins in a day, a group of 10 men, charged with different tasks – from drawing out the wire, straightening it, cutting it, pointing it, and grinding it, to joining it to a pinhead – were able, in Smith's time, to produce over 48,000 pins a day.

Smith was impressed by the great improvements in the productivity of labour that took place during the Industrial Revolution – improvements that saw workers provided with much better equipment, and often saw machines replacing workers.

The jack-of-all-trades could not survive in such a system, and even philosophers began to specialize in the various branches of their subject, such as logic, ethics, epistemology, and metaphysics.

The free market

Because the division of labour increases productivity and makes it possible for everyone to be eligible for some kind of work (since it frees us from training in a craft), Smith argues that it can lead to universal wealth in a well-ordered society. Indeed, he says that in conditions of perfect liberty, the market can lead to a state of perfect equality – one in which everyone is free to pursue his own interests in his own way, so long as it accords with the laws of justice. And by equality Smith is not referring to equality of opportunity, but to equality of condition. In other words, his goal is the creation of a society not divided by competitiveness, but drawn together by bargaining based on mutual self-interest.

Smith's point, therefore, is not that people should have freedom just because they deserve it. His point is that society as a whole benefits from individuals pursuing their own interests. For the "invisible hand" of the market, with its laws of supply and demand, regulates the amount of goods that are available, and prices them far more efficiently than any government could. Put simply, the pursuit of self-interest, far from being incompatible with an equitable society, is, in Smith's view, the only way of guaranteeing it.

In such a society, a government can limit itself to performing just a few essential functions, such as providing defence, criminal justice, and education, and taxes and duties can be reduced accordingly. And just as bargaining can flourish within national boundaries, so it can flourish across them, leading to international trade – a phenomenon that was spreading across the world in Smith's time.

Smith recognized that there were problems with the notion of a free market – in particular with the increasingly common bargain of wages for working time. He also acknowledged that while the division of labour had huge economic benefits, repetitive work is not only boring for the worker, it can destroy a human being – and for this reason he proposed that governments should restrict the extent to which the production line is used. Nevertheless, when *The Wealth of Nations* was first published, its doctrine of free and unregulated trade was seen as revolutionary, not only because of its attack on established commercial and agricultural privileges and monopolies, but also because of its argument that a nation's wealth depends not on its gold reserves, but on its labour – a view that went against all economic thinking in Europe at the time.

Smith's reputation for being a revolutionary was bolstered during the long debate about the nature of society that followed the French Revolution of 1789, prompting the mid-Victorian historian H.T. Buckle to describe *The Wealth of Nations* as "probably the most important book that has ever been written".

Smith's legacy

Critics have argued that Smith was wrong to assume that the "general interest" and "consumer interest" are the same, and that the free market is beneficial to all. What is true is that even though Smith was sympathetic towards the victims of poverty, he never fully succeeded in balancing the interests of producers

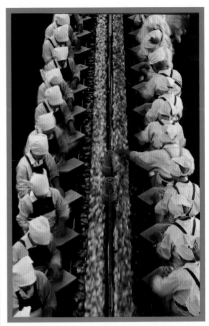

The production line is an incredible money-creating machine, but Smith warns against the dehumanizing effects it can have on workers if it is used without regulation.

and consumers within his social model, or integrating into it the domestic labour, performed mainly by women, that helped to keep society running efficiently.

For these reasons, and with the rise of socialism in the 19th century, Smith's reputation declined, but renewed interest in free market economics in the late 20th century saw a revival of Smith's ideas. Indeed, only today can we fully appreciate his most visionary claim – that a market is more than just a place. A market is a concept, and as such can exist anywhere – not only in a designated place such as a town square. This foreshadows the kind of "virtual" marketplace that only became possible with the advent of telecommunications technology. Today's financial markets and online trading bear witness to Smith's great vision. ∎

THERE ARE TWO WORLDS: OUR BODIES AND THE EXTERNAL WORLD

IMMANUEL KANT (1724–1804)

IN CONTEXT

BRANCH
Metaphysics

APPROACH
Transcendental idealism

BEFORE
1641 René Descartes publishes his *Meditations*, in which he doubts all knowledge apart from the knowledge of his own consciousness.

1739 David Hume publishes his *Treatise of Human Nature*, which suggests limitations on how the human mind perceives reality.

AFTER
19th century The German idealist movement develops in response to Kant's philosophy.

1900s Edmund Husserl develops phenomenology, the study of objects of experience, using Kant's understanding of consciousness.

I mmanuel Kant thought it was "scandalous" that in more than 2,000 years of philosophical thought, nobody had been able to produce an argument to prove that there really is a world out there, external to us. He particularly had in mind the theories of René Descartes and George Berkeley, who both entertained doubts about the existence of an external world.

At the start of his *Meditations*, Descartes argued that we must doubt all knowledge except that of our own existence as thinking beings – even the knowledge that there is an external world. He then went on to counter this sceptical point of view with an argument that claims to prove the existence of God, and therefore the reality of an outside world. However, many philosophers (including Kant) have not found Descartes' proof of God to be valid in its reasoning.

Berkeley, on the other hand, argued that knowledge is indeed possible – but that it comes from experiences our consciousness perceives. We have no justification for believing that these experiences have any external existence outside our own minds.

Time and consciousness

Kant wants to demonstrate that there is an external, material world, and that its existence cannot be doubted. His argument begins as follows: in order for something to exist, it must be determinable in time – that is, we must be able to say when it exists and for how long. But how does this work in the case of my own consciousness?

Although consciousness seems to be constantly changing with a continuous flow of sensations and thoughts, we can use the word "now" to refer to what is currently happening in our consciousness. But "now" is not a determinate time or date. Every time I say "now", consciousness is different.

Here lies the problem: what makes it possible to specify the "when" of my own existence? We cannot experience time itself, directly; rather, we experience time through things that move, change, or stay the same. Consider the hands of a clock, constantly moving slowly around. The moving hands are useless for determining time on their own – they need something against which they change, such as the numbers on a clock face. Every resource I have for measuring my

According to Kant, we can only experience time through things in the world that move or change, such as the hands of a clock. So time is only ever experienced by us indirectly.

constantly changing "now" is found in material objects outside me in space (including my own physical body). Saying that I exist requires a determinate point in time, and this, in turn, requires an actually existing outside world in which time takes place. My level of certainty about the existence of the external world is thus precisely the same as my level of certainty about the existence of consciousness, which Descartes believed was absolutely certain.

The problem of science

Kant also looked at how science understood the exterior world. He admired the awesome progress that the natural sciences had made over the previous two centuries, compared with the relative stagnation in the subject from ancient times until that point. Kant, along with other philosophers, wondered what was suddenly being done correctly in scientific research. The answer given by many thinkers of the period was empiricism. The empiricists, such as John Locke and David Hume, argued that there is no knowledge except that which

See also: René Descartes 116–23 ▪ John Locke 130–33 ▪ George Berkeley 138–41 ▪ David Hume 148–53 ▪ Johann Gottlieb Fichte 176 ▪ Georg Hegel 178–85 ▪ Friedrich Schelling 335 ▪ Arthur Schopenhauer 186–88

comes to us through our experience of the world. They opposed the views of rationalist philosophers, such as Descartes or Gottfried Leibniz, who argued that the mind's ability to reason and deal with concepts is more important for knowledge than experience.

The empiricists claimed that the recent success of science was due to scientists being much more careful in their observations of the world than they had been previously, and making fewer unjustified assumptions based on reason alone. Kant argues that although this is no doubt partly true, it could not be the whole answer, as it is simply false to say that there was no detailed and careful empirical observation in science before the 16th century.

The real issue, Kant argues, is that a new scientific method arose that made empirical observations valuable. This method involves two elements. First, it asserts that concepts such as force or movement can be perfectly described by mathematics. Second, it tests its own conceptions of the world by asking specific questions about nature and observing the answers. »

It is precisely in knowing its limits that philosophy exists.
Immanuel Kant

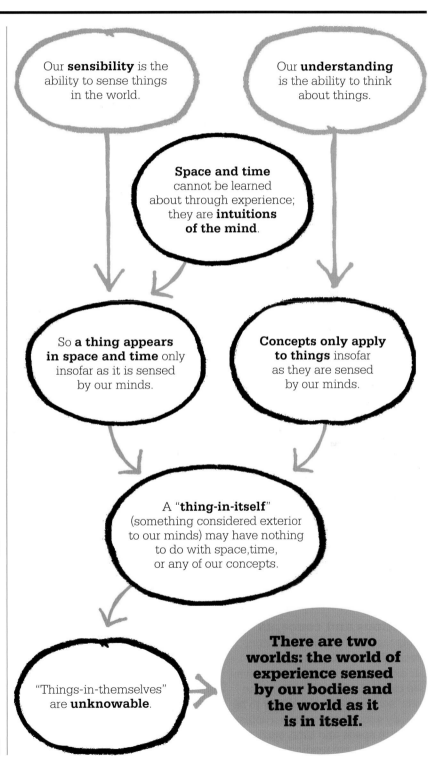

Our **sensibility** is the ability to sense things in the world.

Our **understanding** is the ability to think about things.

Space and time cannot be learned about through experience; they are **intuitions of the mind**.

So **a thing appears in space and time** only insofar as it is sensed by our minds.

Concepts only apply to things insofar as they are sensed by our minds.

A "**thing-in-itself**" (something considered exterior to our minds) may have nothing to do with space, time, or any of our concepts.

"Things-in-themselves" are **unknowable**.

There are two worlds: the world of experience sensed by our bodies and the world as it is in itself.

> Thoughts without content are empty; intuitions without concepts are blind… only from their union can cognition arise.
> **Immanuel Kant**

For example, the experimental physicist Galileo Galilei wanted to test the hypothesis that two things of different weights will nevertheless fall through the air at the same rate. He designed an experiment to test this in such a way that the only possible explanation of the observed result would be the truth or falsity of the hypothesis.

Kant identifies the nature and importance of the scientific method. He believes that this method had put physics and other subjects on the "secure road of a science". However, his investigations do not stop there. His next question is: "Why is our experience of the world such that the scientific method works?" In other words, why is our experience of the world always mathematical in nature, and how is it always possible for human reason to put questions to nature?

Intuitions and concepts

In his most famous work, *Critique of Pure Reason*, Kant argues that our experience of the world involves two elements. The first is what he calls "sensibility" – our ability to be directly acquainted with particular things in space and time, such as this book you are reading now.

These direct acquaintances he calls "intuitions". Second is what Kant calls the "understanding", our ability to have and use concepts. For Kant, a concept is an indirect acquaintance with things as examples of a type of thing, such as the concept of "book" in general. Without concepts we would not know our intuition was of a book; without intuitions we would never know that there were books at all.

Each of these elements has, in turn, two sides. In sensibility, there is my intuition of a particular thing in space and time (like the book) and my intuition of space and time as such (my acquaintance with what space and time are like in general). In understanding, there is

my concept of some type of thing (books) and my concept of a "thing" as such (substance). A concept such as substance defines what it means to be a thing in general rather than defining some type of thing like a book. My intuition of a book and the concept of a book are empirical, for how could I know anything about books unless I had come across them in the world? But my intuition of space and time and the concept of substance are *a priori*, meaning that they are known before or independently of any experience.

A true empiricist would argue against Kant that all acquaintances come from experience – in other words, nothing is *a priori*. They

Kant split knowledge into intuitions, gained from direct sensibility of the world, and concepts, which come indirectly from our understanding. Some of our knowledge – both of sensibility and understanding – comes from empirical evidence, while some is known *a priori*.

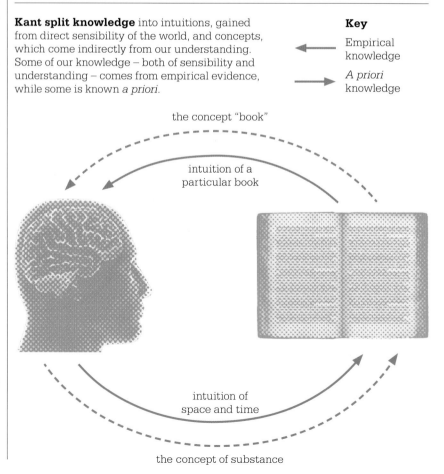

Key
⟵ Empirical knowledge
⟶ *A priori* knowledge

the concept "book"

intuition of a particular book

intuition of space and time

the concept of substance

Our understanding that entities such as trees undergo change presupposes an *a priori* grasp of the concept "substance", according to Kant. Such concepts are the preconditions of our experience.

might say that we learn what space is by observing things in space; and we learn what substance is from our observation that the features of things change without the underlying thing itself changing. For instance, though a tree's leaves turn from green to brown, and eventually fall from the tree, it is still the same tree.

Space and substance

Kant's arguments show that, on the contrary, space is an *a priori* intuition. In order to learn about things outside of me, I need to know that they are outside of me. But that shows that I could not learn about space in this way: how can I locate something outside of me without already knowing what "outside of me" means? Some knowledge of space has to be assumed before I can ever study space empirically. We must be familiar with space *a priori*.

This argument has an extraordinary consequence. Because space itself is *a priori*, it does not belong to things in the world. But our experience of things in space is a feature of our

sensibility. A thing-in-itself – Kant's term for a thing that is considered separately from sensibility, and therefore exterior to our minds – may have nothing to do with space. Kant used similar arguments to prove the same thing of time.

Kant then turns to proving the existence of *a priori* concepts, such as substance. He asks us first to distinguish between two types of alteration: variation and change. Variation concerns the properties that things have: for instance, a tree's leaves may be green or brown. Change is what the tree does: the same tree changes its leaves from green to brown. To make this distinction is already to use the notion of substance: the tree (as substance) changes, but the leaves (as the properties of substance) vary. If we do not accept this distinction, then we cannot accept the validity of the concept of substance. We would be saying that any time there is alteration, something "pops" into or out of existence; the tree with green leaves is annihilated at the same time that the tree with brown leaves begins to exist from nothing.

Kant needs to prove that such a view is impossible. The key to this is time determination. Time cannot be directly experienced (it is not a thing); rather, we experience time through things that alter or do not alter, as Kant has already shown. If we experienced time through the tree with green leaves and also experienced time through the tree with brown leaves without there being any connection between the two, then we would be experiencing two separate real times. Since this is absurd, Kant believes he has demonstrated that the concept of substance is absolutely essential before we can gain any experience of the world. And, since it is

through that experience that we learn anything empirical, the concept of substance could not be empirical: it is rather *a priori*.

The limits of knowledge

A philosophical position that asserts that some state or activity of the mind is prior to and more fundamental than things we experience is called idealism, and Kant calls his own position "transcendental idealism". He insists that space, time, and certain concepts are features of the world we experience (what Kant called the phenomenal world) rather than features of the world itself considered separately from experience (what Kant called the noumenal world).

Kant's claims about *a priori* knowledge have both positive and negative consequences. The positive consequence is that the *a priori* nature of space, time, and certain concepts is what makes our experience of the world possible and reliable. Space and time make our experience mathematical in nature; we can measure it against known values. *A priori* concepts such as substance make it possible to address questions about nature such as "Is that a substance?" and "What properties does it exhibit »

Only from the
human standpoint can
we speak of space.
Immanuel Kant

and according to what laws?" In other words, Kant's transcendental idealism is what makes it possible for our experience to be considered useful to science.

On the negative side, certain types of thinking call themselves science and even resemble science, but fail utterly. This is because they apply to things-in-themselves intuitions about space and time, or concepts such as substance – which according to Kant must be valid for experience, but have no validity with respect to things-in-themselves. Because they resemble science, these types of thinking are a constant temptation to us, and are a trap that many fall into without realizing it. For example, we might wish to claim that God is the cause of the world, but cause and effect is another of the *a priori* concepts, like substance, that Kant believes is entirely valid for our experienced world, but not for

Human reason is troubled by questions that it cannot dismiss, but also cannot answer.
Immanuel Kant

Reason only has insight into that which it produces after a plan of its own.
Immanuel Kant

things-in-themselves. So the existence of God (considered, as it usually is, as a being independent of the experienced world) is not something that could be known. The negative consequence of Kant's philosophy, then, is to place quite severe restrictions on the limits of knowledge.

Transcendental idealism gives us a much more radical way of understanding the distinction between ourselves and the external world. What is external to me is interpreted as not just external to me in space, but external to space itself (and to time, and to all the *a priori* concepts that make my experience of the world possible). And there are two worlds: the "world" of experience, which includes both my thoughts and feelings, and also includes experience of material things such as my body, or books; and the "world" of things-in-themselves, which is precisely not experienced and so not in any sense known, and which we must constantly strive to avoid fooling ourselves about.

Our bodies have a curious role to play in all this. On the one hand, my body as a material thing is a part of the external world. On the other hand, the body is a part of us, and indeed is the medium through which we encounter other things

The Flammarion woodcut depicts a man looking outside of space and time. For Kant, what is external to us is external to space and time also, and can never be known as a thing-in-itself.

Rationalism
The rationalists believed that the use of reason, rather than experience, leads to knowledge of objects in the world.

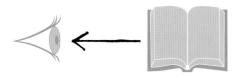

Empiricism
The empiricists believed that knowledge comes from our experience of objects in the world, rather than our reason.

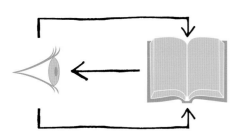

Transcendental Idealism
Kant's theory of transcendental idealism stated that both reason and experience were necessary to understand the world.

Immanuel Kant

Immanuel Kant was born into a family of financially struggling artisans in 1724, and he lived and worked his whole life in the cosmopolitan Baltic port city of Konigsberg, then part of Prussia. Though he never left his native province, he became an internationally famous philosopher within his own lifetime.

Kant studied philosophy, physics, and mathematics at the University of Konigsberg, and taught at the same institution for the next 27 years. In 1792 his unorthodox views led King Friedrich Wilhelm II to ban him from teaching, to which he returned after the king's death five years later. Kant published throughout his career, but is best known for the series of ground-breaking works he produced in his 50s and 60s. Though a bright and sociable man, he never married, and died at the age of 80.

Key works

1781 *Critique of Pure Reason*
1785 *Foundations of the Metaphysics of Morals*
1788 *Critique of Practical Reason*
1790 *Critique of Judgement*

(using our skin, nerves, eyes, ears, and so on). This provides us with one way of understanding the distinction between bodies and the external world: the body as the medium of my sensations is different from other external and material things.

Lasting influence

Kant's book *Critique of Pure Reason* is arguably the most significant single work in the history of modern philosophy. Indeed, the whole subject of philosophy is often divided by many modern thinkers into everything that happened before Kant, and everything that has happened since.

Before Kant, empiricists such as John Locke emphasized what Kant termed sensibility, but rationalists such as Descartes tended to emphasize understanding. Kant argues that our experience of the world always involves both, so it is frequently said that Kant combined rationalism and empiricism.

After Kant, German philosophy in particular progressed rapidly. The idealists Johann Fichte, Friedrich Schelling, and Georg Hegel all took Kant's thought in new directions and, in their turn, influenced the whole of 19th-century thought, from romanticism to Marxism. Kant's sophisticated critique of metaphysical thought was also important in positivism, which held that every justifiable assertion is capable of being scientifically or logically verified.

The fact that Kant locates the *a priori* even within our intuitions of the world was important for 20th-century phenomenologists such as Edmund Husserl and Martin Heidegger, who sought to examine objects of experience independently of any assumptions we may have about them. Kant's work also remains an important reference point for contemporary philosophers today, especially in the branches of metaphysics and epistemology. ■

SOCIETY IS INDEED A CONTRACT
EDMUND BURKE (1729–1797)

IN CONTEXT

BRANCH
Political philosophy

APPROACH
Conservatism

BEFORE
c.350 BCE Aristotle argues that society is like an organism, and that man is by nature a political animal.

5th century St Augustine of Hippo argues that government is a form of punishment for "original sin".

17th century Thomas Hobbes and John Locke develop the idea of the "social contract".

AFTER
19th century French philosopher Joseph de Maistre points out the anti-democratic legacy of Burke since the French Revolution.

20th century British philosopher Michael Oakeshott develops a more liberal form of conservatism.

Many a disaffected person cries "It's not my fault... blame society!" But the meaning of the word "society" is not entirely clear, and it has changed over time. During the 18th century, when the Irish philosopher and statesman Edmund Burke was writing, Europe was becoming increasingly commercialized, and the idea that society is a mutual agreement between its members – like a commercial company – was readily understood. However, this point of view also implies that it is only the material things in life that matter. Burke attempts to redress the balance by reminding us that human beings also enrich their lives through science, art,

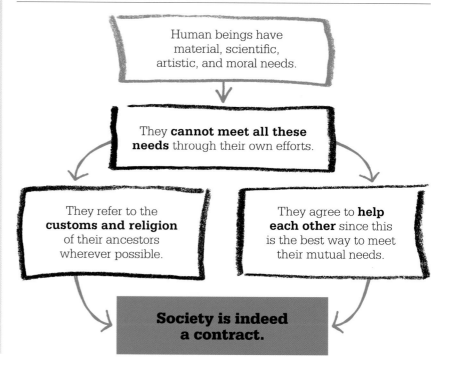

Human beings have material, scientific, artistic, and moral needs.

They **cannot meet all these needs** through their own efforts.

They refer to the **customs and religion** of their ancestors wherever possible.

They agree to **help each other** since this is the best way to meet their mutual needs.

Society is indeed a contract.

See also: John Locke 130–33 ▪ David Hume 148–53 ▪ Jean-Jacques Rousseau 154–59 ▪ Adam Smith 160–63 ▪ John Rawls 294–95

and virtue, and that while society is indeed a contract or partnership, it is not simply concerned with economics, or, as he puts it, "gross animal existence". Society embodies the common good (our agreement on customs, norms, and values), but for Burke "society" means more than just the people living now – it also includes our ancestors and descendants. Moreover, because every political constitution is part of "the great primeval contract of eternal society", God himself is society's ultimate guarantor.

Burke's view has the doctrine of original sin (the idea that we are born sinful) at its core, so he has little sympathy for anyone seeking to blame society for their conduct. Likewise, he dismisses the idea, proposed by John Locke, that we can be perfected by education – as though we are born innocent and merely need to be given the correct influences. For Burke, the fallibility of individual judgment is why we need tradition, to give us the moral bearings we need – an argument that echoes David Hume, who claimed that "custom is the great guide to human life".

Tradition and change
Because society is an organic structure with roots stretching deep into the past, Burke believed its political organization should develop naturally over time. He opposed the idea of sweeping or abrupt political changes that cut through this natural process. For this reason he opposed the French Revolution of 1789, foreseeing its dangers long before the execution of the king and the year-long Reign of Terror. It also prompted him on several occasions to criticize Jean-

Jacques Rousseau, whose book, *The Social Contract*, argued that the contract between citizens and the state can be broken at any time, depending on the will of the people. Another regular target for Burke was the English philosopher and scientist Joseph Priestley, who applauded the French Revolution and pilloried the idea of original sin.

Despite his scepticism about modern commercial society, Burke was a great defender of private property, and was optimistic about the free market. For this reason, he is often hailed as the "father of modern conservatism" – a philosophy that values both economic freedom and tradition. Today, even socialists would agree with Burke that private property is a fundamental social institution, but would disagree with him about its value. Likewise, ecologically-minded philosophers share his belief in the duties of one generation to the next, but with the new agenda of creating a "sustainable society". ▪

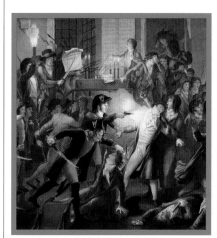

Burke condemned the French Revolution for its wholesale rejection of the past. He believed that change should occur gradually – an idea that became central to modern conservatism.

Edmund Burke

The Anglo-Irish politician Edmund Burke was born and educated in Dublin. From his youth onwards, he was convinced that philosophy was useful training for politics, and in the 1750s he wrote notable essays on aesthetics and the origins of society. He served as an English MP from 1766 until 1794, and he was a prominent member of the Whig party – the more liberal of the two aristocratic parties of the day.

Burke was sympathetic towards the cause of American independence – which sparked a revolution that was entirely justified, in his view – and later became involved in the impeachment trial of Warren Hastings, the Governor-General of India. He remained a scathing critic of colonial malpractice for the rest of his life, and earned a reputation for being the conscience of the British Empire.

Key works

1756 *A Vindication of Natural Society*
1770 *Thoughts on the Present Discontents*
1790 *Reflections on the Revolution in France*

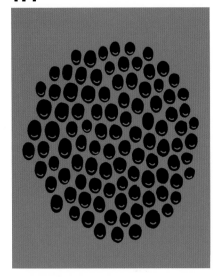

THE GREATEST HAPPINESS FOR THE GREATEST NUMBER
JEREMY BENTHAM (1748–1832)

IN CONTEXT

BRANCH
Ethics

APPROACH
Utilitarianism

BEFORE
Late 4th century BCE
Epicurus states that the main goal of life should be the pursuit of happiness.

Early 17th century Thomas Hobbes argues that a strong legal system, with severe penalties for criminals, leads to a stable and happier society.

Mid-18th century David Hume claims that emotion governs our moral judgement.

AFTER
Mid-19th century John Stuart Mill advocates education for all, arguing that it would improve general happiness.

Late 19th century Henry Sidgwick says that how moral an action is equates directly to the degree of pleasure it brings.

Jeremy Bentham, a legal reformer and philosopher, was convinced that all human activity was driven by only two motivating forces – the avoidance of pain and the pursuit of pleasure. In *The Principles of Morals and Legislation* (1789), he argues that all social and political decisions should be made with the aim of achieving the greatest happiness for the greatest number of people. Bentham believes that the moral worth of such decisions relates directly to their utility, or efficiency, in generating happiness or pleasure. In a society driven by this "utilitarian" approach, he claims that conflicts of interest between individuals can be settled by legislators, guided solely by the principle of creating the broadest possible spread of contentment. If everyone can be made happy, so much the better, but if a choice is necessary, it is always preferable to favour the many over the few.

One of the main benefits of his proposed system, Bentham states, is its simplicity. By adopting his ideas, you avoid the confusions and misinterpretations of more complex political systems that can often lead to injustices and grievances.

Calculating pleasure
More controversially, Bentham proposes a "felicific calculus" that can express mathematically the degree of happiness experienced by each individual. Using this precise method, he states, provides an objective platform for resolving ethical disputes, with decisions being made in favour of the view that is calculated to produce the highest measure of pleasure.

Bentham also insists that all sources of pleasure are of equal value, so that the happiness derived from a good meal or close friendship is equal to that derived from an activity that may require effort or education, such as engaging in philosophical debate or reading poetry. This means that Bentham assumes a fundamental human equality, with complete happiness being accessible to all, regardless of social class or ability. ∎

See also: Epicurus 64–65 ▪ Thomas Hobbes 112–15 ▪ David Hume 148–53 ▪ John Stuart Mill 190–93 ▪ Henry Sidgwick 336

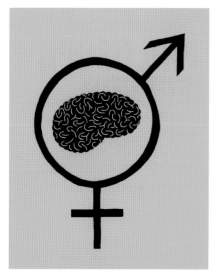

MIND HAS NO GENDER
MARY WOLLSTONECRAFT (1759–1797)

IN CONTEXT

BRANCH
Political philosophy

APPROACH
Feminism

BEFORE
4th century BCE Plato advises that girls should have a similar education to boys.

4th century CE Hypatia, a noted female mathematician and philosopher, teaches in Alexandria, Egypt.

1790 In *Letters on Education*, British historian Catherine Macaulay claims the apparent weakness of women is caused by their mis-education.

AFTER
1869 John Stuart Mill's *The Subjection of Women* argues for equality of the sexes.

Late 20th century A surge of feminist activism begins to overturn most of the social and political inequalities between the sexes in Western society.

For most of recorded history, women have been seen as subordinate to men. But during the 18th century, the justice of this arrangement began to be openly challenged. Among the most prominent voices of dissent was that of the English radical Mary Wollstonecraft.

Many previous thinkers had cited the physical differences between the sexes to justify the social inequality between women and men. However, in the light of new ideas that had been formulated during the 17th century, such as John Locke's view that nearly all knowledge was acquired through experience and education, the validity of such reasoning was being called into question.

Equal education

Wollstonecraft argues that if men and women are given the same education they will acquire the same good character and rational approach to life, because they have fundamentally similar brains and minds. Her book, *A Vindication of the Rights of Woman*, published in 1792, was partly a response to Jean-Jacques Rousseau's *Emile* (1762), which recommends that girls be educated differently to boys, and that they learn deference to them.

Wollstonecraft's demand that women be treated as equal citizens to men – with equal legal, social, and political rights – was still largely treated with derision in the late 18th century. But it did sow the seeds of the suffragette and feminist movements that were to flourish in the 19th and 20th centuries. ∎

Let woman share the rights and she will emulate the virtues of man.
Mary Wollstonecraft

See also: Plato 50–55 ▪ Hypatia of Alexandria 331 ▪ John Stuart Mill 190–93 ▪ Simone de Beauvoir 276–77 ▪ Luce Irigaray 320 ▪ Hélène Cixous 322

WHAT SORT OF PHILOSOPHY ONE CHOOSES DEPENDS ON WHAT SORT OF PERSON ONE IS
JOHANN GOTTLIEB FICHTE (1762–1814)

IN CONTEXT

BRANCH
Epistemology

APPROACH
Idealism

BEFORE
1641 René Descartes discovers that it is impossible to doubt that "I exist". The self is therefore the one and only thing of which we can be sure.

18th century Immanuel Kant develops a philosophy of idealism and the transcendental ego, the "I" that synthesizes information. This forms the basis of Fichte's idealism and notion of the self.

AFTER
20th century Fichte's nationalist ideas become associated with Martin Heidegger and the Nazi regime in Germany.

1950s Isaiah Berlin holds Fichte's idea of true freedom of the self as responsible for modern authoritarianism.

Johann Gottlieb Fichte was an 18th-century German philosopher and student of Immanuel Kant. He examined how it is possible for us to exist as ethical beings with free will, while living in a world that appears to be causally determined; that is to say, in a world where every event follows on necessarily from previous events and conditions, according to unvarying laws of nature.

The idea that there is a world like this "out there", beyond our selves and independent of us, is known as dogmatism. This is an idea that gained ground in the Enlightenment period, but Fichte thinks that it leaves no room for moral values or choice. How can people be considered to have free will, he asks, if everything is determined by something else that exists outside of ourselves?

Fichte argues instead for a version of idealism similar to Kant's, in which our own minds create all that we think of as reality. In this idealist world, the self is an active entity or essence that exists outside of causal influences, and is able to think and choose freely, independently, and spontaneously.

Fichte understands idealism and dogmatism to be entirely different starting points. They can never be "mixed" into one philosophical system, he says; there is no way of proving philosophically which is correct, and neither can be used to refute the other. For this reason one can only "choose" which philosophy one believes in, not for objective, rational reasons, but depending upon "what sort of person one is". ■

Think the I,
and observe what is
involved in doing this.
Johann Gottlieb Fichte

See also: René Descartes 116–23 ▪ Benedictus Spinoza 126–29 ▪ Immanuel Kant 164–71 ▪ Martin Heidegger 252–55 ▪ Isaiah Berlin 280–81

ABOUT NO SUBJECT IS THERE LESS PHILOSOPHIZING THAN ABOUT PHILOSOPHY
FRIEDRICH SCHLEGEL (1772-1829)

The German historian and poet, Friedrich Schlegel, is generally credited with introducing the use of aphorisms (short, ambiguous sayings) into later modern philosophy. In 1798 he observed that there was little philosophizing about philosophy (metaphilosophy), implying that we should question both how Western philosophy functions and its assumption that a linear type of argument is the best approach.

Schlegel disagrees with the approaches of Aristotle and René Descartes, saying they are wrong to assume that there are solid "first principles" that can form a starting point. He also thinks that it is not possible to reach any final answers, because every conclusion of an argument can be endlessly perfected. Describing his own approach, Schlegel says philosophy must always "start in the middle... it is a whole, and the path to recognizing it is no straight line but a circle".

Schlegel's holistic view – seeing philosophy as a whole – fits within the broader context of his Romantic theories about art and life. These value individual human emotion above rational thought, in contrast to most Enlightenment thinking. While his charge against earlier philosophy was not necessarily correct his contemporary, Georg Hegel, took up the cause for reflexivity – the modern name for applying philosophical methods to the subject of philosophy itself. ∎

Philosophy is the art of thinking, and Schlegel points out that its methods affect the kind of answers it can find. Western and Eastern philosophies use very different approaches.

See also: Protagoras 42–43 ∎ Aristotle 56–63 ∎ René Descartes 116–23 ∎ Georg Hegel 178–85 ∎ Martin Heidegger 252–55 ∎ Jacques Derrida 308–13

REALITY
IS A HISTORICAL
PROCESS
GEORG HEGEL (1770–1831)

IN CONTEXT

BRANCH
Metaphysics

APPROACH
Idealism

BEFORE
6th century BCE Heraclitus claims that all things pass into their opposites, an important factor in Hegel's dialectic.

1781 Immanuel Kant publishes his *Critique of Pure Reason*, which shows the limits of human knowledge.

1790s The works of Johann Fichte and Friedrich Schelling lay the foundations for the school of German Idealism.

AFTER
1846 Karl Marx writes *The German Ideology*, which uses Hegel's dialectical method.

1943 Jean-Paul Sartre's existentialist work *Being and Nothingness* relies upon Hegel's notion of the dialectic.

egel was the single most famous philosopher in Germany during the first half of the 19th century. His central idea was that all phenomena, from consciousness to political institutions, are aspects of a single Spirit (by which is meant both "mind" and "idea"). Over time, Spirit recognizes these phenomena as aspects of itself, and reintegrates them. This process of reintegration Hegel calls the "dialectic", and it is one that we (who are all aspects of Spirit) understand as "history". Hegel is therefore a monist, for he believes that all things are aspects of a single thing, and an idealist, for he believes that reality is ultimately something that is not material (in this case Spirit). Hegel's idea radically altered the philosophical landscape, and to fully grasp its implications we need to take a look at the background to his thought.

History and consciousness

Few philosophers would deny that human beings are, to a great extent, historical – that we inherit things from the past, change them, and then pass them on to future generations. Language, for example,

Certain changes, such those brought about by the American Revolution, are explained by Hegel as the progress of Spirit from a lesser stage of its development to a higher stage.

is something that we learn and change as we use it, and the same is true of science – scientists start with a body of theory, and then go on either to confirm or to disconfirm it. The same is also true of social institutions, such as the family, the state, banks, churches, and so on – most of which are modified forms of earlier practices or institutions.

Georg Hegel

Georg Hegel was born in 1770 in Stuttgart, Germany, and studied theology at Tübingen where he met and became friends with the poet Friedrich Hölderlin and the philosopher Friedrich Schelling. He spent several years working as a tutor before an inheritance allowed him to join Schelling at the University of Jena. Hegel was forced to leave Jena when Napoleon's troops occupied the town, and just managed to rescue his major work, *Phenomenology of Spirit*, which catapulted him to a dominant position in German philosophy. In need of funds, he became a newspaper editor and then a school headmaster before being appointed to the chair of philosophy first in Heidelberg and then at the prestigious University of Berlin. At the age of 41 he married Marie von Tucher, with whom he had three children. Hegel died in 1831 during a cholera epidemic.

Key works

1807 *Phenomenology of Spirit*
1812–16 *Science of Logic*
1817 *Encyclopedia of the Philosophical Sciences*

See also: Heraclitus 40 ▪ Johann Gottlieb Fichte 176 ▪ Friedrich Schelling 335 ▪ Arthur Schopenhauer 186–88 ▪ Karl Marx 196–203 ▪ Jean-Paul Sartre 268–71

Human beings, therefore, never begin their existence from scratch, but always within some kind of context – a context that changes, sometimes radically within a single generation. Some things, however, do not immediately appear to be historical, or subject to change.

An example of such a thing is consciousness. We know for certain that what we are conscious of will change, but what it means to be conscious – what kind of a thing it is to be awake, to be aware, to be capable of thinking and making decisions – is something that we tend to believe has always been the same for everyone. Likewise, it seems plausible to claim that the structures of thought are not historical – that the kind of activity that thinking is, and what mental faculties it relies on (memory, perception, understanding, and so on), has always been the same for everyone throughout history. This was certainly what Hegel's great idealist predecessor, Immanuel Kant, believed – and to understand Hegel, we need to know what he thought about Kant's work.

Kant's categories

For Kant, the basic ways in which thought works, and the basic structures of consciousness, are *a priori* – that is, they exist prior to (and so are not are not derived from) experience. This means that they are independent not only of what we are thinking about, or are conscious of, but are independent of any historical influence or development.

Kant calls these structures of thought "categories", and these include the concepts "cause", "substance", "existence", and "reality". For example, experience may give us knowledge about the outside world, but nothing within experience itself teaches us that the outside world actually contains, for example, causes and effects. For Kant, knowledge of the basic structure of the outside world is *a priori* knowledge. It is only possible because we are all born with categories that supply us with a framework for experience – part of which is the assumption that there is an external world. However, Kant continues, this *a priori* framework means that the world as it appears »

To comprehend what is is the task of philosophy, for what is, is reason.
Georg Hegel

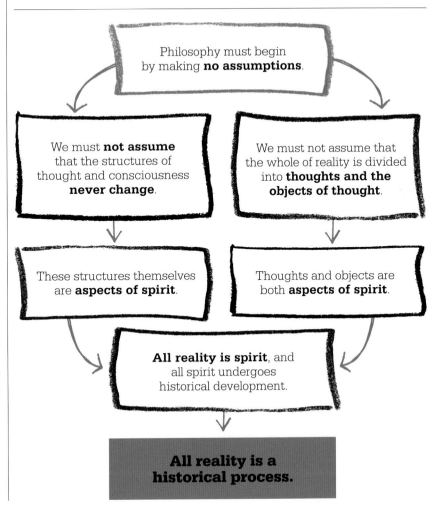

Philosophy must begin by making **no assumptions**.

We must **not assume** that the structures of thought and consciousness **never change**.

We must not assume that the whole of reality is divided into **thoughts and the objects of thought**.

These structures themselves are **aspects of spirit**.

Thoughts and objects are both **aspects of spirit**.

All reality is spirit, and all spirit undergoes historical development.

All reality is a historical process.

Hegel's dialectic shows how opposites find resolution. A state of tyranny, for example, generates a need for freedom – but once freedom has been achieved there can only be anarchy until an element of tyranny is combined with freedom, creating the synthesis "law".

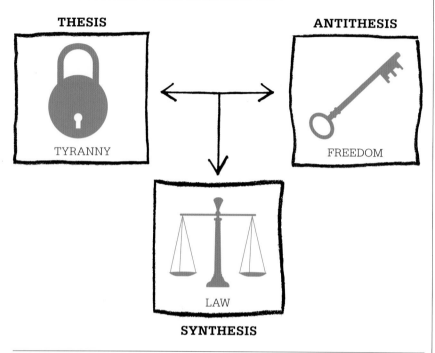

THESIS

TYRANNY

ANTITHESIS

FREEDOM

SYNTHESIS

LAW

they are "dialectical" – meaning that they are always subject to change. Where Kant believes in an unchanging framework of experience, Hegel believes that the framework of experience itself is subject to change – as much, indeed, as the world that we experience. Consciousness, therefore, and not merely what we are conscious of, is part of an evolving process. This process is "dialectical" – a concept that has a very specific meaning in Hegel's philosophical thought.

Hegel's dialectic

The notion of dialectic is central to what Hegel calls his immanent (internal) account of the development of things. He declares that his account will guarantee four things. First, that no assumptions are made. Second, that only the broadest notions possible are employed, the better to avoid asserting anything without justification. Third, that it shows how a general notion gives rise to other, more specific, notions. Fourth, that this process happens entirely from "within" the notion itself. This fourth requirement reveals the core of Hegel's logic – namely that every notion, or "thesis", contains within itself a contradiction, or "antithesis", which is only resolved by the emergence of a newer, richer notion, called a "synthesis", from the original notion itself. One consequence of this immanent process is that when we become aware of the synthesis, we realize that what we saw as the earlier contradiction in the thesis was only an apparent contradiction, one that was caused by some limitation in our understanding of the original notion.

An example of this logical progression appears at the beginning of Hegel's *Science of*

is dependent upon the nature of the human mind, and does not represent the world as it really is – in other words, the world as it is "in itself". This "world as it is in itself" is what Kant calls the noumenal world, and he claims that it is unknowable. All that we can know, according to Kant, is the world as it appears to us through the framework of the categories – and this is what Kant calls the "phenomenal" world, or the world of our everyday experience.

Hegel's critique of Kant

Hegel believes that Kant made great strides forward in eliminating naivety in philosophy, but that his accounts of the "world in itself" and the categories still betray uncritical assumptions. Hegel argues that Kant fails in at least

two respects to be sufficiently thorough in his analysis. First of all, Hegel regards Kant's notion of the "world in itself" as an empty abstraction that means nothing. For Hegel, what exists is whatever comes to be manifested in consciousness – for example, as something sensed or as something thought. Kant's second failure, Hegel argues, is that he makes too many assumptions about the nature and origin of the categories.

Hegel's task is to understand these categories without making any assumptions whatsoever, and the worst assumption that Hegel sees in Kant concerns the relationships of the categories to each other. Kant assumes that the categories are original and distinct, and that they are totally separate from each other – but for Hegel

> Each of the parts of philosophy is a philosophical whole, a circle rounded and complete in itself.
> **Georg Hegel**

Logic, where he introduces the most general and all-inclusive notion of "pure being" – meaning anything that in any sense could be said to be. He then shows that this concept contains a contradiction – namely, that it requires the opposite concept of "nothingness" or "not-being" for it to be fully understood. Hegel then shows that this contradiction is simply a conflict between two aspects of a single, higher concept in which they find resolution. In the case of "being" and "not-being", the concept that resolves them is "becoming". When we say that something "becomes", we mean that it moves from a state of not-being to a state of being – so it turns out that the concept of "being" that we started off with was not really a single concept at all, but merely one aspect of the three-part notion of "becoming". The vital point here is that the concept of "becoming" is not introduced from "outside", as it were, to resolve the contradiction between "being" and "not-being". On the contrary, Hegel's analysis shows that "becoming" was always the meaning of "being" and "not-being", and that all we had to do was analyze these concepts to see their underlying logic.

This resolution of a thesis (being) with its antithesis (not-being) in a synthesis (becoming) is just the beginning of the dialectical process, which goes on to repeat itself at a higher level. That is, any new synthesis turns out, on further analysis, to involve its own contradiction, and this in turn is overcome by a still richer or "higher" notion. All ideas, according to Hegel, are interconnected in this way, and the process of revealing those connections is what Hegel calls his "dialectical method".

In saying that the structures of thought are dialectical, therefore, Hegel means that they are not distinct and irreducible, as Kant maintained, but that they emerge from the broadest, emptiest notions by means of this movement of self-contradiction and resolution.

Dialectic and the world
The discussion of Hegel's dialectic above uses terms such as "emerge", "development", and "movement". On the one hand, these terms reflect something important »

In Hegel's view, a synthesis emerging from an antagonism of thesis and antithesis itself becomes a new thesis, which generates its own antithesis – which finally gives birth to another synthesis. This dialectical process is one in which Spirit comes to ever more accurate understandings of itself – culminating in the philosophy of Hegel, in which it achieves complete understanding.

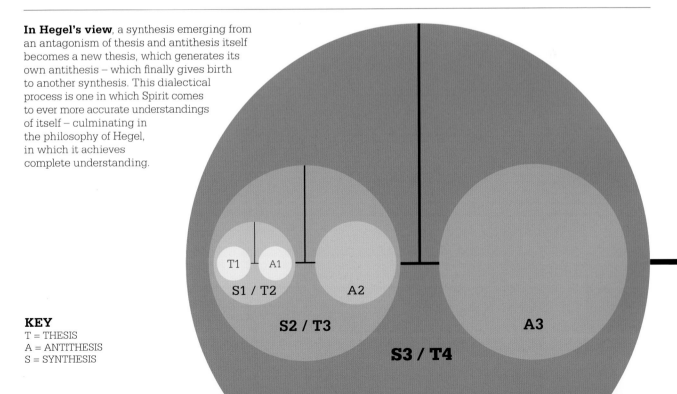

KEY
T = THESIS
A = ANTITHESIS
S = SYNTHESIS

about this method of philosophy – that it starts without assumptions and from the least controversial point, and allows ever richer and truer concepts to reveal themselves through the process of dialectical unfolding. On the other hand, however, Hegel clearly argues that these developments are not simply interesting facts of logic, but are real developments that can be seen at work in history. For example, a man from ancient Greece and a man living in the modern world will obviously think about different things, but Hegel claims that their very ways of thinking are different, and represent different kinds of consciousness – or different stages in the historical development of thought and consciousness.

Hegel's first major work, *Phenomenology of Spirit*, gives an account of the dialectical development of these forms of consciousness. He starts with the types of consciousness that an individual human being might possess, and works up to collective forms of consciousness. He does so in such a way as to show that these types of consciousness are to be found externalized in particular historical periods or events – most famously, for example, in the American and French revolutions.

Indeed, Hegel even argues that at certain times in history, Spirit's next revolutionary change may manifest itself as an individual (such as Napoleon Bonaparte) who, as an individual consciousness, is completely unaware of his or her role in the history of Spirit. And the progress that these individuals make is always characterized by the freeing of aspects of Spirit (in human form) from recurring states

Each stage of world-history is a necessary moment in the Idea of the World Spirit.
Georg Hegel

of oppression – of overcoming tyrannies that may themselves be the result of the overcoming of previous tyrannies.

This extraordinary idea – that the nature of consciousness has changed through time, and changed in accordance with a pattern that is visible in history – means that there is nothing about human beings that is not historical in character. Moreover, this historical development of consciousness cannot simply have happened at random. Since it is a dialectical process, it must in some sense contain both a particular sense of direction and an end point. Hegel calls this end point "Absolute Spirit" – and by this he means a future stage of consciousness which no longer even belongs to individuals, but which instead belongs to reality as a whole.

At this point in its development, knowledge is complete – as it must be, according to Hegel, since Spirit encompasses, through dialectical

Napoleon Bonaparte, according to Hegel, perfectly embodied the *zeitgeist* (spirit of the age) and was able, through his actions, to move history into the next stage of its development.

> Of the Absolute it must be said that it is essentially a result, that only in the end is it what it truly is.
> **Georg Hegel**

synthesis, both the knower and what is known. Furthermore, Spirit grasps this knowledge as nothing other than its own completed essence – the full assimilation of all forms of "otherness" that were always parts of itself, however unknowingly. In other words, Spirit does not simply come to encompass reality – it comes to be aware of itself as having always been nothing other than the movement towards this encompassing of reality. As Hegel writes in *The Phenomenology of Spirit*, "History is a conscious, self-mediating process – [it is] Spirit emptied out into time".

Spirit and nature

But what about the world in which we live, and which seems to go its way quite separately from human history? What does it mean to say that reality itself is historical? According to Hegel, what we ordinarily call "nature" or "the world" is also Spirit. "Nature is to be regarded as a system of stages," he writes, "one arising necessarily from the other and being the proximate truth of the stage from which it results". He goes on to claim that one of the stages of nature is the progression from that which is

"only Life" (nature as a living whole) to that which has "existence as Spirit" (the whole of nature now revealed as always having been, when properly understood, Spirit).

At this stage of nature, a different dialectic begins, namely that of consciousness itself – of the forms that Absolute Spirit takes in its dialectical progression towards self-realization. Hegel's account of this progression begins with consciousness first thinking of itself as an individual thing among other individuals, and occupying a separate space to that of matter or the natural world. Later stages of consciousness, however, are no longer those of individuals, but are those of social or political groups – and so the dialectic continues, refining itself until it reaches the stage of Absolute Spirit.

Spirit and mind

At the time Hegel was writing, there was a dominant philosophical view that there are two kinds of entities in the world – things that exist in the physical world and thoughts about those things – these latter being something like pictures or images of the things. Hegel argues that all versions of this distinction are mistakes, and involve committing ourselves to the ridiculous scenario in which two things are both absolutely different (things and thoughts), but also somehow similar (because the thoughts are images of things).

Hegel argues that it only seems as though the objects of thought are different from thought itself. For Hegel, the illusion of difference and separation between these two apparent "worlds" is shown as such when both thought and nature are revealed as aspects of Spirit. This illusion is overcome in Absolute Spirit, when we see that there is

only one reality – that of Spirit, which knows and reflects on itself, and is both thought and what is thought about.

The "Whole of Spirit", or "Absolute Spirit", is the end point of Hegel's dialectic. However, the preceding stages are not left behind, as it were, but are revealed as insufficiently analyzed aspects of Spirit as a whole. Indeed, what we think of as an individual person is not a separate constituent of reality, but is an aspect of how Spirit develops – or how it "empties itself out into time". Thus, Hegel writes, "The True is the Whole. But the Whole is nothing other than the essence consummating itself through its development". Reality is Spirit – both thought and what is known by thought – and undergoes a process of historical development. ∎

German history had reached its end point in the Prussian state, according to Hegel. However, there was a strong feeling in favour of a united Germany, as personified by the figure of Germania.

EVERY MAN TAKES THE LIMITS OF HIS OWN FIELD OF VISION FOR THE LIMITS OF THE WORLD

ARTHUR SCHOPENHAUER (1788–1860)

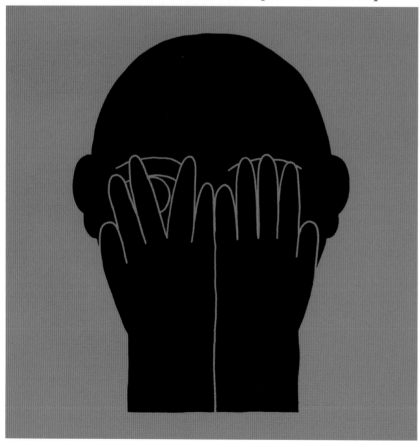

IN CONTEXT

BRANCH
Metaphysics

APPROACH
Idealism

BEFORE
1690 John Locke publishes
*An Essay Concerning Human
Understanding*, explaining
how all our knowledge comes
from experience.

1781 Immanuel Kant's *Critique
of Pure Reason* introduces the
concept of a "thing in itself",
which Schopenhauer used as
a starting point for his ideas.

AFTER
Late 19th century Friedrich
Nietzsche puts forward the
notion of a "Will to power" to
explain human motivations.

Early 20th century Austrian
psychoanalyst Sigmund Freud
explores what lies behind our
basic human urges.

Arthur Schopenhauer was not
part of the mainstream of
early 19th-century German
philosophy. He acknowledged
Immanuel Kant, whom he idolized,
as a major influence, but dismissed
the idealists of his own generation,
who held that reality ultimately
consists of something non-material.
Most of all he detested the idealist
Georg Hegel for his dry writing
style and optimistic philosophy.

Using Kant's metaphysics as
his starting point, Schopenhauer
developed his own view of the
world, which he expressed in clear,
literary language. He took Kant's
view that the world is divided into
what we perceive through our

See also: Empedocles 330 ▪ John Locke 130–33 ▪ Immanuel Kant 164–71 ▪ Georg Hegel 178–85 ▪ Friedrich Nietzsche 214–21

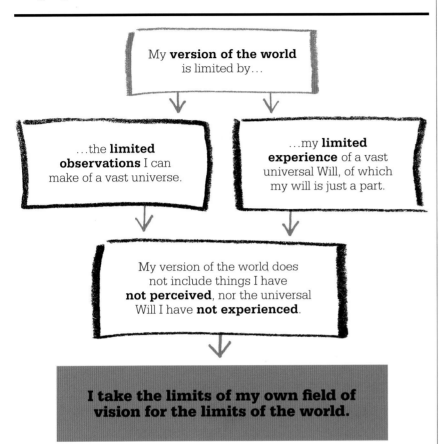

My **version of the world** is limited by…

…the **limited observations** I can make of a vast universe.

…my **limited experience** of a vast universal Will, of which my will is just a part.

My version of the world does not include things I have **not perceived**, nor the universal Will I have **not experienced**.

I take the limits of my own field of vision for the limits of the world.

Arthur Schopenhauer

Born into a wealthy and cosmopolitan family in Danzig (now Gdansk), Schopenhauer was expected to become a merchant like his father. He travelled to France and England before his family settled in Hamburg in 1793. In 1805, after his father's death – possibly by suicide – he felt able to stop working and go to university, where he studied philosophy and psychology. He maintained an uneasy relationship with his mother, who constantly criticized his achievements.

After completing his studies, Schopenhauer taught at Berlin University. He attained a reputation as a philanderer and misogynist; he had several affairs and avoided marriage, and was once convicted of assaulting a woman. In 1831 he moved to Frankfurt, where he lived until his death with a succession of poodles called either Atman ("soul" in Hinduism and Buddhism) or Butz (German for hobgoblin).

Key works

1818 and 1844 *The World as Will and Representation*
1851 *Parerga and Paralipomena*

senses (phenomena), and "things in themselves" (noumena), but he wanted to explain the nature of the phenomenal and noumenal worlds.

Interpreting Kant
According to Kant, we each construct a version of the world from our perceptions – the phenomenal world – but we can never experience the noumenal world as it is "in itself". So we each have a limited vision of the world, as our perceptions are built from information acquired through a limited set of senses. Schopenhauer adds to this that "every man takes the limits of his own field of vision for the limits of the world".

The idea of knowledge being limited to our experience was not an entirely new one; the ancient philosopher Empedocles had said that "each man believes only his experience", and in the 17th century John Locke had asserted that "no man's knowledge here can go beyond his experience". But the reason Schopenhauer gives for this limitation is quite new, and it comes from his interpretation of Kant's phenomenal and noumenal worlds. The important difference between Kant and Schopenhauer is that for Schopenhauer, the phenomenal and noumenal are not two different realities or worlds, but the same world, experienced » differently. It is one world, with two aspects: Will and Representation. This is most easily evidenced by our bodies, which we experience in two ways: we perceive them as objects (Representations), and experience them from within (as Will).

Schopenhauer says that an act of will, such as wishing to raise my arm, and the resulting movement, are not in two different worlds – the noumenal and phenomenal – but the same event experienced in two different ways. One is experienced from inside, the other observed from outside. When we look at things outside ourselves, although we see only their objective Representation, not their inner reality or Will, the world as a whole still has the same simultaneous outer and inner existences.

A universal Will

Schopenhauer uses the word "will" to express a pure energy that has no driving direction, and yet is responsible for everything that manifests itself in the phenomenal world. He believes, like Kant, that space and time belong in the phenomenal world – they are

Schopenhauer studied the Hindu *Bhagavad Gita*, in which Krishna the charioteer tells Arjuna that a man is a slave to his desires unless he can free himself from his cravings.

concepts within our minds, not things outside of them – so the Will of the world does not mark time, or follow causal or spatial laws. This means it must be timeless and indivisible, and so must our individual wills. It follows, then, that the Will of the universe and individual will are one and the same thing, and the phenomenal world is controlled by this vast, timeless, motiveless Will.

Eastern influence

At this point in his argument, Schopenhauer's pessimism shows through. Where contemporaries such as Hegel saw will as a positive force, Schopenhauer sees humanity at the mercy of a mindless, aimless universal Will. It lies behind our most basic urges, he insists, and is what causes us to live lives of constant disappointment and frustration as we attempt to relieve our cravings. For Schopenhauer, the world is neither good nor bad, but meaningless, and humans who struggle to find happiness achieve at best gratification and at worst pain and suffering.

The only escape from this miserable condition, according to Schopenhauer, is nonexistence or at least a loss of will for gratification. He proposes that relief can be found through aesthetic contemplation, especially in music, which is the one art that does not attempt to represent the phenomenal world. Schopenhauer's philosophy here echoes the Buddhist concept of nirvana (a transcendent state free from desire or suffering). He had studied Eastern thinkers and religions in great detail.

From his idea of one universal Will, Schopenhauer develops a moral philosophy that may be somewhat surprising, considering his otherwise misanthropic and

> The fundament upon which all our knowledge and learning rests is the inexplicable.
> **Arthur Schopenhauer**

pessimistic character. He realizes that if we can recognize that our separateness from the universe is essentially an illusion – because all our individual wills and the Will of the universe are one and the same thing – we can learn empathy with everyone and everything else, and moral goodness can arise from a universal compassion. Here, again, Schopenhauer's thinking reflects the ideals of Eastern philosophy.

Lasting legacy

Schopenhauer was largely ignored by other German philosophers in his lifetime, and his ideas were overshadowed by those of Hegel, though he did have an influence on writers and musicians. Towards the end of the 19th century, the primacy he gave to Will became a theme in philosophy once more. Friedrich Nietzsche in particular acknowledged his influence, and Henri Bergson and the American pragmatists also owe something to his analysis of the world as Will. Perhaps Schopenhauer's greatest influence, however, was in the field of psychology, where his ideas about our basic urges and their frustration influenced the psychoanalytic theories of both Sigmund Freud and Carl Jung. ■

THEOLOGY IS ANTHROPOLOGY
LUDWIG ANDREAS FEUERBACH (1804–1872)

IN CONTEXT

BRANCH
Philosophy of religion

APPROACH
Atheism

BEFORE
c.600 BCE Thales is the first Western philosopher to deny that the universe owes its existence to a god.

c.500 BCE The Indian school of atheistic philosophy known as Carvaka is established.

c.400 BCE The ancient Greek philosopher Diagoras of Melos puts forward arguments in defence of atheism.

AFTER
Mid-19th century Karl Marx uses Feuerbach's reasoning in his philosophy of political revolution.

Late 19th century The psychoanalyst Sigmund Freud argues that religion is a projection of human wishes.

The 19th-century German philosopher Ludwig Feuerbach is best known for his book *The Essence of Christianity* (1841), which inspired revolutionary thinkers such as Karl Marx and Friedrich Engels. The book incorporates much of the philosophical thinking of Georg Hegel, but where Hegel saw an Absolute Spirit as the guiding force in nature, Feuerbach sees no reason to look beyond our experience to explain existence. For Feuerbach, humans are not an externalized form of an Absolute Spirit, but the opposite: we have created the idea of a great spirit, a god, from our own longings and desires.

Imagining God
Feuerbach suggests that in our yearning for all that is best in humankind – love, compassion, kindness, and so on – we have imagined a being that incorporates all of these qualities in the highest possible degree, and then called it "God". Theology (the study of God) is therefore nothing more than anthropology (the study of humanity). Not only have we deceived ourselves into thinking that a divine being exists, we have also forgotten or forsaken what we are ourselves. We have lost sight of the fact that these virtues actually exist in humans, not gods. For this reason we should focus less on heavenly righteousness and more on human justice – it is people in this life, on this Earth, that deserve our attention. ∎

The Israelites of the Bible, in their need for certainty and reassurance, created a false god – the golden calf – to worship. Feuerbach argues that all gods are created in the same way.

See also: Thales of Miletus 22–23 ▪ Georg Hegel 178–85 ▪ Karl Marx 196–203

OVER HIS OWN BODY AND MIND, THE INDIVIDUAL IS SOVEREIGN

JOHN STUART MILL (1806–1873)

IN CONTEXT

BRANCH
Political philosophy

APPROACH
Utilitarianism

BEFORE
1651 In *Leviathan*, Thomas Hobbes says that people are "brutish" and must be controlled by a social contract.

1689 John Locke's book, *Two Treatises of Government,* looks at social contract theory in the context of empiricism.

1789 Jeremy Bentham advocates the "greatest happiness principle".

AFTER
1930s Economist J.M. Keynes, influenced by Mill, develops liberal economic theories.

1971 John Rawls publishes *A Theory of Justice*, based on the idea that laws should be those everyone would accept.

John Stuart Mill was born into an intellectually privileged family, and he was aware from an early age of the British traditions of philosophy that had emerged during the Enlightenment of the 18th century. John Locke and David Hume had established a philosophy whose new empiricism stood in stark contrast to the rationalism of continental European philosophers. But during the late 18th century, Romantic ideas from Europe began to influence British moral and political philosophy. The most obvious product of this influence was utilitarianism, which was a very British interpretation of the political philosophy that had

See also: Thomas Hobbes 112–15 ▪ John Locke 130–33 ▪ Jeremy Bentham 174 ▪ Bertrand Russell 236–39 ▪ Karl Popper 262–65 ▪ John Rawls 294–95

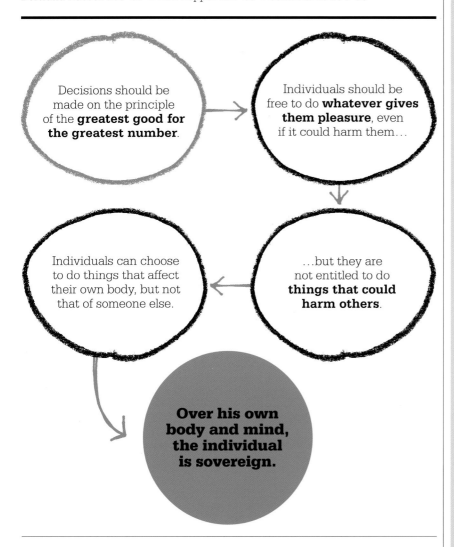

Decisions should be made on the principle of the **greatest good for the greatest number**.

Individuals should be free to do **whatever gives them pleasure**, even if it could harm them…

…but they are not entitled to do **things that could harm others**.

Individuals can choose to do things that affect their own body, but not that of someone else.

Over his own body and mind, the individual is sovereign.

John Stuart Mill

John Stuart Mill was born in London in 1806. His father was the Scottish philosopher and historian James Mill, who founded the movement of "philosophical radicals" with Jeremy Bentham. John was educated at home by his father, whose demanding programme began with teaching Greek to John when he was only three years old.

After years of intense study, Mill suffered a breakdown at the age of 20. He left university to work for the East India Company, where he stayed until his retirement in 1857, as it gave him a living and time to write. During this period he met Harriet Taylor, advocate of women's rights, who – after a relationship of 20 years – eventually became his wife. Mill served as a Member of Parliament from 1865 to 1868, putting into practice his moral and political philosophy.

Key works

1843 *System of Logic*
1848 *Principles of Political Economy*
1859 *On Liberty*
1861 *Utilitarianism*
1869 *The Subjection of Women*
1874 *On Nature*

shaped the 18th-century revolutions of both Europe and America. Its originator, Jeremy Bentham, was a friend of the Mill family, and he influenced John's home education.

Victorian liberalism

As a philosopher Mill sets himself the task of synthesizing a valuable intellectual heritage with the new 19th-century Romanticism. His approach is less sceptical than that of Hume (who argued that all knowledge comes from sense experience, and nothing is certain) and less dogmatic than Bentham (who insisted that everything be judged on its usefulness), but their empiricism and utilitarianism informed his thinking. Mill's moral and political philosophy is less extreme than his predecessors', aiming for reform rather than revolution, and it formed the basis of British Victorian liberalism.

After completing his first philosophical work, the exhaustive six-volume *System of Logic*, Mill » turned his attention to moral philosophy, particularly Bentham's theories of utilitarianism. He had been struck by the elegant simplicity of Bentham's principle of "the greatest happiness for the greatest number", and was a firm believer in its usefulness. He describes his interpretation of how utilitarianism might be applied as similar to Jesus of Nazareth's "golden rule": do as you would be done by, and love your neighbour as yourself. This, he says, constitutes "the ideal perfection of utilitarian morality".

Legislating for liberty

Mill supports Bentham's happiness principle, but he thinks it lacks practicality. Bentham had seen the idea as depending upon an abstract "felicific calculus" (an algorithm for calculating happiness), but Mill

wants to find out how it might be implemented in the real world. He is interested in the social and political implications of the principle, rather than merely its use in making moral decisions. How would legislation promoting the "greatest happiness of the greatest number" actually affect the individual? Might laws that sought to do this, enacting a kind of majority rule, actually prevent some people from achieving happiness?

Mill thinks that the solution is for education and public opinion to work together to establish an "indissoluble association" between an individual's happiness and the good of society. As a result, people would always be motivated to act not only for their own good or happiness, but towards that of everyone. He concludes that society

> It is better to be Socrates dissatisfied than a fool satisfied.
> **John Stuart Mill**

should therefore allow all individuals the freedom to pursue happiness. Furthermore, he says that this right should be protected by the government, and that legislation should be drawn up to protect the individual's freedom to pursue personal goals. There is, however, one situation in which this freedom should be curtailed, Mill says, and that is where one person's action impinges on the happiness of others. This is known as the "harm principle". He underlines this by pointing out that in these cases, a person's "own good, either physical or moral, is not a sufficient warrant".

Quantifying happiness

Mill then turns his attention to how best to measure happiness. Bentham had considered the duration and intensity of pleasures in his felicific calculus, but Mill thinks it is also important to consider the quality of pleasure. By this, he is referring to the difference between a simple satisfaction of desires and sensual pleasures, and happiness gained

The good samaritan helps his enemy in a biblical parable that demonstrates Mill's golden rule: do as you would be done by. He believed this would raise society's overall level of happiness.

through intellectual and cultural pursuits. In the "happiness equation" he gives more weight to higher, intellectual pleasures than to baser, physical ones.

In line with his empiricist background, Mill then tries to pin down the essence of happiness. What is it, he asks, that each individual is striving to achieve? What causes happiness? He decides that "the sole evidence it is possible to produce that anything is desirable, is that people do actually desire it." This seems a rather unsatisfactory explanation, but he goes on to distinguish between two different desires: unmotivated desires (the things we want that will give us pleasure) and conscientious actions (the things we do out a sense of duty or charity, often against our immediate inclination, that ultimately bring us pleasure). In the first case, we desire something as a part of our happiness, but in the second we desire it as a means to our happiness, which is felt only when the act reaches its virtuous end.

Practical utilitarianism

Mill was not a purely academic philosopher, and he believed his ideas should be put into practice, so he considered what this might mean in terms of government and legislation. He saw any restriction of the individual's freedom to pursue happiness as a tyranny, whether this was the collective tyranny of the majority (through democratic election) or the singular rule of a despot. He therefore suggested practical measures to restrict the power of society over the individual, and to protect the rights of the individual to free expression.

In his time as a Member of Parliament, Mill proposed many reforms which were not to come

The National Society for Women's Suffrage was set up in Britain in 1868, a year after Mill tried to secure their legal right to vote by arguing for an amendment to the 1867 Reform Act.

about until much later, but his speeches brought the liberal applications of his utilitarian philosophy to the attention of a wide public. As a philosopher and politician, he argued strongly in defence of free speech, for the promotion of basic human rights, and against slavery – all of which were obvious practical applications of his utilitarianism. Strongly influenced by his wife Harriet Taylor-Mill, he was the first British parliamentarian to propose votes for women as part of his government reforms. His liberalist philosophy also encompassed economics, and contrary to his father's economic theories, he advocated a free-market economy where government intervention is kept to a minimum.

A softer revolution

Mill places the individual, rather than society, at the centre of his utilitarian philosophy. What is important is that individuals are free to think and act as they please, without interference, even if what they do is harmful to them. Every individual, says Mill in his essay *On Liberty*, is "sovereign over his own body

and mind". His ideas came to embody Victorian liberalism, softening the radical ideas that had led to revolutions in Europe and America, and combining them with the idea of freedom from interference by authority. This, for Mill, is the basis for just governance and the means to social progress, which was an important Victorian ideal. He believes that if society leaves individuals to live in a way that makes them happy, it enables them to achieve their potential. This in turn benefits society, as the achievements of individual talents contribute to the good of all.

In his own lifetime Mill was regarded as a significant philosopher, and he is now considered by many to be the architect of Victorian liberalism. His utilitarian-inspired philosophy had a direct influence on social, political, philosophical, and economic thinking well into the 20th century. Modern economics has been shaped from various interpretations of his application of utilitarianism to the free market, notably by the British economist John Maynard Keynes. In the field of ethics, philosophers such as Bertrand Russell, Karl Popper, William James, and John Rawls all took Mill as their starting point. ∎

One person with a belief is a social power equal to 99 who have only interests.
John Stuart Mill

ANXIETY IS THE DIZZINESS OF FREEDOM
SØREN KIERKEGAARD (1813–1855)

IN CONTEXT

BRANCH
Metaphysics

APPROACH
Existentialism

BEFORE
1788 Immanuel Kant stresses the importance of freedom in moral philosophy in his *Critique of Practical Reason*.

1807–22 Georg Hegel suggests a historical consciousness, or *Geist*, establishing a relationship between human consciousness and the world in which it lives.

AFTER
1927 Martin Heidegger explores the concepts of *Angst* and existential guilt in his book *Being and Time*.

1938 Jean-Paul Sartre lays down the foundations of his existentialist philosophy.

1946 Ludwig Wittgenstein acknowledges Kierkegaard's work in *Culture and Value*.

When making decisions, we have **absolute freedom** of choice.

We realize that we can choose to do **nothing, or anything**.

Our minds **reel** at the thought of this absolute freedom.

A feeling of dread or **anxiety** accompanies the thought.

Anxiety is the dizziness of freedom.

Søren Kierkegaard's philosophy developed in reaction to the German idealist thinking that dominated continental Europe in the mid-19th century, particularly that of Georg Hegel. Kierkegaard wanted to refute Hegel's idea of a complete philosophical system, which defined humankind as part of an inevitable historical development, by arguing for a more subjective approach. He wants to examine what "it means to be a human being", not as part of some great philosophical system, but as a self-determining individual.

Kierkegaard believes that our lives are determined by our actions, which are themselves determined by our choices, so how we make

See also: Immanuel Kant 164–71 ▪ Georg Hegel 178–85 ▪ Friedrich Nietzsche 214–21 ▪ Martin Heidegger 252–55 ▪ Jean-Paul Sartre 268–71 ▪ Simone De Beauvoir 276–77 ▪ Albert Camus 284–85

those choices is critical to our lives. Like Hegel, he sees moral decisions as a choice between the hedonistic (self-gratifying) and the ethical. But where Hegel thought this choice was largely determined by the historical and environmental conditions of our times, Kierkegaard believes that moral choices are absolutely free, and above all subjective. It is our will alone that determines our judgement, he says. However, far from being a reason for happiness, this complete freedom of choice provokes in us a feeling of anxiety or dread.

Kierkegaard explains this feeling in his book, *The Concept of Anxiety*. As an example, he asks us to consider a man standing on a cliff or tall building. If this man looks over the edge, he experiences two different kinds of fear: the fear of falling, and fear brought on by the impulse to throw himself off the edge. This second type of fear, or anxiety, arises from the realization that he has absolute freedom to choose whether to jump or not, and this fear is as dizzying as his vertigo. Kierkegaard suggests that

we experience the same anxiety in all our moral choices, when we realize that we have the freedom to make even the most terrifying decisions. He describes this anxiety as "the dizziness of freedom", and goes on to explain that although it induces despair, it can also shake us from our unthinking responses by making us more aware of the available choices. In this way it increases our self-awareness and sense of personal responsibility.

The father of existentialism

Kierkegaard's ideas were largely rejected by his contemporaries, but proved highly influential to later generations. His insistence on the importance and freedom of our choices, and our continual search for meaning and purpose, was to provide the framework for existentialism. This philosophy, developed by Friedrich Nietzsche and Martin Heidegger, was later fully defined by Jean-Paul Sartre. It explores the ways in which we can live meaningfully in a godless universe, where every act is a

Hamlet is caught on the edge of a terrible choice: whether to kill his uncle or leave his father's death unavenged. Shakespeare's play demonstrates the anxiety of true freedom of choice.

choice, except the act of our own birth. Unlike these later thinkers, Kierkegaard did not abandon his faith in God, but he was the first to acknowledge the realization of self-consciousness and the "dizziness" or fear of absolute freedom. ▪

Søren Kierkegaard

Søren Kierkegaard was born in Copenhagen in 1813, in what became known as the Danish Golden Age of culture. His father, a wealthy tradesman, was both pious and melancholic, and his son inherited these traits, which were to greatly influence his philosophy. Kierkegaard studied theology at the University of Copenhagen, but attended lectures in philosophy. When he came into a sizeable inheritance, he decided to devote his life to philosophy. In 1837 he met and fell in love with Regine Olsen, and three years later they became

engaged, but Kierkegaard broke off the engagement the following year, saying that his melancholy made him unsuitable for married life. Though he never lost his faith in God, he continually criticized the Danish national church for hypocrisy. In 1855 he fell unconscious in the street, and died just over a month later.

Key works

1843 *Fear and Trembling*
1843 *Either/Or*
1844 *The Concept of Anxiety*
1847 *Works of Love*

THE HISTORY OF ALL HITHERTO EXISTING SOCIETY IS THE HISTORY OF CLASS STRUGGLES

KARL MARX (1818–1883)

Can the complex history
of the human species be
reduced to a single formula?
One of the greatest thinkers of the
19th century, Karl Marx, believed
that it could. He opened the first
chapter of his most famous work,
The Communist Manifesto, with
the claim that all historical change
comes about as the result of an
ongoing conflict between dominant
(upper) and subordinate (lower)
social classes, and that the roots
of this conflict lie in economics.

Marx believed that he had
gained a uniquely important
insight into the nature of society

through the ages. Earlier approaches
to history had emphasized the role
of individual heroes and leaders, or
stressed the role played by ideas,
but Marx focused on a long
succession of group conflicts,
including those between ancient
masters and slaves, medieval lords
and serfs, and modern employers
and their employees. It was conflicts
between these classes, he claimed,
that caused revolutionary change.

The Communist Manifesto

Marx wrote the *Manifesto* with
the German philosopher Friedrich
Engels, whom he had met when
they were both studying academic
philosophy in Germany during the
late 1830s. Engels offered financial
support, ideas, and superior writing
skills, but Marx was acknowledged
as the real genius behind their
combined publications.

In their private manuscripts
from the early and mid-1840s, Marx
and Engels emphasized that while
previous philosophers had only
sought to interpret the world, the
whole point of their activities was
to change it. During the 1850s and
60s Marx refined his ideas in many
short documents, including *The
Communist Manifesto*, a pamphlet
of about 40 pages.

The *Manifesto* seeks to explain
the values and political plans of
communism – a new belief system
put forward by a small and relatively
new group of radical German
socialists. The *Manifesto* claims
that society had simplified into
two classes in direct conflict: the
bourgeoisie (the capital-owning
class) and the proletariat (the
working class).

The word "bourgeoisie" is
derived from the French word
burgeis, or burgher: a property-
owning tradesman who had risen
above the general populace to own

Intellectual debate was widespread in
Germany at the time Marx was writing,
though he himself believed that it was
the task of philosophy not to discuss
ideas, but to bring about real change.

and run his own business. Marx
describes how the discovery and
colonization of America, the opening
of the Indian and Chinese markets,
and the increase in the commodities
that could be exchanged had, by
the mid-19th century, led to the
rapid development of commerce
and industry. Craftsmen no longer
produced enough goods for the
growing needs of new markets, and
so the manufacturing system had
taken their place. As the *Manifesto*
relates, "the markets kept growing,
demand ever rising".

Values of the bourgeoisie

Marx claims that the bourgeoisie,
who controlled all this trade, had left
no link between people other "than
naked self-interest, than callous
'cash payment'". People were once
valued for who they were, but the
bourgeoisie "has resolved personal
worth into exchange value". Moral,
religious, and even sentimental
values had been cast aside, as

See also: Niccolò Machiavelli 102–07 ▪ Jean-Jacques Rousseau 154–59 ▪ Adam Smith 160–63 ▪ Georg Hegel 178–85 ▪ Ludwig Andreas Feuerbach 189 ▪ Friedrich Nietzsche 214–21

everyone – from scientists and lawyers to priests and poets – had been transformed into nothing but a paid labourer. In place of religious and political "illusions", Marx writes, the bourgeoisie had "substituted naked, shameless, direct, brutal exploitation". Charters that had once protected people's freedom had been cast aside for one "unconscionable freedom – Free Trade".

The only solution, according to Marx, was for all the instruments of economic production (such as land, raw materials, tools, and factories) to become common property, so that every member of society could work according to their capacities, and consume according to their needs. This was the only way to prevent the rich from living at the expense of the poor.

Dialectical change

The philosophy behind Marx's reasoning on the process of change came largely from his predecessor, Georg Hegel, who had described reality not as a state of affairs, but as a process of continual change. The change was caused, he said, by the fact that every idea or state of affairs (known as the "thesis") »

From each according to his abilities, to each according to his needs.
Karl Marx

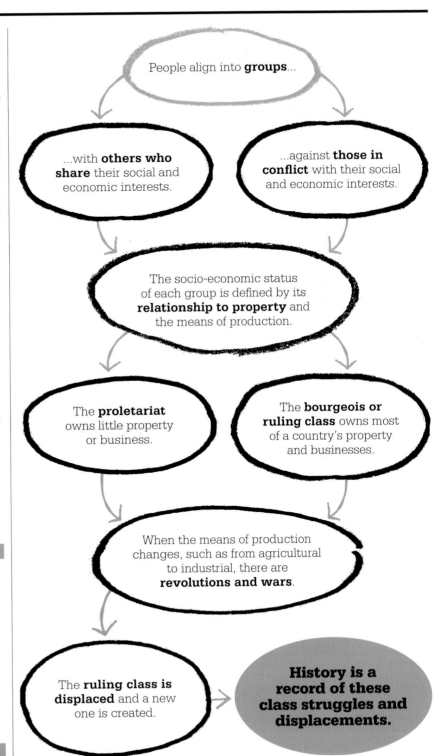

People align into **groups**...

...with **others who share** their social and economic interests.

...against **those in conflict** with their social and economic interests.

The socio-economic status of each group is defined by its **relationship to property** and the means of production.

The **proletariat** owns little property or business.

The **bourgeois or ruling class** owns most of a country's property and businesses.

When the means of production changes, such as from agricultural to industrial, there are **revolutions and wars**.

The **ruling class is displaced** and a new one is created.

History is a record of these class struggles and displacements.

contains within it an internal conflict (the "antithesis") that eventually forces a change to occur, leading to a new idea or state of affairs (the "synthesis"). This process is known as the dialectic.

Hegel believed that we can never experience things in the world as they are, but only as they appear to us. For him, existence primarily consists of mind or spirit, so the journey of history, through countless cycles of the dialectic, is essentially the progress of spirit, or *Geist*, towards a state of absolute harmony. But it is here that Hegel and Marx part company. Marx insists that the process is not a journey of spiritual development, but of real historical change. Marx claims that the final, conflict-free state that lies at the end of the process is not the spiritual bliss that Hegel predicted, but the perfect society, where everyone works harmoniously towards the good of a greater whole.

The formation of classes

In earlier ages, humans had been entirely responsible for producing everything they needed – such as clothing, food, and habitation – for themselves, but as the early societies began to form, people came to rely more on one another. This led to the form of "bargain making" described by the Scottish economist and philosopher Adam Smith, as people exchanged goods or labour. Marx agrees with Smith that this system of exchange led people to specialize in their labour, but he points out that this new specialization (or "job") had also come to define them. Whatever a person's specialization or job, be it agricultural labourer or hereditary landowner, it had come to dictate where he or she lived, what they ate, and what they wore; it also dictated with whom in society they shared interests, and with whom their interests lay in conflict. Over time, this led to the formation of distinct socio-economic classes, locked into conflict.

According to Marx, there have been four major stages in human history, which he sees as based on four different forms of property ownership: the original tribal system of common property; the

> The ruling ideas of each age have ever been the ideas of its ruling class.
> **Karl Marx**

ancient communal and state system of ownership (where both slavery and private property began); the feudal or estate system of property; and the modern system of capitalist production. Each of these stages represents a different form of economic system, or "mode of production", and the transitions between them are marked in history by stormy political events, such as wars and revolutions, as one ruling class is displaced by another. *The Communist Manifesto* popularized the idea that through understanding the system of property ownership in any one society, in any particular era, we can acquire the key to understanding its social relations.

Rise of cultural institutions

Marx also believes that an analysis of the economic basis of any society allows us to see that as its system of property alters, so too do its "superstructures" – such as its politics, laws, art, religions, and

The wealthy bourgeoisie enjoyed the luxuries of life in the late 18th and 19th centuries, while the workers in their companies and on their estates endured terrible poverty.

> The abolition of religion as the illusory happiness of the people is required for real happiness.
> **Karl Marx**

philosophies. These develop to serve the interests of the ruling class, promoting its values and interests, and diverting attention away from political realities. However, even this ruling class is not, in fact, determining events or institutions. Hegel had said that every age is held in the sway of the *Zeitgeist*, or spirit of the age, and Marx agrees. But where Hegel saw the *Zeitgeist* as determined by an Absolute Spirit developing over time, Marx sees it as defined by the social and economic relations of an era. These define the ideas or "consciousness" of individuals and societies. In Marx's view, people do not make a stamp on their era, moulding it into a particular shape; the era defines the people.

Marx's revision of Hegel's philosophy from a journey of spirit to one of social and economic modes of production was also influenced by another German philosopher, Ludwig Feuerbach. Feuerbach believed that traditional religion is intellectually false – it is not corroborated in any way by reasoning – and that it contributes to the general sum of human misery. He claimed that people make gods in their own image from an amalgamation of humanity's greatest virtues, and then cling to these gods and invented religions, preferring their "dreams" to the real world. People become alienated from themselves, through an unfavourable comparison of their selves to a god that they have forgotten they created.

Marx agrees that people cling to religion because they long for a place in which the self is not despised or alienated, but he says that this is not due to some authoritarian god, but to material facts in their actual, daily lives. The answer for Marx lies not only in the end of religion, but in total social and political change.

A Marxist utopia

In addition to its general account of human history leading to the rise of the bourgeois and proletarian classes, *The Communist Manifesto* makes a variety of other claims about politics, society, and economics. For example, it argues that the capitalist system is not merely exploitative, but also inherently financially unstable, leading to the recurrence of increasingly severe commercial crises, the growing poverty of the workforce, and the emergence of the proletariat as the one genuinely revolutionary class. For the first time in history, this revolutionary class would represent the vast majority of humanity.

These developments are seen as underpinned by the increasingly complex nature of the process of production. Marx predicted that as technology improved, it would lead to increasing unemployment, alienating more and more people from the means of production. This would split society in two, between the large numbers of impoverished people and the few who owned and controlled the means of production. Following the rules of the dialectic, this conflict would result in a violent revolution to establish a new, classless society. This would »

The Industrial Revolution saw the formalization of specialized skills into paid employment. People then formed into groups, or classes, made up of those with similar socio-economic status.

Socialist-inspired revolutions swept through Europe just after the publication of *The Communist Manifesto*. These included the February Revolution of 1848 in Paris.

be the utopian, conflict-free society that marked the end of the dialectic. Marx thought this perfect society would not require government, but only administration, and this would be carried out by the leaders of the revolution: the communist "party" (by which he means those who adhered to the cause, rather than any specific organization). Within this new kind of state (which Marx called the "dictatorship of the proletariat") people would enjoy genuine democracy and social ownership of wealth. Shortly after this final change in the mode of production to a perfect society, Marx predicted, political power as it had previously been understood would come to an end, because there would be no good reason for political dissent or criminality.

Political power

Marx predicted that the outcome of the intense class struggles in Europe between the bourgeoisie and the wage-earning working class would become evident only when the great mass of people had become property-less and were obliged to sell their labour for wages. The juxtaposition of poverty with the great wealth of the few would become increasingly obvious, he thought, and communism would become increasingly attractive.

However, Marx did not expect the opponents of communism to give up their privileges easily. In every period of history, the ruling class has enjoyed the advantage of controlling both the government and the law as a way of reinforcing their economic dominance. The modern state, he said, was actually a "committee for managing the affairs of the bourgeois class", and struggles by excluded groups to have their own interests taken into account – such as the battle to extend the right to vote – were simply short-term ways in which the more fundamental economic conflict

found expression. Marx saw political interests and parties as merely vehicles for the economic interests of the ruling classes, which were forced to appear as though they were acting in the general interest in order to gain and maintain power.

The road to revolution

Marx's originality lies in his combination of pre-existing ideas rather than the creation of new ones. His system uses insights from German idealist philosophers, especially Georg Hegel and Ludwig Feuerbach; from French political theorists, such as Jean-Jacques Rousseau; and from British political economists, particularly Adam Smith. Socialism had become a recognized political doctrine in the first half of the 19th century, and from this Marx derives several insights about property, class, exploitation, and commercial crises.

Class conflict was certainly in the air when Marx composed the *Manifesto*. It was written just before a succession of revolutions

> A spectre is haunting Europe – the spectre of communism.
> **Karl Marx**

against the monarchies of many continental European countries broke out in 1848 and 1849. In the preceding decades, a significant number of people had migrated from the countryside to the towns in search of work, although continental Europe had not yet seen the industrial development that had taken place in Britain. A wave of discontent felt by the poor against the status quo was exploited by a variety of liberal and nationalist politicians, and revolutions rippled across Europe, although ultimately these uprisings were defeated and led to little permanent change.

However, the *Manifesto* acquired an iconic status during the 20th century, inspiring revolutions in Russia, China, and many other countries. The brilliance of Marx's theories has been proved wrong in practice: the extent of repression in Stalinist Russia, in Mao Zedong's China, and in Pol Pot's Cambodia, has widely discredited his political and historical theories.

Criticism of Marxism

Although Marx did not foresee communism being implemented in such a barbaric manner in these primarily agricultural societies, his

Marxist states of the 20th century promoted themselves as utopias. They produced a proliferation of paintings and statues glorifying the achievements of their happy, newly liberated citizens.

ideas are nevertheless still open to a variety of criticisms. First, Marx always argued for the inevitability of revolution. This was the essential part of the dialectic, but it is clearly too simplistic, as human creativity is always able to produce a variety of choices, and the dialectic fails to allow for the possibility of improvement by gradual reform.

Second, Marx tended to invest the proletariat with wholly good attributes, and to suggest that a communist society would give rise somehow to a new type of human being. He never explained how the dictatorship of this perfect proletariat would be different from earlier, brutal forms of dictatorship, nor how it would avoid the corrupting effects of power.

Third, Marx rarely discussed the possibility that new threats to liberty might emerge after a successful revolution; he assumed that poverty was the only real cause of criminality. His critics have also alleged that he did not sufficiently understand the forces of nationalism, and that he gave no proper account of the role of personal leadership in politics. In fact, the 20th-century communist movement was to produce immensely powerful personality cults in virtually every country in which communists came to power.

Lasting influence

Despite the criticism and crises that Marx's theories have provoked, his ideas have been hugely influential. As a powerful critic of commercial capitalism, and as an economic and socialist theorist, Marx is still considered relevant to politics and economics today. Many would agree with the 20th-century Russian-British philosopher, Isaiah Berlin, that the *The Communist Manifesto* is "a work of genius". ∎

Karl Marx

The most famous revolutionary thinker of the 19th century was born in the German city of Trier. The son of a Jewish lawyer who had converted to Christianity, Marx studied law at Bonn University, where he met his future wife, Jenny von Westphalen. He then studied at the University of Berlin, before working as a journalist. The favour he bestowed on democracy in his writing led to censorship by the Prussian royal family, and he was forced into exile in France and Belgium. During this time he developed a unique theory of communism in collaboration with his German compatriot Friedrich Engels.

Marx returned to Germany during the 1848–49 revolutions, but after they were quashed he lived in exile in London for the rest of his life. He and his wife lived in extreme poverty, and when Marx died stateless at the age of 64, there were only 11 mourners at his funeral.

Key works

1846 *The German Ideology*
1847 *The Poverty of Philosophy*
1848 *The Communist Manifesto*
1867 *Das Kapital: Volume 1*

MUST THE CITIZEN EVER RESIGN HIS CONSCIENCE TO THE LEGISLATOR?
HENRY DAVID THOREAU (1817–1862)

IN CONTEXT

BRANCH
Political philosophy

APPROACH
Non-conformism

BEFORE
c.340 BCE Aristotle claims that the city-state is more important than the individual.

1651 Thomas Hobbes says that society without strong government reverts to anarchy.

1762 In *The Social Contract,* Jean-Jacques Rousseau proposes government by the will of the people.

AFTER
1907 Mahatma Gandhi cites Thoreau as an influence on his campaign of passive resistance in South Africa.

1964 Martin Luther King is awarded the Nobel Peace Prize for his campaign to end racial discrimination through civil disobedience and non-cooperation.

Almost a century after Jean-Jacques Rousseau claimed that nature was essentially benign, American philosopher Henry Thoreau developed the idea further, arguing that "all good things are wild and free", and that the laws of man suppress rather than protect civil liberties. He saw that political parties were necessarily one-sided, and that their policies often ran contrary to our moral beliefs. For this reason, he believed it was the individual's duty to protest against unjust laws, and argued that passively allowing such laws to be enacted effectively gave them justification. "Any fool can make a rule, and any fool will mind it," as he said about English grammar, but the principle runs through his political philosophy too.

In his essay *Civil Disobedience,* written in 1849, Thoreau proposes a citizen's right to conscientious objection through non-cooperation and non-violent resistance – which he put into practice by refusing to pay taxes that supported the war in Mexico and perpetuated slavery.

Thoreau's ideas contrasted sharply with those of his contemporary Karl Marx, and with the revolutionary spirit in Europe at the time, which called for violent action. But they were later adopted by numerous leaders of resistance movements, such as Mahatma Gandhi and Martin Luther King. ∎

Mahatma Gandhi's campaign of civil disobedience against British rule in India included the Salt March of 1930, undertaken in protest against unjust laws controlling salt production.

See also: Jean-Jacques Rousseau 154–59 ▪ Adam Smith 160–63 ▪ Edmund Burke 172–73 ▪ Karl Marx 196–203 ▪ Isaiah Berlin 280–81 ▪ John Rawls 294–95

CONSIDER WHAT EFFECTS THINGS HAVE
CHARLES SANDERS PEIRCE (1839–1914)

IN CONTEXT

BRANCH
Epistemology

APPROACH
Pragmatism

BEFORE
17th century John Locke challenges rationalism by tracing the origin of our ideas to sense impressions.

18th century Immanuel Kant argues that speculation about what lies beyond our experience is meaningless.

AFTER
1890s William James and John Dewey take up the philosophy of pragmatism.

1920s Logical positivists in Vienna formulate the theory of verification – that the meaning of a statement is the method by which it is verified.

1980s Richard Rorty's version of pragmatism argues that the very notion of truth can be dispensed with.

C harles Sanders Peirce was the scientist, logician, and philosopher of science who pioneered the philosophical movement known as pragmatism. Deeply sceptical of metaphysical ideas – such as the idea that there is a "real" world beyond the world we experience – he once asked his readers to consider what is wrong with the following theory: a diamond is actually soft, and only becomes hard when it is touched.

Peirce argued that there is "no falsity" in such thinking, for there is no way of disproving it. However, he claimed that the meaning of a concept (such as "diamond" or "hard") is derived from the object or quality that the concept relates to – and the effects it has on our senses. Whether we think of the diamond as "soft until touched" or "always hard" before our experience, therefore, is irrelevant. Under both theories the diamond feels the same, and can be used in exactly the same way. However, the first theory is far more difficult to work with, and so is of less value to us.

This idea, that the meaning of a concept is the sensory effect of its object, is known as the pragmatic maxim, and it became the founding principle of pragmatism – the belief that the "truth" is the account of reality that works best for us.

One of the key things Peirce was trying to accomplish was to show that many debates in science, philosophy, and theology are meaningless. He claimed that they are often debates about words, rather than reality, because they are debates in which no effect on the senses can be specified. ∎

Nothing is vital for science; nothing can be.
Charles Sanders Peirce

See also: John Locke 130–33 ▪ Immanuel Kant 164–71 ▪ William James 206–09 ▪ John Dewey 228–31 ▪ Richard Rorty 314–19

ACT AS IF WHAT YOU DO MAKES A DIFFERENCE

WILLIAM JAMES (1842–1910)

IN CONTEXT

BRANCH
Epistemology

APPROACH
Pragmatism

BEFORE
1843 John Stuart Mill's
A System of Logic studies the
ways in which we come to
believe something is true.

1870s Charles Sanders Peirce
describes his new pragmatist
philosophy in *How to Make
Our Ideas Clear*.

AFTER
1907 Henri Bergson's *Creative
Evolution* describes reality as a
flow rather than a state.

1921 Bertrand Russell explores
reality as pure experience in
The Analysis of Mind.

1925 John Dewey develops a
personal version of pragmatism,
known as "instrumentalism",
in *Experience and Nature*.

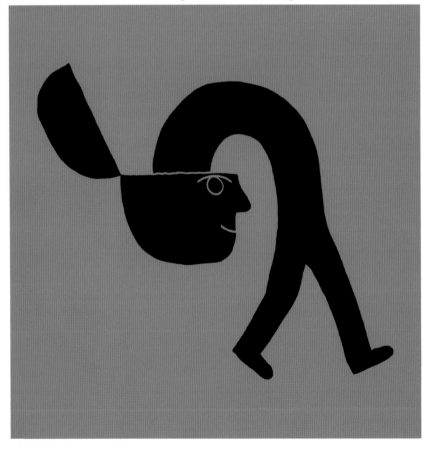

O ver the course of the 19th
century, as the United
States began to find its
feet as an independent nation,
philosophers from New England
such as Henry David Thoreau and
Ralph Waldo Emerson gave a
recognizably American slant to
European Romantic ideas. But it
was the following generation of
philosophers, who lived almost a
century after the Declaration of
Independence, that came up with
something truly original.

The first of these, Charles
Sanders Peirce, proposed a theory
of knowledge he called pragmatism,
but his work was hardly noticed at
the time; it fell to his lifelong friend

See also: John Stuart Mill 190–93 ▪ Charles Sanders Peirce 205 ▪ Henri Bergson 226–27 ▪ John Dewey 228–31 ▪
Bertrand Russell 236–39 ▪ Ludwig Wittgenstein 246–51 ▪ Richard Rorty 314–19

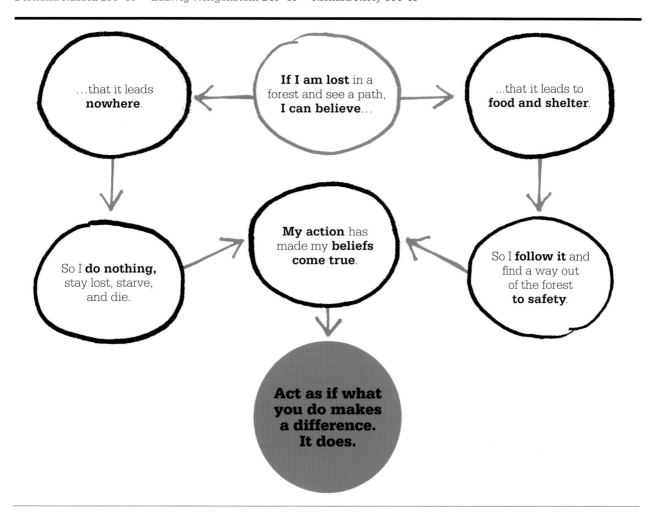

William James – godson to Ralph Emerson – to champion Peirce's ideas and develop them further.

Truth and usefulness

Central to Peirce's pragmatism was the theory that we do not acquire knowledge simply by observing, but by doing, and that we rely on that knowledge only so long as it is useful, in the sense that it adequately explains things for us. When it no longer fulfils that function, or better explanations make it redundant, we replace it. For example, we can see by looking back in history how our ideas about the world have changed constantly, from thinking that Earth is flat to knowing it to be round; from assuming that Earth is the centre of the universe, to realizing that it is just one planet in a vast cosmos. The older assumptions worked perfectly adequately as explanations in their time, yet they are not true, and the universe itself has not changed. This demonstrates how knowledge as an explanatory tool is different from facts. Peirce examined the nature of knowledge in this way, but James was to apply this reasoning to the notion of truth. »

Every way of classifying a thing is but a way of handling it for some particular purpose.
William James

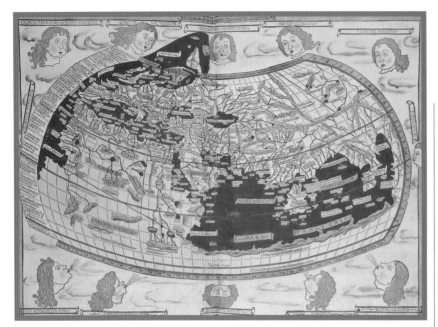

The idea of a flat Earth served well as a "truth" for several thousand years, despite the fact that Earth is a sphere. James claims that an idea's usefulness determines its truthfulness.

James also thinks that belief in an idea is an important factor in choosing to act upon it, and in this way belief is a part of the process that makes an idea true. If I am faced with a difficult decision, my belief in a particular idea will lead to a particular course of action and so contribute to its success. It is because of this that James defines "true beliefs" as those that prove useful to the believer. Again, he is careful to distinguish these from facts, which he says "are not true. They simply are. Truth is the function of the beliefs that start and terminate among them."

For James, the truth of an idea depends on how useful it is; that is to say, whether or not it does what is required of it. If an idea does not contradict the known facts – such as laws of science – and it does provide a means of predicting things accurately enough for our purposes, he says there can be no reason not to consider it true, in the same way that Peirce considered knowledge as a useful tool irrespective of the facts.

This interpretation of truth not only distinguishes it from fact, but also leads James to propose that "the truth of an idea is not a stagnant property inherent in it. Truth *happens* to an idea. It becomes true, is made true by events. Its verity is in fact an event, a process." Any idea, if acted upon, is found to be true by the action we take; putting the idea into practice is the process by which it becomes true.

The right to believe
Every time we try to establish a new belief, it would be useful if we had all the available evidence and the time to make a considered decision. But in much of life we do not have that luxury; either there is not enough time to examine the known facts, or there is not enough

---

William James

Born in New York City, William James was brought up in a wealthy and intellectual family; his father was a famously eccentric theologian, and his brother Henry became a well-known author. During his childhood he lived for several years in Europe, where he pursued a love of painting, but at the age of 19 he abandoned this to study science. His studies at Harvard Medical School were interrupted by the ill health and depression that were to prevent him from ever practising medicine, but he eventually graduated and in 1872 took a teaching post in

physiology at Harvard University. His increasing interest in the subjects of psychology and philosophy led him to write acclaimed publications in these fields, and he was awarded a professorship in philosophy at Harvard in 1880. He taught there until his retirement in 1907.

Key works

1890 *The Principles of Psychology*
1896 *The Will to Believe*
1902 *The Varieties of Religious Experience*
1907 *Pragmatism*

evidence, and we are forced to a decision. We have to rely on our beliefs to guide our actions, and James says that we have "the right to believe" in these cases.

James explains this by taking the example of a man lost and starving in a forest. When he sees a path, it is important for him to believe that the path will lead him out of the forest and to habitation, because if he does not believe it, he will not take the path, and will remain lost and starving. But if he does, he will save himself. By acting on his idea that the path will lead him to safety, it becomes true. In this way our actions and decisions make our belief in an idea become true. This is why James asserts "act as if what you do makes a difference" – to which he adds the typically concise and good-humoured rider, "it does".

We must, however, approach this idea with caution: a shallow interpretation of what James is

Religious belief can bring about extraordinary changes in people's lives, such as the healing of the sick at places of pilgrimage. This occurs regardless of whether or not a god actually exists.

saying could give the impression that any belief, no matter how outlandish, could become true by acting upon it – which of course is not what he meant. There are certain conditions that an idea must fulfil before it can be considered a justifiable belief. The available evidence must weigh in its favour, and the idea must be sufficient to withstand criticism. In the process of acting upon the belief, it must continually justify itself by its usefulness in increasing our understanding or predicting results. And even then, it is only in retrospect that we can safely say that the belief has become true through our acting upon it.

Reality as a process

James was a psychologist as well as a philosopher, and he sees the implications of his ideas in terms of human psychology as much as in the theory of knowledge. He recognized the psychological necessity for humans to hold certain beliefs, particularly religious ones. James thinks that while it is not justifiable as a fact, belief in a god is useful to its believer if it allows him or her to lead a more fulfilled life, or to overcome the fear of death. These things – a more fulfilled life and a fearless confrontation of death – become true; they happen as the result of a belief, and the decisions and actions based upon it.

Along with his pragmatic notion of truth, and very much connected with it, James proposes a type of metaphysics that he calls "radical empiricism". This approach takes reality to be a dynamic, active process, in the same way that truth is a process. Like the traditional empiricists before him, James rejected the rationalist notion that the changing world is in some way unreal, but he also went further to

The pragmatic method means looking away from principles and looking towards consequences.
William James

state that "for pragmatism, [reality] is still in the making", as truth is constantly being made to happen. This "stream" of reality, he believes, is not susceptible to empirical analysis either, both because it is in continual flux and because the act of observing it affects the truth of the analysis. In James's radical empiricism, from which both mind and matter are formed, the ultimate stuff of reality is pure experience.

Continuing influence

Pragmatism, proposed by Peirce and expounded by James, established America as a significant centre for philosophical thought in the 20th century. James's pragmatic interpretation of truth influenced the philosophy of John Dewey, and spawned a "neopragmatist" school of thought in America that includes philosophers such as Richard Rorty. In Europe, Bertrand Russell and Ludwig Wittgenstein were indebted to James's metaphysics. His work in psychology was equally influential, and often intimately connected with his philosophy, notably his concept of the "stream of consciousness", which in turn influenced writers such as Virginia Woolf and James Joyce. ■

THE MOD

WORLD

1900–1950

ERN

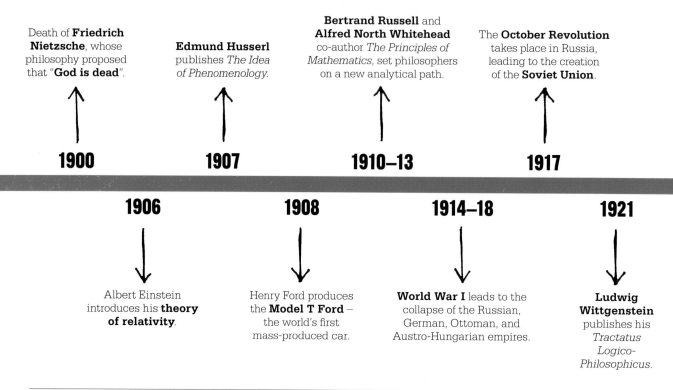

Death of **Friedrich Nietzsche**, whose philosophy proposed that "**God is dead**".

1900

Edmund Husserl publishes *The Idea of Phenomenology*.

1907

Bertrand Russell and **Alfred North Whitehead** co-author *The Principles of Mathematics*, set philosophers on a new analytical path.

1910–13

The **October Revolution** takes place in Russia, leading to the creation of the **Soviet Union**.

1917

1906

Albert Einstein introduces his **theory of relativity**.

1908

Henry Ford produces the **Model T Ford** – the world's first mass-produced car.

1914–18

World War I leads to the collapse of the Russian, German, Ottoman, and Austro-Hungarian empires.

1921

Ludwig Wittgenstein publishes his *Tractatus Logico-Philosophicus*.

Towards the end of the 19th century, philosophy once again reached a turning point. Science, and particularly Charles Darwin's theory of evolution (1859), had thrown into doubt the idea of the universe as God's creation, with humankind as the peak of his creative genius. Moral and political philosophy had become entirely human-centred, with Karl Marx declaring religion "the opiate of the people". Following in the footsteps of Arthur Schopenhauer, Friedrich Nietzsche believed that Western philosophy, with its roots in Greek and Judaeo-Christian traditions, was ill-equipped to explain this modern world view. He proposed a radical new approach to finding meaning in life, one that involved casting aside old values and

traditions. In doing so, he set the agenda for much of the philosophy of the 20th century.

A new analytical tradition

To some extent, the traditional concerns of philosophy – such as asking what exists – were answered by science in the early 20th century. Albert Einstein's theories offered a more detailed explanation of the nature of the universe, and Sigmund Freud's psychoanalytic theories gave people a radically new insight into the workings of the mind.

As a result, philosophers turned their attention to questions of moral and political philosophy or, since philosophy had become the province of professional academics, to the more abstract business of logic and linguistic analysis. At the vanguard of this movement of logical

analysis – which became known as analytic philosophy – was the work of Gottlob Frege, who linked the philosophical process of logic with mathematics. His ideas were enthusiastically received by a British philosopher and mathematician, Bertrand Russell.

Russell applied the principles of logic that Frege had outlined to a thorough analysis of mathematics in the *Principia Mathematica*, which he wrote with Alfred North Whitehead, and then – in a move that revolutionized philosophical thinking – he applied the same principles to language. The process of linguistic analysis was to become the major theme in 20th century British philosophy.

One of Russell's pupils, Ludwig Wittgenstein, developed Russell's work on logic and language, but

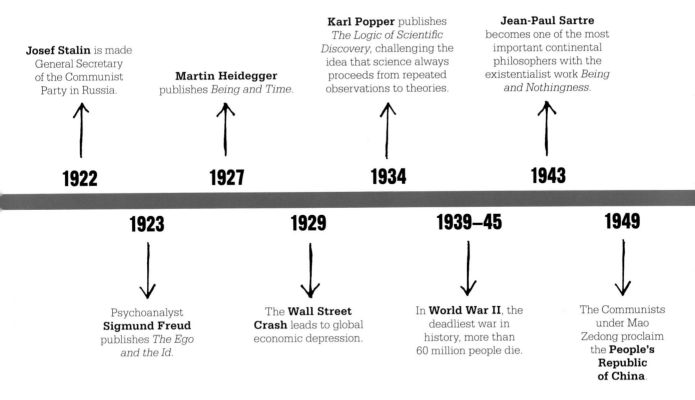

Josef Stalin is made General Secretary of the Communist Party in Russia.

1922

Martin Heidegger publishes *Being and Time*.

1927

Karl Popper publishes *The Logic of Scientific Discovery*, challenging the idea that science always proceeds from repeated observations to theories.

1934

Jean-Paul Sartre becomes one of the most important continental philosophers with the existentialist work *Being and Nothingness*.

1943

1923

Psychoanalyst **Sigmund Freud** publishes *The Ego and the Id*.

1929

The **Wall Street Crash** leads to global economic depression.

1939–45

In **World War II**, the deadliest war in history, more than 60 million people die.

1949

The Communists under Mao Zedong proclaim the **People's Republic of China**.

---

also made key contributions in areas as diverse as perception, ethics, and aesthetics, becoming one of the greatest thinkers of the 20th century. Another, slightly younger Viennese philosopher, Karl Popper, took his cue from Einstein, and strengthened the link between scientific thinking and philosophy.

Meanwhile, in Germany, philosophers rose to the challenge posed by Nietzsche's ideas with a philosophy based on the experience of the individual in a godless universe: existentialism. Edmund Husserl's phenomenology (the study of experience) laid the groundwork, and this was carried forward by Martin Heidegger, who was also greatly influenced by the Danish philosopher, Søren Kierkegaard. Heidegger's work, produced in the 1920s and 30s, was largely rejected in the mid-20th century due to his connections with the Nazi party during World War II, but his works were key to the development of existentialism, and were important to late 20th-century culture.

Wars and revolutions
Philosophy was as affected by the massive political upheavals of the 20th century as any other cultural activity, but it also contributed to the ideologies that shaped the modern world. The revolution that formed the Soviet Union in the 1920s had its roots in Marxism, a 19th-century political philosophy. This theory became more prevalent globally than any single religion, dominating the policy of China's Communist Party until around 1982, and replacing traditional philosophies across Asia.

Liberal democracies in Europe during the 1930s were threatened by fascism, forcing many thinkers to flee from the continent to Britain and the US. Philosophers turned their attention to left-wing or liberal politics in reaction to the oppression they experienced under totalitarian regimes. World War II and the Cold War that followed it coloured the moral philosophy of the second half of the 20th century.

In France, existentialism was made fashionable by Jean-Paul Sartre, Simone de Beauvoir, and Albert Camus, who were all novelists. This trend was in keeping with the French view of philosophy as part of an essentially literary culture. It was also fundamental to the direction that continental philosophy was to take in the last decades of the 20th century. ∎

MAN
IS SOMETHING TO BE
SURPASSED
FRIEDRICH NIETZSCHE (1844–1900)

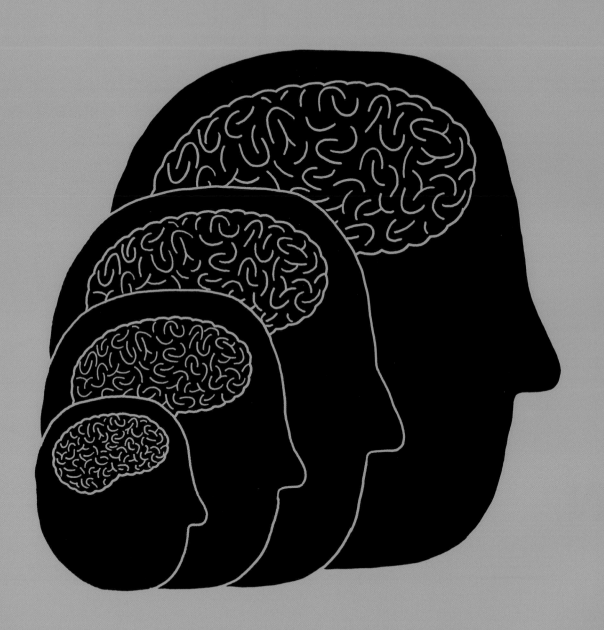

IN CONTEXT

BRANCH
Ethics

APPROACH
Existentialism

BEFORE
380 BCE Plato explores the
distinction between reality
and appearance in his
dialogue, *The Republic*.

1st century CE *The Sermon
on the Mount*, in Matthew's
gospel in the Bible, advocates
turning away from this world
to the greater reality of the
world to come.

1781 Immanuel Kant's *Critique
of Pure Reason* argues that we
can never know how the world
is "in itself".

AFTER
1930s Nietzsche's work is
used to help construct the
mythology of Nazism.

1966 Michel Foucault's *The
Order of Things* discusses
the overcoming of "man".

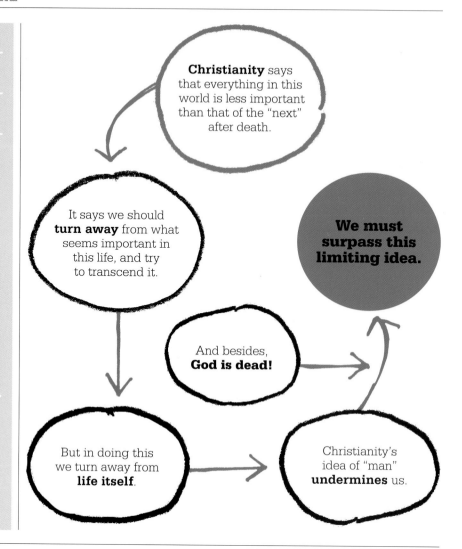

Christianity says that everything in this world is less important than that of the "next" after death.

It says we should **turn away** from what seems important in this life, and try to transcend it.

We must surpass this limiting idea.

And besides, **God is dead!**

But in doing this we turn away from **life itself**.

Christianity's idea of "man" **undermines** us.

Nietzsche's idea that man
is something to be
surpassed appears in
Thus Spoke Zarathustra, perhaps
his most famous book. It was
written in three parts in 1883–84,
with a fourth part added in 1885.
The German philosopher used it
to launch a sustained attack on
the history of Western thought.
He targets three linked ideas in
particular: first, the idea we
have of "man" or human nature;
second, the idea we have of God;
and third, the ideas we have about
morality, or ethics.

Elsewhere Nietzsche writes about
philosophizing "with a hammer",
and here he certainly attempts to
shatter many of the most cherished
views of the Western philosophical
tradition, especially in relation to
these three things. He does so in a
style that is astonishingly hot-headed
and fevered, so that at times the
book seems closer to prophecy than
philosophy. It was written quickly,
with Part I taking him only a few
days to set down on paper. Even so,
while Nietzsche's book does not
have the calm, analytical tone that
people have perhaps come to

expect of philosophical works, the
author still succeeds in setting out
a remarkably consistent and hugely
challenging vision.

Zarathustra descends
The name of Nietzsche's prophet,
Zarathustra, is an alternative name
for the ancient Persian prophet
Zoroaster. The book begins by
telling us that at the age of 30,
Zarathustra goes to live in the
mountains. For ten years he
delights in the solitude, but one
dawn, he wakes to find that he is
weary of the wisdom he has

See also: Plato 50–55 ▪ Immanuel Kant 164–71 ▪ Søren Kierkegaard 194–95 ▪ Albert Camus 284–85 ▪ Michel Foucault 302–03 ▪ Jacques Derrida 308–13

accumulated alone on the mountain. So he decides to descend to the market place to share this wisdom with the rest of humankind.

On the way down to the town, at the foot of the hill, he meets with an old hermit. The two men have already met, ten years before, when Zarathustra first ascended the mountain. The hermit sees that Zarathustra has changed during the past decade: when he climbed the mountain, the hermit says, Zarathustra carried ashes; but now, as he descends, he is carrying fire.

Then the hermit asks Zarathustra a question: why are you going to the trouble of sharing your wisdom? He advises Zarathustra to stay in the mountains, warning him that nobody will understand his message. Zarathustra then asks a question: what does the hermit do in the mountains? The hermit replies that he sings, weeps, laughs, mumbles, and praises God. On hearing this, Zarathustra himself laughs. Then he wishes the hermit well and continues on his way down the mountain. As he goes,

Zarathustra says to himself, "How can it be possible! This old hermit has not yet heard that God is dead."

Behold the Superman

The idea of the death of God may be the most famous of all Nietzsche's ideas, and it is closely related both to the idea that man is something to be surpassed and to Nietzsche's distinctive understanding of morality. The relationship between these things becomes clear as the story of Zarathustra continues.

When he reaches the town, Zarathustra sees that there is a crowd gathered around a tightrope walker who is about to perform, and he joins them. Before the acrobat has a chance to walk across his rope, Zarathustra stands up. It is at this point that he says, "Behold! I teach you the Superman!" He continues by telling the crowd the real point he wishes to convey: "Man is something to surpassed...". Zarathustra follows this with a long speech, but when he gets to the end, the crowd only laughs, imagining that the prophet is »

The prophet Zoroaster (c.628–551 BCE), also known as Zarathustra, founded a religion based on the struggle between good and evil. Nietzsche's Zarathustra places himself "beyond good and evil".

Friedrich Nietzsche

Nietzsche was born in Prussia in 1844 to a religious family; his father, uncle, and grandfathers were all Lutheran ministers. His father and younger brother died when he was a young child, and he was brought up by his mother, grandmother, and two aunts. At the age of 24 he became a professor at Basel University, where he met the composer Richard Wagner, who influenced him strongly until Wagner's anti-semitism forced Nietzsche to end their friendship. In 1870 he contracted diphtheria and dysentery, and thereafter suffered continual ill health. He

was forced to resign his professorship in 1879, and for the next ten years travelled in Europe. In 1889 he collapsed in the street while attempting to prevent a horse from being whipped, and suffered some form of mental breakdown from which he never recovered. He died in 1900 aged 56.

Key works

1872 *The Birth of Tragedy*
1883–85 *Thus Spoke Zarathustra*
1886 *Beyond Good and Evil*
1888 *Twilight of the Idols*

just another showman, or perhaps even a warm-up performer for the tightrope-walker.

In opening his book in this unusual way, Nietzsche seems to be betraying his own unease with the reception that his philosophy will receive, as if he is afraid that he will be seen as a philosophical showman without anything real to say. If we want to avoid making the same mistake as the crowd gathered around Zarathustra, and actually understand what Nietzsche is saying, it is necessary to explore some of Nietzsche's core beliefs.

Overturning old values

Nietzsche believes that certain concepts have become inextricably entangled: humankind, morality, and God. When his character Zarathustra says that God is dead, he is not simply launching an attack upon religion, but doing something much bolder. "God" here does not only mean the god that philosophers talk about or the religious pray to; it means the sum

total of the higher values that we might hold. The death of God is not just the death of a deity; it is also the death of all the so-called higher values that we have inherited.

One of the central purposes of Nietzsche's philosophy is what he calls the "revaluation of all values", an attempt to call into question all of the ways that we are accustomed to thinking about ethics and the meanings and purposes of life. Nietzsche repeatedly maintains that in doing so he is setting out a philosophy of cheerfulness, which, although it overturns everything we have thought up until now about good and evil, nevertheless seeks to affirm life. He claims that many of the things that we think are "good" are, in fact, ways of limiting, or of turning away from, life.

We may think it is not "good" to make a fool of ourselves in public, and so resist the urge to dance joyfully in the street. We may believe that the desires of the flesh are sinful, and so punish ourselves when they arise. We may stay in

mind-numbing jobs, not because we need to, but because we feel it is our duty to do so. Nietzsche wants to put an end to such life-denying philosophies, so that humankind can see itself in a different way.

Blaspheming against life

After Zarathustra proclaims the coming of the Superman, he swiftly moves to condemn religion. In the past, he says, the greatest blasphemy was to blaspheme against God; but now the greatest blasphemy is to blaspheme against life itself. This is the error that Zarathustra believes he made upon the hillside: in turning away from the world, and in offering up prayers to a God who is not there, he was sinning against life.

The history behind this death of God, or loss of faith in our higher values, is told in Nietzsche's essay, *How the "Real World" at last Became a Myth*, which was published in *Twilight of the Idols*. The essay carries the subtitle "History of an Error", and it is an extraordinarily condensed one-page history of

Man is a rope tied between the animal and the Superman – a rope over an abyss.
Friedrich Nietzsche

Existing between the levels of animal and Superman, human life, Nietzsche says, is "a dangerous wayfaring, a dangerous looking-back, a dangerous trembling and halting".

Western philosophy. The story begins, Nietzsche says, with the Greek philosopher Plato.

The real world

Plato divided the world into an "apparent" world that appears to us through our senses, and a "real" world that we can grasp through the intellect. For Plato, the world we perceive through the senses is not "real" because it is changeable and subject to decay. Plato suggests that there is also an unchanging, permanent "real world" that can be attained with the help of the intellect. This idea comes from Plato's study of mathematics. The form or idea of a triangle, for example, is eternal and can be grasped by the intellect. We know that a triangle is a three-sided, two-dimensional figure whose angles add up to 180°, and that this will always be true, whether anyone is thinking about it or not and however many triangles exist in the world. On the other hand, the triangular things that do exist in the world (such as sandwiches, pyramids, and triangular shapes drawn on a chalkboard), are triangular only insofar as they are reflections of this idea or form of the triangle.

Influenced by mathematics in this way, Plato proposed that the intellect can gain access to a whole world of Ideal Forms, which is permanent and unchanging, whereas the senses have access only to the world of appearances. So, for example, if we want to know about goodness, we need to have an intellectual appreciation of the Form of Goodness, of which the various examples of goodness in the world are only reflections. This is an idea that has had far-reaching consequences for our understanding of the world; not least

Some religions and philosophies insist that a more important "real world" exists elsewhere. Nietzsche sees this as a myth that tragically prevents us from living fully now, in this world.

For Plato, everything in this world, even beauty, is only a "shadow" of Forms in another world.

Christianity sees this life as merely a forerunner to the more important "life after death".

because, as Nietzsche points out, this way of dividing up the world makes the "real world" of the intellect the place where everything of value resides. In contrast, it makes the "apparent world" of the senses a world that is, relatively speaking, unimportant.

Christian values

Nietzsche traces the fortunes of this tendency to split the world into two and finds that the same idea appears within Christian thought. In place of the "real world" of Plato's Forms, Christianity substitutes an alternative "real world"; a future world of heaven that is promised to the virtuous. Nietzsche believes that

Christianity views the world we live in now as somehow less real than heaven, but in this version of the "two worlds" idea the "real world" is attainable, albeit after death and on condition that we follow Christian rules in this life. The present world is devalued, as it is with Plato, except insofar as it acts as a stepping stone to the world beyond. Nietzsche claims that Christianity asks us to deny the present life in favour of the promise of a life to come.

Both the Platonic and Christian versions of the idea that the world is divided into a "real" and an "apparent" one have profoundly affected our thoughts about ourselves. The suggestion that »

The Superman is someone of enormous strength and independence in mind and body; Nietzsche denied any had existed, but named Napoleon, Shakespeare, and Socrates as models.

absolutely unattainable – even to the wise or the virtuous, in this world or the next – then it is "an idea grown useless, superfluous". As a result, it is an idea that we need to do away with. If God is dead, Nietzsche is perhaps the person who stumbles across the corpse; nevertheless, it is Kant whose fingerprints are all over the murder weapon.

Philosophy's longest error
Once we have dispensed with the idea of the "real world", the long-held distinction between the "real world" and the "apparent world" begins to break down. In *How the "Real World" at last Became a Myth*, Nietzsche goes onto explain this as follows: "We have abolished the real world; what world is left? The apparent world, perhaps? … But no! With the real world we have also abolished the apparent world." Nietzsche now sees the beginning of the end of philosophy's "longest error": its infatuation with the distinction between "appearance" and "reality", and the idea of two worlds. The end of this error, Nietzsche writes, is the zenith of mankind – the high point of all humanity. It is at this point – in an essay written six years after *Thus Spake Zarathustra* – that Nietzsche writes "Zarathustra begins".

This is a key moment for Nietzsche because when we grasp the fact that there is only one world, we suddenly see the error that had put all values beyond this world. We are then forced to reconsider all our values and even what it means to be human. And when we see through these philosophical

everything of value in the world is somehow "beyond" the reach of this world leads to a way of thinking that is fundamentally life-denying. As a result of this Platonic and Christian heritage, we have come to see the world we live in as a world that we should resent and disdain, a world from which we should turn away, transcend, and certainly not enjoy. But in doing so, we have turned away from life itself in favour of a myth or an invention, an imagined "real world" that is situated elsewhere. Nietzsche calls priests of all religions "preachers of death", because their teachings encourage us to turn from this world, and from life to death. But why does Nietzsche insist that God is dead? To answer this, we must

look to the work of the 18th-century German philosopher Immanuel Kant, whose ideas are critical to understanding the philosophy behind Nietzsche's work.

A world beyond reach
Kant was interested in the limits of knowledge. In his book *Critique of Pure Reason*, he argued that we cannot know the world as it is "in itself". We cannot attain it with the intellect, as Plato believed; nor is it promised to us after death as in the Christian view. It exists (we assume), but it is forever out of reach. The reasons that Kant uses to come up with this conclusion are complex, but what is important from Nietzsche's point of view is that, if the real world is said to be

illusions, the old idea of "man" can be surpassed. The Superman is Nietzsche's vision of a fundamentally life-affirming way of being. It is one that can become the bearer of meaning not in the world beyond, but here; Superman is "the meaning of the Earth".

Creating ourselves

Nietzsche's writings did not reach a large audience in his lifetime, so much so that he had to pay for the publication of the final part of *Thus Spoke Zarathustra* himself. But around 30 years after his death in 1900, the idea of the Superman fed into the rhetoric of Nazism through Hitler's readings of Nietzsche's work. Nietzsche's ideas about the Superman, and particularly his call for an eradication of the Jewish-Christian morality that held sway throughout Europe would have been attractive to Hitler as validation for his own aims. But where Nietzsche seemed to be searching for a return to the more rustic, life-affirming values of pagan Europe, Hitler took his writings as an excuse for unbridled violence and transgression on a grand scale. The consensus amongst scholars is that Nietzsche himself would have been horrified by this turn of events. Writing in an era of extraordinary nationalism, patriotism, and colonial expansion, Nietzsche was one of the few thinkers to call these assumptions into question. At one point in *Thus Spoke Zarathustra* he makes it clear that he considers nationalism a form of alienation or failure. "Only where the state ends," Zarathustra says, "there begins the human being who is not superfluous".

Nietzsche's open-ended idea of human possibility was important to many philosophers in the period following World War II. His ideas about religion and the importance of self-evaluation can be traced especially in the work of succeeding existentialists such as the French philosopher Jean-Paul Sartre. Like Nietzsche's Superman, Sartre says that we must each define the meaning of our own existence.

The degree of introspection achieved by Nietzsche had never been achieved by anyone.
Sigmund Freud

Nietzsche's damning criticisms of the Western philosophical tradition have had a huge impact not only on philosophy, but also on European and world culture, and they went on to influence countless artists and writers in the 20th century. ∎

Nietzsche's writings were edited and censored by his anti-semitic sister Elizabeth, who controlled his archive after he became insane. This allowed the Nazis to wilfully misinterpret them.

MEN WITH SELF-CONFIDENCE COME AND SEE AND CONQUER

AHAD HA'AM (1856–1927)

IN CONTEXT

BRANCH
Ethics

APPROACH
Cultural Zionism

BEFORE
5th century BCE Socrates combines both confidence and an admission of his own foolishness.

1511 Desiderius Erasmus writes *The Praise of Folly*, a satirical work which appears to praise foolish behaviour.

1711 The English poet Alexander Pope writes that "Fools rush in where angels fear to tread."

1843 In his book *Fear and Trembling*, Søren Kierkegaard writes about founding faith "on the strength of the absurd".

AFTER
1961 Michel Foucault writes *Madness and Civilization*, a philosophical study of the history of folly.

had Ha'am was the pen name of the Ukrainian-born Jewish philosopher Asher Ginzberg, a leading Zionist thinker who advocated a Jewish spiritual renaissance. In 1890 he claimed in a semi-satirical essay that although we worship wisdom, self-confidence matters more.

In any difficult or dangerous situation, he says, the wise are those who hold back, weighing up the advantages and disadvantages of any action. Meanwhile (and greatly to the disapproval of the wise) it is the self-confident who forge ahead, and often win the day. Ha'am wants to suggest – and when reading him we should remember that this is a suggestion that is meant half-seriously and half-satirically – that individual folly can often yield a result, simply because of the self-confidence that goes along with it.

Wisdom and confidence

Although in his original essay Ha'am seemed to celebrate the potential advantages of foolishness, this was a view from which he later distanced himself, perhaps afraid that others might read what was essentially an exercise in satire as if it were written with high-minded seriousness. Self-confidence is only warranted, he later made clear, when the difficulties of an undertaking are fully understood and evaluated.

Ha'am was fond of quoting an old Yiddish proverb: "an act of folly which turns out well is still an act of folly". On some occasions we act foolishly, without fully understanding the difficulties of the task we are undertaking, but we win through because luck is on our side. However, says Ha'am, this does not make our prior foolishness in any way commendable.

If we want our actions to bring results, it may indeed be the case that we need to develop and use the kind of self-confidence that can occasionally be seen in acts of folly. At the same time, we must always temper this self-confidence with wisdom, or our acts will lack true effectiveness in the world. ∎

See also: Socrates 46–49 ▪ Søren Kierkegaard 194–95 ▪ Michel Foucault 302–03 ▪ Luce Irigaray 320

EVERY MESSAGE IS MADE OF SIGNS
FERDINAND DE SAUSSURE (1857–1913)

IN CONTEXT

BRANCH
Philosophy of language

APPROACH
Semiotics

BEFORE
c.400 BCE Plato explores the relationship between names and things.

c.250 BCE Stoic philosophers develop an early theory of linguistic signs.

1632 Portuguese philosopher John Poinsot writes his *Treatise on Signs*.

AFTER
1950s Saussure's analysis of the structures of language influences Noam Chomsky's theory of generative grammar, which aims to expose the rules of a language that govern its possible word combinations.

1960s Roland Barthes explores the literary implications of signs and semiotics.

Saussure was a 19th-century Swiss philosopher who saw language as made up of systems of "signs", with the signs acting as the basic units of the language. His studies formed the basis of a new theory, known as semiotics. This new theory of signs was developed by other philosophers during the 20th century such as Russia's Roman Jakobson, who summed up the semiotic approach when he said that "every message is made of signs".

Saussure said that a sign is made up of two things. Firstly, a "signifier", which is a sound-image. This is not the actual sound, but the mental "image" we have of the sound. Secondly, the "signified", or concept. Here Saussure turns his back on a long tradition that says language is about the relationships between words and things, because he is saying that both aspects of a sign are mental (our concept of a "dog" for example, and a sound-image of the sound "dog"). Saussure claims that any message – for example "my dog is called Fred" – is a system of signs. This means that it is a system of relationships between sound-images and concepts. However, Saussure states that the relationship between the signified and the signifier is arbitrary – so there is nothing particularly "doggy" about the sound "dog", which is why the word can be *chien* in French, or *gou* in Chinese.

Saussure's work on language became the basis of modern linguistics, and influenced many philosophers and literary theorists. ∎

In the lives of individuals and of societies, language is a factor of greater importance than any other.
Ferdinand de Saussure

See also: Plato 50–55 ▪ Charles Sanders Peirce 205 ▪ Ludwig Wittgenstein 246–51 ▪ Roland Barthes 290–91 ▪ Julia Kristeva 323

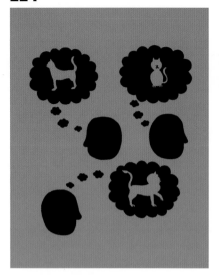

EXPERIENCE BY ITSELF IS NOT SCIENCE
EDMUND HUSSERL (1859–1938)

IN CONTEXT

BRANCH
Ontology

APPROACH
Phenomenology

BEFORE
5th century BCE Socrates uses argument to try to answer philosophical questions with certainty.

17th century René Descartes uses doubt as a starting point for his philosophical method.

1874 Franz Brentano, Husserl's teacher, claims that philosophy needs a new scientific method.

AFTER
From 1920s Martin Heidegger, Husserl's student, develops his teacher's method of phenomenology, leading to the birth of existentialism.

From 1930s Husserl's phenomenology reaches France, influencing thinkers such as Emmanuel Levinas and Maurice Merleau-Ponty.

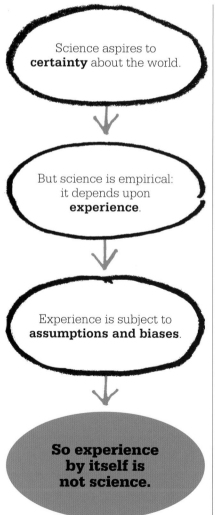

Science aspires to **certainty** about the world.

But science is empirical: it depends upon **experience**.

Experience is subject to **assumptions and biases**.

So experience by itself is not science.

Husserl was a philosopher haunted by a dream that has preoccupied thinkers since the time of the ancient Greek philosopher Socrates: the dream of certainty. For Socrates, the problem was this: although we easily reach agreement on questions about things we can measure (for example, "how many olives are there in this jar?"), when it comes to philosophical questions such as "what is justice?" or "what is beauty?", it seems that there is no clear way of reaching agreement. And if we cannot know for certain what justice is, then how can we say anything about it at all?

The problem of certainty
Husserl was a philosopher who started life as a mathematician. He dreamed that problems such as "what is justice?" might be solved with the same degree of certainty with which we are able to solve mathematical problems such as "how many olives are in the jar?" In other words, he hoped to put all the sciences – by which he meant all branches of human knowledge and activity, from maths, chemistry, and physics to ethics and politics – on a completely secure footing.

See also: René Descartes 116–23 ▪ Franz Brentano 336 ▪ Martin Heidegger 252–55 ▪ Emmanuel Levinas 273 ▪ Maurice Merleau-Ponty 274–75

Scientific theories are based on experience. But Husserl believed that experience alone did not add up to science, because as any scientist knows, experience is full of all kinds of assumptions, biases, and misconceptions. Husserl wanted to drive out all of these uncertainties to give science absolutely certain foundations.

To do this, Husserl made use of the philosophy of the 17th-century philosopher René Descartes. Like Husserl, Descartes wanted to free philosophy from all assumptions, biases, and doubts. Descartes wrote that although almost everything could be doubted, he could not doubt that he was doubting.

Phenomenology

Husserl takes up a similar approach to Descartes, but uses it differently. He suggests that if we adopt a scientific attitude to experience, laying aside every single assumption that we have (even including the assumption that an external world exists outside of us), then we can

Mathematics does not rely on empirical evidence, which is full of assumptions, to reach its conclusions. Husserl wanted to put all science (and all knowledge) on a similar foundation.

We entirely lack a rational science of man and of the human community.
Edmund Husserl

start philosophy with a clean slate, free of all assumptions. Husserl calls this approach phenomenology: a philosophical investigation of the phenomena of experience. We need to look at experience with a scientific attitude, laying to one side (or "bracketing out" as Husserl calls it) every single one of our assumptions. And if we look carefully and patiently enough, we can build a secure foundation of knowledge that might help us deal with the philosophical problems that have been with us since the very beginnings of philosophy.

However, different philosophers following Husserl's method came to different results, and there was little agreement as to what the method actually was, or how one carried it out. Towards the end of his career, Husserl wrote that the dream of putting the sciences on firm foundations was over. But although Husserl's phenomenology failed to provide philosophers with a scientific approach to experience, or to solve philosophy's most enduring problems, it nevertheless gave birth to one of the richest traditions in 20th-century thought. ∎

Edmund Husserl

Husserl was born in 1859 in Moravia, then a part of the Austrian empire. He started his career studying mathematics and astronomy, but after finishing his doctorate in mathematics he decided to take up philosophy.

In 1887 Husserl married Malvine Steinschneider, with whom he had three children. He also became Privatdozent (private lecturer) at Halle, where he remained until 1901. He then accepted an associate professorship at the University of Göttingen, before becoming a professor of philosophy at the University of Freiburg in 1916, where Martin Heidegger was among his students. In 1933, Husserl was suspended from the university on account of his Jewish background, a decision in which Heidegger was implicated. Husserl continued to write until his death in 1938.

Key works

1901 *Logical Investigations*
1907 *The Idea of Phenomenology*
1911 *Philosophy as a Rigorous Science*
1913 *Ideas toward a Pure Phenomenology*

INTUITION GOES IN THE VERY DIRECTION OF LIFE
HENRI BERGSON (1859–1941)

IN CONTEXT

BRANCH
Epistemology

APPROACH
Vitalism

BEFORE
13th century John Duns Scotus distinguishes between intuitive and abstract thought, and claims that intuitive thought takes precedence.

1781 Immanuel Kant publishes *Critique of Pure Reason*, claiming that absolute knowledge is impossible.

AFTER
1890s William James begins to explore the philosophy of everyday experience, popularizing pragmatism.

1927 Alfred North Whitehead writes *Process philosophy*, suggesting that the existence of the natural world should be understood in terms of process and change, not things or fixed stabilities.

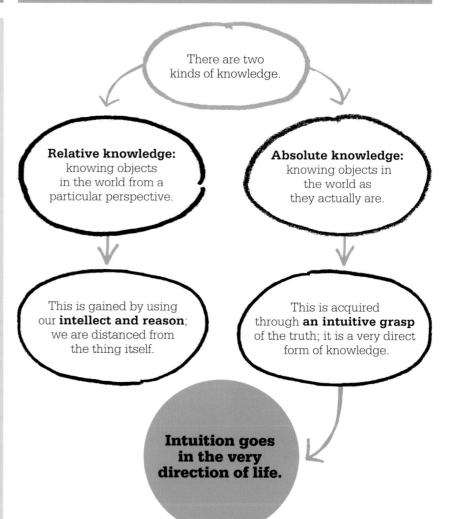

There are two kinds of knowledge.

Relative knowledge: knowing objects in the world from a particular perspective.

Absolute knowledge: knowing objects in the world as they actually are.

This is gained by using our **intellect and reason**; we are distanced from the thing itself.

This is acquired through **an intuitive grasp** of the truth; it is a very direct form of knowledge.

Intuition goes in the very direction of life.

See also: John Duns Scotus 333 ▪ Immanuel Kant 164–71 ▪ William James 206–09 ▪ Alfred North Whitehead 336 ▪ Gilles Deleuze 338

Henri Bergson's 1910 book *Creative Evolution* explored his vitalism, or theory of life. In it, Bergson wanted to discover whether it is possible to really know something – not just to know about it, but to know it as it actually is.

Ever since the philosopher Immanuel Kant published *The Critique of Pure Reason* in 1781, many philosophers have claimed that it is impossible for us to know things as they actually are. This is because Kant showed that we can know how things are relative to we ourselves, given the kinds of minds we have; but we cannot ever step outside of ourselves to achieve an absolute view of the world's actual "things-in-themselves".

Two forms of knowledge

Bergson, however, does not agree with Kant. He says that there are two different kinds of knowledge: relative knowledge, which involves knowing something from our own unique particular perspective; and absolute knowledge, which is knowing things as they actually are. Bergson believes that these are reached by different methods, the first through analysis or intellect, and the second through intuition. Kant's mistake, Bergson believes, is that he does not recognize the full importance of our faculty of intuition, which allows us to grasp an object's uniqueness through direct connection. Our intuition is linked to what Bergson called our *élan vital*, a life-force (vitalism) that interprets the flux of experience in terms of time rather than space.

Suppose you want to get to know a city, he says. You could compile a record of it by taking photographs of every part, from every possible perspective, before reconstructing these images to give some idea of the city as a whole. But you would be grasping it at one remove, not as a living city. If, on the other hand, you were simply to stroll around the streets, paying attention in the right way, you might acquire knowledge of the city itself – a direct knowledge of the city as it actually is. This direct knowledge, for Bergson, is knowledge of the essence of the city.

Capturing the essence of a city, person, or object may only be possible through direct knowledge gained from intuition, not analysis. Bergson says we underestimate the value of our intuition.

But how do we practise intuition? Essentially, it is a matter of seeing the world in terms of our sense of unfolding time. While walking through the city, we have a sense of our own inner time, and we also have an inner sense of the various unfolding times of the city through which we are walking. As these times overlap, Bergson believes that we can make a direct connection with the essence of life itself. ▪

Henri Bergson

Henri Bergson was one of the most influential French philosophers of his time. Born in France in 1859, he was the son of an English mother and a Polish father. His early intellectual interests lay in mathematics, at which he excelled. Despite this, he took up philosophy as a career, initially teaching in schools. When his book *Matter and Memory* was published in 1896, he was elected to the Collège de France and became a university lecturer. He also had a successful political career, and represented the French government during the establishment of the League of Nations in 1920. His work was widely translated and influenced many other philosophers and psychologists, including William James. He was awarded the Nobel Prize for Literature in 1927, and died in 1941 at the age of 81.

Key works

1896 *Matter and Memory*
1903 *An Introduction to Metaphysics*
1907 *Creative Evolution*
1932 *The Two Sources of Morality and Religion*

WE ONLY THINK WHEN WE ARE CONFRONTED WITH PROBLEMS

JOHN DEWEY (1859–1952)

IN CONTEXT

BRANCH
Epistemology

APPROACH
Pragmatism

BEFORE
1859 Charles Darwin's *On the Origin of Species* puts human beings in a new, naturalistic perspective.

1878 Charles Sanders Peirce's essay *How to Make our Ideas Clear* lays the foundations of the pragmatist movement.

1907 William James publishes *Pragmatism: A New Name for Some Old Ways of Thinking*, popularizing the philosophical term "pragmatism".

AFTER
From 1970 Jürgen Habermas applies pragmatic principles to social theory.

1979 Richard Rorty combines pragmatism with analytic philosophy in *Philosophy and the Mirror of Nature*.

John Dewey belongs to the philosophical school known as pragmatism, which arose in the USA in the late 19th century. The founder is generally considered to be the philosopher Charles Sanders Peirce, who wrote a groundbreaking essay in 1878 called *How to Make our Ideas Clear*.

Pragmatism starts from the position that the purpose of philosophy, or "thinking", is not to provide us with a true picture of the world, but to help us to act more effectively within it. If we are taking a pragmatic perspective, we should not be asking "is this the

See also: Heraclitus 40 ▪ Charles Sanders Peirce 205 ▪ William James 206–09 ▪ Jürgen Habermas 306–07 ▪ Richard Rorty 314–19

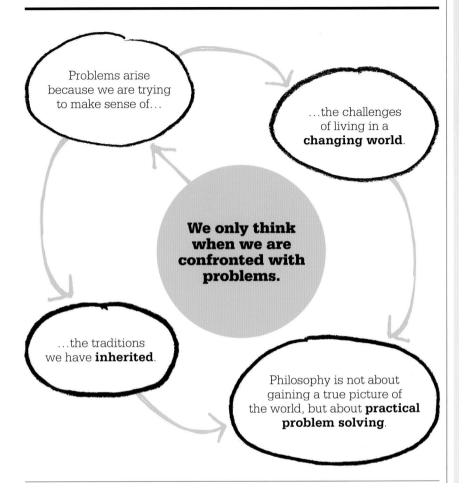

Problems arise because we are trying to make sense of…

…the challenges of living in a **changing world**.

We only think when we are confronted with problems.

…the traditions we have **inherited**.

Philosophy is not about gaining a true picture of the world, but about **practical problem solving**.

John Dewey

John Dewey was born in Vermont, USA, in 1859. He studied at the University of Vermont, and then worked as a schoolteacher for three years before returning to undertake further study in psychology and philosophy. He taught at various leading universities for the remainder of his life, and wrote extensively on a broad range of topics, from education to democracy, psychology, and art. In addition to his work as a scholar, he set up an educational institution – the University of Chicago Laboratory Schools –which put into practice his educational philosophy of learning by doing. This institution is still running today. Dewey's broad range of interests, and his abilities as a communicator, allowed his influence on American public life to extend far beyond the Laboratory Schools. He continued to write about philosophy and social issues until he died in 1952 at the age of 92.

Key works

1910 *How We Think*
1925 *Experience and Nature*
1929 *The Quest for Certainty*
1934 *Art as Experience*

way things are?" but rather, "what are the practical implications of adopting this perspective?"

For Dewey, philosophical problems are not abstract problems divorced from people's lives. He sees them as problems that occur because humans are living beings trying to make sense of their world, struggling to decide how best to act within it. Philosophy starts from our everyday human hopes and aspirations, and from the problems that arise in the course of our lives. This being the case, Dewey thinks that philosophy should also be a way of finding

practical responses to these problems. He believes that philosophizing is not about being a "spectator" who looks at the world from afar, but about actively engaging in the problems of life.

Evolving creatures

Dewey was strongly influenced by the evolutionary thought of the naturalist Charles Darwin, who published *On The Origin of Species* in 1859. Darwin described humans as living creatures who are a part of the natural world. Like the other animals, humans have evolved in response to their changing » environments. For Dewey, one of the implications of Darwin's thought is that it requires us to think of human beings not as fixed essences created by God, but instead as natural beings. We are not souls who belong in some other, non-material world, but evolved organisms who are trying to do our best to survive in a world of which we are inescapably a part.

Everything changes

Dewey also takes from Darwin the idea that nature as a whole is a system that is in a constant state of change; an idea that itself echoes the philosophy of the ancient Greek philosopher Heraclitus. When Dewey comes to think about what philosophical problems are, and how they arise, he takes this insight as a starting point.

Dewey discusses the idea that we only think when confronted with problems in an essay entitled *Kant and the Philosophic Method* (1884). We are, he says, organisms that find ourselves having to respond to a world that is subject to constant change and flux. Existence is a risk, or a gamble, and the world is fundamentally unstable. We depend upon our environment to be able to survive and thrive, but

> We do not solve philosophical problems, we get over them.
> **John Dewey**

the many environments in which we find ourselves are themselves always changing. Not only this, but these environments do not change in a predictable fashion. For several years there may be a good crop of wheat, for instance, but then the harvest fails. A sailor may set sail under fine weather, only to find that a storm suddenly blows up out of nowhere. We are healthy for years, and then disease strikes us when we least expect it.

In the face of this uncertainty, Dewey says that there are two different strategies we can adopt. We can either appeal to higher beings and hidden forces in the universe for help, or we can seek to understand the world and gain control of our environment.

Appeasing the gods

The first of these strategies involves attempting to affect the world by means of magical rites, ceremonies, and sacrifices. This approach to the uncertainty of the world, Dewey believes, forms the basis of both religion and ethics.

In the story that Dewey tells, our ancestors worshipped gods and spirits as a way of trying to ally themselves with the "powers that dispense fortune". This scenario is played out in stories from around the world, in myths and legends such as those about unfortunate seafarers who pray to gods or saints to calm the storm, and thereby survive. In the same way, Dewey believes, ethics arises out of the attempts our ancestors made to appease hidden forces; but where they made sacrifices, we strike bargains with the gods, promising to be good if they spare us from harm.

The alternative response to the uncertainties of our changing world is to develop various techniques of mastering the world, so that we

We no longer employ sacrifice as a way to ask for help from the gods, but many people find themselves offering up a silent promise to be good in return for help from some higher being.

can live in it more easily. We can learn the art of forecasting the weather, and build houses to shelter ourselves from its extremes, and so on. Rather than attempting to ally ourselves with the hidden powers of the universe, this strategy involves finding ways of revealing how our environment works, and then working out how to transform it to our benefit.

Dewey points out that it is important to realize that we can never completely control our environment or transform it to such an extent that we can drive out all uncertainty. At best, he says, we can modify the risky, uncertain nature of the world in which we find ourselves. But life is inescapably risky.

A luminous philosophy

For much of human history, Dewey writes, these two approaches to dealing with the riskiness of life have existed in tension with each other, and they have given rise to two different kinds of knowledge:

Scientific experiments, such as Benjamin Franklin's attempt to harness electricity in the 1740s, help us gain control over the world. Dewey thought philosophy should be equally useful.

He is critical of any philosophical approaches that ultimately make our experience more puzzling, or the world more mysterious. Second, he thinks we should judge a philosophical theory by asking to what extent it succeeds in addressing the problems of living. Is it useful to us, in our everyday lives? Does it, for instance, "yield the enrichment and increase of power" that we have come to expect from new scientific theories?

A practical influence

A number of philosophers, such as Bertrand Russell, have criticized pragmatism by claiming that it has simply given up on the long philosophical quest for truth. Nevertheless, Dewey's philosophy has been enormously influential in America. Given that Dewey places such an overriding emphasis on responding to the practical problems of life, it is perhaps unsurprising that much of his influence has been in practical realms, such as in education and in politics. ∎

Education is not an affair of telling and being told, but an active and constructive process.
John Dewey

on the one hand, ethics and religion; and on the other hand, arts and technologies. Or, more simply, tradition and science. Philosophy, in Dewey's view, is the process by means of which we try to work through the contradictions between these two different kinds of response to the problems in our lives. These contradictions are not just theoretical; they are also practical. For example, I may have inherited innumerable traditional beliefs about ethics, meaning, and what constitutes a "good life", but I may find that these beliefs are in tension with the knowledge and understanding that I have gained from studying the sciences. In this context philosophy can be seen as the art of finding both theoretical and practical responses to these problems and contradictions.

There are two ways in which to judge whether a form of philosophy is successful. First, we should ask whether it has made the world more intelligible. Does this particular philosophical theory make our experience "more luminous", Dewey asks, or does it make it "more opaque"? Here Dewey is agreeing with Peirce that philosophy's purpose is to make our ideas and our everyday experience clearer and easier to understand.

THOSE WHO CANNOT REMEMBER THE PAST ARE CONDEMNED TO REPEAT IT
GEORGE SANTAYANA (1863–1952)

IN CONTEXT

BRANCH
Philosophy of history

APPROACH
Naturalism

BEFORE
55 BCE Lucretius, a Roman poet, explores the origins of societies and civilizations.

1730s The Italian philosopher Giovanni Vico claims that all civilizations pass through three stages: the age of the gods; the age of aristocrats and heroes; and democracy. This is due to "an uninterrupted order of causes and effects".

1807–22 Georg Hegel writes of history as the continual progress of mind or spirit.

AFTER
2004 In his book, *Memory, History, Forgetting,* French philosopher Paul Ricoeur explores the necessity not only of remembering, but also of forgetting the past.

I n *The Life of Reason* (1905), the Spanish-American philosopher George Santayana wrote that those who cannot remember the past are condemned to repeat it. Santayana's naturalistic approach means that he sees knowledge and belief as arising not from reasoning, but through interaction between our minds and the material environment. Santayana is often misquoted as saying that those

who *do not* remember the past are condemned to repeat it, and this is sometimes understood to mean that we must do our best to remember past atrocities. But Santayana is actually making a point about progress. For progress to be possible, we must not only remember past experiences, but also be able to learn from them; to see different ways of doing things. The psyche structures new beliefs through experiences, and this is how we prevent ourselves from repeating mistakes.

Real progress, Santayana believes, is not so much a matter of revolution as of adaptation, taking what we have learned from the past and using it to build the future. Civilization is cumulative, always building on what has gone before, in the same way that a symphony builds note by note into a whole. ∎

Progress is only possible through an understanding of the past coupled with a sense of possible alternatives. The AT&T Building, New York, uses old architectural patterns in new ways.

See also: Georg Hegel 178–85 ▪ Karl Marx 196–203 ▪ William James 206–09 ▪ Bertrand Russell 236–39

IT IS ONLY SUFFERING THAT MAKES US PERSONS
MIGUEL DE UNAMUNO (1864–1936)

The Spanish philosopher, novelist, and poet, Miguel de Unamuno, is perhaps best known for his book *The Tragic Sense of Life* (1913). In this he writes that all consciousness is consciousness of death (we are painfully aware of our lack of immortality) and of suffering. What makes us human is the fact that we suffer.

At first glance, it may seem as if this idea is close to that of Siddhartha Gautama, the Buddha, who also said that suffering is an inescapable part of all human life. But Unamuno's response to suffering is very different. Unlike the Buddha, Unamuno does not see suffering as a problem to be overcome through practising detachment. Instead he argues that suffering is an essential part of what it means to exist as a human being, and a vital experience.

If all consciousness amounts to consciousness of human mortality and suffering, as Unamuno claims, and if consciousness is what makes us distinctively human, then the only way we can lend our lives a kind of weight and substance is to embrace this suffering. If we turn away from it, we are not only turning away from what makes us human, we are also turning away from consciousness itself.

Love or happiness
There is also an ethical dimension to Unamuno's ideas on suffering. He claims that it is essential to acknowledge our pain, because it is only when we face the fact of our own suffering that we become capable of truly loving other suffering beings. This presents us with a stark choice. On the one hand, we can choose happiness and do our best to turn away from suffering. On the other hand, we can choose suffering and love.

The first choice may be easier, but it is a choice that ultimately limits us – indeed, severs us from an essential part of ourselves. The second choice is more difficult, but it is one that opens the way to the possibility of a life of depth and significance. ∎

See also: Siddhartha Gautama 30–33 ▪ St Augustine of Hippo 72–73 ▪ Martin Heidegger 252–55 ▪ Albert Camus 284–85 ▪ Jean-Paul Sartre 268–71

BELIEVE IN LIFE
WILLIAM DU BOIS (1868–1963)

IN CONTEXT

BRANCH
Ethics

APPROACH
Pragmatism

BEFORE
4th century BCE Aristotle explores the ancient Greek ethical concept of *eudaimonia* or "human flourishing".

1845 Publication of *Narrative of the Life of Frederick Douglass, an American Slave* boosts support for the abolition of slavery in the United States.

Late 19th and early 20th century Pragmatists, such as Charles Sanders Peirce and William James, argue that we should judge the value of ideas in terms of their usefulness.

AFTER
1950s and 1960s Martin Luther King Jr, as a leader of the African-American Civil Rights movement, adopts a policy of non-violent direct action to address social segregation.

In 1957, close to the end of his long life, the American academic, political radical, and civil rights activist, William Du Bois, wrote what has become known as his last message to the world. Knowing that he did not have much longer to live, he penned a short passage to be read at his funeral. In this message, Du Bois expresses his hope that any good he has done will survive long enough to justify his life, and that those things he has left undone, or has done badly, may be taken up by others to be bettered or completed.

"Always," Du Bois writes, "human beings will live and progress to a greater, broader, and fuller life." This is a statement of belief rather than a statement of fact. It is as if Du Bois is saying that we must believe in the possibility of a fuller life, or in the possibility of progress, to be able to progress at all. In this idea, Du Bois shows the influence of the American philosophical movement known as Pragmatism, which claims that what matters is not just our thoughts and beliefs, but also the practical implications of these thoughts and beliefs.

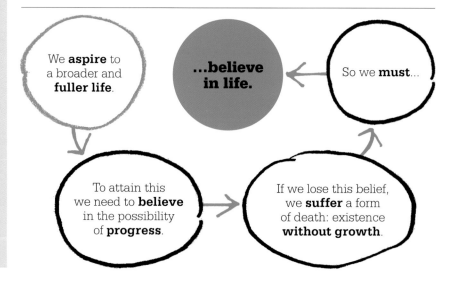

We **aspire** to a broader and **fuller life**.

...believe in life.

So we **must**...

To attain this we need to **believe** in the possibility of **progress**.

If we lose this belief, we **suffer** a form of death: existence **without growth**.

See also: Aristotle 56–63 ▪ Charles Sanders Peirce 205 ▪ William James 206–09 ▪ John Dewey 228–31

> The problem of the 20th century is the problem of the colour line.
> **William Du Bois**

Du Bois goes on to say that the "only possible death" is to lose one's belief in the prospects for human progress. But there are also hints of deeper philosophical roots here, going all the way back to the ancient Greek idea of *eudaimonia* or "human flourishing"; for the philosopher Aristotle, this involved living a life of excellence based upon virtue and reason.

Political activist

Du Bois considers two of the major impediments to a life of excellence to be racism and social inequality.

He rejects scientific racism – the idea that black people are inferior genetically to white people – that was prevalent throughout most of his life. As racial inequality has no basis in biological science, he regards it as a purely social problem, one that can be addressed only by committed political and social activism.

Du Bois is tireless in his search for solutions to the problem of all forms of social inequality. He argues that social inequality is one of the major causes of crime, claiming that lack of education and

Martin Luther King Jr cited Du Bois' writings as a key influence behind his decision to become actively involved in the battle to demolish racial divisions and establish social equality in the US.

employment are correlated with high levels of criminal activity. In his final message to the world, Du Bois reminds us that the task of bringing about a more just society is still incomplete. He states that it is up to future generations to believe in life, so that we can continue to contribute to the fulfilment of "human flourishing". ∎

William Du Bois

Du Bois showed exceptional academic promise from an early age. He won a scholarship to Fisk University, and spent two years in Germany studying in Berlin before attending Harvard, where he wrote a dissertation on the slave trade. He was the first African-American to graduate from Harvard with a doctorate.

Alongside an active career as a university teacher and writer, Du Bois was involved in the Civil Rights movement and in radical politics. His political judgement has sometimes been called into question: he famously wrote a

glowing eulogy on the death of the Soviet dictator Josef Stalin. Nevertheless, Du Bois remains a key figure in the struggle for racial equality, thanks to what Martin Luther King Jr called his "divine dissatisfaction with all forms of injustice".

Key works

1903 *The Souls of Black Folk*
1915 *The Negro*
1924 *The Gift of Black Folk*
1940 *Dusk of Dawn: An Essay Toward an Autobiography of a Race Concept*

THE ROAD TO HAPPINESS LIES IN AN ORGANIZED DIMINUTION OF WORK

BERTRAND RUSSELL (1872–1970)

IN CONTEXT

BRANCH
Ethics

APPROACH
Analytic philosophy

BEFORE
1867 Karl Marx publishes the first volume of *Capital*.

1905 In *The Protestant Ethic and the Spirit of Capitalism*, German sociologist Max Weber argues that the Protestant work ethic was partly responsible for the growth of capitalism.

AFTER
1990s Growth of the trend of "downshifting", promoting fewer working hours.

2005 Tom Hodgkinson, editor of the British magazine *The Idler*, publishes his leisure-praising book *How To Be Idle*.

2009 British philosopher Alain de Botton explores our working lives in *The Pleasures and Sorrows of Work*.

T he British philosopher Bertrand Russell was no stranger to hard work. His collected writings fill countless volumes; he was responsible for some of the most important developments in 20th-century philosophy, including the founding of the school of analytic philosophy; and throughout his long life – he died aged 97 – he was a tireless social activist. So why is this most active of thinkers suggesting that we should work less?

Russell's essay *In Praise of Idleness* was first published in 1932, in the middle of the Great

Depression, a period of global economic crisis following the Wall Street Crash of 1929. It might seem distasteful to promote the virtues of idleness at such a time, when unemployment was rising to a third of the working population in some parts of the world. For Russell, however, the economic chaos of the time was itself the result of a set of deep-rooted and mistaken attitudes about work. Indeed, he claims that many of our ideas about work are little more than superstitions, which should be swept away by rigorous thinking.

What is work?

Russell begins by defining work, which he says is of two kinds. First, there is work aimed at "altering the position of matter at or near the earth's surface relative to other such matter". This is the most fundamental sense of work – that of manual labour. The second kind of work is "telling other people to alter the position of matter relative to other such matter". This second kind of work, Russell says, can be extended indefinitely – not only can you have people employed to supervise people who move matter, but others can be employed to supervise the supervisors, or give advice on how to employ other people, while still more can be employed to manage the people who give advice on how to employ people, and so on. The first kind of work, he says, tends to be unpleasant and badly paid, while the second tends to be more pleasant, and better paid. These two types of work define two types of worker – the labourer and the supervisor – and these in turn relate to two social classes – the working

class and the middle class. But to these Russell adds a third class, who he claims has a lot to answer for – that of the leisured landowner who avoids all work, and who depends on the labour of others to support his or her idleness.

According to Russell, history is littered with examples of people working hard all their lives and being allowed to keep just enough for themselves and their families to survive, while any surplus they produce is appropriated by warriors, priests, and the leisured ruling classes. And it is always these beneficiaries of the system, says »

The Great Depression was the worst economic depression of the 20th century. For Russell, it highlighted the need for a critique of capitalism and a re-evaluation of the ethics of work.

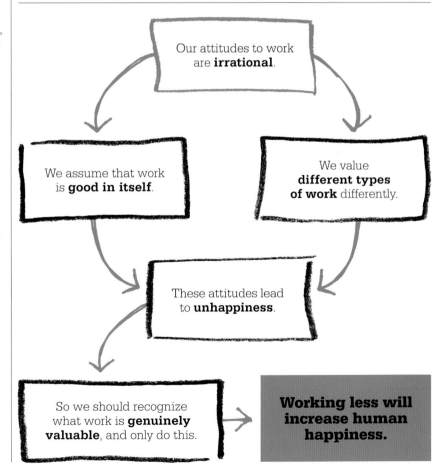

Our attitudes to work are **irrational**.

We assume that work is **good in itself**.

We value **different types of work** differently.

These attitudes lead to **unhappiness**.

So we should recognize what work is **genuinely valuable**, and only do this.

Working less will increase human happiness.

Russell, who are heard extolling the virtues of "honest toil", giving a moral gloss to a system that is manifestly unjust. And this fact alone, according to Russell, should prompt us to re-evaluate the ethics of work, for by embracing "honest toil" we comply with and even promote our own oppression.

Russell's account of society, with its emphasis on the struggle between classes, owes something to the thought of the 19th-century philosopher Karl Marx, although Russell was always uneasy with Marxism, and his essay is as critical of Marxist states as it is of capitalist states. His view also owes much to Max Weber's book *The Protestant Ethic and the Spirit of Capitalism*, first published in 1905, particularly Weber's examination of the moral claims that underlie our attitudes to work – claims that Russell insists should be challenged.

For example, not only do we see work as a duty and an obligation, we also see different types of work as occupying a hierarchy of virtue. Manual work is generally considered less virtuous than more skilled or intellectual work, and we tend to reward people in accordance with

this perceived virtue rather than for what they produce. And given that we consider work itself to be inherently virtuous, we tend to see the unemployed as lacking in virtue.

The more we think about it, the more it seems that our attitudes towards work are both complex and incoherent. What, then, can be done? Russell's suggestion is that we look at work not in terms of these curious moral ideas that are a relic of earlier times, but in terms of what makes for a full and satisfying human life. And when we do this, Russell believes, it is hard to avoid the conclusion that we should all simply work less. What, Russell asks, if the working day were only four hours long? Our present system is such that part of the population can be overworked, and so miserable, while another part can be totally unemployed, and so also miserable. This, it seems, does not benefit anyone.

The importance of play
Russell's view is that reducing our working hours would free us to pursue more creative interests. "Moving matter about," Russell writes, "is emphatically not one of

> Immense harm is caused by the belief that work is virtuous.
> **Bertrand Russell**

the ends of human life." If we allow work to occupy every waking hour, we are not living fully. Russell believes that leisure, previously something known only to the privileged few, is necessary for a rich and meaningful life. It might be objected that nobody would know what to do with their time if they worked only for four hours a day, but Russell regrets this. If this is true, he says, "it is a condemnation of our civilization," suggesting that our capacity for play and light-heartedness has been eclipsed by the cult of efficiency. A society that took leisure seriously,

Bertrand Russell

Bertrand Russell was born in Wales in 1872 to an aristocratic family. He had an early interest in mathematics, and went on to study the subject at Cambridge. There he met the philosopher Alfred North Whitehead, with whom he later collaborated on the *Principia Mathematica*, a book that established him as one of the leading philosophers of his era. It was also at Cambridge that he met, and deeply influenced, the philosopher Ludwig Wittgenstein.

Russell wanted philosophy to speak to ordinary people. He was a social activist, a pacifist, an educationalist, an advocate of atheism, and a campaigner against nuclear arms, as well as the author of numerous popular works of philosophy. He died of influenza in February, 1970.

Key works

1903 *The Principles of Mathematics*
1910, 1912, and 1913 (3 vols) *Principia Mathematica*
1914 *Our Knowledge of the External World*
1927 *The Analysis of Matter*
1956 *Logic and Knowledge*

> The morality of work is the morality of slaves, and the modern world has no need of slavery.
> **Bertrand Russell**

Russell believes, would be one that took education seriously – because education is surely about more than training for the workplace. It would be one that took the arts seriously, because there would be time to produce works of quality without the struggle that artists have for economic independence. Moreover, it would be one that took the need for enjoyment seriously. Indeed, Russell believes that such a society would be one in which we would lose the taste for war because, if nothing else, war would involve "long and severe work for all."

The balanced life

Russell's essay may appear to present something of a Utopian vision of a world in which work is reduced to a minimum. It is not entirely clear how, even if it were possible to reduce the working day to four hours, this change would lead to the social revolution that Russell claims. Nor is Russell's faith in the idea that industrialization can ultimately free us from manual

Leisure time, for Russell, should no longer be spent merely recovering from work. On the contrary, it should constitute the largest part of our lives and be a source of play and creativity.

labour entirely convincing. The raw materials for industrial production still need to come from somewhere. They need to be mined and refined and exported to the place of production, all of which depends on manual labour. Despite these problems, Russell's reminder that we need to look more closely at our attitudes to work is one that remains relevant today. We take as "natural" the length of the working week and the fact that some kinds of work are rewarded more than others. For many of us, neither our

work nor our leisure are as fulfilling as we believe they could be, and at the same time we cannot help feeling that idleness is a vice. Russell's idea reminds us that not only do we need to scrutinize our working lives, but that there is a virtue and a usefulness to lounging, loafing, and idling. As Russell says: "Hitherto we have continued to be as energetic as we were before there were machines; in this we have been foolish, but there is no reason to go on being foolish forever." ∎

LOVE IS A BRIDGE FROM POORER TO RICHER KNOWLEDGE
MAX SCHELER (1874–1928)

IN CONTEXT

BRANCH
Ethics

APPROACH
Phenomenology

BEFORE
c.380 BCE Plato writes his
Symposium, a philosophical
exploration of the nature of
love and knowledge.

17th century Blaise Pascal
writes of the logic of the
human heart.

Early 20th century Edmund
Husserl develops his new
phenomenological method
for studying the experience
of the human mind.

AFTER
1953 Polish philosopher Karol
Wojtyza (later Pope John Paul
II) writes his PhD thesis on
Scheler, acknowledging the
philosopher's influence on
Roman Catholicism.

The German philosopher
Max Scheler belongs to the
philosophical movement
known as phenomenology. This
attempts to investigate all the
phenomena of our inner experience;
it is the study of our consciousness
and its structures.

Scheler says that phenomenology
has tended to focus too exclusively
on the intellect in examining
the structures of consciousness,
and has overlooked something
fundamental: the experience of
love, or of the human heart. He
introduces the idea that love forms
a bridge from poorer to richer
knowledge in an essay entitled
Love and Knowledge (1923).

Scheler's starting point, which
is taken from the 17th-century
French philosopher Blaise Pascal, is
that there is a specific logic to the
human heart. This logic is different
from the logic of the intellect.

A spiritual midwife
It is love, Scheler believes, that
makes things apparent to our
experience and that makes
knowledge possible. Scheler writes
that love is "a kind of spiritual
midwife" that is capable of
drawing us towards knowledge,
both knowledge of ourselves and
knowledge of the world. It is the
"primary determinant" of a person's
ethics, possibilities, and fate.

At root, in Scheler's view, to
be human is not to be a "thinking
thing" as the French philosopher
Descartes said in the 17th century,
but a being who loves. ■

Philosophy is a love-
determined movement
towards participation in
the essential reality
of all possibles.
Max Scheler

See also: Plato 50–55 ▪ Blaise Pascal 124–25 ▪ Edmund Husserl 224–25

ONLY AS AN INDIVIDUAL CAN MAN BECOME A PHILOSOPHER
KARL JASPERS (1883–1969)

IN CONTEXT

BRANCH
Epistemology

APPROACH
Existentialism

BEFORE
1800s Søren Kierkegaard writes of philosophy as a matter of the individual's struggle with truth.

1880s Friedrich Nietzsche says that "God is dead", there are no absolute truths, and we must rethink all our values.

1920s Martin Heidegger claims that philosophy is a matter of our relationship with our own existence.

AFTER
From 1940 Hannah Arendt's ideas of freedom are influenced by Jaspers' philosophy.

From 1950 Hans-Georg Gadamer explores the idea that philosophy progresses through a fusion of individual perspectives.

For some, philosophy is a way to discover objective truths about the world. For German philosopher and psychiatrist Karl Jaspers, on the other hand, philosophy is a personal struggle. Strongly influenced by the philosophers Kierkegaard and Nietzsche, Jaspers is an existentialist who suggests that philosophy is a matter of our own attempts to realize truth. Since philosophy is an individual struggle, he writes in his 1941 book *On my Philosophy*, we can philosophize only as individuals. We cannot turn to anybody else to tell us the truth; we must discover it for ourselves, by our own efforts.

A community of individuals
Although in this sense truth is something that we realize alone, it is in communication with others that we realize the fruits of our efforts and raise our consciousness beyond its limits. Jaspers considers his own philosophy "true" only so far as it aids communication with others. And while other people cannot provide us with a form of "ready-made truth", philosophy remains a collective endeavour. For Jaspers, each individual's search for truth is carried out in community with all those "companions in thought" who have undergone the same personal struggle. ∎

The philosopher lives in the invisible realm of the spirit, struggling to realize truth. The thoughts of other, companion, philosophers act as signposts towards potential paths to understanding.

See also: Søren Kierkegaard 194–95 ▪ Friedrich Nietzsche 214–21 ▪ Martin Heidegger 252–55 ▪ Hans-Georg Gadamer 260–61 ▪ Hannah Arendt 272

LIFE IS A SERIES OF COLLISIONS WITH THE FUTURE
JOSE ORTEGA Y GASSET (1883–1955)

IN CONTEXT

BRANCH
Ontology

APPROACH
Existentialism

BEFORE
1641 In his *Meditations*, René Descartes argues that there are two worlds: the world of mind and the world of matter.

Early 1900s Edmund Husserl establishes phenomenology. He claims that philosophers must look at the world anew, putting all preconceptions aside.

AFTER
1920s Martin Heidegger explores questions about what our existence means for us, citing Ortega as an influence.

1930s onward Ortega's philosophy becomes popular in Spain and Latin America, influencing philosophers Xavier Zubiri, José Gaos, Ignacio Ellacuría, and María Zambrano, among others.

Ortega y Gasset's philosophy is about *life*. He is not interested in analysing the world in a cool and detached fashion. Instead, he wants to explore how philosophy can engage creatively with life. Reason, Ortega believes, is not something passive, but something active – something that allows us to get to grips with the circumstances in which we find ourselves, and allows us to change our lives for the better.

In his *Meditations on Quixote*, published in 1914, Ortega writes: "I am myself and my circumstances." Descartes said that it was possible to imagine ourselves as thinking beings, and yet to doubt the existence of the external world, including our own bodies. But Ortega says that it makes no sense to see ourselves as separate from the world. If we want to think seriously about ourselves, we have to see that we are always immersed

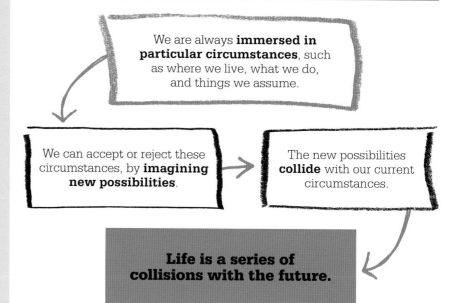

We are always **immersed in particular circumstances**, such as where we live, what we do, and things we assume.

We can accept or reject these circumstances, by **imagining new possibilities**.

The new possibilities **collide** with our current circumstances.

Life is a series of collisions with the future.

See also: René Descartes 116–23 ▪ Immanuel Kant 164–71 ▪ Edmund Husserl 224–25 ▪ Martin Heidegger 252–55 ▪ Jean-Paul Sartre 268–71

in particular circumstances – circumstances that are often oppressive and limiting. These limitations are not only those of our physical surroundings, but also of our thoughts, which contain prejudices, and our behaviour, which is shaped by habit.

While many people live without reflecting on the nature of their circumstances, Ortega says that philosophers should not only strive to understand their circumstances better, they should actively seek to change them. Indeed, he claims that the philosopher's duty is to expose the assumptions that lie behind all our beliefs.

The energy of life

In order to transform the world and to engage creatively with our own existence, Ortega says that we must look at our lives with fresh eyes. This means not only looking anew at our external circumstances, but also looking inside ourselves to reconsider our beliefs and prejudices. Only when we have done this will we be able to commit ourselves to creating new possibilities.

Every act of hope, such as celebrating Christmas on the front line in World War I, is a testament to our ability to overcome our circumstances. For Ortega, this is "vital reason" in action.

I am myself and my circumstances.
José Ortega y Gasset

However, there is a limit to the amount that we can change the world. Our habitual thinking runs deep, and even if we free ourselves enough to imagine new possibilities and new futures, our external circumstances may stand in the way of realizing these possibilities. The futures that we imagine will always collide with the reality of the circumstances in which we find ourselves. This is why Ortega sees life as a series of collisions with the future.

Ortega's idea is challenging on both a personal and a political level. It reminds us that we have a duty to attempt to change our circumstances, even though we may encounter difficulties in doing so, and even though our attempts may not always succeed. In *The Revolt of the Masses*, he warns that democracy carries within it the threat of tyranny by the majority, and that to live by majority rule – to live "like everyone else" – is to live without a personal vision or moral code. Unless we engage creatively with our own lives, we are hardly living at all. This is why for Ortega, reason is vital – it holds the energy of life itself. ∎

José Ortega y Gasset

José Ortega y Gasset was born in Madrid, Spain, in 1883. He studied philosophy first in Madrid, then at various German universities – where he became influenced by the philosophy of Immanuel Kant – before settling in Spain as a university professor.

Throughout his life, Ortega earned a living not only as a philosopher but as a journalist and essayist. He was also actively engaged in Spanish politics in the 1920s and 1930s, but his involvement came to an end with the outbreak of the Spanish Civil War in 1936. Ortega then went into exile in Argentina, where he stayed, disillusioned with politics, until 1945. After three years in Portugal, he returned to Madrid in 1948, where he founded the Institute of Humanities. He continued working as a philosopher and journalist for the remainder of his life.

Key works

1914 *Meditations on Quixote*
1925 *The Dehumanization of Art*
1930 *The Revolt of the Masses*
1935 *History as a System*
1957 *What is Philosophy?*

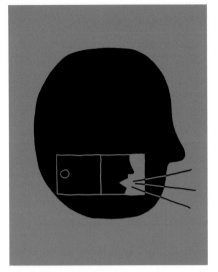

TO PHILOSOPHIZE, FIRST ONE MUST CONFESS
HAJIME TANABE (1885–1962)

Before you read on, confess! This may seem like a strange idea, but it is one that Japanese philosopher Tanabe Hajime wants us to take seriously. If we want to philosophize, Tanabe believes, we cannot do so without making a confession. But what is it that we should confess, and why?

To answer these questions, we need to look at the roots of Tanabe's philosophy in both the European and the Japanese traditions of philosophy. In terms of its European roots, Tanabe traces his thought back to the Greek philosopher Socrates who lived in the 5th century BCE. Socrates is important

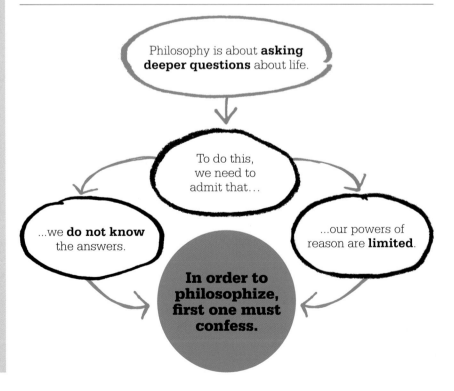

Philosophy is about **asking deeper questions** about life.

To do this, we need to admit that...

...we **do not know** the answers.

...our powers of reason are **limited**.

In order to philosophize, first one must confess.

See also: Siddharta Gautama 30–33 ▪ Socrates 46–49 ▪ St Augustine of Hippo 72–73 ▪ Edmund Husserl 224–25 ▪ Martin Heidegger 252–55 ▪ Jacques Derrida 308–13

The Buddha Amitabha, here shown between Kannon (Compassion) and Seishi (Wisdom), is the principal buddha of the Pure Land school of Buddhism, to which Shinran belonged.

to Tanabe because of the way he frankly confessed that he knew nothing. According to the story, the oracle at Delphi said that Socrates was the wisest man in Athens, and Socrates, who was certain of his own ignorance, set out to prove the oracle wrong. After innumerable conversations with people in Athens, he came to the conclusion that he was indeed the wisest person in the city, because he alone could accept that he knew nothing.

The Japanese roots of Tanabe's idea go back to the thought of the Buddhist monk Shinran, who belonged to what is known as the Pure Land school of Buddhism. Shinran's innovation was his claim that enlightenment is impossible if we rely on our own power. Instead, we must confess our own ignorance and limitations, so that we are open to what both Shinran and Tanabe call *tariki*, or "other power". In the context of Pure Land Buddhism, this other power is that of the Buddha Amitabha. In the context of Tanabe's philosophy, confession leads to a recognition of "absolute nothingness", and ultimately to self-awakening and wisdom.

Forsaking ourselves

For Tanabe, then, philosophy is not about discussing the finer points of logic, or about arguing or debating anything – it is not, in fact, an "intellectual" discipline. For Tanabe, it is something much more fundamental – a process of relating, in the deepest possible sense, to our very own being – an idea that is partly shaped by his reading of Martin Heidegger.

For a problem to belong to philosophy, there must be something inconceivable in it.
Hajime Tanabe

It is only through confessing, Tanabe believes, that we can rediscover our true being – a process he describes in directly religious terms as a form of death and resurrection. This death and resurrection is the rebirth of the mind through "other power", and its passing from the limited view of the "self" to the perspective of enlightenment. However, this shift is not simply a preparation for philosophy – on the contrary, it is the very work of philosophy itself, which is rooted in scepticism and the "forsaking of ourselves to the grace of other power". Philosophy, in other words, is not an activity that we engage in, but something that happens through us when we gain access to our true selves by letting go of the self – a phenomenon that Tanabe calls "action without an acting subject."

Continual confession is, Tanabe writes, "the ultimate conclusion" to which the recognition of our limitations drives us. In other words, Tanabe asks us not to find new answers to old philosophical questions, but to re-evaluate the very nature of philosophy. ▪

Hajime Tanabe

Hajime Tanabe was born in Tokyo, Japan, in 1885. After studying at Tokyo University, he was appointed associate professor of philosophy at Kyoto University, where he was an active member of what became known as the Kyoto School of philosophy. In the 1920s, he spent time in Germany studying with the philosophers Edmund Husserl and Martin Heidegger, and after his return to Japan he was appointed to the post of full professor. He was deeply affected by World War II, and when it ended in 1945 he retired from teaching philosophy. Tanabe's book *Philosophy as Metanoetics* was published a year later, in 1946. After his retirement, Tanabe dedicated the remainder of his life to meditation and writing.

Key works

1946 *Philosophy as Metanoetics*

THE LIMITS OF MY LANGUAGE ARE THE LIMITS OF MY WORLD

LUDWIG WITTGENSTEIN (1889–1951)

IN CONTEXT

BRANCH
Philosophy of language

APPROACH
Logic

BEFORE
4th century BCE Aristotle sets the foundations of logic.

Late 19th century Gottlob Frege develops the foundations of modern logic.

Early 20th century Bertrand Russell develops notation that translates natural language into logical propositions.

AFTER
1920s Ideas in the *Tractatus* are used by philosophers of the Vienna Circle, such as Moritz Schlick and Rudolf Carnap, to develop Logical Positivism.

From 1930 Wittgenstein rejects the ideas expressed in the *Tractatus,* and begins to explore very different ways of viewing language.

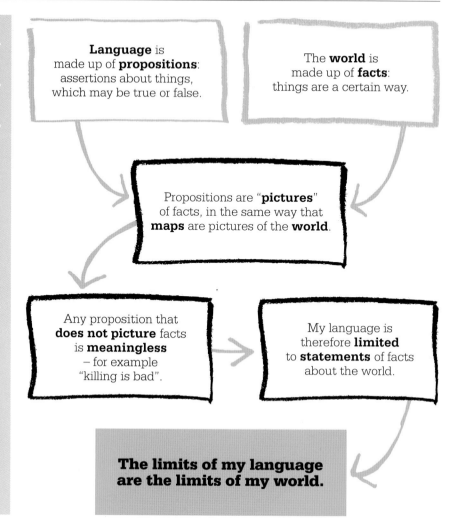

Language is made up of **propositions**: assertions about things, which may be true or false.

The **world** is made up of **facts**: things are a certain way.

Propositions are "**pictures**" of facts, in the same way that **maps** are pictures of the **world**.

Any proposition that **does not picture** facts is **meaningless** – for example "killing is bad".

My language is therefore **limited** to **statements** of facts about the world.

The limits of my language are the limits of my world.

Wittgenstein's *Tractatus Logico-Philosophicus* is perhaps one of the most forbidding texts in the history of 20th-century philosophy. Only around 70 pages long in its English translation, the book is made up of a series of highly condensed and technical numbered remarks.

In order to appreciate the full significance of the *Tractatus,* it is important to set it within its philosophical context. The fact that Wittgenstein is talking about the "limits" of my language and my world sets him firmly within the philosophical tradition that stems from the 18th-century German philosopher Immanuel Kant. In *The Critique of Pure Reason*, Kant set out to explore the limits of knowledge by posing questions such as "What can I know?" and "What things will lie forever outside of human understanding?" One reason that Kant asked such questions was that he believed many problems in philosophy arose because we fail to recognize the limitations of human understanding. By turning our attention back onto ourselves and asking about the necessary limits of our knowledge, we can then either resolve, or even perhaps dissolve, nearly all of the philosophical problems of the past.

The *Tractatus* tackles the same kind of task that Kant did, but does so in a far more radical fashion. Wittgenstein states that he is setting out to make clear what can be meaningfully said. In much the same way that Kant strives to set the limits of reason, Wittgenstein wants to set the limits of language and, by implication, of all thought. He does this because he suspects that a great deal of philosophical

See also: Aristotle 56–63 ▪ Immanuel Kant 164–71 ▪ Gottlob Frege 336 ▪ Bertrand Russell 236–39 ▪ Rudolf Carnap 257

> The solution of
> the problem of life is
> seen in the vanishing
> of the problem.
> **Ludwig Wittgenstein**

discussion and disagreement is based on some fundamental errors in how we go about thinking and talking about the world.

Logical structure

For all of their apparent complexity, Wittgenstein's central ideas in the *Tractatus* are essentially based on a fairly simple principle, that both language and the world are formally structured, and that these structures can be broken down into their component parts. Wittgenstein attempts to lay bare the structures both of the world and of language, and then to show the way they relate to each other. Having done this, he attempts to draw a number of wide-reaching philosophical conclusions.

If we are to understand what Wittgenstein means when he says that limits of my language are the limits of my world, we need to ask what he means by the words

The ancient Egyptians arranged symbols and stylized images of objects in the world, known as hieroglyphs, into logically structured sequences to create a form of written language.

"world" and "language", because he does not use these words in the everyday sense we might expect. When he talks about language, the debt Wittgenstein owes to the British philosopher Bertrand Russell becomes apparent. For Russell, who was an important figure in the development of philosophical logic, everyday language was inadequate for talking clearly and precisely about the world. He believed that logic was a "perfect language", which excluded all traces of ambiguity, so he developed a way of translating everyday language into what he considered a logical form.

Logic is concerned with what are known in philosophy as propositions. We can think of propositions as assertions that it is possible for us to consider as being either true or false. For example, the statement "the elephant is very angry" is a proposition, but the word "elephant" is not. According to Wittgenstein's

Tractatus, meaningful language must consist solely of propositions. "The totality of propositions," he writes, "is language."

Knowing a little about what Wittgenstein means by language, we can now explore what he means by "the world". The *Tractatus* begins with the claim that "the world is all that is the case". This might appear to be straightforward and robustly matter-of-fact, but taken on its own, it is not entirely clear what Wittgenstein means by this statement. He goes on to write that "the world is the totality of facts, not of things". Here we can see a parallel between the way that Wittgenstein treats language and the way he is treating the world. It may be a fact, for example, that the elephant is angry, or that there is an elephant in the room, but an elephant just by itself is not a fact.

From this point, it begins to become clear how the structure of language and that of the world »

Logic is not
a body of doctrine
but a mirror-image
of the world.
Ludwig Wittgenstein

A digital image, although not the same sort of object as the one it depicts, has the same "logical form". Words only represent reality for Wittgenstein if, again, both have the same logical form.

might be related. Wittgenstein says that language "pictures" the world. He formulated this idea during World War I, when he read in a newspaper about a court case in Paris. The case concerned a car accident, and the events were re-enacted for those present in court using model cars and model pedestrians to represent the cars and pedestrians in the real world. The model cars and the model pedestrians were able to depict their counterparts, because they were related to each other in exactly the same way as the real cars and real pedestrians involved in the accident. Similarly, all the elements depicted on a map are related to each other in exactly the same way as they are in the landscape that the map represents. What a picture shares with that which it is depicting, Wittgenstein says, is a logical form.

It is important here to realize that we are talking about logical pictures, and not about visual pictures. Wittgenstein presents a useful example to show what he

means. The sound waves generated by a performance of a symphony, the score of that symphony, and the pattern formed by the grooves on a gramophone recording of the symphony all share between them the same logical form. Wittgenstein states, "A picture is laid against reality like a measure." In this way it can depict the world.

Of course, our picture may be incorrect. It may not agree with reality, for example, by appearing to show that the elephant is not angry when the elephant is, in fact, very angry. There is no middle ground here for Wittgenstein. Because he starts with propositions that are, by their very nature, true or false, pictures also are either true or false.

Language and the world, then, both have a logical form; and language can speak about the world by picturing the world, and picturing it in a fashion that agrees with reality. It is at this point that Wittgenstein's idea gets really interesting, and it is here that we can see why Wittgenstein is interested in the limits of language.

Consider the following idea: "You should give half of your salary to charity." This is not picturing anything in the world in the sense meant by Wittgenstein. What can be said – what Wittgenstein calls the "totality of true propositions" – is merely the sum of all those things that are the case, or the natural sciences.

Discussion about religious and ethical values is, for Wittgenstein, strictly meaningless. Because the things that we are attempting to talk about when we discuss such topics are beyond the limits of the world, they also lie beyond the limits of our language. Wittgenstein writes, "It is clear that ethics cannot be put into language."

Beyond words
Some readers of Wittgenstein, at this point, claim that he is a champion of the sciences, driving out vague concepts involved in talk of ethics, religion, and the like. But something more complex is going on. Wittgenstein does not think that the "problems of life" are

> ## ❝
> ## What we cannot speak about we must pass over in silence.
> ## Ludwig Wittgenstein
> ## ❞

nonsensical. Instead, he believes that these are the most important problems of all. It is simply that they cannot be put into words, and because of this, they cannot become a part of philosophy. Wittgenstein writes that these things, even though we cannot speak of them, nevertheless make themselves manifest, adding that "they are what is mystical".

All of this, however, has serious repercussions for the propositions that lie within the *Tractatus* itself. After all, these are not propositions that picture the world. Even logic, one of Wittgenstein's major tools, does not say anything about the world. Is the *Tractatus*, therefore, nonsense? Wittgenstein himself was fearless in following his argument to its conclusion, ultimately recognizing that the answer to such a question must be yes. Anybody who understands the *Tractatus* properly, he claims, will eventually see that the propositions used in it are nonsense, too. They are like the steps of a philosophical ladder that helps us to climb altogether beyond the problems of philosophy, but which we can kick away once we have ascended.

Change of direction

After completing the *Tractatus*, Wittgenstein concluded that there were no more philosophical problems left to resolve, and so abandoned the discipline. However, over the course of the 1920s and 1930s, he began to question his earlier thinking, becoming one of its fiercest critics. In particular, he questioned his once firmly held belief that language consists solely of propositions, a view that ignores much of what we do in our everyday speech – from telling jokes, to cajoling, to scolding.

Nevertheless, despite all of its problems, the *Tractatus* remains one of the most challenging and compelling works of Western philosophy – and ultimately one of the most mysterious. ∎

Philosophy demands logical, unambiguous language. Wittgenstein concludes, therefore, that it can only be made up of propositions, or statements of fact, such as "the cat sat on the mat", which can be clearly divided into their component parts.

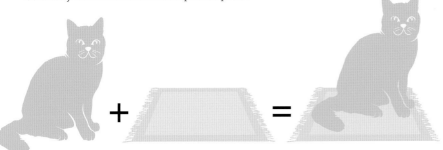

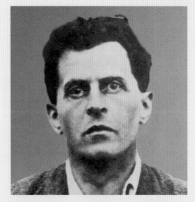

Ludwig Wittgenstein

Born into a wealthy Viennese family in 1889, Wittgenstein first studied engineering and in 1908 travelled to England to continue his education in Manchester. However, he soon developed an interest in logic, and by 1911 had moved to Cambridge to study under the philosopher Bertrand Russell.

During World War I, he served on the Russian front and in Italy, where he was taken prisoner. Around this time, he began the *Tractatus Logico-Philosophicus,* which was published in 1921.

Believing that the *Tractatus* resolved all the problems of philosophy, Wittgenstein now embarked on an itinerant career as a schoolteacher, gardener, and architect. But after developing criticisms of his earlier ideas, he resumed his work at Cambridge in 1929, becoming a professor there in 1939. He died in 1951.

Key works

1921 *Tractatus Logico-Philosophicus*
1953 *Philosophical Investigations*
1958 *The Blue and Brown Books*
1977 *Remarks on Colour*

WE ARE OURSELVES THE ENTITIES TO BE ANALYSED

MARTIN HEIDEGGER (1889–1976)

IN CONTEXT

BRANCH
Ontology

APPROACH
Phenomenology

BEFORE
c.350 BCE Diogenes of Sinope uses a plucked chicken to parody Plato's followers' claim that a human being is a "featherless biped".

1900–13 Edmund Husserl proposes his phenomenological theories and method in *Logical Investigations* and *Ideas I*.

AFTER
1940s Jean-Paul Sartre publishes *Being and Nothingness*, which looks at the connection between "being" and human freedom.

1960 Hans-Georg Gadamer's *Truth and Method,* inspired by Heidegger, explores the nature of human understanding.

It is said that in ancient Athens the followers of Plato gathered one day to ask themselves the following question: "What is a human being?" After a great deal of thought, they came up with the following answer: "a human being is a featherless biped". Everybody seemed content with this definition until Diogenes the Cynic burst into the lecture hall with a live plucked chicken, shouting, "Behold! I present you with a human being". After the commotion had died down, the philosophers reconvened and refined their definition. A human being, they said, is a featherless biped with broad nails.

See also: Plato 50–55 ▪ Diogenes of Sinope 66 ▪ Edmund Husserl 224–25 ▪ Hans-Georg Gadamer 260–61 ▪ Ernst Cassirer 337 ▪ Jean-Paul Sartre 268–71 ▪ Hannah Arendt 272 ▪ Richard Rorty 314–19

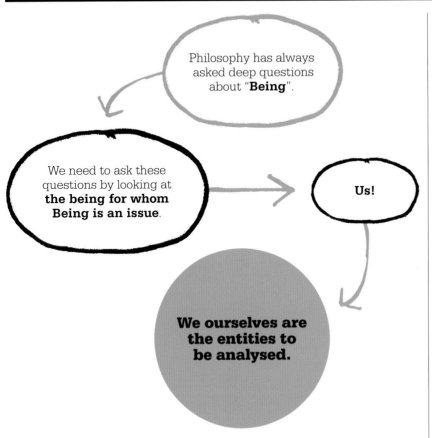

Philosophy has always asked deep questions about "**Being**".

We need to ask these questions by looking at **the being for whom Being is an issue**.

Us!

We ourselves are the entities to be analysed.

The question of existence never gets straightened out except through existing itself.
Martin Heidegger

experience of them. For example, phenomenology would not look directly at the question "what is a human being?" but would instead look at the question "what is it like to be human?"

The human existence

For Heidegger, this constitutes the fundamental question of philosophy. He was most interested in the philosophical subject of ontology (from the Greek word *ontos*, meaning "being"), which looks at questions about being or existence. Examples of ontological questions might be: "what does it mean to say that something exists?" and "what are the different kinds of things that exist?" Heidegger wanted use the question "what is it like to be human?" as a way of answering deeper questions about existence in general.

In his book, *Being and Time*, Heidegger claims that when other philosophers have asked ontological questions, they have tended to use approaches that are too abstract and shallow. If we want to know what it means to say that something exists, we need to start looking »

This curious story from the history of early philosophy shows the kinds of difficulties philosophers have sometimes been faced with when attempting to give abstract, general definitions of what it is to be human. Even without the intervention of Diogenes, it seems clear that describing ourselves as featherless bipeds does not really capture much of what it means to be human.

An insider's perspective

It is this question – how we might go about analyzing what it is to be human – that concerned the philosopher Martin Heidegger. When Heidegger came to answer the question, he did so in a way

that was strikingly different from many of his predecessors. Instead of attempting an abstract definition that looks at human life from the outside, he attempts to provide a much more concrete analysis of "being" from what could be called an insider's position. He says that since we exist in the thick of things – in the midst of life – if we want to understand what it is to be human, we have to do so by looking at human life from within this life.

Heidegger was a student of Husserl, and he followed Husserl's method of phenomenology. This is a philosophical approach that looks at phenomena – how things appear – through examining our

We should raise anew
the question of the
meaning of being.
Martin Heidegger

We try to make sense of the world
by engaging with projects and tasks
that lend life a unity. Being human,
Heidegger says, means to be immersed
in the day-to-day world.

at the question from the perspective
of those beings for whom being is
an issue. We can assume that
although cats, dogs, and toadstools
are beings, they do not wonder
about their being: they do not fret
over ontological questions; they do
not ask "what does it mean to say
that something exists?" But there
is, Heidegger points out, one being
that does wonder about these

things, and that is the human being.
In saying that we are ourselves the
entities to be analysed, Heidegger is
saying that we if we want to explore
questions of being, we have to start
with ourselves, by looking at what
it means for us to exist.

Being and time

When Heidegger asks about
the meaning of being, he is not
asking about abstract ideas, but
about something very direct and
immediate. In the opening pages of
his book, he says that the meaning
of our being must be tied up with
time; we are essentially temporal

beings. When we are born, we find
ourselves in the world as if we had
been thrown here on a trajectory
we have not chosen. We simply find
that we have come to exist, in an
ongoing world that pre-existed us,
so that at our birth we are presented
with a particular historical, material,
and spiritual environment. We
attempt to make sense of this world
by engaging in various pastimes –
for example, we might learn Latin, or
attempt to find true love, or decide
to build ourselves a house. Through
these time-consuming projects we
literally project ourselves towards
different possible futures; we define
our existence. However, sometimes
we become aware that there is an
outermost limit to all our projects, a
point at which everything we plan
will come to an end, whether finished
or unfinished. This point is the
point of our death. Death, Heidegger
says, is the outermost horizon of our
being: everything we can do or see
or think takes place within this
horizon. We cannot see beyond it.

Heidegger's technical vocabulary
is famously difficult to understand,
but this is largely because he is
attempting to explore complex
philosophical questions in a concrete
or non-abstract way; he wants to
relate to our actual experience. To
say that "the furthest horizon of our

being is death" is to say something about what it is like to live a human life, and it captures some idea of what we are in a way that many philosophical definitions – "featherless biped" or "political animal", for example – overlook.

Living authentically

It is to Heidegger that we owe the philosophical distinction between authentic and inauthentic existence. Most of the time we are wrapped up in various ongoing projects, and forget about death. But in seeing our life purely in terms of the projects in which we are engaged, we miss a more fundamental dimension of our existence, and to that extent, Heidegger says, we are existing inauthentically. When we become aware of death as the ultimate limit of our possibilities, we start to reach a deeper understanding of what it means to exist.

For example, when a good friend dies, we may look at our own lives and realize that the various projects which absorb us from day to day feel meaningless, and that there is a deeper dimension to life that is

All being is a "being-towards-death", but only humans recognize this. Our lives are temporal, and it is only once we realize this that we can live a meaningful and authentic life.

Dying is not an event; it is a phenomenon to be understood existentially.
Martin Heidegger

missing. And so we may find ourselves changing our priorities and projecting ourselves towards different futures.

A deeper language

Heidegger's later philosophy continues to tackle questions of being, but it turns away from his earlier, exacting approach to take a more poetic look at the same kinds of questions. Philosophy, he comes to suspect, simply cannot reflect this deeply on our own being. In order to ask questions about human existence, we must use the richer, deeper language of poetry, which engages us in a way that goes far beyond the mere exchange of information.

Heidegger was one of the 20th century's most influential philosophers. His early attempt to analyse what it means to be human, and how one might live an authentic life, inspired philosophers such as Sartre, Levinas, and Gadamer, and contributed to the birth of existentialism. His later, more poetic, thinking has also had a powerful influence on ecological philosophers, who believe it offers a way of thinking about what it means to be a human being within a world under threat of environmental destruction. ∎

Martin Heidegger

Heidegger is acknowledged to be one of the most important philosophers of the 20th century. He was born in 1889 in Messkirch, Germany, and had early aspirations to be a priest, but after coming across the writings of Husserl he took up philosophy instead. He quickly became well-known as an inspirational lecturer, and was nicknamed "the magician of Messkirch". In the 1930s he became rector of Freiburg University and a member of the Nazi party. The extent and nature of his involvement with Nazism remains controversial, as is the question of how far his philosophy is implicated in the ideologies of Nazism.

Heidegger spent the last 30 years of his life travelling and writing, exchanging ideas with friends such as Hannah Arendt and the physicist Werner Heisenberg. He died in Freiburg in 1976, aged 86.

Key works

1927 *Being and Time*
1936–46 *Overcoming Metaphyics*
1955–56 *The Principle of Reason*
1955–57 *Identity and Difference*

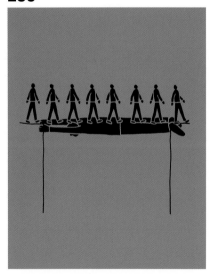

THE INDIVIDUAL'S ONLY TRUE MORAL CHOICE IS THROUGH SELF-SACRIFICE FOR THE COMMUNITY
TETSURO WATSUJI (1889–1960)

IN CONTEXT

BRANCH
Ethics

APPROACH
Existentialism

BEFORE
13th century Japanese philosopher Dōgen writes about "forgetting the self".

Late 19th century Friedrich Nietzsche writes about the influence of "climate" on philosophy; this idea becomes important to Watsuji's thought.

1927 Martin Heidegger publishes *Being and Time*. Watsuji goes on to rethink Heidegger's book in the light of his ideas on "climate".

AFTER
Late 20th century Japanese philosopher Yuasa Yasuo further develops Watsuji's ethics of community.

Tetsuro Watsuji was one of the leading philosophers in Japan in the early part of the 20th century, and he wrote on both Eastern and Western philosophy. He studied in Japan and Europe, and like many Japanese philosophers of his time, his work shows a creative synthesis of these two very different traditions.

Forgetting the self

Watsuji's studies of Western approaches to ethics convinced him that thinkers in the West tend to take an individualistic approach to human nature, and so also to ethics. But for Watsuji, individuals can only be understood as expressions of their particular times, relationships, and social contexts, which together constitute a "climate". He explores the idea of human nature in terms of our relationships with the wider

Samurai warriors often sacrificed their own lives in battle in order to save the state, in an act of extreme loyalty and self-negation that Watsuji called *kenshin*, or "absolute self-sacrifice".

community, which form a network within which we exist; Watsuji calls this "betweenness". For Watsuji ethics is a matter not of individual action, but of the forgetting or sacrifice of one's self, so that the individual can work for the benefit of the wider community.

Watsuji's nationalist ethics and insistence on the superiority of the Japanese race led to his fall from favour following World War II, although he later distanced himself from these views. ■

See also: Søren Kierkegaard 194–95 ▪ Friedrich Nietzsche 214–21 ▪ Nishida Kitaro 336–37 ▪ Hajime Tanabe 244–45 ▪ Martin Heidegger 252–55

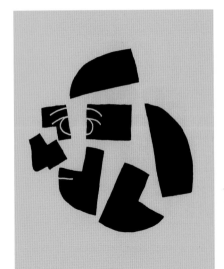

LOGIC IS THE LAST SCIENTIFIC INGREDIENT OF PHILOSOPHY
RUDOLF CARNAP (1891–1970)

IN CONTEXT

BRANCH
Philosophy of science

APPROACH
Logical positivism

BEFORE
1890 Gottlob Frege starts to explore the logical structures of language.

1921 Ludwig Wittgenstein writes that philosophy is the study of the limits of language.

AFTER
1930s Karl Popper proposes that science works by means of falsifiability: no amount of positive proofs can prove something to be true, whereas one negative result confirms that a theory is incorrect.

1960s Thomas Kuhn explores the social dimensions of scientific progress, undermining some of the tenets of logical positivism.

One of the problems for 20th-century philosophy is determining a role for philosophy given the success of the natural sciences. This is one of the main concerns of German-born Rudolf Carnap in *The Physical Language as the Universal Language of Science* (1934), which suggests that philosophy's proper function – and its primary contribution to science – is the logical analysis and clarification of scientific concepts.

Carnap claims that many apparently deep philosophical problems – such as metaphysical ones – are meaningless, because they cannot be proved or disproved through experience. He adds that they are also in fact pseudo-problems caused by logical confusions in the way we use language.

Logical language
Logical positivism accepts as true only strictly logical statements that can be empirically verified. For Carnap, philosophy's real task is therefore the logical analysis of language (in order to discover and

In logic,
there are no morals.
Rudolf Carnap

rule out those questions that are, strictly speaking, meaningless), and to find ways of talking clearly and unambiguously about the sciences.

Some philosophers, such as Willard Quine and Karl Popper, have argued that Carnap's standards for what can be said meaningfully are too exacting and present an idealized view of how science operates, which is not reflected in practice. Nevertheless, Carnap's reminder that language can fool us into seeing problems that are not really there is an important one. ∎

See also: Gottlob Frege 336 ▪ Ludwig Wittgenstein 246–51 ▪ Karl Popper 262–65 ▪ Willard Van Orman Quine 278–79 ▪ Thomas Kuhn 293

THE ONLY WAY OF KNOWING A PERSON IS TO LOVE THEM WITHOUT HOPE
WALTER BENJAMIN (1892–1940)

IN CONTEXT

BRANCH
Ethics

APPROACH
Frankfurt School

BEFORE
c.380 BCE Plato writes his *Symposium*, considered the first sustained philosophical account of love.

1863 The French writer Charles Baudelaire explores the idea of the *flâneur*, the "person who walks the city to experience it".

AFTER
1955 Guy Debord establishes psychogeography, the study of the effects of geography on an individual's emotions and behaviour.

1972 Italian novelist Italo Calvino explores the relationships between cities and signs in his book *Invisible Cities*.

The German philosopher Walter Benjamin was an affiliate of the Frankfurt School, a group of neo-Marxist social theorists who explored the significance of mass culture and communication. Benjamin was also fascinated by the techniques of film and literature, and his 1926 essay *One-Way Street* is an experiment in literary construction. Here he puts together a collection of observations – intellectual and empirical – that apparently occur to him as he walks down an imaginary city street.

The construction of life currently lies far more in the hands of facts than of convictions.
Walter Benjamin

In the essay Benjamin does not set out a grand theory. Instead he wants to surprise us with ideas, in the same way that we might be surprised by something catching our eye while on a walk. Towards the end of the essay, he says that "Quotations in my work are like wayside robbers who leap out, brandishing weapons, and relieve the idler of his certainty."

Illuminating love
The idea that the only way of knowing a person is to love them hopelessly appears in the middle of the essay, under the heading "Arc Lamp". In a flare of light, Benjamin pauses and thinks just this, and no more – the essay moves immediately afterwards to a new section. We are forced to guess what he means. Is he saying that knowledge arises out of love? Or that it is only when we stop hoping for some outcome that we can clearly see the beloved? We cannot know. All we can do is walk down the street alongside Benjamin, experiencing the flare of light of these passing thoughts. ∎

See also: Plato 50–55 ∎ Karl Marx 196–203 ∎ Theodor Adorno 266–67 ∎ Roland Barthes 290–91

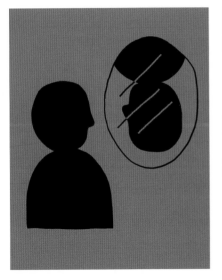

THAT WHICH IS CANNOT BE TRUE
HERBERT MARCUSE (1898–1979)

IN CONTEXT

BRANCH
Political philosophy

APPROACH
Frankfurt School

BEFORE
1821 Georg Hegel writes in his *Philosophy of Right* that what is actual is rational and what is rational is actual.

1867 Karl Marx publishes the first volume of *Capital* (*Das Kapital*), setting out his view of the "laws of motion" within capitalist societies, and asserting that capitalism is guilty of exploiting humans.

1940s Martin Heidegger begins to explore the problems of technology.

AFTER
2000 Slavoj Žižek explores the relationship between technology, capitalist society, and totalitarianism.

At first glance, nothing seems to be more irrational than Marcuse's claim that "that which is" cannot be true, which appears in his 1941 book, *Reason and Revolution*. If that which is cannot be true, the reader is tempted to ask, then what is? But Marcuse's idea is partly an attempt to overturn the claim made by the German philosopher Hegel that what is rational is actual, and also that what is actual is rational.

Marcuse believes this is a dangerous idea because it leads us to think that what is actually the case – such as our existing political system – is necessarily rational. He reminds us that those things we take as reasonable may be far more unreasonable than we like to admit. He also wants to shake us up into realizing the irrational nature of many of the things that we take for granted.

Subversive reason
In particular, Marcuse is deeply uneasy with capitalist societies and with what he calls their "terrifying harmony of freedom and oppression, productivity and destruction, growth and regression". We assume that the societies we live in are based upon reason and justice, but when we look more closely, we may find that they are neither as just nor as reasonable as we believe.

Marcuse is not discounting reason, but trying to point out that reason is subversive, and that we can use it to call into question the society in which we live. The aim of philosophy, for Marcuse, is a "rationalist theory of society". ∎

Fast cars are the kind of consumables that Marcuse accuses us of using to recognize ourselves; he says we find "our soul" in these items, becoming mere extensions of the things we create.

See also: Georg Hegel 178–85 ▪ Karl Marx 196–203 ▪ Martin Heidegger 252–55 ▪ Slavoj Žižek 326

HISTORY DOES NOT BELONG TO US BUT WE BELONG TO IT

HANS-GEORG GADAMER (1900–2002)

G adamer is associated in particular with one form of philosophy: "hermeneutics". Derived from the Greek word *hermeneuo*, meaning "interpret", this is the study of how humans interpret the world.

Gadamer studied philosophy under Martin Heidegger, who said that the task of philosophy is to interpret our existence. This interpretation is always a process of deepening our understanding by starting from what we already know. The process is similar to how we might interpret a poem. We start

by reading it carefully in the light of our present understanding. If we come to a line that seems strange or particularly striking, we might need to reach for a deeper level of understanding. As we interpret individual lines, our sense of the poem as a whole might begin to change; and as our sense of the poem as a whole changes, so might our understanding of individual lines. This is known as the "hermeneutic circle".

Heidegger's approach to philosophy moved in this circular fashion, and this was the approach

We understand the world through **interpretation**.

This always takes place within a **particular historical era**, which gives us particular **prejudices and biases**.

We cannot understand things outside of these prejudices and biases.

History does not belong to us, but we belong to it.

See also: Immanuel Kant 164–71 ▪ Georg Hegel 178–85 ▪ Martin Heidegger 252–55 ▪ Jürgen Habermas 306–07 ▪ Jacques Derrida 308–13 ▪ Richard Rorty 314–19

When viewing historical objects we should not view time as a gulf to be bridged, says Gadamer. Its distance is filled with the continuity of tradition, which sheds light on our understanding.

that Gadamer later explored in his book *Truth and Method*. Gadamer goes on to point out that our understanding is always from the point of view of a particular point in history. Our prejudices and beliefs, the kinds of questions that we think are worth asking, and the kinds of answers with which we are satisfied are all the product of our history. We cannot stand outside of history and culture, so we can never reach an absolutely objective perspective.

But these prejudices should not be seen as a bad thing. They are, after all, our starting point, and our current understanding and sense of meaning are based upon these prejudices and biases. Even if it were possible to get rid of all our prejudices, we would not find that we would then see things clearly. Without any given framework for interpretation, we would not be able to see anything at all.

Conversing with history

Gadamer sees the process of understanding our lives and our selves as similar to having a "conversation with history". As we read historical texts that have existed for centuries, the differences in their traditions and assumptions reveal our own cultural norms and prejudices, leading us to broaden and deepen our understanding of our own lives in the present. For instance, if I pick up a book by Plato, and read it carefully, I might find not only that I am deepening my understanding of Plato, but also that my own prejudices and biases become clear, and perhaps begin to shift. Not only am I reading Plato, but Plato is reading me. Through this dialogue, or what Gadamer calls "the fusion of horizons", my understanding of the world reaches a deeper, richer level. ▪

Because an experience is itself within the whole of life, the whole of life is present in it too.
Hans-Georg Gadamer

Hans-Georg Gadamer

Gadamer was born in Marburg in 1900, but grew up in Breslau, Germany (now Wroclaw, Poland). He studied philosophy first in Breslau and then in Marburg, where he wrote a second doctoral dissertation under the tutelage of the philosopher Martin Heidegger, who was an enormous influence on his work. He became an associate professor at Marburg, beginning a long academic career which eventually included succeeding the philosopher Karl Jaspers as Professor of Philosophy in Heidelberg in 1949. His most important book, *Truth and Method*, was published when he was 60. It attacked the idea that science offered the only route to truth and its publication brought him wider international fame. A sociable and lively man, Gadamer remained active right up until his death in Heidelberg at the age of 102.

Key works

1960 *Truth and Method*
1976 *Philosophical Hermeneutics*
1980 *Dialogue and Dialectic*
1981 *Reason in the Age of Science*

IN SO FAR AS A SCIENTIFIC STATEMENT SPEAKS ABOUT REALITY, IT MUST BE FALSIFIABLE

KARL POPPER (1902–1994)

IN CONTEXT

BRANCH
Philosophy of science

APPROACH
Analytic philosophy

BEFORE
4th century BCE Aristotle
stresses the importance of
observation and measurement
to understanding the world.

1620 Francis Bacon sets
out the inductive methods of
science in *Novum Organum*.

1748 David Hume's
*Enquiry concerning Human
Understanding* raises the
problem of induction.

AFTER
1962 Thomas Kuhn criticizes
Popper in *The Structure of
Scientific Revolutions*.

1978 Paul Feyerabend, in
Against Method, questions the
very idea of scientific method.

We often think that science works by "proving" truths about the world. We might imagine that a good scientific theory is one that we can prove conclusively to be true. The philosopher Karl Popper, however, insists that this is not the case. Instead, he says that what makes a theory scientific is that it is capable of being falsified, or being shown to be wrong by experience.

Popper is interested in the method by which science finds out about the world. Science depends on experiment and experience, and if we want to do science well, we need to pay close attention to what philosopher David Hume called

See also: Socrates 46–49 ▪ Aristotle 56–63 ▪ Francis Bacon 110–11 ▪ David Hume 148–53 ▪ Rudolf Carnap 257 ▪ Thomas Kuhn 293 ▪ Paul Feyerabend 297

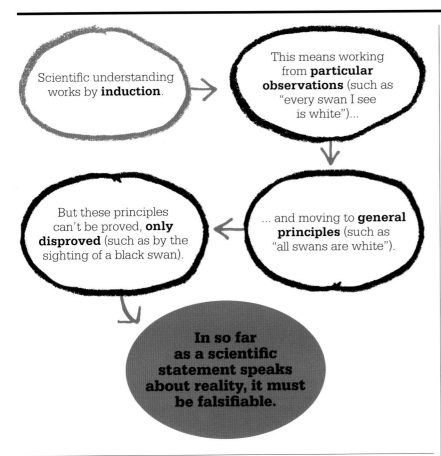

Scientific understanding works by **induction**.

This means working from **particular observations** (such as "every swan I see is white")...

... and moving to **general principles** (such as "all swans are white").

But these principles can't be proved, **only disproved** (such as by the sighting of a black swan).

In so far as a scientific statement speaks about reality, it must be falsifiable.

Black swans were first encountered by Europeans in the 17th century. This falsified the idea that all swans are white, which at the time was held to be universally true.

the "regularities" of nature – the fact that events unfold in the world in particular patterns and sequences that can be systematically explored. Science, in other words, is empirical, or based on experience, and to understand how it works we need to understand how experience in general leads to knowledge.

Consider the following statement: "If you drop a tennis ball from a second-floor window, it will fall to the ground." Leaving aside any chance events (such as the ball being snatched away by a passing eagle), we can be fairly sure that this claim is a reasonable one. It would be a strange person who said, "Hold on, are you sure it will

fall to the ground?" But how do we know that this is what will happen when we drop the tennis ball? What kind of knowledge is this?

The short answer is that we know it will fall because that is what it always does. Leaving aside chance events, no-one has ever found that a tennis ball hovers or rises upwards when it is released. We know it falls to the ground because experience has shown us that this will happen. And not only can we be sure that the ball will fall to the ground, we can also be sure about how it will fall to the ground. For example, if we know the force of gravity, and how high the window is above the ground, we can

calculate the speed at which the ball will fall. Nothing about the event is even remotely mysterious.

Nevertheless, the question remains: can we be certain that the next time we drop the ball it will fall to the ground? No matter how often we conduct the experiment, and no matter how confident we become about its outcome, we can never prove that the result will be the same in the future.

Inductive reasoning
This inability to speak with any certainty about the future is called the problem of induction, and it was first recognised by Hume in the 18th century. So what is inductive reasoning?

Induction is the process of moving from a set of observed facts about the world to more general conclusions about the world. We expect that if we drop the ball it will fall to the ground because, at least according to Hume, we are generalizing from innumerable » experiences of similar occasions on which we have found things like balls to fall to the ground when we release them.

Deductive reasoning

Another form of reasoning, which philosophers contrast with induction, is deductive reasoning. While induction moves from the particular case to the general, deduction moves from the general case to the particular. For instance, a piece of deductive reasoning might start from two premises, such as: "If it is an apple, then it is a fruit (since all apples are fruit)" and "This is an apple". Given the nature of these premises, the statement "This is an apple" leads inescapably to the conclusion "It is a fruit".

Philosophers like to simplify deductive arguments by writing them out in notation. So the general form of the argument above would be "If P then Q; since P, therefore Q". In our example, "P" stands for "It is an apple", and "Q" stands for

"It is a fruit". Given the starting points "If P then Q" and "P", then the conclusion "Q" is necessary, or unavoidably true. Another example would be: "If it is raining, the cat will meow (since all cats meow in the rain). It is raining, therefore the cat will meow".

All arguments of this kind are considered by philosophers to be valid arguments, because their conclusions follow inevitably from their premises. However, the fact that an argument is valid does not mean that its conclusions are true. For example, the argument "If it is a cat, then it is banana-flavoured; this is a cat, therefore it is banana-flavoured" is valid, because it follows a valid form. But most people would agree that the conclusion is false. And a closer look shows that there is a problem, from an empirical perspective, with the premise "If it is a cat, then it is banana-flavoured", because cats, in our world at least, are not banana-flavoured. In other words, because the premise is

> Every solution to a problem creates new unsolved problems.
> **Karl Popper**

untrue, even though the argument itself is valid, the conclusion is also untrue. Other worlds can be imagined in which cats are in fact banana-flavoured, and for this reason the statement that cats are not banana-flavoured is said to be contingently true, rather than logically or necessarily true, which would demand that it be true in all possible worlds. Nevertheless, arguments that are valid and have true premises are called "sound"

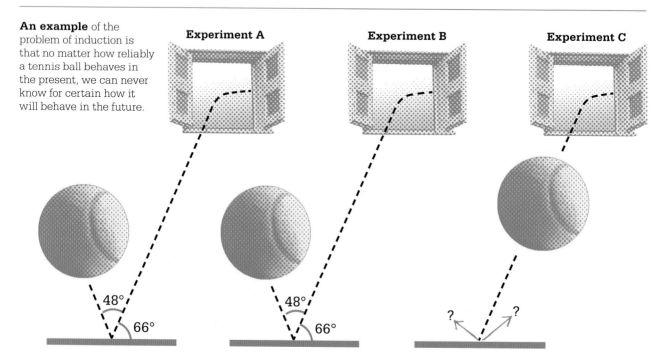

An example of the problem of induction is that no matter how reliably a tennis ball behaves in the present, we can never know for certain how it will behave in the future.

Experiment A

Experiment B

Experiment C

48°   66°

48°   66°

?   ?

> Science may be described as the art of systematic over-simplification.
> **Karl Popper**

arguments. The banana-flavoured cat argument, as we have seen, is valid but not sound – whereas the argument about apples and fruit is both valid and sound.

Falsifiability

Deductive arguments could be said to be like computer programs – the conclusions they reach are only as good as the data that is fed into them. Deductive reasoning has an important role to play in the sciences, but on its own, it cannot say anything about the world. It can only say "If this is the case, then that is the case." And if we want to use such arguments in the

sciences, we still have to rely on induction for our premises, and so science is lumbered with the problem of induction.

For this reason, according to Popper, we cannot prove our theories to be true. Moreover, what makes a theory scientific is not that it can be proved at all, but that it can be tested against reality and shown to be potentially false. In other words, a falsifiable theory is not a theory that is false, but one that can only be shown to be false by observation.

Theories that are untestable (for example, that we each have an invisible spirit guide, or that God created the universe) are not part of the natural sciences. This does not mean that they are worthless, only that they are not the kinds of theories that the sciences deal with.

The idea of falsifiability does not mean we are unjustified in having a belief in theories that cannot be falsified. Beliefs that stand up to repeated testing, and that resist our attempts at falsification, can be taken to be reliable. But even the best theories are always open to the possibility that a new result will show them to be false.

Experiments can show that certain phenomena reliably follow others in nature. But Popper claims that no experiment can ever verify a theory, or even show that it is probable.

Popper's work has not been without its critics. Some scientists claim that he presents an idealized view of how they go about their work, and that science is practised very differently from how Popper suggests. Nevertheless, his idea of falsifiability is still used in distinguishing between scientific and non-scientific claims, and Popper remains perhaps the most important philosopher of science of the 20th century. ■

Karl Popper

Karl Popper was born in Vienna, Austria, in 1902. He studied philosophy at the University of Vienna, after which he spent six years as a schoolteacher. It was during this time that he published *The Logic of Scientific Discovery*, which established him as one of the foremost philosophers of science. In 1937, he emigrated to New Zealand, where he lived until the end of World War II, and where he wrote his study of totalitarianism, *The Open Society and Its Enemies*. In 1946, he moved to England to teach, first at the London School of Economics, then

at the University of London. He was knighted in 1965, and remained in England for the rest of his life. Although he retired in 1969, he continued to write and publish until his death in 1994.

Key works

1934 *The Logic of Scientific Discovery*
1945 *The Open Society and Its Enemies*
1957 *The Poverty of Historicism*
1963 *Conjectures and Refutations: The Growth of Scientific Knowledge*

INTELLIGENCE IS A MORAL CATEGORY
THEODOR ADORNO (1903–1969)

IN CONTEXT

BRANCH
Ethics

APPROACH
Frankfurt School

BEFORE
1st century CE Saint Paul writes about being a "fool for Christ".

500–1450 The idea of the "holy fool", who represents an alternative view of the world, becomes popular throughout Medieval Europe.

20th century The global rise of differing forms of mass-media communication raises new ethical questions.

AFTER
1994 Portuguese neuroscientist Antonio Damasio publishes *Descartes' Error: Emotion, Reason, and the Human Brain*.

21st century Slavoj Žižek explores the political, social, and ethical dimensions of popular culture.

The idea of the holy fool has a long tradition in the West, dating all the way back to Saint Paul's letter to the Corinthians in which he asks his followers to be "fools for Christ's sake". Throughout the Middle Ages this idea was developed into the popular cultural figure of the saint or sage who was foolish or lacked intelligence, but who was morally good or pure.

In his book *Minima Moralia*, the German philosopher Theodor Adorno calls into question this long tradition. He is suspicious of attempts to (as he puts it) "absolve and beatify the blockhead", and wants to make the case that goodness involves our entire being, both our feeling and our understanding.

The problem with the idea of the holy fool, Adorno says, is that it divides us into different parts, and in doing so makes us incapable of acting judiciously at all. In reality, judgement is measured by the extent to which we manage to make feeling and understanding cohere. Adorno's view implies that evil acts are not just failures of feeling, but also failures of intelligence and understanding.

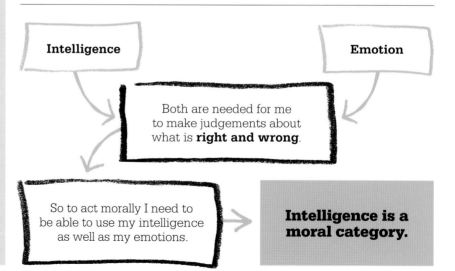

Intelligence

Emotion

Both are needed for me to make judgements about what is **right and wrong**.

So to act morally I need to be able to use my intelligence as well as my emotions.

Intelligence is a moral category.

See also: René Descartes 116–23 ▪ Georg Hegel 178–85 ▪ Karl Marx 196–203 ▪ Slavoj Žižek 326

Adorno was a member of the Frankfurt School, a group of philosophers who were interested in the development of capitalism. He condemned forms of mass communication such as television and radio, claiming that these have led to the erosion of both intelligence and feeling, and to a decline in the ability to make moral choices and judgements. If we choose to switch off our brains by watching blockbuster movies (insofar as we can choose at all, given the prevailing cultural conditions in which we live), for Adorno, this is a moral choice. Popular culture, he believes, not only makes us stupid; it also makes us unable to act morally.

Essential emotions

Adorno believes that the opposite error to that of imagining that there might be such a thing as a holy fool is imagining that we can judge on intelligence alone, without emotion. This might happen in a court of law; judges have been known to instruct the jury to put all emotion to one side, so that they can come to a cool and measured decision.

> The power of judgement is measured by the cohesion of self.
> **Theodor Adorno**

Lighthearted television is inherently dangerous, says Adorno, because it distorts the world and imbues us with stereotypes and biases that we begin to take on as our own.

But in Adorno's view, we can no more make wise judgements by abandoning emotion than we can by abandoning intelligence.

When the last trace of emotion has been driven out of our thinking, Adorno writes, we are left with nothing to think about, and the idea that intelligence might benefit "from the decay of the emotions" is simply mistaken. For this reason Adorno believes that the sciences, which are a form of knowledge that do not make reference to our emotions, have, like popular culture, had a dehumanizing effect upon us.

Unexpectedly, it may in fact be the sciences that will ultimately demonstrate the wisdom of Adorno's central concerns about the severing of intelligence and feeling. Since the 1990s, scientists such as Antonio Damasio have studied emotions and the brain, providing increasing evidence of the many mechanisms by which emotions guide decision-making. So if we are to judge wisely or even to judge at all, we must employ both emotion and intelligence. ▪

Theodor Adorno

Born in 1903 in Frankfurt, Theodor Adorno's two passions from an early age were philosophy and music; his mother and aunt were both accomplished musicians. At university Adorno studied musicology and philosophy, graduating in 1924. He had ambitions to be a composer, but setbacks in his musical career led him increasingly towards philosophy. One area in which Adorno's interests converged was in his criticism of the industry surrounding popular culture, demonstrated in his notorious essay *On Jazz*, published in 1936.

In 1938, during the rise of Nazism in Germany, Adorno emigrated to New York, and then moved to Los Angeles, where he taught at the University of California. He returned to Germany after the end of World War II, and took up a professorship at Frankfurt. Adorno died at the age of 66 while on holiday in Switzerland in 1969.

Key works

1949 *Philosophy of New Music*
1951 *Minima Moralia*
1966 *Negative Dialectics*
1970 *Aesthetic Theory*

EXISTENCE PRECEDES ESSENCE

JEAN-PAUL SARTRE (1905–1980)

IN CONTEXT

BRANCH
Ethics

APPROACH
Existentialism

BEFORE
4th century BCE Aristotle asks the question "How should we live?"

1840s Søren Kierkegaard writes *Either/Or*, exploring the role played by choice in shaping our lives.

1920s Martin Heidegger says that what is important is our relationship with our own existence.

AFTER
1949 Sartre's friend and companion, Simone de Beauvoir, publishes *The Second Sex*, which applies Sartre's ideas to the question of the relationship between men and women.

S ince ancient times, the question of what it is to be human and what makes us so distinct from all other types of being has been one of the main preoccupations of philosophers. Their approach to the question assumes that there is such a thing as human nature, or an essence of what it is to be human. It also tends to assume that this human nature is fixed across time and space. In other words, it assumes that there is a universal essence of what it is to be human, and that this essence can be found in every single human that has ever existed, or will ever exist. According to this view, all human beings, regardless of their

See also: Aristotle 56–63 ▪ Søren Kierkegaard 194–95 ▪ Martin Heidegger 252–55 ▪ Simone de Beauvoir 276–77 ▪ Albert Camus 284–85

When we **make** something we do so for a **purpose**.

There is **no** God.

The purpose (or **essence**) of a made thing comes before its **existence**.

We are not made by **God**.

We are **not made** for any purpose…

…so our existence precedes our essence.

We have to **create** our purpose for **ourselves**.

Jean-Paul Sartre

Born in Paris, Sartre was just 15 months old when his father died. Brought up by his mother and grandfather, he proved a gifted student, and gained entry to the prestigious École Normale Supérieure. There he met his lifelong companion and fellow philosopher Simone de Beauvoir. After graduation, he worked as a teacher and was appointed Professor of Philosophy at the University of Le Havre in 1931.

During World War II, Sartre was drafted into the army and briefly imprisoned. After his release in 1941, he joined the resistance movement.

After 1945, Sartre's writing became increasingly political and he founded the literary and political journal *Modern Times*. He was offered, but declined, the Nobel Prize for Literature in 1964. Such was his influence and popularity that more than 50,000 people attended his funeral in 1980.

Key works

1938 *Nausea*
1943 *Being and Nothingness*
1946 *Existentialism and Humanism*
1960 *Critique of Dialectical Reason*

circumstances, possess the same fundamental qualities and are guided by the same basic values. For Sartre, however, thinking about human nature in this way risks missing what is most important about human beings, and that is our freedom.

To clarify what he means by this, Sartre gives the following illustration. He asks us to imagine a paper-knife – the kind of knife that might be used to open an envelope. This knife has been made by a craftsman who has had the idea of creating such a tool, and who had a clear understanding of what is required of a paper-knife. It needs to be sharp enough to cut through paper, but not so sharp as to be dangerous. It needs to be easy to wield, made of an appropriate substance – metal, bamboo, or wood, perhaps, but not butter, wax, or feathers – and fashioned to function efficiently. Sartre says that it is inconceivable for a paper-knife to exist without its maker knowing what it is going to be used for. Therefore the essence of a paper-knife – or all of the things that make it a paper-knife and not a steak knife or a paper aeroplane – comes before the existence of any particular paper-knife.

Humans, of course, are not paper-knives. For Sartre, there is no preordained plan that makes » us the kind of beings that we are. We are not made for any particular purpose. We exist, but not because of our purpose or essence like a paper-knife does; our existence precedes our essence.

Defining ourselves

This is where we begin to see the connection between Sartre's claim that "existence precedes essence" and his atheism. Sartre points out that religious approaches to the question of human nature often work by means of an analogy with human craftsmanship – that human nature in the mind of God is analogous to the nature of the paper-knife in the mind of the craftsman who makes it. Even many non-religious theories of human nature, Sartre claims, still have their roots in religious ways of thinking, because they continue to insist that essence comes before existence, or that we are made for a specific purpose. In claiming that existence comes before essence, Sartre is setting out a position that he believes is more consistent with his atheism. There is no universal, fixed human nature, he declares, because no God exists who could ordain such a nature.

Here Sartre is relying on a very specific definition of human nature, identifying the nature of something with its purpose. He is rejecting the concept of what philosophers call teleology in human nature – that it is something that we can think about in terms of the purpose of human existence. Nevertheless, there is a sense in which Sartre is offering a theory of human nature, by claiming that we are the kinds of beings who are compelled to assign a purpose to our lives. With no divine power to prescribe that purpose, we must define ourselves.

Defining ourselves, however, is not just a matter of being able to say what we are as human beings. Instead, it is a matter of shaping ourselves into whatever kind of being we choose to become. This is what makes us, at root, different from all the other kinds of being in the world – we can become whatever we choose to make of ourselves. A rock is simply a rock; a cauliflower is simply a cauliflower; and a mouse is simply a mouse. But human beings possess the ability to actively shape themselves.

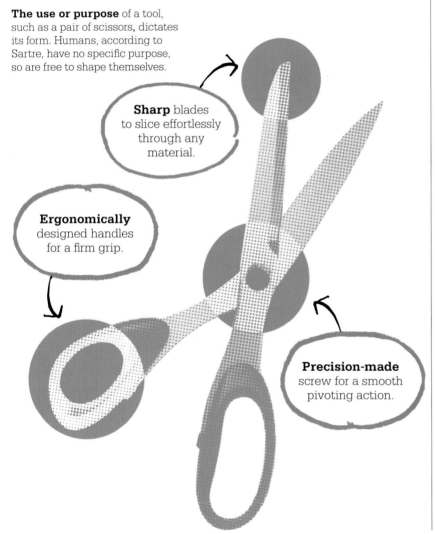

The use or purpose of a tool, such as a pair of scissors, dictates its form. Humans, according to Sartre, have no specific purpose, so are free to shape themselves.

Sharp blades to slice effortlessly through any material.

Ergonomically designed handles for a firm grip.

Precision-made screw for a smooth pivoting action.

First of all man exists, turns up, appears on the scene, and only afterwards defines himself.
Jean-Paul Sartre

Sartre's idea that we are free to shape our own lives influenced the students that took to the streets of Paris in May 1968 to protest against the draconian powers of the university authorities.

Because Sartre's philosophy releases us from the constraint of a human nature that is preordained, it is also one of freedom. We are free to choose how to shape ourselves, although we do have to accept some limitations. No amount of willing myself to grow wings, for example, will ever cause that to happen. But even within the range of realistic choices we have, we often find that we are constrained and simply make decisions based upon habit, or because of the way in which we have become accustomed to see ourselves.

Sartre wants us to break free of habitual ways of thinking, telling us to face up to the implications of living in a world in which nothing is preordained. To avoid falling into unconscious patterns of behaviour, he believes we must continually face up to choices about how to act.

Responsible freedom
By making choices, we are also creating a template for how we think a human life ought to be. If I decide

As far as men go,
it is not what they are that
interests me, but what
they can become.
Jean-Paul Sartre

to become a philosopher, then I am not just deciding for myself. I am implicitly saying that being a philosopher is a worthwhile activity. This means that freedom is the greatest responsibility of all. We are not just responsible for the impact that our choices have upon ourselves, but also for their impact on the whole of mankind. And, with no external principles or rules to justify our actions, we have no excuses to hide behind for the choices that we make. For this reason, Sartre declares that we are "condemned to be free".

Sartre's philosophy of linking freedom with responsibility has been labelled as pessimistic, but he refutes that charge. Indeed, he states that it is the most optimistic philosophy possible, because despite bearing responsibility for the impact of our actions upon others, we are able to choose to exercise sole control over how we fashion our world and ourselves.

Sartre's ideas were particularly influential on the writings of his companion and fellow philosopher Simone de Beauvoir, but they also had a marked impact on French cultural and daily life. Young people especially were thrilled by his call to use their freedom to fashion their existence. He inspired them to challenge the traditionalist, authoritarian attitudes that prevailed in France in the 1950s and 1960s. Sartre is cited as a key influence on the streets protests in Paris in May 1968, which helped to bring down the conservative government and herald a more liberal climate throughout France.

Engagement with political issues was an important part of Sartre's life. His constantly changing affiliations, as well as his perpetual movement between politics, philosophy, and literature, are themselves perhaps testament to a life lived in the light of the idea that existence precedes essence. ■

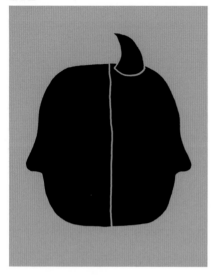

THE BANALITY OF EVIL
HANNAH ARENDT (1906–1975)

IN CONTEXT

BRANCH
Ethics

APPROACH
Existentialism

BEFORE
c.350 St Augustine of Hippo writes that evil is not a force, but comes from a lack of goodness.

1200s Thomas Aquinas writes *Disputed questions on evil*, exploring the idea of evil as a lack of something, rather than a thing in itself.

AFTER
1971 American social scientist Philip Zimbardo conducts the notorious "Stanford Prison Experiment" in which ordinary students are persuaded to participate in "evil" acts that would normally be considered unthinkable both to themselves and to others.

I n 1961, the philosopher Hannah Arendt witnessed the trial of Adolph Eichmann, one of the architects of the Holocaust. In her book *Eichmann in Jerusalem*, Arendt writes of the apparent "everydayness" of Eichmann. The figure before her in the dock did not resemble the kind of monster we might imagine. In fact, he would not have looked out of place in a café or in the street.

A failure of judgement
After witnessing the trial, Arendt came to the conclusion that evil does not come from malevolence or a delight in doing wrong. Instead, she suggests, the reasons people act in such ways is that they fall victim to failures of thinking and judgement. Oppressive political systems are able to take advantage of our tendencies towards such failures, and can make acts that we might usually consider to be "unthinkable" seem normal.

The idea that evil is banal does not strip evil acts of their horror. Instead, refusing to see people

Eichmann committed atrocities not through a hatred of the Jewish community, Arendt suggests, but because he unthinkingly followed orders, disengaging from their effects.

who commit terrible acts as "monsters", brings these acts closer to our everyday lives, challenging us to consider how evil may be something of which we are all capable. We should guard against the failures of our political regimes, says Arendt, and the possible failures in our own thinking and judgement. ∎

See also: St Augustine of Hippo 72–73 ▪ Thomas Aquinas 88–95 ▪ Theodor Adorno 266–67

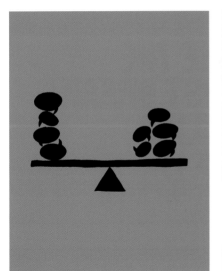

REASON LIVES IN LANGUAGE

EMMANUEL LEVINAS (1906–1995)

IN CONTEXT

BRANCH
Ethics

APPROACH
Phenomenology

BEFORE
1920s Edmund Husserl explores our relationship to other human beings from a phenomenological perspective.

1920s Austrian philosopher Martin Buber claims that meaning arises out of our relationship with others.

AFTER
From 1960 Levinas's work on relationships influences the thoughts of French feminist philosophers such as Luce Irigaray and Julia Kristeva.

From 1970 Levinas's ideas on responsibility influence psychotherapy.

2001 Jacques Derrida explores responsibility in relation to humanitarian questions such as political asylum.

L evinas's ideas are most easily understood through looking at an example. Imagine that you are walking down a street on a cold winter evening, and you see a beggar huddled in a doorway. She may not even be asking for change, but somehow you can't help feeling some obligation to respond to this stranger's need. You may choose to ignore her, but even if you do, something has already been communicated to you: the fact that this is a person who needs your help.

Inevitable communication

Levinas was a Jew Lithuanian who lived through the Holocaust. He says that reason lives in language in *Totality and Infinity* (1961), explaining that "language" is the way that we communicate with others even before we have started to speak. Whenever I see the face of another person, the fact that this is another human being and that I have a responsibility for them is instantly communicated. I can turn away from this responsibility, but I cannot escape it. This is why reason arises out of the face-to-face relationships we have with other people. It is because we are faced by the needs of other human beings that we must offer justifications for our actions. Even if you do not give your change to the beggar, you find yourself having to justify your choice. ∎

Nothing else in our lives so disrupts our consciousness as an encounter with another person, who, simply by being there, calls to us and asks us to account for ourselves.

See also: Edmund Husserl 224–25 ▪ Roland Barthes 290–91 ▪ Luce Irigaray 320 ▪ Hélène Cixous 322 ▪ Julia Kristeva 323

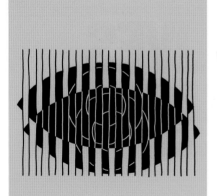

IN ORDER TO SEE THE WORLD, WE MUST BREAK WITH OUR FAMILIAR ACCEPTANCE OF IT
MAURICE MERLEAU-PONTY (1908–1961)

The idea that philosophy begins with our ability to wonder at the world goes back as far as ancient Greece. Usually we take our everyday lives for granted, but Aristotle claimed that if we want to understand the world more deeply, we have to put aside our familiar acceptance of things. And nowhere, perhaps, is this harder to do than in the realm of our experience. After all, what could be more reliable than the facts of direct perception?

French philosopher Merleau-Ponty was interested in looking more closely at our experience of the world, and in questioning our everyday assumptions. This puts him in the tradition known as phenomenology, an approach to philosophy pioneered by Edmund

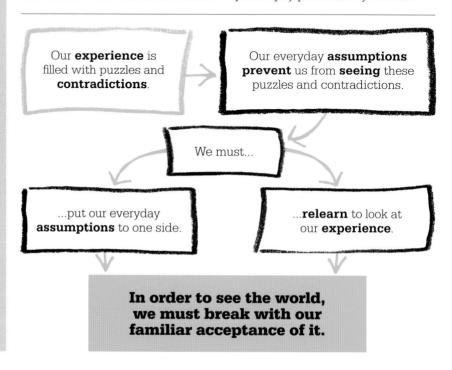

Our **experience** is filled with puzzles and **contradictions**.

Our everyday **assumptions prevent** us from **seeing** these puzzles and contradictions.

We must...

...put our everyday **assumptions** to one side.

...**relearn** to look at our **experience**.

In order to see the world, we must break with our familiar acceptance of it.

See also: Aristotle 56–63 ▪ Edmund Husserl 224–25 ▪ Ludwig Wittgenstein 246–51 ▪ Martin Heidegger 252–55 ▪ Jean-Paul Sartre 268–71

Man is in the world and only in the world does he know himself.
Maurice Merleau-Ponty

Husserl at the beginning of the 20th century. Husserl wanted to explore first-person experience in a systematic way, while putting all assumptions about it to one side.

The body-subject

Merleau-Ponty takes up Husserl's approach, but with one important difference. He is concerned that Husserl ignores what is most important about our experience – the fact that it consists not just of mental experience, but also of bodily experience. In his most important book, *The Phenomenology of Perception*, Merleau-Ponty explores this idea and comes to the conclusion that the mind and body are not separate entities – a thought that contradicts a long philosophical tradition championed by Descartes. For Merleau-Ponty, we have to see that thought and perception are embodied, and that the world, consciousness, and the body are all part of a single system. And his alternative to the disembodied mind proposed by Descartes is what he calls the body-subject. In other words, Merleau-Ponty rejects the dualist's view that the world is made of two separate entities, called mind and matter.

Cognitive science

Because he was interested in seeing the world anew, Merleau-Ponty took an interest in cases of abnormal experience. For example, he believed that the phantom limb phenomenon (in which an amputee "feels" his missing limb) shows that the body cannot simply be a machine. If it were, the body would no longer acknowledge the missing part – but it still exists for the subject because the limb has always been bound up with the subject's will. In other words, the body is never "just" a body – it is always a "lived" body.

Merleau-Ponty's focus on the role of the body in experience, and his insights into the nature of the mind as fundamentally embodied, have led to a revival of interest in his work among cognitive scientists. Many recent developments in cognitive science seem to bear out his idea that, once we break with our familiar acceptance of the world, experience is very strange indeed. ▪

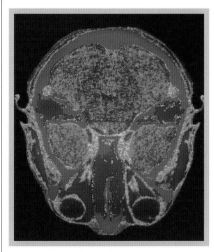

MRI scans of the brain provide doctors with life-saving information. However, in Merleau-Ponty's view, no amount of physical information can give us a complete account of experience.

Maurice Merleau-Ponty

Maurice Merleau-Ponty was born in Rochefort-sur-Mer, France, in 1908. He attended the École Normale Supérieure along with Jean-Paul Sartre and Simone de Beauvoir, and graduated in philosophy in 1930. He worked as a teacher at various schools, until joining the infantry during World War II. His major work, *The Phenomenology of Perception*, was published in 1945, after which he taught philosophy at the University of Lyon.

Merleau-Ponty's interests extended beyond philosophy to include subjects such as education and child psychology. He was also a regular contributor to the journal *Les Temps modernes*. In 1952, Merleau-Ponty became the youngest-ever Chair of Philosophy at the College de France, and remained in the post until his death in 1961, at the age of only 53.

Key works

1942 *The Structure of Behaviour*
1945 *The Phenomenology of Perception*
1964 *The Visible and the Invisible*

MAN IS DEFINED AS A HUMAN BEING AND WOMAN AS A FEMALE
SIMONE DE BEAUVOIR (1908–1986)

IN CONTEXT

BRANCH
Ethics

APPROACH
Feminism

BEFORE
c.350 BCE Aristotle says, "The female is a female by virtue of a certain lack of qualities."

1792 Mary Wollstonecraft publishes A *Vindication of the Rights of Woman*, illustrating the equality of the sexes.

1920s Martin Heidegger sets out a "philosophy of existence," prefiguring existentialism.

1940s Jean-Paul Sartre says "existence precedes essence".

AFTER
1970s Luce Irigaray explores the philosophical implications of sexual difference.

From 1980 Julia Kristeva breaks down the notions of "male" and "female" as characterized by de Beauvoir.

French philosopher Simone de Beauvoir writes in her book *The Second Sex* that throughout history, the standard measure of what we take to be human – both in philosophy and in society at large – has been a peculiarly male view. Some philosophers, such as Aristotle, have been explicit in equating full humanity with maleness. Others have not said as much, but have nevertheless taken maleness as the standard against which humanity is to be judged. It is for this reason that de Beauvoir says that the Self (or "I") of philosophical knowledge is by default male, and his binary pair – the female – is therefore something else, which she calls the Other. The Self is active and knowing, whereas the Other is all that the Self rejects: passivity, voicelessness, and powerlessness.

De Beauvoir is also concerned with the way that women are judged to be equal only insofar as they are like men. Even those who

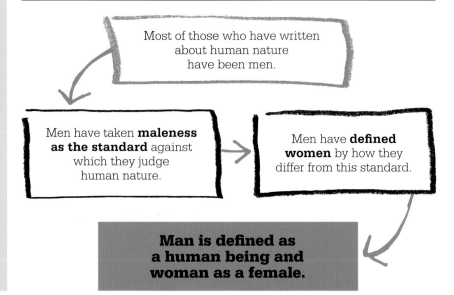

Most of those who have written about human nature have been men.

Men have taken **maleness as the standard** against which they judge human nature.

Men have **defined women** by how they differ from this standard.

Man is defined as a human being and woman as a female.

See also: Hypatia of Alexandria 331 ▪ Mary Wollstonecraft 175 ▪ Jean-Paul Sartre 268–71 ▪ Luce Irigaray 320 ▪ Hélène Cixous 322 ▪ Martha Nussbaum 339

Representation of the world is the work of men; they describe it from their own point of view.
Simone de Beauvoir

have written on behalf of the equality of women, she says, have done so by arguing that equality means that women can be and do the same as men. She claims that this idea is mistaken, because it ignores the fact that women and men are different. De Beauvoir's philosophical background was in phenomenology, the study of how things appear to our experience. This view maintains that each of us constructs the world from within the frame of our own consciousness; we constitute things and meanings from the stream of our experiences. Consequently de Beauvoir maintains that the relationship that we have to our own bodies, to others, and to the world, as well as to philosophy itself, is strongly influenced by whether we are male or female.

Existential feminism

Simone De Beauvoir was also an existentialist, believing that we are born without purpose and must carve out an authentic existence for ourselves, choosing what to become. In applying this idea to the notion of "woman", she asks us to separate the biological entity (the bodily form which females are born into) from femininity, which is a social

construct. Since any construct is open to change and interpretation, this means that there are many ways of "being a woman"; there is room for existential choice. In the introduction to *The Second Sex* de Beauvoir notes society's awareness of this fluidity: "We are exhorted to be women, remain women, become women. It would appear, then, that every female human being is not necessarily a woman". She later states the position explicitly: "One is not born but becomes a woman".

De Beauvoir says that women must free themselves both from the idea that they must be like men, and from the passivity that society has induced in them. Living a truly authentic existence carries more risk than accepting a role handed down by society, but it is the only path to equality and freedom. ▪

The many myths of woman as mother, wife, virgin, symbol of nature and so on trap women, claimed de Beauvoir, into impossible ideals, while denying their individual selves and situations.

Simone de Beauvoir

The existentialist philosopher Simone de Beauvoir was born in Paris in 1908. She studied philosophy at the Sorbonne University, and it was here that she met Jean-Paul Sartre, with whom she began a lifelong relationship. Both a philosopher and an award-winning novelist, she often explored philosophical themes within fictional works such as *She Came to Stay* and *The Mandarins*. Her most famous work, *The Second Sex*, brought an existentialist approach to feminist ideas. Despite initially being vilified by the political right and left, and being placed on the Vatican's Index of Forbidden Books, it became one of the most important feminist works of the 20th century. De Beauvoir was a prolific writer, producing travel books, memoirs, a four-volume autobiography, and political essays over the course of her life. She died at the age of 78, and was buried in Montparnasse cemetery.

Key works

1944 *Pyrrhus and Cineas*
1947 *The Ethics of Ambiguity*
1949 *The Second Sex*
1954 *The Mandarins*

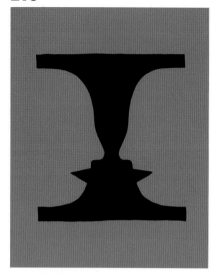

LANGUAGE IS A SOCIAL ART
WILLARD VAN ORMAN QUINE (1908–2000)

IN CONTEXT

IN CONTEXT

BRANCH
Philosophy of language

APPROACH
Analytic philosophy

BEFORE
c.400 BCE Plato's *Cratylus* investigates the relationship between words and things.

19th century Søren Kierkegaard stresses the importance of the study of language for philosophy.

1950s Ludwig Wittgenstein writes that there is no such thing as a private language.

AFTER
1980s Richard Rorty suggests that knowledge is more like "conversation" than the representation of reality.

1990s In *Consciousness Explained*, Quine's former student Daniel Dennett says that both meaning and inner experience can only be understood as social acts.

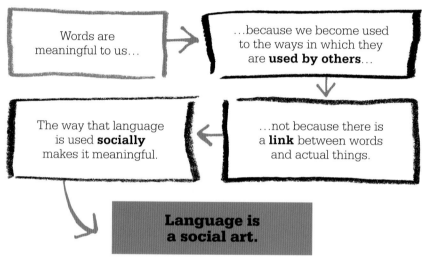

Words are meaningful to us…

…because we become used to the ways in which they are **used by others**…

The way that language is used **socially** makes it meaningful.

…not because there is a **link** between words and actual things.

Language is a social art.

Some philosophers assert that language is about the relationship between words and things. Quine, however, disagrees. Language is not about the relationship between objects and verbal signifiers, but about knowing what to say and when to say it. It is, he says in his 1968 essay *Ontological Relativity*, a social art.

Quine suggests the following thought experiment. Imagine that we come across some people – perhaps natives of another country – who speak a language we do not share. We are sitting with a group of these people when a rabbit appears, and one of the natives says "gavagai". We wonder if there can be a connection between the event – the appearance of the rabbit – and the fact that the native says "gavagai". As time goes on, we note that every time a rabbit appears, somebody says "gavagai", so we conclude that "gavagai" can be reliably translated as rabbit. But, Quine insists, we are wrong. "Gavagai" could mean all manner of things. It could mean "oh, look, dinner!" for example, or it could mean "behold, a fluffy creature!"

See also: Plato 50–55 ▪ Søren Kierkegaard 194–95 ▪ Ferdinand de Saussure 223 ▪ Ludwig Wittgenstein 246–51 ▪ Roland Barthes 290–91 ▪ Daniel Dennett 339

If we wanted to determine the meaning of "gavagai", we could try another method. We could point to other fluffy creatures (or other things on the dinner menu) and see if our utterance of "gavagai" met with assent or dissent. But even if we were to reach a position where, in each and every occasion on which "gavagai" was uttered, we ourselves would utter the word "rabbit", we still could not be sure that this was an appropriate translation. "Gavagai" could mean "set of rabbit parts" or "wood-living rabbit" or "rabbit or hare"; it might even refer to a short prayer that must be uttered whenever a rabbit is seen.

Unsettled language

In attempting to establish the precise meaning of this mysterious "gavagai", therefore, we might think that the solution would be to learn the language of our informants thoroughly, so that we could be absolutely sure of the contexts in which the word was spoken. But this would only result in multiplying the problem, because we could not

No word has a fixed meaning, according to Quine. When the word "rabbit" is spoken, it may mean any one of a number of things, depending on the context in which it is said.

be sure that the other words we found ourselves using to explain the meaning of "gavagai" were themselves accurate translations.

Quine refers to this problem as the "indeterminacy of translation", and it has unsettling implications. It suggests that ultimately words do not have meanings. The sense of somebody uttering "gavagai" (or, for that matter, "rabbit"), and of this utterance being meaningful comes not from some mysterious link between words and things, but from the patterns of our behaviour, and the fact that we have learned to participate in language as a social art. ▪

Willard Van Orman Quine

Born in 1908 in Ohio, USA, Quine studied at Harvard with Alfred North Whitehead, a philosopher of logic and mathematics. While there he also met Bertrand Russell, who was to become a profound influence on his thought. After completing his PhD in 1932, Quine travelled throughout Europe, meeting many of its most eminent philosophers, including several of the Vienna Circle.

Returning to teach at Harvard, Quine's philosophical career was briefly interrupted during World War II when he spent four years decrypting messages for the US Navy intelligence. A great traveller, he was said to be prouder of the fact that he had visited 118 countries than of his many awards and fellowships. Quine became professor of philosophy at Harvard in 1956, and taught there until his death in 2000, aged 92.

Key works

1952 *Methods of Logic*
1953 *From a Logical Point of View*
1960 *Word and Object*
1990 *The Pursuit of Truth*

THE FUNDAMENTAL SENSE OF FREEDOM IS FREEDOM FROM CHAINS
ISAIAH BERLIN (1909–1997)

IN CONTEXT

BRANCH
Ethics

APPROACH
Analytic philosophy

BEFORE
1651 In his book *Leviathan*, Thomas Hobbes considers the relationship between freedom and state power.

1844 Søren Kierkegaard argues that our freedom to make moral decisions is a chief cause of unhappiness.

1859 In his book *On Liberty*, John Stuart Mill distinguishes between freedom from coercion and freedom to act.

1941 Psychoanalyst Erich Fromm explores positive and negative liberty in his book *The Fear of Freedom*.

AFTER
Present day The development of new surveillance technology raises fresh questions about the nature of freedom.

Freedom is both positive and negative.

Positive: we are free to control our own destiny and choose our own goals.

Negative: we are free from external obstacles and domination, or "chains".

But our individual goals sometimes **conflict** or lead to the **domination** of others.

When our own positive freedom leads to a **decrease** in others' negative freedom, it becomes **oppression**.

The fundamental sense of freedom is freedom from chains.

What does it mean to be free? This is the question explored by the British philosopher Isaiah Berlin in his famous essay *Two Concepts of Liberty*, written in 1958. Here he makes a distinction between what he calls "positive" and "negative"

freedom. Although he is not the first to draw this distinction, he does so with great originality, and uses it to expose apparent inconsistencies in our everyday notion of freedom.

For Berlin, "negative" freedom is what he calls our "fundamental sense" of freedom. This kind of

See also: Jean-Jacques Rousseau 154–59 ▪ John Stuart Mill 190–93 ▪ Søren Kierkegaard 194–95 ▪ Karl Marx 196–203 ▪ Jean-Paul Sartre 268–71

Soviet propaganda often depicted workers liberated from capitalism. From a capitalist view, however, such images showed a triumph of negative freedom over positive freedom.

freedom is freedom from external obstacles: I am free because I am not chained to a rock, because I am not in prison, and so on. This is freedom from something else. But Berlin points out that when we talk about freedom, we usually mean something more subtle than this. Freedom is also a matter of self-determination, of being a person with hopes, and intentions, and purposes that are one's own. This "positive" freedom is about being in control of one's own destiny. After all, I am not free just because all the doors of my house are unlocked. And this positive freedom is not exclusively personal, because self-determination can also be desired at the level of the group or of the state.

For Berlin, the problem is that these two forms of freedom are often in conflict. Think, for example, of the freedom that comes from the discipline of learning how to play the tuba. As a beginner, I can do little more than struggle with my own inability to play – but eventually I can play with a kind of liberated gusto. Or think of the fact that people frequently exercise their "positive" freedom by voting for a particular government, knowing that their "negative" freedom will be restricted when that government comes to power.

The goals of life

Berlin points to another problem. Who is to say what a suitable goal of "positive" freedom should be? Authoritarian or totalitarian regimes often have an inflexible view of the purpose of human life, and so restrict "negative" freedoms to maximize their idea of human happiness. Indeed, political oppression frequently arises from an abstract idea of what the good life is, followed by state intervention to make that idea a reality.

Berlin's response to this is twofold. First, it is important to recognize that the various freedoms we may desire will always be in conflict, for there is no such thing as "the goal of life" – only the goals of particular individuals. This fact, he claims, is obscured by philosophers who look for a universal basis for morality, but confuse "right action" with the purpose of life itself. Second, we need to keep alive the fundamental sense of freedom as an absence of "bullying and domination", so that we do not find our ideals turning into chains for ourselves and for others. ■

Isaiah Berlin

Isaiah Berlin was born in Riga, Latvia, in 1909. He spent the first part of his life in Russia, firstly under the Russian empire, and then under the rule of the new Communist state. Due to rising anti-Semitism, however, and problems with the Soviet régime, his family emigrated to Britain in 1921. Berlin was an outstanding student at Oxford University, where he remained as a lecturer. He was a philosopher with broad interests, ranging from art and literature to politics. His essay *Two Concepts of Liberty* was delivered in 1958 at Oxford University, and it is often considered one of the classics of 20th-century political theory. He is celebrated for being one of the foremost scholars of liberalism.

Key works

1953 *The Hedgehog and the Fox: An Essay on Tolstoy's View of History*
1958 *Two Concepts of Liberty*
1990 *The Crooked Timber of Humanity: Chapters in the History of Ideas*
2000 *The Power of Ideas*
2006 *Political Ideas in the Romantic Age*

THINK LIKE A MOUNTAIN
ARNE NAESS (1912–2009)

The injunction to think like a mountain has become closely associated with the concept of "deep ecology" – a term coined in 1973 by the Norwegian philosopher and environmental campaigner, Arne Naess. He uses the term to stress his belief that we must first recognize we are part of nature, and not separate from it, if we are to avoid environmental catastrophe. But the notion of thinking like a mountain goes back to 1949, when it was expressed by American ecologist Aldo Leopold in *The Sand County Almanac*.

Working as a forester in New Mexico in the early part of the 20th century, Leopold shot a female wolf on the mountainside. "We reached the old wolf in time to watch a fierce green fire dying in her eyes," he wrote. "I realized then, and have known ever since, that there was something new to me in those eyes – something known only to her and to the mountain." It was from this experience that Leopold came to the idea that we should think like a mountain, recognizing not just our needs or those of our fellow humans, but those of the

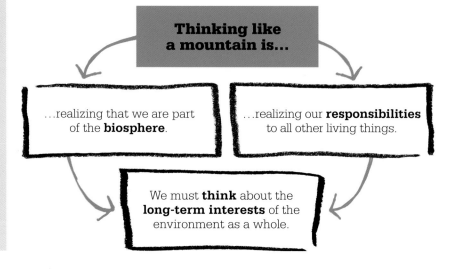

Thinking like a mountain is...

…realizing that we are part of the **biosphere**.

…realizing our **responsibilities** to all other living things.

We must **think** about the **long-term interests** of the environment as a whole.

See also: Laozi 24–25 ▪ Benedictus Spinoza 126–29 ▪ Friedrich Schelling 335

> The thinking for the future has to be loyal to nature.
> **Arne Naess**

entire natural world. He implies that often we miss the broader implications of our actions, only considering the immediate benefits to ourselves. To "think like a mountain" means identifying with the wider environment and being aware of its role in our lives.

Harmonizing with nature

Naess takes up Leopold's idea by proposing his "deep ecology". He states that we only protect our environment by undergoing the kind of transformation of which Leopold writes. Naess urges us to move towards seeing ourselves as part of the whole biosphere. Instead of viewing the world with a kind of detachment, we must find our place in nature, by acknowledging the intrinsic value of all elements of the world we inhabit.

Naess introduces the "ecological self", a sense of self that is rooted in an awareness of our relationship to a "larger community of all living beings". He claims that broadening our identification with the world to include wolves, frogs, spiders, and perhaps even mountains, leads to a more joyful and meaningful life.

Naess's "deep ecology" has had a powerful effect on environmental philosophy and on the development of environmental activism. For those of us who live in cities, it may seem hard or even impossible to connect with an "ecological self". Nevertheless, it may be possible. As the Zen master Robert Aitken Roshi wrote in 1984, "When one thinks like a mountain, one thinks also like the black bear, so that honey dribbles down your fur as you catch the bus to work." ∎

The natural world, for Naess, is not something that we should strive to control and manipulate for our own gain. Living well involves living as an equal with all the elements of our environment.

Arne Naess

Widely acknowledged as the leading Norwegian philosopher of the 20th century, Arne Naess became the youngest-ever full professor at the University of Oslo at the age of 27. He was also a noted mountaineer and led a successful expedition to the summit of Tirich Mir in northern Pakistan in 1950.

It was only after Naess retired from his teaching post in 1970 that he actively developed his thinking about the natural world and became involved in direct action on environmental issues. In 1970, he chained himself to the rocks by the Mardalsfossen Waterfall in Norway to protest against the building of a nearby dam. Elected as chairperson of Greenpeace Norway in 1988, he was knighted in 2005.

Key works

1968 *Scepticism*
1974 *Ecology, Society and Lifestyle*
1988 *Thinking Like a Mountain* (with John Seed, Pat Fleming and Joanna Macy)
2002 *Life's Philosophy: Reason and Feeling in a Deeper World*

LIFE WILL BE LIVED ALL THE BETTER IF IT HAS NO MEANING
ALBERT CAMUS (1913–1960)

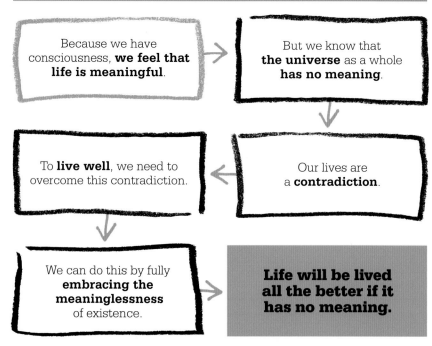

Because we have consciousness, **we feel that life is meaningful**.

But we know that **the universe** as a whole **has no meaning**.

Our lives are a **contradiction**.

To **live well**, we need to overcome this contradiction.

We can do this by fully **embracing the meaninglessness** of existence.

Life will be lived all the better if it has no meaning.

Some people believe that philosophy's task is to search for the meaning of life. But the French philosopher and novelist Albert Camus thought that philosophy should recognize instead that life is inherently meaningless. While at first this seems a depressing view, Camus believes that only by embracing this idea are we capable of living as fully as possible.

Camus' idea appears in his essay *The Myth of Sisyphus*. Sisyphus was a Greek king who fell out of favour with the gods, and so was sentenced to a terrible fate in the Underworld. His task was to roll an enormous rock to the top of a hill, only to watch it roll back to the bottom. Sisyphus then had to trudge down the hill to begin the task again, repeating this for all

See also: Søren Kierkegaard 194–95 ▪ Friedrich Nietzsche 214–21 ▪ Martin Heidegger 252–55 ▪ Jean-Paul Sartre 268–71

Sisyphus was condemned eternally to push a rock up a hill, but Camus thought he might find freedom even in this grim situation if he accepted the meaninglessness of his eternal task.

eternity. Camus was fascinated by this myth, because it seemed to him to encapsulate something of the meaninglessness and absurdity of our lives. He sees life as an endless struggle to perform tasks that are essentially meaningless.

Camus recognizes that much of what we do certainly seems meaningful, but what he is suggesting is quite subtle. On the one hand, we are conscious beings who cannot help living our lives as if they are meaningful. On the other hand, these meanings do not reside out there in the universe; they reside only in our minds. The universe as a whole has no meaning and no purpose; it just is. But because, unlike other living things, we have consciousness, we are the kinds of beings who find meaning and purpose everywhere.

Recognizing the absurd

The absurd, for Camus, is the feeling that we have when we recognize that the meanings we give to life do not exist beyond our own consciousness. It is the result of a contradiction between our own sense of life's meaning, and our knowledge that nevertheless the universe as a whole is meaningless.

Camus explores what it might mean to live in the light of this contradiction. He claims that it is

> The struggle towards the heights is enough to fill a man's heart.
> **Albert Camus**

only once we can accept the fact that life is meaningless and absurd that we are in a position to live fully. In embracing the absurd, our lives become a constant revolt against the meaninglessness of the universe, and we can live freely.

This idea was further developed by the philosopher Thomas Nagel, who said that the absurdity of life lies in the nature of consciousness, because however seriously we take life, we always know that there is some perspective from which this seriousness can be questioned. ■

Albert Camus

Camus was born in Algeria in 1913. His father was killed a year later in World War I, and Camus was brought up by his mother in extreme poverty. He studied philosophy at the University of Algiers, where he suffered the first attack of the tuberculosis which was to recur throughout his life. At the age of 25 he went to live in France, where he became involved in politics. He joined the French Communist Party in 1935 but was expelled in 1937. During World War II he worked for the French Resistance, editing an underground newspaper and writing many of his best-known novels, including *The Stranger*. He wrote many plays, novels, and essays, and was awarded the Nobel Prize for Literature in 1957. Camus died in a car crash aged 46, having discarded a train ticket to accept a lift back to Paris with a friend.

Key works

1942 *The Myth of Sisyphus*
1942 *The Stranger*
1947 *The Plague*
1951 *The Rebel*
1956 *The Fall*

CONTEM PHILOSO

1950–PRESENT

PORARY
PHY

Frantz Fanon
publishes *Black Skin, White Masks.*

1952

The **Vietnam War** begins. The USSR and China support communist North Vietnam, while the USA supports South Vietnam.

1955

Thomas Kuhn
publishes *The Structure of Scientific Revolutions.*

1962

China's Great Proletarian **Cultural Revolution** "purges" China of everything Western, capitalist, traditionalist, or religious.

1966

1953

Simone de Beauvoir
publishes her groundbreaking feminist work, *The Second Sex.*

1961

The Berlin Wall is constructed, dividing East and West Germany until its fall in 1989.

1964

The **Civil Rights Act** 1964 becomes law in the USA, prohibiting discrimination by race.

1967

Jacques Derrida, the founder of deconstruction, publishes *Writing and Difference.*

The closing decades of the 20th century were notable for accelerating advances in technology and the subsequent improvement in communications of all kinds. The increasing power of the mass media, especially television, since the end of World War II had fuelled a rise in popular culture with its associated anti-establishment ideals, and this in turn was prompting political and social change. From the 1960s onwards, the old order was being questioned in Europe and the US, and dissent gathered momentum in Eastern Europe.

By the 1980s, relations between the East and West were thawing, and the Cold War was coming to a close; the fall of the Berlin Wall in 1989 offered hope for the new decade. But the 1990s was a period of ethnic and religious unrest, culminating in the US declaring a "War on Terror" at the start of the new millennium.

Elitist philosophies
Culture in the West went through similarly significant changes. The gap between popular and "high" culture widened after the 1960s, as the intellectual avant-garde often decided to disregard public taste. Philosophy followed a similarly elitist path, particularly after the death of Jean-Paul Sartre, whose Marxist existentialism – beloved of 1960s intellectuals – now had less of an audience.

Continental philosophy was dominated in the 1970s and 80s by structuralism, a movement that grew from literature-based French philosophy. Central to this movement was the notion of "deconstructing" texts and revealing them to be inherently unstable, with many contradictory meanings. The theory's principal proponents – French theorists Louis Althusser, Jacques Derrida, and Michel Foucault – linked their textual analyses with left-wing politics, while the analyst Jacques Lacan gave structuralism a psychoanalytic perspective. Their ideas were soon taken up by a generation of writers and artists working under the banner of "postmodernism", which rejected all possibility of a single, objective truth, viewpoint, or narrative.

Structuralism's contribution to philosophy was not enthusiastically received by philosophers in the English-speaking world, who viewed the work at best with

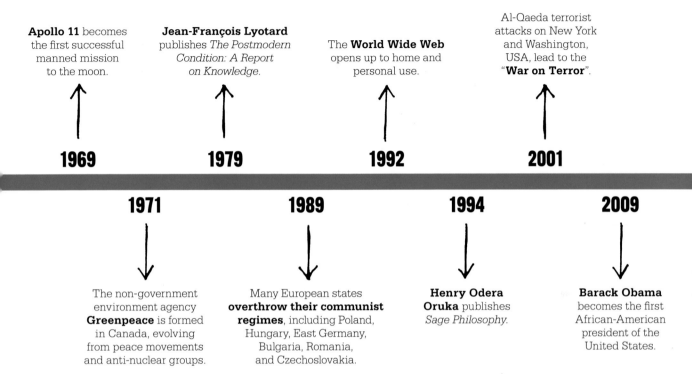

Apollo 11 becomes the first successful manned mission to the moon.

1969

Jean-François Lyotard publishes *The Postmodern Condition: A Report on Knowledge*.

1979

The **World Wide Web** opens up to home and personal use.

1992

Al-Qaeda terrorist attacks on New York and Washington, USA, lead to the "**War on Terror**".

2001

1971

The non-government environment agency **Greenpeace** is formed in Canada, evolving from peace movements and anti-nuclear groups.

1989

Many European states **overthrow their communist regimes**, including Poland, Hungary, East Germany, Bulgaria, Romania, and Czechoslovakia.

1994

Henry Odera Oruka publishes *Sage Philosophy*.

2009

Barack Obama becomes the first African-American president of the United States.

suspicion, and largely with derision. Within a philosophical tradition of linguistic analysis, continental structuralism seemed ultimately simplistic – although it was often written in impenetrable prose that belied its literary roots.

The squabbles of philosophers did not inspire the popular culture of the time. This may have been because postmodernism was largely incomprehensible to the general public. Their most common experience of it was postmodern art, which was highly conceptual and accompanied by knowing references by an intellectual elite. It seemed to deliberately exclude any possibility of mass appreciation, and became seen as an abstract philosophy only enjoyed by professional academics and artists, and out of touch with the world most people lived in. The

public, as well as businesses and governments, wanted more down-to-earth guidance from philosophy.

A more practical approach

Though postmodern philosophy may not have found favour with the majority of the general public, some philosophers of the period chose to focus on more pressing social, political, and ethical questions that had more relevance to people's everyday lives. Thinkers in post-colonial Africa such as Frantz Fanon began to examine race, identity, and the problems that were inherent in any struggle for liberation. Later thinkers, such as Henry Odera Oruka, would begin to amass a new history of African philosophy, questioning the rules governing philosophy itself, and what it should include.

Continuing in the tradition of Simone de Beauvoir's existential feminist philosophy, French philosophers such as Hélène Cixous and Luce Irigaray added a postmodern perspective to feminism, but other thinkers on both sides of the Atlantic left postmodernism completely to one side. Some, such as American philosopher John Rawls and Germany's Jürgen Habermas, returned to examining important everyday concepts in depth, such as justice and communication.

The more practical approach to philosophy in the 21st century has led to a renewed public interest in the subject. There is no way of predicting what direction it will take, but philosophy is certain to continue to provide the world with thought-provoking ideas. ∎

LANGUAGE IS A SKIN
ROLAND BARTHES (1915–1980)

IN CONTEXT

BRANCH
Philosophy of language

APPROACH
Semiotics

BEFORE
380 BCE Plato's *Symposium*
is the first sustained
philosophical discussion
of love in the West.

4th century CE St Augustine
of Hippo writes extensively on
the nature of love.

1916 Ferdinand de Saussure's
Course in General Linguistics
establishes modern semiotics
and the study of language as
a series of signs.

1966 French psychoanalyst
Jacques Lacan looks at
the relationship between
Alcibiades, Socrates, and
Agathon in his *Écrits*.

AFTER
1990s Julia Kristeva explores
the relationship between love,
semiotics, and psychoanalysis.

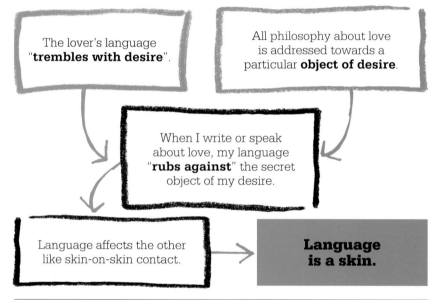

The lover's language "**trembles with desire**".

All philosophy about love is addressed towards a particular **object of desire**.

When I write or speak about love, my language "**rubs against**" the secret object of my desire.

Language affects the other like skin-on-skin contact.

Language is a skin.

The strangest, but most popular, book written by philosopher and literary critic Roland Barthes is *A Lover's Discourse*. As the French title, *Fragments d'un discours amoureux*, suggests, this is a book told in fragments and snapshots, somewhat like the essay *One-Way Street* by the German philosopher Walter Benjamin. *A Lover's Discourse* is not so much a book of philosophy as it is a love story; but it is a love story without any real story. There are no characters, and there is nothing in the way of a plot. There are only the reflections of a lover in what Barthes calls "extreme solitude".

At the very beginning of the book, Barthes makes clear that a plot is not possible, because the solitary thoughts of a lover come in outbursts that are often contradictory and lack any clear order. As a lover, Barthes suggests, I might even find myself plotting against myself. The lover is somebody who might be

See also: Plato 50–55 ▪ St Augustine of Hippo 72–73 ▪ Ferdinand de Saussure 223 ▪ Walter Benjamin 258 ▪ Jacques Derrida 308–13 ▪ Julia Kristeva 323

> Every lover
> is mad.
> **Roland Barthes**

affectionately described as having "lost the plot". So instead of using a plot, or narrative, Barthes arranges his book like a extraordinary encyclopaedia of contradictory and disordered outbursts, any of which might serve as the point the reader might suddenly exclaim, "That's so true! I recognize that scene..."

The language of love
It is in this context that Barthes suggests "language is a skin". Language, at least the language of the lover, is not something that simply talks about the world in a neutral fashion, but it is something that, as Barthes says, "trembles with desire". Barthes writes of how "I rub my language against the other. It is as if I had words instead of fingers, or fingers at the tip of my words." Even if I write cool, detached philosophy about love, Barthes claims, there is buried in my philosophical coolness a secret address to a particular person, an object of my desire, even if this somebody is "a phantom or a creature still to come".

Barthes gives an example of this secret address (although not, it should be said, in the context of a particularly detached philosophical discussion) from Plato's dialogue, *The Symposium*. This is an account of a discussion on the subject of love that takes place in the house of the poet Agathon. A statesman called Alcibiades turns up to the discussion both late and drunk, and sits down on a couch with Agathon and the philosopher Socrates. The drunken speech he gives is full of praise for Socrates, but it is Agathon that Alcibiades desires; it is against Agathon, so to speak, that Alcibiades' language is rubbing.

But what of the language that we use when talking of other things? Is only the lover's language a skin that trembles with hidden desire, or is this also true of other types of language? Barthes does not tell us, leaving us to consider the idea for ourselves. ∎

The lover's language is like a skin, says Barthes, which is inhabited by the lover. Its words are able to move the beloved – and only the beloved – in an almost physical or tactile way.

Roland Barthes

Barthes was born in Cherbourg, France, in 1915. He attended the University of Sorbonne in Paris from 1935, graduating in 1939, but by this time he had already contracted the tuberculosis that would afflict him for the remainder of his life. His illness made it difficult to acquire teaching qualifications, but it exempted him from military service during World War II. After the war, having finally qualified as a teacher, he taught in France, Romania, and Egypt. He returned to live in France full time in 1952, and there started to write the pieces that were collected together and published under the title *Mythologies* in 1957.

Barthes' reputation grew steadily through the 1960s, in France and internationally, and he taught both at home and abroad. He died at the age of 64, when he was run over by a laundry van after lunching with President Mitterrand.

Key works

1957 *Mythologies*
1973 *The Pleasure of the Text*
1977 *A Lover's Discourse*

HOW WOULD WE MANAGE WITHOUT A CULTURE?

MARY MIDGLEY (1919–)

IN CONTEXT

BRANCH
Philosophy of science

APPROACH
Analytic philosophy

BEFORE
4th century BCE Aristotle
defines human beings as
"political animals", suggesting
that not only are we natural
beings, but that the creation of
culture is a part of our nature.

1st century BCE Roman poet
Titus Lucretius Carus writes
On the Nature of the Universe,
exploring the natural roots of
human culture.

1859 Naturalist Charles
Darwin publishes *On the
Origin of Species*, arguing that
all life has evolved through a
process of natural selection.

AFTER
1980s onwards Richard
Dawkins and Mary Midgley
debate the implications of
Darwinism for our view of
human nature.

In her book *Beast and Man*, published in 1978, the British philosopher Mary Midgley assesses the impact the natural sciences have on our understanding of human nature. It is often claimed that the findings of the sciences, particularly those of paleontology and evolutionary biology, undermine our views of what it is to be human. Midgley wants to address these fears, and she does so by stressing both the things that set us apart from other animals and the things that we share with the rest of the animal kingdom.

One of the questions that she tackles is that of the relationship between nature and culture in human life. Her concern is to address the fact that many people see nature and culture as somehow opposed, as if culture is something non-natural that is added onto our animal natures.

Midgley disagrees with the idea that culture is something of a wholly different order to nature. Insteadc she wants to argue that culture is a natural phenomenon. In other words, we have evolved to be the kinds of creatures who have cultures. It could be said that we spin culture as naturally as spiders spin webs. If this is so, then we can no more do without culture than a spider can do without its web: our need for culture is both innate and natural. In this way, Midgley hopes both to account for human uniqueness, and also to put us in the larger context of our evolutionary past. ∎

> We mistakenly cut ourselves off from other animals, trying not to believe we have an animal nature.
> **Mary Midgley**

See also: Plato 50–55 ▪ Aristotle 56–63 ▪ Ludwig Wittgenstein 246–51

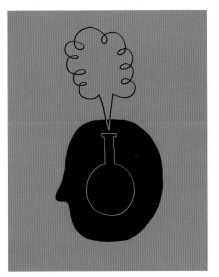

NORMAL SCIENCE DOES NOT AIM AT NOVELTIES OF FACT OR THEORY
THOMAS KUHN (1922–1996)

American physicist and historian of science Thomas Kuhn is best known for his book *The Structure of Scientific Revolutions*, published in 1962. The book is both an exploration of turning points in the history of science and an attempt to set out a theory of how revolutions in science take place.

Paradigm shifts

Science, in Kuhn's view, alternates between periods of "normal science" and periods of "crisis". Normal science is the routine process by which scientists working within a theoretical framework – or "paradigm" – accumulate results that do not call the theoretical underpinnings of their framework into question. Sometimes, of course, anomalous, or unfamiliar, results are encountered, but these are usually considered to be errors on the part of the scientists concerned – proof, according to Kuhn, that normal science does not aim at novelties. Over time, however, anomalous results can accumulate until a crisis point is reached. Following the crisis, if a new theory has been formulated, there is a shift in the paradigm, and the new theoretical framework replaces the old. Eventually this framework is taken for granted, and normal science resumes – until further anomalies arise. An example of such a shift was the shattering of the classical view of space and time following the confirmation of Einstein's theories of relativity. ∎

Nicolaus Copernicus's claim that Earth orbits the Sun was a revolution in scientific thinking. It led to scientists abandoning the belief that our planet is at the centre of the universe.

See also: Francis Bacon 110–11 ▪ Rudolf Carnap 257 ▪ Karl Popper 262–65 ▪ Paul Feyerabend 297 ▪ Richard Rorty 314–19

THE PRINCIPLES OF JUSTICE ARE CHOSEN BEHIND A VEIL OF IGNORANCE
JOHN RAWLS (1921–2002)

IN CONTEXT

BRANCH
Political philosophy

APPROACH
Social contract theory

BEFORE
c.380 BCE Plato discusses the nature of justice and the just society in *The Republic*.

1651 Thomas Hobbes sets out a theory of social contract in his book *Leviathan*.

1689 John Locke develops Hobbes's theory in his *Second Treatise of Government*.

1762 Jean-Jacques Rousseau writes *The Social Contract*. His views are later adopted by French revolutionaries.

AFTER
1974 Robert Nozick criticizes Rawls' "original position" in his influential book *Anarchy, State, and Utopia*.

2001 Rawls defends his views in his last book, *Justice as Fairness: A Restatement*.

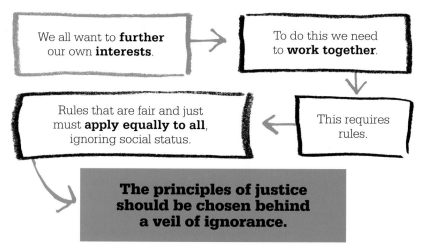

We all want to **further** our own **interests**.

To do this we need to **work together**.

This requires rules.

Rules that are fair and just must **apply equally to all**, ignoring social status.

The principles of justice should be chosen behind a veil of ignorance.

I n his book *A Theory of Justice*, first published in 1971, political philosopher John Rawls argues for a re-evaluation of justice in terms of what he calls "justice as fairness". His approach falls into the tradition known as social contract theory, which sees the rule of law as a form of contract that individuals enter into because it yields benefits that exceed what they can attain individually. Rawls' version of this theory involves a thought experiment in which people are made ignorant of their place in society, or placed in what he calls the "original position" in which the social contract is made. From this Rawls establishes principles of justice on which, he claims, all rational beings should agree.

The original position
Imagine that a group of strangers is marooned on a desert island, and that, after giving up hope of being rescued, they decide to start a new society from scratch. Each of the survivors wants to further their own interests, but each also sees that they can only do so by working together in some way – in other words, by forming a social contract. The question is: how do they go

See also: Plato 50–55 ▪ Thomas Hobbes 112–15 ▪ John Locke 130–33 ▪ Jean-Jacques Rousseau 154–59 ▪ Noam Chomsky 304–05

about establishing the principles of justice? What rules do they lay down? If they are interested in a truly rational and impartial justice, then there are countless rules that have to be discounted immediately. For example, the rule "If your name is John, you must always eat last", is neither rational nor impartial, even if it may be to your advantage if your name is "John".

In such a position, says Rawls, what we need to do is cast a "veil of ignorance" over all the facts of our lives, such as who we are, and where we were born, and then ask what kind of rules it would be best for us to live by. Rawls' point is that the only rules that could rationally be agreed on by all

parties are ones that genuinely honour impartiality, and don't, for example, take race, class, creed, natural talent, or disability into account. In other words, if I don't know what my place in society will be, rational self-interest compels me to vote for a world in which everyone is treated fairly.

Rationality versus charity

It is important to note that for Rawls this is not a story about how justice has actually arisen in the world. Instead, he gives us a way of testing our theories of justice against an impartial benchmark. If they fail to measure up, his point is that it is our reason, and not simply our charity, that has failed. ∎

John Rawls

John Rawls was born in 1921 in Maryland, USA. He studied at Princeton University, then joined the army and served in the Pacific during World War II. After the war, in which he saw the ruins of Hiroshima, he resigned from the army and returned to studying philosophy, earning his PhD from Princeton in 1950.

Rawls undertook further study at Oxford University, where he met philosopher Isaiah Berlin, before returning to the US to teach. After a period at Cornell and MIT, he moved to Harvard, where he wrote *A Theory of Justice*. While at Harvard, he also taught up-and-coming philosophers Thomas Nagel and Martha Nussbaum.

In 1995 Rawls suffered the first of several strokes, but continued working until his death in 2002.

Key works

1971 *A Theory of Justice*
1993 *Political Liberalism*
1999 *The Law of Peoples*
2000 *Lectures on the History of Moral Philosophy*
2001 *Justice as Fairness: A Restatement*

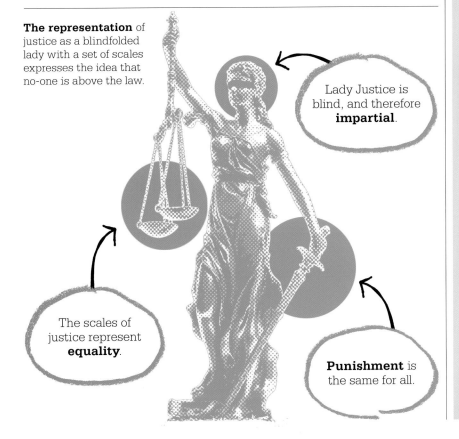

The representation of justice as a blindfolded lady with a set of scales expresses the idea that no-one is above the law.

Lady Justice is blind, and therefore **impartial**.

The scales of justice represent **equality**.

Punishment is the same for all.

ART IS A FORM OF LIFE
RICHARD WOLLHEIM (1923–2003)

IN CONTEXT

BRANCH
Aesthetics

APPROACH
Analytic philosophy

BEFORE
c.380 BCE Plato's *Republic* explores the relationship between art forms and political institutions.

1953 Ludwig Wittgenstein's *Philosophical Investigations* introduces and explores his concept of "forms of life".

1964 Arthur Danto publishes his philosophical essay *The Artworld*, which analyses artistic endeavour from an institutional viewpoint.

AFTER
1969 American philosopher George Dickie develops further the institutional theory of artistic creativity in his essay *Defining Art*.

The British philosopher of art, Richard Wollheim, believes that we should resist the tendency to see art as an abstract idea that needs to be analysed and explained. If we are to fully understand art, he believes, we must always define it in relation to its social context. By describing art as a "form of life", in *Art and its Objects* (1968), he uses a term coined by the Austrian-born philosopher Ludwig Wittgenstein to describe the nature of language. For Wittgenstein, language is a "form of life", because the way we use it is always a reflection of our individual experiences, habits, and skills. He is attempting to resist the tendency of philosophy to make simplistic generalizations about language and instead is pointing to the many different roles language plays in our lives.

Social setting
Wollheim is making the same point as Wittgenstein, but in relation to works of art. Artists, he states, are conditioned by their context – their

What we consider art may depend on the context in which we view it. Andy Warhol's *32 Campbell's Soup Cans* creates fine art from images usually associated with commerce.

beliefs, histories, emotional dispositions, physical needs, and communities – and the world that they interpret is a world of constant change. For Wollheim, one implication of this is that there can be no general "artistic impulse" or instinct for the creation of art that is totally independent of the institutions in which it operates. ∎

See also: Plato 50–55 ▪ Ludwig Wittgenstein 246–51

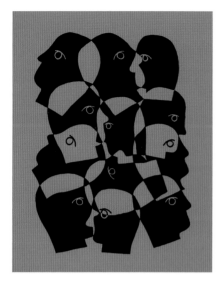

ANYTHING GOES
PAUL FEYERABEND (1924–1994)

IN CONTEXT

BRANCH
Philosophy of science

APPROACH
Analytic philosophy

BEFORE
1934 In *The Logic of Scientific Discovery*, Karl Popper defines "falsifiability" as a criterion for any scientific theory.

1962 Thomas Kuhn introduces the idea of "paradigm shifts" in science in *The Structure of Scientific Revolutions*.

1960s and early 1970s
Feyerabend develops his ideas in discussion with his friend and fellow philosopher of science, Imre Lakatos.

AFTER
From 1980s Feyerabend's ideas contribute to the theories of the mind proposed by American philosophers Patricia and Paul Churchland.

Born in Austria, Feyerabend became a student of Karl Popper at the London School of Economics, but he went on to depart significantly from Popper's rational model of science. During his time at the University of California in the 1960s and 1970s, Feyerabend became friendly with the German-born philosopher Thomas Kuhn, who argued that scientific progress is not gradual, but always jumps in "paradigm shifts" or revolutions that lead to whole new frameworks for scientific thinking. Feyerabend goes even further, suggesting that when this occurs, all the scientific concepts and terms are altered, so there is no permanent framework of meaning.

Anarchy in science
Feyerabend's most famous book *Against Method: Outline of an Anarchistic Theory of Knowledge*, was first published in 1975. Here he sets out his vision of what he calls "epistemological anarchism". Epistemology is the branch of philosophy that deals with questions and theories about knowledge, and Feyerabend's "anarchism" is rooted in the idea that all of the methodologies used in the sciences are limited in scope. As a result, there is no such thing as "scientific method". If we look at how science has developed and progressed in practice, the only "method" that we can discern is that "anything goes". Science, Feyerabend maintains, has never progressed according to strict rules, and if the philosophy of science demands such rules, it will limit scientific progress. ∎

Science and myth overlap in many ways.
Paul Feyerabend

See also: Karl Popper 262–65 ∎ Thomas Kuhn 293

KNOWLEDGE IS PRODUCED TO BE SOLD

JEAN-FRANCOIS LYOTARD (1924–1998)

IN CONTEXT

BRANCH
Epistemology

APPROACH
Postmodernism

BEFORE
1870s The term "postmodern" is first used in the context of art criticism.

1939–45 Technological advances in World War II lay the ground for the computer revolution of the 20th century.

1953 Ludwig Wittgenstein writes in his *Philosophical Investigations* about "language games" – an idea that Lyotard uses to develop his idea of meta-narratives.

AFTER
1984 American literary critic Fredric Jameson writes *Postmodernism, or the Cultural Logic of Late Capitalism*.

From 1990s The World Wide Web offers unprecedented access to information.

The idea that knowledge is produced to be sold appears in Jean-François Lyotard's book *The Postmodern Condition: A Report on Knowledge*. The book was originally written for the Council of Universities in Quebec, Canada, and the use of the term "postmodern" in its title is significant. Although Lyotard did not invent the term, which had been used by various art critics since the 1870s, his book was responsible for broadening its range and increasing its popularity. His use of the word in the title of this book is often said to mark the beginning of postmodern thought.

The term "postmodernism" has since been used in so many different ways that it is now hard to know exactly what it means,

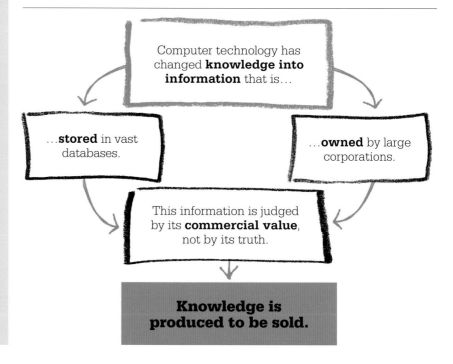

Computer technology has changed **knowledge into information** that is…

…**stored** in vast databases.

…**owned** by large corporations.

This information is judged by its **commercial value**, not by its truth.

Knowledge is produced to be sold.

See also: Immanuel Kant 164–71 ▪ Georg Hegel 178–85 ▪ Friedrich Nietzsche 214–21 ▪ Ludwig Wittgenstein 246–51 ▪ Martin Heidegger 252–55 ▪ Gilles Deleuze 338

When knowledge becomes data it is no longer the indefinable matter of minds, but a commodity that can be transferred, stored, bought, or sold.

but Lyotard's definition is very clear. Postmodernism, he writes, is a matter of "incredulity towards meta-narratives". Meta-narratives are overarching, single stories that attempt to sum up the whole of human history, or that attempt to put all of our knowledge into a single framework. Marxism (the view that history can be seen as a series of struggles between social classes) is an example of a meta-narrative. Another is the idea that humanity's story is one of progress towards deeper knowledge and social justice, brought about by greater scientific understanding.

Externalized knowledge
Our incredulity towards these meta-narratives implies a new scepticism. Lyotard suggests that this is due to a shift in the way we have related to knowledge since World War II, and to the huge change in the technologies we use to deal with it. Computers have fundamentally transformed our attitudes, as knowledge has become information that can be stored in databases, moved to and fro, and bought and sold. This is what Lyotard calls the "mercantilization" of knowledge.

This has several implications. The first, Lyotard points out, is that knowledge is becoming externalized. It is no longer something that helps towards the development of minds; something that might be able to transform us. Knowledge is also becoming disconnected from questions of truth. It is being judged not in terms of how true it is, but in terms of how well it serves certain ends. When we cease to ask questions about knowledge such as "is it true?" and start asking questions such as "how can this be sold?", knowledge becomes a commodity. Lyotard is concerned that once this happens, private corporations may begin to seek to control the flow of knowledge, and decide who can access what types of knowledge, and when. ▪

Jean-François Lyotard

Jean-François Lyotard was born in Versailles, France in 1924. He studied philosophy and literature at the Sorbonne, Paris, becoming friends with Gilles Deleuze. After graduating, he taught philosophy in schools for several years in France and Algeria.

Lyotard became involved in radical left-wing politics in the 1950s, and was a well-known defender of the 1954–62 Algerian revolution, but his philosophical development ultimately led him to become disillusioned with the meta-narratives of Marxism. In the 1970s he began working as a university professor, teaching philosophy first at the Sorbonne and then in many other countries around the world, including the USA, Canada, Brazil, and France. Lyotard retired as Professor Emeritus at the University of Paris VIII, and died of leukaemia in 1998.

Key works

1971 *Discourse, Figure*
1974 *Libidinal Economy*
1979 *The Postmodern Condition: A Report on Knowledge*
1983 *The Differend*

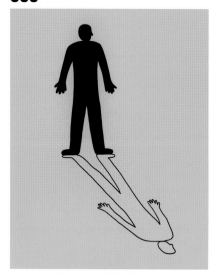

FOR THE BLACK MAN, THERE IS ONLY ONE DESTINY AND IT IS WHITE

FRANTZ FANON (1925–1961)

Philosopher and psychiatrist Frantz Fanon first published his psychoanalytic study of colonialism and racism, *Black Skin, White Masks*, in 1952. In the book Fanon attempts to explore the psychological and social legacy of colonialism among non-white communities around the world.

In saying that "for the black man, there is only one destiny", and this destiny is white, Fanon is saying at least two things. First, he says that "the black man wants to be like the white man"; that is, the aspirations of many colonized peoples have been formed by the dominant colonial culture. European colonial cultures tended to equate "blackness" with impurity, which shaped the self-view of those who were subject to colonial rule, so that they came to see the colour of their skin as a sign of inferiority.

The only way out of this predicament seems to be an aspiration to achieve a "white existence"; but this will always fail, because the fact of having dark skin will always mean that one will fail to be accepted as white. For

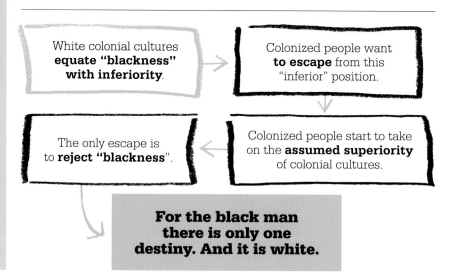

White colonial cultures **equate "blackness" with inferiority**.

Colonized people want **to escape** from this "inferior" position.

Colonized people start to take on the **assumed superiority** of colonial cultures.

The only escape is to **reject "blackness"**.

For the black man there is only one destiny. And it is white.

See also: Aristotle 56–63 ▪ Jean-Paul Sartre 268–71 ▪ Maurice Merleau-Ponty 274–75 ▪ Edward Said 321

> There is a fact: white men consider themselves superior to black men.
> **Frantz Fanon**

Fanon, this aspiration to achieve "a white existence" not only fails to address racism and inequality, but it also masks or even condones these things by implying that there is an "unarguable superiority" to white existence.

At the same time, Fanon is saying something more complex. It might be thought that, given this tendency to aspire to a kind of "white existence", the solution would be to argue for an independent view of what it means to be black. Yet this, too, is subject to all kinds of problems. Elsewhere in his book,

Fanon writes that "the black man's soul is a white man's artefact". In other words, the idea of what it means to be black is the creation of patterns of fundamentally racist European thought.

Here Fanon is, in part, responding to what was known in France as the *négritude* (or "blackness") movement. This was a movement of French and French-speaking black writers from the 1930s who wanted to reject the racism and colonialism of mainstream French culture, and argued for an independent, shared black culture. But Fanon believes that this idea of *négritude* is one that fails to truly address the problems of racism that it seeks to overcome, because the way that it thinks about "blackness" simply repeats the fantasies of mainstream white culture.

Human rights

In one sense, Fanon believes that the solution can only come when we move beyond racial thinking; that if we remain trapped within the idea of race we cannot ever

address these injustices. "I find myself in the world and I recognize that I have one right alone," Fanon writes at the end of his book; "that of demanding human behaviour from the other." Fanon's thought has been of widespread importance in anti-colonial and anti-racist movements, and has influenced social activists such as anti-apartheid campaigner Steve Biko and scholars such as Edward Said. ▪

The inferiority associated with being black led many colonized people to adopt the "mother country's cultural standards", says Fanon, and even to aspire to a "white existence".

Frantz Fanon

Frantz Fanon was born in 1925 in Martinique, a Caribbean island that was at that time a French colony. He left Martinique to fight with the Free French Forces in World War II, after which he studied both medicine and psychiatry in Lyon, France. He also attended lectures on literature and philosophy, including those given by the philosopher Merleau-Ponty. The young Fanon had thought of himself as French, and the racism he encountered on first

entering France surprised him. It played a huge role in shaping his philosophy, and one year after qualifying as a psychiatrist in 1951, he published his book *Black Skin, White Masks*.

In 1953 Fanon moved to Algeria where he worked as a hospital psychiatrist. After two years spent listening to his patients' tales of the torture they had endured during the 1954–62 Algerian War of Independence, he resigned his government-funded post, moved to Tunisia, and began working for the Algerian independence movement. In the late 1950s, he

developed leukaemia. During his illness, he wrote his final book, *The Wretched of the Earth*, arguing for a different world. It was published in the year of his death with a preface by Jean-Paul Sartre, a friend who had first influenced Fanon, then been influenced by him.

Key works

1952 *Black Skin, White Masks*
1959 *A Dying Colonialism*
1961 *The Wretched of the Earth*
1969 *Toward the African Revolution* (collected short works)

MAN IS AN INVENTION OF RECENT DATE

MICHEL FOUCAULT (1926–1984)

IN CONTEXT

BRANCH
Epistemology

APPROACH
Discursive archaeology

BEFORE
Late 18th century Immanuel Kant lays the foundation for the 19th-century model of "man".

1859 Charles Darwin's *On the Origin of Species* causes a revolution in how we understand ourselves.

1883 Friedrich Nietzsche, in *Thus Spoke Zarathustra,* announces that man is something to be surpassed.

AFTER
1985 American philosopher Donna Haraway's *A Cyborg Manifesto* attempts to imagine a post-human future.

1991 Daniel Dennett's *Consciousness Explained* calls into question many of our most cherished notions about consciousness.

We treat the idea of "man" or humankind as if it is a **natural** and **eternal** idea.

But an **archaeology of our thinking** shows that the idea of "man" arose as an object of study at the beginning of the 19th century.

Man is an invention of recent date.

The idea that man is an invention of recent date appears in *The Order of Things: An Archaeology of the Human Sciences* by French philosopher Michel Foucault. To understand what Foucault means by this, we need to know what he means by archaeology, and why he thinks that we should apply it to the history of thought.

Foucault is interested in how our discourse – the way in which we talk and think about things – is formed by a set of largely unconscious rules that arise out of the historical conditions in which

we find ourselves. What we take to be the "common sense" background to how we think and talk about the world is in fact shaped by these rules and these conditions. However, the rules and conditions change over time, and consequently so do our discourses. For this reason, an "archaeology" is needed to unearth both the limits and the conditions of how people thought and talked about the world in previous ages. We cannot take concepts that we use in our present context (for example, the concept of "human nature") and assume that they are somehow eternal, and that all we

See also: Immanuel Kant 164–71 ▪ Friedrich Nietzsche 214–21 ▪ Martin Heidegger 252–55 ▪ Maurice Merleau-Ponty 274–75 ▪ Daniel Dennett 339

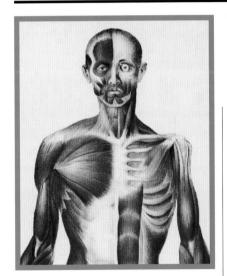

The **19th century** saw a revolution in anatomy, as shown in this illustration from a medical text book. Foucault believes that our modern concept of man dates from this period.

by abandoning the old question "Why is the world the way it is?" and asking "Why do we see the world the way we do?" We take our idea of what it is to be human as fundamental and unchanging, but it is in fact only a recent invention. Foucault locates the beginning of our particular idea of "man" at the beginning of the 19th century, around the time of the birth of the natural sciences. This idea of "man" is, Foucault considers, paradoxical: we see ourselves both as objects in the world, and so as objects of study, and as subjects who experience and study the world – strange creatures that look in two directions at once.

The human self-image

Foucault suggests that not only is this idea of "man" an invention of recent date, it is also an invention that may be close to coming to its

need is a "history of ideas" to trace their genealogy. For Foucault, it is simply wrong to assume that our current ideas can be usefully applied to any previous point in history. The ways in which we use the words "man", "mankind", and "human nature", Foucault believes, are examples of this.

The roots of this idea lie firmly in the philosophy of Immanuel Kant, who turned philosophy on its head

end – one that may soon be erased "like a face drawn in the sand at the edge of the sea".

Is Foucault right? In a time of rapid advances in computing and human-machine interfaces, and when philosophers informed by cognitive science, such as Daniel Dennett and Dan Wegner, are questioning the very nature of subjectivity, it is hard not to feel that, even if the face in the sand is not about to be erased, the tide is lapping alarmingly at its edges. ▪

> Man is neither the oldest nor the most constant problem that has been posed for human knowledge.
> **Michel Foucault**

Michel Foucault

Foucault was born in Poitiers, France, in 1926 to a family of doctors. After World War II, he entered the École Normale Supérieure, where he studied philosophy under Maurice Merleau-Ponty. In 1954 he spent time in Uppsala, Sweden, and then lived for a time both in Poland and Germany, only returning to France in 1960.

He received a PhD in 1961 for his study *A History of Madness*, which argued that the distinction between madness and sanity is not real, but a social construct. After the month-long student

strikes in Paris of 1968, he became involved in political activism, and continued to work both as a lecturer and an activist for the rest of his life.

Key works

1961 *A History of Madness*
1963 *The Birth of the Clinic: An Archaeology of Medical Perception*
1966 *The Order of Things: An Archaeology of the Human Sciences*
1975 *Discipline and Punish: The Birth of the Prison*

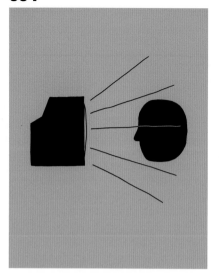

IF WE CHOOSE, WE CAN LIVE IN A WORLD OF COMFORTING ILLUSION
NOAM CHOMSKY (1928–)

IN CONTEXT

BRANCH
Ethics

APPROACH
Universalism

BEFORE
c.380 BCE In *The Republic*, Plato claims that many of us live in a world of illusion.

1739 David Hume publishes *A Treatise of Human Nature*. Though an empiricist, he claims that there must be some fixed principles from which morality derives.

1785 Immanuel Kant, in his *Groundwork of the Metaphysic of Morals*, argues that morality should be based on universality.

Early 20th century John Dewey argues that politics is the shadow cast on society by big business.

1971 John Rawls revives Kant's notion of universality in his *A Theory of Justice*.

Although originally famous for his work in linguistics, Noam Chomsky is today best known for his analyses of political power. Since the publication of his first political book, *American Power and the New Mandarins*, in 1969, he has claimed that there is often a mismatch between the way that states exert power and the rhetorical claims that they make. He maintains that rhetorical claims by governments are not by themselves sufficient for us to reach the truth about political power. Governments may speak the language of "facts" as a way of justifying their actions, but unless their claims are supported by evidence, then they are only illusions, and the actions to which they lead lack justification. If we are to understand more clearly how states operate, it is necessary to move beyond the battle between

If we assume that our own government is naturally **more ethical** than other governments...

... we are choosing to live in a world of comforting illusion.

To **break** with this illusion we need to...

... look at the evidence for what **our government** actually does.

... apply the same ethical principles that we apply to **other governments** to our own.

See also: Plato 50–55 ▪ David Hume 148–53 ▪ Immanuel Kant 164–71 ▪ John Dewey 228–31 ▪ John Rawls 294–95

> States are not moral agents; people are.
> **Noam Chomsky**

rival forms of rhetoric, and instead to look at history, at institutional structures, at official policy documents, and so forth.

Ethics and universality

Chomsky's ethical analyses are based on what he calls the "principle of universality". At root, this principle is relatively simple. It says that at the very least we should apply to ourselves the same standards that we apply to others. This is a principle that Chomsky claims has always been central to any responsible system of ethics. The central psychological insight here is that we are fond of using ethical language as a way of protesting about others, but that we are less inclined to pass judgment on ourselves. Nevertheless, if we claim to uphold any set of ethical or moral standards, and if we wish to be consistent, then we must apply to others the standards we apply to ourselves. In terms of government, this means that we must analyse our political actions rigorously, instead of allowing ourselves to be blinded by rhetoric.

This is both a moral and an intellectual imperative. For Chomsky, these are closely related. He points out that if anyone making a moral claim is also violating universality, then their claim cannot be taken seriously and should be rejected.

If we are to cut through the rhetoric and examine political morality in a rigorous fashion, it seems that universality is a necessary starting point. Some of Chomsky's specific claims about the nature of global power have caused considerable controversy, but this does not invalidate his central insight. For if we wish to call his specific claims into question, then we should do so in the light of universality and of all the available evidence. If his claims turn out to be false, then they should be rejected or modified; but if they turn out to be true, then they should be acted upon. ∎

Uncle Sam, the personification of the United States, is one of countless props used by governments to foster public support. Chomsky warns that such images can distract us from the truth.

Noam Chomsky

Chomsky was born in 1928 in Pennsylvania, USA, and was raised in a multilingual Jewish household. He studied mathematics, philosophy, and linguistics at the University of Pennsylvania, where he wrote a groundbreaking thesis on philosophical linguistics. In 1957, his book *Syntactic Structures* secured his reputation as one of the leading figures in linguistics, and revolutionized the field.

Although continuing to teach and publish in linguistics, Chomsky became increasingly involved in politics. He was a prominent opponent of the Vietnam War, which prompted him to publish his critique of US intellectual culture, *The Responsibility of Intellectuals*, in 1967. Today, he continues to write and lecture on linguistics, philosophy, politics, and international affairs.

Key works

1967 *The Responsibility of Intellectuals*
1969 *American Power and the New Mandarins*
2001 *9-11*
2006 *Failed States: The Abuse of Power and the Assault on Democracy*

SOCIETY IS DEPENDENT UPON A CRITICISM OF ITS OWN TRADITIONS
JURGEN HABERMAS (1929–)

IN CONTEXT

BRANCH
Political philosophy

APPROACH
Social theory

BEFORE
1789 The French Revolution begins, marking the end of a "representational" power structure in France.

1791 Jeremy Bentham writes *Of Publicity*, an early exploration of the idea of the "public".

1842 Karl Marx writes his essay *On Freedom of the Press*.

AFTER
1986 Edward Said criticizes Habermas and the Frankfurt School for their Eurocentric views and their silence on racist theory and imperialism.

1999 Canadian author Naomi Klein's *No Logo* explores the fate of the public sphere in an era dominated by advertising and the mass media.

According to the German philosopher Jürgen Habermas, modern society depends not only on technological advances, but also upon our ability to criticize and reason collectively about our own traditions. Reason, says Habermas, lies at the heart of our everyday communications. Somebody says or does something, and we say, "Why did you do that?" or "Why did you say that?" We continually ask for justifications, which is why Habermas talks about "communicative" reason.

Coffee houses became a focus of social and political life in the major cities of 18th-century Europe. Noted as places where "the dissaffected met", attempts were frequently made to close them.

Reason, for him, is not about discovering abstract truths, but about the need we have to justify ourselves to others.

Creating a public sphere
In the 1960s and 1970s, Habermas concluded that there was a link between communicative reason and what he calls the "public sphere". Up until the 18th century, he states, European culture was largely "representational", meaning that the ruling classes sought to "represent" themselves to their subjects with displays of power that required no justification, such as impressive pageants or grand architectural projects. But in the 18th century, a variety of public spaces emerged that were outside state control, including literary salons and coffee houses. These were places where individuals could gather to engage in conversation or reasoned debate. This growth of the public sphere led to increased opportunities to question the authority of representational state culture. The public sphere became a "third space", a buffer between the private space of our immediate friends and family, and the space occupied by state control.

See also: Jeremy Bentham 174 ▪ Karl Marx 196–203 ▪ Theodor Adorno 266–67 ▪ Edgar Morin 338 ▪ Niklas Luhmann 339 ▪ Noam Chomsky 304–05 ▪ Edward Said 321

By establishing a public sphere, we also open up more opportunities for recognizing that we have interests in common with other private individuals – interests that the state may fail to serve. This can lead to questioning the actions of the state. Habermas believes that the growth of the public sphere helped to trigger the French Revolution in 1789.

The expansion of the public sphere, from the 18th century onwards, has led to a growth of democratically elected political institutions, independent courts, and bills of rights. But Habermas believes that many of these brakes on the arbitrary use of power are now under threat. Newspapers, for example, can offer opportunities for reasoned dialogue between private individuals, but if the press is controlled by large corporations, such opportunities may diminish. Informed debate on issues of substance is replaced with celebrity gossip, and we are transformed from critical, rational agents into mindless consumers. ■

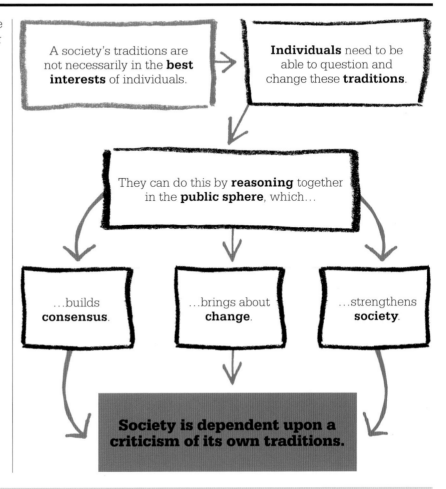

A society's traditions are not necessarily in the **best interests** of individuals.

Individuals need to be able to question and change these **traditions**.

They can do this by **reasoning** together in the **public sphere**, which…

…builds **consensus**.

…brings about **change**.

…strengthens **society**.

Society is dependent upon a criticism of its own traditions.

Jürgen Habermas

Jürgen Habermas grew up in Germany under the Nazi regime. His realization that "we had been living in a criminal system", following the Nuremburg trials (1945–46), was to have a lasting effect on his philosophy.

On completing his doctorate in 1954, he studied with members of the Frankfurt School, including Max Horkheimer and Theodor Adorno. During the 1960s and 1970s, he lectured at universities in Bonn and Gottingen. In 1982, he became Professor of Philosophy at the University at Frankfurt, where he taught until his retirement in 1993. More recently, Habermas has himself taken an active role in the public sphere, entering into debates on Holocaust denial and global terrorism.

Key works

1962 *The Structural Transformation of the Public Sphere*
1981 *The Theory of Communicative Action*
1985 *The Philosophical Discourse of Modernity*
2005 *Between Naturalism and Religion*

THERE IS NOTHING

OUTSIDE OF THE TEXT

JACQUES DERRIDA (1930–2004)

IN CONTEXT

BRANCH
Epistemology

APPROACH
Deconstruction

BEFORE
4th century BCE Plato's *Meno* explores the idea of "aporia".

Early 20th century Charles Sanders Peirce and Ferdinand de Saussure begin the study of signs and symbols (semiotics), which would become a key influence on *Of Grammatology*.

1961 Emmanuel Levinas publishes *Totality and Infinity*, which Derrida would respond to in *Writing and Difference*. Levinas becomes a growing influence in Derrida's later explorations of ethics.

AFTER
1992 English philosopher Simon Critchley's *Ethics of Deconstruction* explores aspects of Derrida's work.

We are all mediators, translators
Jacques Derrida

J acques Derrida remains one of the most controversial 20th-century philosophers. His name is associated, first and foremost, with "deconstruction", a complex and nuanced approach to how we read and understand the nature of written texts. If we are to understand what Derrida means when he says in his famous book *Of Grammatology* that there is nothing outside of the text (the original French is *"il n'y a pas de hors-texte"*, also translated as "there is no outside-text"), we need to take a closer look at Derrida's deconstructive approach in general.

Often when we pick up a book, whether a philosophy book or a novel, we imagine that what we have in our hands is something that we can understand or interpret as a relatively self-contained whole. When it comes to philosophical texts, we might be expected to imagine that these are especially systematic and logical. Imagine that you go into a bookshop and pick up a copy of *Of Grammatology*. You would think that, if you were to read the book, by the end of it you would have a reasonable grasp of what "grammatology" itself might be, what Derrida's main ideas were on the subject, and what this said about the world. But, for Derrida, texts do not work in this way.

Aporia and différance
Even the most straightforward texts (and *Of Grammatology* is not one such text) are riddled with what Derrida calls "aporias". The word "aporia" comes from the Ancient Greek, where it means something like "contradiction", "puzzle", or "impasse." For Derrida, all written texts have such gaps, holes, and contradictions and his method of deconstruction is a way of reading texts while looking out for these puzzles and impasses. In exploring these contradictions as they appear in different texts,

Derrida aims to broaden our understanding of what texts are and what they do, and to show the complexity that lies behind even the most apparently simple works. Deconstruction is a way of reading texts to bring these hidden paradoxes and contradictions out into the open. This is not, however, just a matter of how we read philosophy and literature; there are much broader implications to Derrida's approach that bring into question the relationship between language, thought, and even ethics.

At this point, it would help to introduce an important technical term from Derrida's vocabulary: *"différance"*. This may look like a typographical error – and indeed, when the term *différance* first entered the French dictionary, the story goes that even Derrida's mother sternly said to him, "But Jacques, that is not how you spell it!" But in fact *différance* is a word that Derrida coined himself to point to a curious aspect of language.

"Différance" (with an "a") is a play both on the French *"différence"* (with an "e"), meaning "to differ", and the French *"deférrer"* meaning "to defer". To understand how this

A typesetter can check plates of type closely before they are printed, but the ideas they express are full of "aporias", or contradictions, says Derrida, which no amount of analysis can eliminate.

The meaning of what we write is, for Derrida, changed by what we write next. Even the deceptively simple act of writing a letter can lead to a deferral of meaning in the text itself.

word works, it would be useful to consider how this deferring and differing might actually take place in practice. Let us start with deferring. Imagine that I say "The cat…", then I add, "that my friend saw…". After a pause, I say, "in the garden was black and white…", and so on. The precise meaning of the word "cat" as I am using it is continually deferred, or put off, as more information is given. If I had been cut off after saying "The cat…" and had not mentioned my friend or the garden, the meaning of "cat" would have been different. The more I add to what I say, in other words, the more the meaning of what I have already said is revised. Meaning is deferred in language.

But there is something else going on as well. The meaning of "cat", Derrida believes, cannot be considered as something that rests in the relationship between my words and actual things in the world. The word takes its »

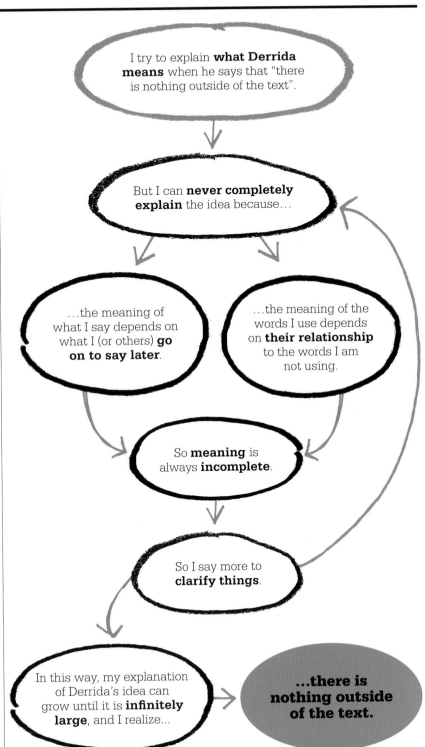

I try to explain **what Derrida means** when he says that "there is nothing outside of the text".

But I can **never completely explain** the idea because…

…the meaning of what I say depends on what I (or others) **go on to say later**.

…the meaning of the words I use depends on **their relationship** to the words I am not using.

So **meaning** is always **incomplete**.

So I say more to **clarify things**.

In this way, my explanation of Derrida's idea can grow until it is **infinitely large**, and I realize…

…**there is nothing outside of the text.**

> We think only in signs
> **Jacques Derrida**

meaning from its position in a whole system of language. So when I say "cat", this is meaningful not because of some mysterious link between the word and an actual cat, but because this term differs from, for example, "dog" or "lion" or "zebra".

Taken together, these two ideas of deferring and differing say something quite strange about language in general. On the one hand, the meaning of anything we say is ultimately always deferred, because it depends on what else we say; and the meaning of that, in turn, depends on what else we say, and so on. And on the other hand, the meaning of any particular term we use depends on all the things that we don't mean. So meaning is not self-contained within the text itself.

The written word
For Derrida, *différance* is an aspect of language that we become aware of thanks to writing. Since ancient Greek times, philosophers have been suspicious of written language. In Plato's dialogue, the *Phaedrus*, Socrates tells a legend about the invention of writing, and says that writing provides only "the appearance of wisdom" and not its reality. Writing, when philosophers have thought about it at all, has tended to be seen simply as a pale reflection of the spoken word; the

latter has been taken as the primary means of communication. Derrida wants to reverse this; according to him, the written word shows us something about language that the spoken word does not.

The traditional emphasis on speech as a means of transmitting philosophical ideas has fooled us all, Derrida believes, into thinking that we have immediate access to meaning. We think that meaning is about "presence" – when we speak with another person, we imagine that they make their thoughts "present" for us, and that we are doing the same for them. If there is any confusion, we ask the other person to clarify. And if there are any puzzles, or aporias, we either ask for clarification, or these simply slide past us without our noticing. This leads us to think that meaning in general is about presence – to think, for example, that the real meaning of "cat" can be found in the presence of a cat on my lap.

But when we deal with a written text, we are freed from this naïve belief in presence. Without the author there to make their excuses and explain for us, we start to notice the complexities and the

puzzles and the impasses. All of a sudden, language begins to look a little more complicated.

Questioning meaning
When Derrida says that there is nothing outside of the text, he does not mean that all that matters is the world of books, that somehow the world "of flesh and bone" does not matter. Nor is he trying to play down the importance of any social concerns that might lie behind the text. So what exactly is he saying?

First, Derrida is suggesting that if we take seriously the idea that meaning is a matter of *différance*, of differing and of deferring, then if we want to engage with the question of how we ought think about the world, we must always keep alive to the fact that meaning is never as straightforward as we think it is, and that this meaning is always open to being prised apart by deconstruction.

Second, Derrida is suggesting that in our thinking, our writing, and our speaking, we are always implicated in all manner of political, historical, and ethical questions that we may not even recognize or acknowledge. For this reason, some

Derrida's own thesis that there is nothing outside of the text is open to be analysed using his own deconstructive methods. Even the idea as explained in this book is subject to *différance*.

Derrida registered his opposition to the Vietnam War in a lecture given in the US in 1968. His involvement in numerous political issues and debates informed much of his later work.

philosophers have suggested that deconstruction is essentially an ethical practice. In reading a text deconstructively, we call into question the claims that it is making, and we open up difficult ethical issues that may have remained hidden. Certainly in his later life, Derrida turned his attention to some of the very real ethical puzzles and contradictions that are raised by ideas such as "hospitality" and "forgiveness".

Critics of Derrida

Given that Derrida's idea is based on the notion that meaning can never be completely present in the text, it is perhaps not surprising that Derrida's work can often be difficult. Michel Foucault, one of Derrida's contemporaries, attacked Derrida's thinking for being wilfully obscure; he protested that often it was impossible to say exactly what Derrida's thesis actually was. The

latter's response to this, perhaps, might be to say that the idea of having a thesis is itself based on the idea of "presence" that he is attempting to call into question. This may seem like dodging the issue; but if we take Derrida's idea seriously, then we have to admit that the idea that there is nothing outside of the text is itself not outside of the text. To take this idea seriously, then, is to treat it sceptically, to deconstruct it, and to explore the puzzles, impasses, and contradictions that – according to Derrida himself – lurk within it. ∎

I never give in to the temptation to be difficult just for the sake of being difficult
Jacques Derrida

Jacques Derrida

Jacques Derrida was born to Jewish parents in the then French colony of Algeria. He was interested in philosophy from an early age, but also nurtured dreams of becoming a professional footballer. Eventually it was philosophy that won out and, in 1951, he entered the École Normale Supérieure in Paris. There he formed a friendship with Louis Althusser, also of Algerian origin, who, like Derrida, went on to become one of the most prominent thinkers of his day.

The publication in 1967 of *Of Grammatology*, *Writing and Difference*, and *Speech and Phenomena* sealed Derrida's international reputation. A regular visiting lecturer at a number of European and American universities, he took up the post of Professor of Humanities at the University of California, Irvine, in 1986. His later work increasingly focused on issues of ethics, partly due to the influence of Emmanuel Levinas.

Key works

1967 *Of Grammatology*
1967 *Writing and Difference*
1967 *Speech and Phenomena*
1994 *The Politics of Friendship*

THERE IS NOTHING DEEP DOWN INSIDE US EXCEPT WHAT WE HAVE PUT THERE OURSELVES

RICHARD RORTY (1931–2007)

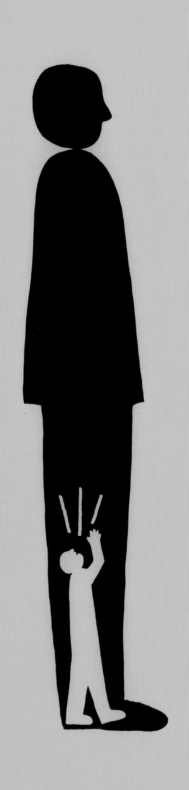

IN CONTEXT

BRANCH
Ethics

APPROACH
Pragmatism

BEFORE
5th century BCE Socrates disputes the nature of justice, goodness, and other concepts with the citizens of Athens.

4th century BCE Aristotle writes a treatise on the nature of the soul.

1878 Charles Sanders Peirce coins the term "pragmatism".

1956 American philosopher Wilfrid Sellars publishes *Empiricism and the Philosophy of Mind*, calling into question the "myth of the given".

AFTER
1994 South-African-born philosopher John McDowell publishes *Mind and World*, a book strongly influenced by Rorty's work.

The soul is a curious thing. Even if we cannot say much about our souls or describe what a soul is like, many of us nonetheless hold firmly to the belief that, somewhere deep down, we each have such a thing. Not only this, we might claim that this thing is the fundamental self ("me") and, at the same time, is somehow connected directly with the truth or reality.

The tendency to picture ourselves as possessing a kind of "double" – a soul or a deep self that "uses Reality's own language" – is explored by American philosopher Richard Rorty in the introduction to his book, *The Consequences of Pragmatism* (1982). Rorty argues that, to the extent that we have such a thing at all, a soul is a human invention; it is something that we have put there ourselves.

Knowledge as a mirror

Rorty was a philosopher who worked within the American tradition of pragmatism. In considering a statement, most philosophical traditions ask "is this true?" , in the sense of: "does this correctly represent the way things are?". But

Philosophy makes progress not by becoming more rigorous but by becoming more imaginative.
Richard Rorty

pragmatists consider statements in quite a different way, asking instead: "what are the practical implications of accepting this as true?"

Rorty's first major book, *Philosophy and the Mirror of Nature*, published in 1979, was an attempt to argue against the idea that knowledge is a matter of correctly representing the world, like some kind of mental mirror. Rorty argues that this view of knowledge cannot be upheld, for two reasons. First, we assume that our experience of the world is directly "given" to us – we assume that what we experience is the raw

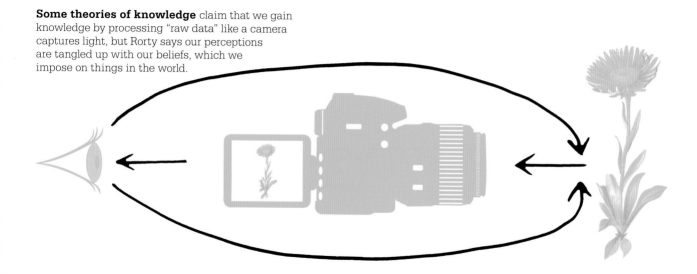

Some theories of knowledge claim that we gain knowledge by processing "raw data" like a camera captures light, but Rorty says our perceptions are tangled up with our beliefs, which we impose on things in the world.

See also: Socrates 46–49 ▪ Aristotle 56–63 ▪ Charles Sanders Peirce 205 ▪ William James 206–09 ▪ John Dewey 228–31 ▪ Jürgen Habermas 306–07

data of how the world is. Second, we assume that once this raw data has been collected, our reason (or some other faculty of mind) then starts to work on it, reconstructing how this knowledge fits together as a whole, and mirroring what is in the world.

Rorty follows the philosopher Wilfrid Sellars in claiming that the idea of experience as "given" is a myth. We cannot ever access anything like raw data – it is not possible for us to experience a dog, for instance, outside of thought or language. We only become aware of something through conceptualizing it, and our concepts are learned through language. Our perceptions are therefore inextricably tangled up with the habitual ways that we use language to divide up the world.

Rorty suggests that knowledge is not so much a way of mirroring nature as "a matter of conversation and social practice". When we decide what counts as knowledge, our judgement rests not on how strongly a "fact" correlates to the world, so much as whether it is something "that society lets us say". What we can and cannot count as knowledge is therefore limited by the social contexts that we live in, by our histories, and by what those around us will allow us to claim. "Truth," said Rorty, "is what your contemporaries let you get away with saying."

Reasons for judgement

But does truth really reduce down to a matter of what we can get away with? Rorty is aware that there are some disturbing implications here, especially in questions of ethics. Imagine, for instance, that I kidnap my neighbour's pet hamster and »

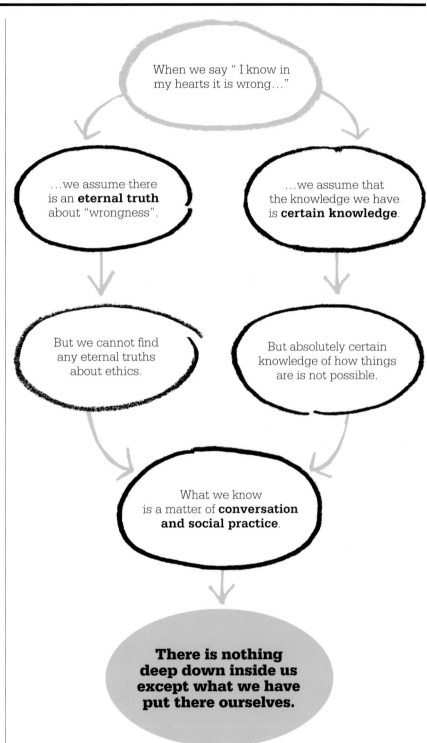

When we say " I know in my hearts it is wrong…"

…we assume there is an **eternal truth** about "wrongness".

…we assume that the knowledge we have is **certain knowledge**.

But we cannot find any eternal truths about ethics.

But absolutely certain knowledge of how things are is not possible.

What we know is a matter of **conversation and social practice**.

There is nothing deep down inside us except what we have put there ourselves.

Using children as soldiers may seem intrinsically wrong, but Rorty says there are no ethical absolutes. Ethics is a matter of doing our best, in solidarity with others, to realize a better world.

subject it to all manner of cruel tortures, simply for the fun of hearing it squeak. We might all agree that doing such a thing to the poor hamster (or, for that matter, doing such a thing to my neighbour) is a morally blameable act. We might claim that there is something absolutely and fundamentally wrong about doing such a thing to another living being; and we might all agree that we ought not let other people get away with such things.

But when we look at the reasons that we give for saying that this is a morally blameable act, things become interesting. For example, imagine that you are asked by a particularly awkward moral philosopher why it is wrong to treat hamsters (or horses, or humans) in this way. At first you might suggest all manner of reasons. But philosophy being what it is, and

What sort of a world can we prepare for our great-grandchildren?
Richard Rorty

moral philosophers being the kinds of beings they are, you might find that for every reason you can think of, your philosopher friend has a counter-reason or leads you into some kind of contradiction.

This is, in fact, precisely what the philosopher Socrates did in ancient Athens. Socrates wanted to find out what concepts such as "goodness" and "justice" really were, so he questioned people who used these concepts, to find out whether they really knew what these things were. As the dialogues of Plato show, most of the people Socrates talked to were surprisingly unclear about what it was they were actually talking about, despite their earlier conviction that they fully grasped the relevant concepts. In the same way, after an hour or two of being interrogated by a modern-day Socrates about how to treat hamsters, you might blurt out in frustration the following sentence: "But I just know, in my heart of hearts, that it is wrong!"

My heart of hearts
We say or think this kind of thing relatively frequently, but it is not immediately clear what exactly we mean. To examine the idea more closely, we can break it down into three parts. First, it seems that

when we say "I know, in my heart of hearts, that it is wrong", we are speaking as if there is something out there in the world that is "wrongness", and that this thing is knowable. Or, as some philosophers put it, we are speaking as if there is an essence of "wrongness" to which this particular instance of wrongness corresponds.

Second, by saying that we just "know" in our heart of hearts, we imply that this mysterious entity – our "heart of hearts" – is a thing that, for reasons unknown, has a particular grasp of truth.

Third, we seem to be speaking as if there is a straightforward relationship between our "heart of hearts" and this "wrongness" that lies out there in the world, such that if we know something in our heart of hearts, we can have access to an absolutely certain kind of knowledge. In other words, this is just another version of the idea that knowledge is a way of mirroring the world. And this, Rorty believes, is unacceptable.

A world without absolutes
In order for his beliefs to be consistent, Rorty has to give up on the idea of fundamental moral truths. There can be no absolute right or wrong if knowledge is

If we can rely on one another, we need not rely on anything else.
Richard Rorty

"what society lets us say". Rorty recognizes that this is a difficult thing to accept. But is it necessary to believe that on doing something morally wrong you are betraying something deep within you? Must you believe that there is "some truth about life, or some absolute moral law, that you are violating" in order to maintain even a shred of human decency? Rorty thinks not. He maintains that we are finite beings, whose existence is limited to a short time on Earth, and none of us have a hotline to some deeper, more fundamental moral truth. However, this does not imply that the problems of life have either

We do not need to believe in an absolute moral law in order to live as ethical beings. Conversation, social hope, and solidarity with others allow us to form a working definition of "the good".

gone away or ceased to matter. These problems are still with us, and in the absence of absolute moral laws we are thrown back upon our own resources. We are left, Rorty writes, with "our loyalty to other human beings clinging together against the dark". There is no absolute sense of rightness and wrongness to be discovered. So we simply have to hold on to our hopes and loyalties, and continue to participate in involved conversations in which we talk about these difficult issues.

Perhaps, Rorty is saying, these things are enough: the humility that comes from recognizing that there is no absolute standard of truth; the solidarity we have with others; and our hopes that we may be able to contribute to, and to bequeath to those who come after us, a world that is worth living in. ■

Richard Rorty

Richard Rorty was born in New York, USA in 1931. His parents were political activists, and Rorty describes his early years as being spent reading about Leon Trotsky, the Russian revolutionary. He said that he knew by the age of 12 that "the point of being human was to spend one's life fighting social injustice". He began attending the University of Chicago early, at the age of 15, going on to take a PhD at Yale in 1956. He was then drafted into the army for two years, before becoming a lecturer. He wrote his most important book, *Philosophy and the Mirror of Nature*, while professor of philosophy at Princeton. He wrote widely on philosophy, literature, and politics and, unusually for a 20th-century philosopher, drew on both the so-called analytic and the continental traditions. Rorty died of cancer aged 75.

Key works

1979 *Philosophy and the Mirror of Nature*
1989 *Contingency, Irony, and Solidarity*
1998 *Achieving Our Country*
1999 *Philosophy and Social Hope*

EVERY DESIRE HAS A RELATION TO MADNESS
LUCE IRIGARAY (1932–)

IN CONTEXT

BRANCH
Political philosophy

APPROACH
Feminism

BEFORE
1792 Mary Wollstonecraft's
*A Vindication of the Rights of
Woman* first initiates serious
debate about the place of
women in society.

1890s Austrian psychologist
Sigmund Freud establishes
his psychoanalytic method,
which will greatly influence
Irigaray's work.

1949 Simone de Beauvoir's
The Second Sex explores
the implications of sexual
difference.

AFTER
1993 Luce Irigaray turns to
non-Western modes of thought
about sexual difference in
An Ethics of Sexual Difference.

The Belgian philosopher and analyst Luce Irigaray is concerned above all else with the idea of sexual difference. A former student of Jacques Lacan, a psychoanalyst who famously explored the linguistic structure of the unconscious, Irigaray claims that all language is essentially masculine in nature.

In *Sex and Genealogies* (1993) she writes: "Everywhere, in everything, men's speech, men's values, dreams, and desires are law." Irigaray's feminist work can be seen as a struggle to find authentically female ways of speaking, dreaming, and desiring, that are free from male-centredness.

Wisdom and desire
To address this problem, Irigaray suggests that all thinking – even the most apparently sober and objective-sounding philosophy, with its talk of wisdom, certainty, rectitude, and moderation – is underpinned by desire. In failing to acknowledge the desire that underpins it, traditional male-centred philosophy has also failed to acknowledge that beneath its apparent rationality simmer all manner of irrational impulses.

Irigaray suggests that each sex has its own relationship to desire, and as a result each sex has a relation to madness. This calls into question the long tradition of equating maleness with this rationality, and femaleness with irrationality. It also opens the way to the possibility of new ways of writing and thinking about philosophy, for both men and women. ∎

One must assume the feminine role deliberately.
Luce Irigaray

See also: Mary Wollstonecraft 175 ▪ Ludwig Wittgenstein 246–51 ▪ Simone de Beauvoir 276–77 ▪ Hélène Cixous 322 ▪ Julia Kristeva 323

EVERY EMPIRE TELLS ITSELF AND THE WORLD THAT IT IS UNLIKE ALL OTHER EMPIRES
EDWARD SAID (1935–2003)

The Palestinian writer Edward Said was one of the 20th century's foremost critics of imperialism. In 1978 he published *Orientalism*, which explored how the depictions of Islamic societies by 19th-century European scholars were closely related to the imperialist ideologies of European states.

In his later work, Said remained critical of all forms of imperialism, past and present. He points out that although we may be critical of empires of the past, these empires saw themselves as bringing civilization to the world – a view not shared by the people they claimed to be helping. Empires plunder and control, while masking their abuses of power by talking about their "civilizing" missions. If this is the case, Said warns, we should be wary of present-day claims by any state undertaking foreign interventions. ∎

The British Empire was one of many 19th-century empires that claimed to believe it was bringing the benefits of civilization to the countries it colonized, such as India.

See also: Frantz Fanon 300–01 ▪ Michel Foucault 302–03 ▪ Noam Chomsky 304–05

THOUGHT HAS ALWAYS WORKED BY OPPOSITION
HELENE CIXOUS (1937–)

IN CONTEXT

BRANCH
Epistemology

APPROACH
Feminism

BEFORE
1949 Simone de Beauvoir's *The Second Sex* explores the philosophical implications of sexual difference.

1962 French anthropologist Claude Lévi-Strauss writes *The Savage Mind*, a study of binary oppositions in culture.

1967 Controversial French philosopher Jacques Derrida publishes *Of Grammatology*, introducing the concept of deconstruction, which Cixous uses in her study of gender.

AFTER
1970s The French literary movement of *écriture féminine* ("women's writing") explores appropriate use of language in feminist thinking, taking its inspiration from Cixous.

In 1975, the French poet, novelist, playwright, and philosopher Hélène Cixous wrote *Sorties*, her influential exploration of the oppositions that often define the way we think about the world. For Cixous, a thread that runs through centuries of thought is our tendency to group elements of our world into opposing pairs, such as culture/nature, day/night, and head/heart. Cixous claims that these pairs of elements are always by implication ranked hierarchically, underpinned by a tendency to see one element as being dominant or superior and associated with maleness and activity, while the other element or weaker aspect is associated with femaleness and passivity.

Time for change

Cixous believes that the authority of this hierarchical pattern of thinking is now being called into question by a new blossoming of feminist thought. She questions what the implications of this change might be, not only for our

Woman must write herself and bring woman into literature.
Hélène Cixous

philosophical systems, but also for our social and political institutions. Cixous herself, however, refuses to play the game of setting up binary oppositions, of victors and losers, as a structural framework for our thinking. Instead she conjures up the image of "millions of species of mole as yet not recognized", tunnelling away under the edifices of our world view. And what will happen when these edifices start to crumble? Cixous does not say. It is as if she is telling us that we can make no assumptions, that the only thing we can do is wait and see. ■

See also: Mary Wollstonecraft 175 ▪ Simone de Beauvoir 276–77 ▪ Jacques Derrida 308–13 ▪ Julia Kristeva 323 ▪ Martha Nussbaum 339

WHO PLAYS GOD IN PRESENT-DAY FEMINISM?
JULIA KRISTEVA (1941–)

IN CONTEXT

BRANCH
Political philosophy

APPROACH
Feminism

BEFORE
1792 Mary Wollstonecraft's
*A Vindication of the Rights
of Woman* initiates serious
debate about the nature of the
roles women are conditioned
to play in society.

1807 Georg Hegel explores
the dialectic between
"master" and "slave" in
Phenomenology of Spirit.

1949 Simone de Beauvoir's
The Second Sex is published,
rapidly becoming a key text in
the French feminist movement.

AFTER
1997 In their book *Fashionable
Nonsense*, physics professors
Alan Sokal and Jean Bricmont
criticize Kristeva's misuse
of scientific language.

Bulgarian-born philosopher
and psychoanalyst Julia
Kristeva is often regarded
as one of the leading voices in
French feminism. Nevertheless,
the question of whether, or in what
way, Kristeva is a feminist thinker
has been subject to considerable
debate. Part of the reason for this
is that for Kristeva herself, the very
notion of feminism is problematic.
Feminism has arisen out of the
conflict women have had with
the structures that are associated
with male dominance or power.
Because of these roots, Kristeva
warns, feminism tends to carry
with it some of the same male-
centred presuppositions that it is
seeking to question.

If the feminist movement is
to realize its goals fully, Kristeva
believes that it is essential for it to
be more self-critical. She warns
that by seeking to fight what she
calls the "power principle" of a
male-dominated world, feminism
is at risk of adopting yet another
form of this principle. Kristeva is
convinced that for any movement
to be successful in achieving true
emancipation, it must constantly
question its relationship to power
and established social systems –
and, if necessary "renounce belief
in its own identity". If the feminist
movement fails to take these steps,
Kristeva fears that it is in serious
danger of developing into little
more than an additional strand
in the ongoing game of power. ∎

Margaret Thatcher, like many
women who have achieved positions
of great power, modified her public
image to incorporate classic male
concepts of strength and authority.

See also: Mary Wollstonecraft 175 ▪ Georg Hegel 178–85 ▪
Simone de Beauvoir 276–77 ▪ Hélène Cixous 322 ▪ Martha Nussbaum 339

PHILOSOPHY IS NOT ONLY A WRITTEN ENTERPRISE
HENRY ODERA ORUKA (1944–1995)

IN CONTEXT

BRANCH
Metaphilosophy

APPROACH
Ethnography

BEFORE
600–400 BCE Greek thinkers such as Thales, Pythagoras, and Plato all study in Egypt, Africa, which was a centre of philosophical study in the ancient world.

AFTER
20th century After the retreat of European colonial power, African philosophy begins to flourish across the continent. The growth of anthropology and ethnography also leads to a deeper understanding of indigenous traditions of thought in Africa.

Late 20th century Ghanaian philosopher Kwasi Wiredu argues that philosophic sagacity and folk wisdom must be distinguished from philosophy proper.

Henry Odera Oruka was born in Kenya in 1944 and he was interested in metaphilosophy, or philosophizing about philosophy. In his book *Sage Philosophy* (1994), he looks at why philosophy in sub-Saharan Africa has often been overlooked, and concludes that it is because it is primarily an oral tradition, while

Oruka claims that philosophy has decreed the thoughts of certain races to be more important than others, but it must encompass the sayings of African sages just as it does Greek sages.

philosophers in general tend to work with written texts. Some people have claimed that philosophy is necessarily connected with written recording, but Oruka disagrees.

In order to explore philosophy within the oral traditions of Africa, Oruka proposed an approach that he called "philosophic sagacity". He borrowed the ethnographic approach of anthropology, where people are observed in their everyday settings, and their thoughts and actions recorded in context. Oruka himself travelled into villages and recorded conversations with people who were considered wise by their local community. His aim was to find out whether they had systematic views underpinning their perspectives. Those sages who had critically examined their ideas about traditional philosophical topics, such as God or freedom, and found a rational foundation for them could, Oruka believes, be considered philosophic sages. These systematic views deserve to be explored in the light of wider philosophical concerns and questions. ∎

See also: Socrates 46–49 ▪ Friedrich Schlegel 177 ▪ Jacques Derrida 308–13

IN SUFFERING, THE ANIMALS ARE OUR EQUALS
PETER SINGER (1946–)

IN CONTEXT

BRANCH
Ethics

APPROACH
Utilitarianism

BEFORE
c.560 BCE Indian sage and Jainist leader Mahavira calls for strict vegetarianism.

1789 Jeremy Bentham sets out the theory of utilitarianism in his book, *Introduction to the Principles of Morals and Legislation*, arguing: "each to count for one, and none for more than one".

1861 In his book *Utilitarianism*, John Stuart Mill develops Bentham's utilitarianism from an approach that considers individual acts to one that considers moral rules.

AFTER
1983 American philosopher Tom Regan publishes *The Case for Animal Rights*.

The Australian philosopher Peter Singer became known as one of the most active advocates of animal rights following the publication of his book *Animal Liberation* in 1975. Singer takes a utilitarian approach to ethics, following the tradition developed by Englishman Jeremy Bentham in the late 18th century.

Utilitarianism asks us to judge the moral value of an act by the consequences of that act. For Bentham, the way to do this is by calculating the sum of pleasure or pain that results from our actions, like a mathematical equation.

Animals are sentient beings

Singer's utilitarianism is based on what he refers to as an "equal consideration of interests". Pain, he says, is pain, whether it is yours or mine or anybody else's. The extent to which non-human animals can feel pain is the extent to which we should take their interests into account when making decisions that affect their lives, and we should refrain from activities that cause such pain. However, like all utilitarians, Singer applies the "greatest happiness principle", which says that we should make decisions in such a way that they result in the greatest happiness for the greatest number. Singer points out that he has never said that no experiment on an animal could ever be justified; rather that we should judge all actions by their consequences, and "the interests of animals count among those consequences"; they form part of the equation. ∎

The value of life is a notoriously difficult ethical question.
Peter Singer

See also: Jeremy Bentham 174 ▪ John Stuart Mill 190–93

ALL THE BEST MARXIST ANALYSES ARE ALWAYS ANALYSES OF A FAILURE
SLAVOJ ZIZEK (1949–)

IN CONTEXT

BRANCH
Political philosophy

APPROACH
Marxism

BEFORE
1807 Georg Hegel publishes *The Phenomenology of the Spirit*, laying the groundwork for Marxist thought.

1848 Karl Marx and Friedrich Engels publish their *Communist Manifesto*.

1867 Marx publishes the first volume of *Capital* (*Das Kapital*), a treatise on political economy.

1899 In *The Interpretation of Dreams*, psychoanalyst Sigmund Freud claims that much of human behaviour is driven by unconscious forces.

1966 Psychoanalytical theorist Jacques Lacan, one of Žižek's major influences, revisits Freud's ideas in *Écrits*.

The idea that all the best Marxist analyses have traditionally been analyses of failure appears in an interview with Slovenian philosopher Slavoj Žižek given in 2008. In this interview, Žižek was asked about the events in Czechoslovakia in 1968, when a period of reform, aimed at decentralizing and democratizing the country, was brutally brought to an end by the Soviet Union and its allies.

Žižek's claim is that the crushing of the reforms became the very thing that later sustained a myth held by the political left – namely that, had the reforms gone ahead, some kind of social and political paradise would have followed. According to Žižek, those on the political left are prone to dwelling on their failures, because doing so allows myths to be generated about what would have happened if they had succeeded. Žižek says that these failures allow those on the left to maintain a "safe moralistic position", because their failures mean that they are never in

The Soviet invasion of Czechoslovakia in 1968 led to the end of the short-lived "Prague Spring" period of liberalization. All moves towards democracy were suppressed until 1989.

power, or truly tested by action. He describes this stance as the "comfortable position of resistance", which allows an avoidance of the real issues – such as re-evaluating the nature of political revolution. For Žižek, a dedicated Marxist, serious questions about the nature of political power are obscured by endlessly trying to justify utopia's elusiveness. ∎

See also: Immanuel Kant 164–71 ▪ Georg Hegel 178–85 ▪ Karl Marx 196–203 ▪ Martin Heidegger 252–55

DIRECTO

RY

DIRECTORY

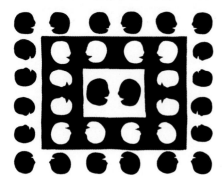

Though the ideas already presented in this book show the broad range of philosophical thought expressed by some of history's best minds, there are many more people who have helped to shape the story of philosophy. Some of these thinkers – such as Empedocles, Plotinus, or William of Ockham – have had ideas that form the starting point for other, more well-known theories, and their influence on later philosophers is clear. Some, such as Friedrich Schelling or Gilles Deleuze, have taken the works of previous philosophers and added an interesting twist that sheds new light on the subject. Whatever their relationship is to the history of philosophy, the people discussed below have all helped to broaden the boundaries of philosophical thought.

ANAXIMANDER
c.610–546 BCE

Born in Miletus, in what is now southwest Turkey, Anaximander was a pupil of Thales, the "father" of Western philosophy. Like Thales, he thought there was a single basic substance from which everything had evolved. He decided it must be infinite and eternal and called it *apeiron* ("indefinite"). Anaximander also challenged Thales' suggestion that Earth was supported by a sea of water, reasoning that this sea would have to be supported by something else. Lacking evidence for this supporting structure, he declared that Earth was an object hanging in space. He went on to publish what is believed to be the first map of the world.
See also: Thales of Miletus 22–23

ANAXIMENES OF MILETUS
c.585–528 BCE

Like other Milesian philosophers, Anaximenes searched for the fundamental material from which the universe was made. He opted for air, pointing out that just as air gives life to the human body, so a universal kind of air gives life to the cosmos. He was the first thinker on record to use observed evidence to support his ideas. Blowing with pursed lips produced cold air; with relaxed lips, warm air. He argued, therefore, that when something condenses, it cools; when it expands it heats up. Likewise, when air condenses, it becomes visible; first as mist, then as rain, and ultimately, he believed, as rock, thus giving birth to Earth.
See also: Thales of Miletus 22–23

ANAXAGORAS
c.500–428 BCE

Born in Ionia, off the southern coast of present-day Turkey, Anaxagoras played a key role in making Athens the world centre of philosophy and scientific enquiry. Central to his thinking were his views on the material world and cosmology. He reasoned that everything in the material world was made up of a small part of everything else, otherwise it could not have come into being. Sentenced to death for impiety after insisting that the sun was a fiery rock, he fled Athens and spent his final years in exile.
See also: Thales of Miletus 22–23

EMPEDOCLES
c.490–430 BCE

Empedocles was a member of a high-ranking political family in the then-Greek colony of Sicily. His knowledge of the natural world led to him being credited with miraculous powers, such as the ability to cure diseases and control the weather. He reasserted the notion of Heraclitus that we live in an ever-changing world, as opposed to Parmenides' theory that everything is ultimately one fixed entity. He believed that four elements – fire, water, earth, and air – continually combine, move apart, and recombine in a finite number of ways. This idea remained part of Western thinking up until the Renaissance period.
See also: Thales of Miletus 22–23 ▪ Heraclitus 40 ▪ Parmenides 41

ZENO OF ELEA
c.490–430 BCE

Little is known about Zeno of Elea, other than his paradoxes of motion, which are mentioned by Aristotle. Zeno is thought to have produced more than 40 of these, although only a few survive. In them, he defended the claim of his teacher Parmenides that the changing and varied world we perceive around us is not reality – which is in fact motionless, uniform, and simple. Movement, Zeno believed, is an illusion of the senses. Each of his paradoxes began from the position that he wished to refute – that movement, and hence change, is real – then continued by revealing the contradictory consequences that lead to the rejection of this notion.
See also: Heraclitus 40 ▪ Parmenides 41 ▪ Aristotle 56–63

PYRRHO
c.360–272 BCE

Pyrrho was born on the Ionian island of Elis. He was exposed to Asian culture while serving on Alexander the Great's military campaigns, and was also the first noted philosopher to place doubt at the centre of to his thinking. Pyrrho treated the suspension of judgment about beliefs as the only reasonable reaction to the fallibility of the senses, and to the fact that both sides of any argument can seem to be equally valid. Pyrrho left no writings, but he did inspire the Sceptical school in ancient Greek philosophy, which developed the idea that the suspension of belief leads to a tranquil mind.
See also: Socrates 46–49 ▪ Al-Ghazâlî 332

PLOTINUS
c.205–270 CE

Born in Egypt, Plotinus studied in Alexandria, then considered the intellectual hub of the world. He later moved to Rome, where he taught his own brand of Platonism, known as Neo-Platonism. Plotinus divided the cosmos into layers, with the indefinable source of all being – the "One" – at the top, followed by Mind, Soul, Nature, and finally the Material World. He believed in reincarnation and the immortality of the soul; by striving for enlightenment individuals could achieve mystical union with the "One", and so escape the cycle of rebirth. His ideas, presented in the *Enneads*, were widely influential, particularly those that supported Christianity, which was taking root in the Roman Empire at the time.
See also: Siddhartha Gautama 30–33 ▪ Plato 50–55

WANG BI
226–249 CE

In 220 CE, the ruling Chinese Han Dynasty collapsed, heralding an era of moral confusion. Philosopher Wang Bi helped to bring order to this chaos by reconciling two dominant schools of thought. He argued that Daoist texts should not be read literally, but more like works of poetry, thus making them compatible with the highly practical Confucian ideals of political and moral wisdom. His fresh appraisals of Daoism and Confucianism ensured the survival of both, and paved the way for the spread of Buddhism across China.
See also: Laozi 24–25 ▪ Siddhartha Gautama 30–33 ▪ Confucius 34–39

IAMBLICHUS
c.245–325 CE

A Syrian Neo-Platonist philosopher, Iamblichus was reputedly born into an influential aristocratic family. He founded a school near modern-day Antioch, where he taught a curriculum based mainly on the ideas of Plato and Aristotle, although he is best known for his expansion of the theories of Pythagoras, which he recorded in his *Collection of Pythagorean Doctrines*. Iamblichus introduced the concept of the soul being embodied in matter, both of which he believed to be divine. Salvation, or the return of the soul to its pure immortal form, he stated, was achieved through the performance of specific religious rituals, and not just the contemplation of abstract ideas alone.
See also: Pythagoras 26–29 ▪ Plato 50–55 ▪ Plotinus 331

HYPATIA OF ALEXANDRIA
c.370–415 CE

Hypatia taught mathematics, astronomy, and philosophy at the Museum of Alexandria, eventually succeeding her father as its head. Although she was an esteemed Neo-Platonist intellectual and the first notable female mathematician, it was her martyrdom that ensured her fame. She was murdered by a Christian mob, who blamed her for the religious turmoil resulting from conflict between her friend, the Roman prefect Orestos, and Cyril, Bishop of Alexandria. No works of hers survive, but she is credited with inventing a graduated brass hydrometer and the plane astrolabe.
See also: Plato 50–55 ▪ Plotinus 331

PROCLUS
c.412–485 CE

Born in Constantinople, Proclus succeeded his Platonist teacher Syrianus as head of the Academy at Athens. His *Commentary on Euclid* is the main account of the early development of Greek geometry, and his *Commentary on Plato's Timaeus* has been described as the most important ancient Neo-Platonist text. A scientist, mathematician, lawyer, and poet, with a deep interest in religion, he was to become an influence on many thinkers in both the medieval Islamic and the Christian schools of philosophy.
See also: Plato 50–55 ▪ Boethius 74–75 ▪ Thomas Aquinas 88–95

JOHN PHILOPONUS
490–570 CE

Almost nothing is known about Philoponus's early life other than he studied in Alexandria with the Aristotelian Ammonius Hermiae. A philosopher and natural scientist, Philoponus's methods of enquiry were shaped by Christian beliefs. By arguing that the universe had an absolute beginning, and that this beginning was caused by God, he became the first serious critic of Aristotle, opening up paths of enquiry which became major influences on future scientists, notably the Italian astronomer Galileo Galilei. Unpopular with his colleagues, he later gave up philosophy and turned to theology, again causing controversy by suggesting that the Trinity was not one but three separate Gods.
See also: Aristotle 56–63 ▪ Thomas Aquinas 88–95

AL-KINDI
801–873 CE

The Iraqi polymath Al-Kindî was one of the first Islamic scholars to introduce ancient Greek ideas to the Islamic world. He worked at Baghdad's House of Wisdom, where he supervised the translation of the great Classical texts into Arabic. He wrote extensively on a variety of subjects, most notably psychology and cosmology, mixing his own Neo-Platonist approach with the authority of Aristotelian argument. He had a special interest in the compatibility of philosophy and Islamic theology, and many of his works are concerned with the nature of God and the human soul, as well as prophetic knowledge.
See also: Al-Fârâbî 332 ▪ Avicenna 76–79 ▪ Averroes 82–83

JOHANNES SCOTUS ERIUGENA
c.815–877CE

His Latin name is often translated as John the Scot, but the theologian and philosopher Johannes Scotus Eriugena was Irish – the medieval Latin for Ireland being "Scotia". He argued that there was no conflict between knowledge that was derived from reason and knowledge from divine revelation. He even set out to demonstrate that all Christian doctrine had in fact a rational basis. This brought him into conflict with the Church, on the grounds that his theories made both revelation and faith redundant. Eriugena's defence was that reason is the judge of all authority, and that it is needed for us to interpret revelation.
See also: Plato 50–55 ▪ St Augustine of Hippo 72–73

AL-FARABI
c.872–950 CE

It is disputed whether Al-Fârâbî was born in what is now Iran or in Kazakhstan, but it is certain that he arrived in Baghdad in 901, where he spent much of his life. Although a Neo-Platonist, he was also highly influenced by Aristotle and wrote commentaries on his work, as well as on other subjects, including medicine, science, and music. He regarded philosophy as a calling conferred by Allah and as the only route to true knowledge. In this life, he said, philosophers have a duty to guide people in all matters of daily life; his book *The Ideas of the Citizens of the Virtuous City* describes a Platonic utopia ruled by philosopher prophets.
See also: Aristotle 56–63 ▪ Avicenna 76–79 ▪ Averroes 82–83

AL-GHAZALI
c.1058–1111

Born what is now Iran, Al-Ghazâlî was head of the prestigious Nizamiyyah school in Baghdad from 1092 to 1096, when he wrote *The Opinions of the Philosophers*, which explains the Neo-Platonist and Aristotelian views of Islamic scholars. His lectures brought him great respect and wealth, but after concluding that truth comes from faith and mystical practices, and not from philosophy, he abandoned his teaching post and possessions to become a wandering Sufi preacher. He came to believe that all causal links between events were only made possible by the will of God.
See also: Aristotle 56–63 ▪ Avicenna 76–79 ▪ Averroes 82–83 ▪ Moses Maimonides 84–85

PIERRE ABELARD
1079–1142

Remembered less for his philosophy than for his tragic love affair with his pupil Héloïse, Pierre Abélard was nevertheless a remarkable thinker. A brilliant student, he attended the Cathedral School of Nôtre Dame, Paris, and became a charismatic teacher. By the age of 22, he had set up his own school, and went on to become head at Nôtre Dame in 1115. Renowned for his skills in argument, Abélard stood against the popular belief in universal forms, inherited from Plato, stating that terms such as "oak tree", are just words that do not denote anything real about the many particular oaks that exist.
See also: Plato 50–55 ▪ Aristotle 56–63 ▪ Boethius 74–75 ▪ William of Ockham 334

ROBERT GROSSETESTE
1175–1253

The child of a poor English peasant family, Grosseteste's formidable intelligence was spotted by the Mayor of Lincoln, who arranged for him to be educated. Evidence indicates that he studied at Oxford University and in Paris, before joining the clergy and going on to become Bishop of Lincoln. An outspoken critic of the Church in his time, Grosseteste is noted for his scientific thinking. He was one of the first medieval philosophers to grasp Aristotle's dual path of scientific reasoning: generalizing from particular observations into a universal law, and then back again from universal laws to the prediction of particulars.
See also: Aristotle 56–63

IBN BAJJA
c.1095–1138

A political advisor, poet, scientist, and philosopher, Ibn Bâjja was one of the great thinkers of Moorish Spain. Born in Saragossa, he used the ideas of Plato and Aristotle in his treatises, and influenced Averroes. He set out to show the compatibility between reason and faith, stating that the path to true knowledge, and therefore enlightenment and a link with the divine, came only from thinking and acting rationally. But, Ibn Bâjja warned, each individual must make their own journey to enlightenment. If the enlightened attempt to pass their wisdom directly to others, they place themselves at risk of contamination by the ignorant.
See also: Plato 50–55 ▪ Aristotle 56–63 ▪ Averroes 82–83

RAMON LLULL
1232–1316

Educated at the Majorcan royal court in Mallorca, Llull developed a mystical version of Neo-Platonism. After a vision of Christ, he joined the Franciscan order and worked as a missionary in North Africa. Convinced that rational argument could persuade Muslims and Jews to convert to Christianity, Llull wrote *Ars Magna*. In this work, he used complex reasoning to generate different combinations of the basic tenets of all monotheistic religions, hoping to demonstrate the truths of Christianity. He was convinced that if everybody was of one faith, all human knowledge would combine into a single system.
See also: Plato 50–55 ▪ St Anselm 80–81 ▪ Meister Eckhart 333

MEISTER ECKHART
c.1260–1327

Little is known about the early life of the German theologian Meister Eckhart, other than he studied in Paris, joined the Dominican order, and held various administrative and teaching posts around Europe. A follower of Thomas Aquinas, he is best known for his vivid sermons, which dwelt on the presence of God within the human soul, and for the mystical imagery of his prose. He was accused of heresy, and during his trial he acknowledged that the florid and emotive language he used to inspire his listeners might have led him to stray from the path of orthodoxy. It is thought that he died before a verdict was delivered.
See also: St Anselm 80–81 ▪ Thomas Aquinas 88–95 ▪ Ramon Llull 333 ▪ Nikolaus von Kues 96

JOHN DUNS SCOTUS
c.1266–1308

Duns Scotus, a Franciscan friar, was among the most influential of the medieval philosophers. Born in Scotland, he taught at Oxford University and later in Paris. Duns Scotus's arguments were noted for their rigour and intricacy. He argued against Thomas Aquinas that attributes, when applied to God, retain the same meaning as when used of ordinary objects. On the issue of universals, he stated that we can perceive particulars directly, without the assistance of general concepts. He also claimed that knowledge can be acquired by the proper use of the senses, without the need for divine "illumination".
See also: Plato 50–55 ▪ Aristotle 56–63 ▪ Thomas Aquinas 88–95

WILLIAM OF OCKHAM
c.1285–1347

The English theologian and philosopher William of Ockham studied and taught at Oxford. He was a Franciscan friar, and was excommunicated for claiming that the pope had no authority to exercise temporal power. He is best known to students of philosophy for the principle that bears his name: Ockham's Razor, which states that the best possible explanation of anything is always the simplest. In his support for the idea that universals are abstractions from experience of particulars, he is regarded as a forerunner of British empiricism, a movement begun in the 17th century by John Locke.
See also: Plato 50–55 ▪ Aristotle 56–63 ▪ Francis Bacon 110–11 ▪ John Locke 130–33

NICOLAUS OF AUTRECOURT
c.1298–1369

Born near Verdun, France, Nicolaus of Autrecourt studied theology at the Sorbonne in Paris. Unusually for a philosopher of the medieval period, he explored the logic of scepticism, concluding that truth and the truth of its contradiction are not logically compatible, so that absolute truth or knowledge, and the causal links between events or reactions, cannot be uncovered by logic alone. In 1346, Pope Clement VI condemned his ideas as heretical. He was ordered to recant his statements and his books were burnt in public. With the exception of his *Universal Treatise* and a few letters, little of his work survives.
See also: Pyrrho 331 ▪ Al-Ghazâlî 332 ▪ David Hume 148–53

MOSES OF NARBONNE
DIED c.1362

Moses of Narbonne, also known as Moses ben Joshua, was a Jewish philosopher and physician. Born in Perpignan, in the Catalan region of France, he later moved to Spain. He believed that Judaism was a guide to the highest degree of truth. He also stated that the Torah (the first part of the Hebrew Bible and the basis of Jewish law) has two levels of meaning: the literal and the metaphysical. The latter is not accessible to the layman.
See also: Averroes 82–83 ▪ Moses Maimonides 84–85

GIOVANNI PICO DELLA MIRANDOLA
1463–1494

Pico della Mirandola was a member of the Platonic Academy in Florence and is best known for his *Oration on the Dignity of Man,* which argued that the potential of the individual was limitless, the only restrictions being self-imposed. It was written as an introduction to *900 Theses*, his compendium of intellectual achievement, in which he aimed to reconcile Platonic and Aristotelian thinking. Papal objections to the inclusion of the merits of paganism saw Mirandola briefly jailed, after which he was forced to flee France.
See also: Plato 50–55 ▪ Aristotle 56–63 ▪ Desiderius Erasmus 97

FRANCISCO DE VITORIA
1480–1546

A Dominican friar, Francisco de Vitoria was a follower of Thomas Aquinas and founder of the School of Salamanca. Called the "father of international law", he is primarily known for developing a code for international relations. He grew up at the time of Spain's unification and its colonization of the Americas. Although he did not argue against Spain's right to build an empire, he thought that Christianity should not be imposed on the indigenous peoples of South America and that they should be afforded rights to property and self-government.
See also: Thomas Aquinas 88–95

GIORDANO BRUNO
1548–1600

The Italian astronomer and thinker Giordano Bruno was influenced by Nikolaus von Kues and the *Corpus Hermeticum* – a set of occult treatises believed, at the time, to predate ancient Greek philosophy. From von Kues, he took the idea of an infinite universe, in which our solar system is just one of many supporting intelligent life. God, argued Bruno, is a part of, not separate from, a universe made up of "monads", or animate atoms. These views, and his interest in astrology and magic, led to him being found guilty of heresy and burned at the stake.
See also: Nikolaus von Kues 96 ▪ Gottfried Leibniz 134–35

FRANCISCO SUAREZ
1548–1617

Born in Granada, Spain, the Jesuit philosopher Francisco Suárez wrote on many topics, but is best known for his writings on metaphysics. In the controversy over universal forms that dominated so much philosophy of the time, he argued that only particulars exist. Suárez also maintained that between Thomas Aquinas's two types of divine knowledge – the knowledge of what is actual and the knowledge of what is possible – there exists "middle knowledge" of what would have been the case had things been different. He believed that God has "middle knowledge" of all our actions, without this meaning that God caused them to happen or that they are unavoidable.

See also: Plato 50–55 ▪ Aristotle 56–63 ▪ Thomas Aquinas 88–95

BERNARD MANDEVILLE
c.1670–1733

Bernard Mandeville was a Dutch philosopher, satirist, and physician, who made his home in London. His best-known work, *The Fable of Bees* (1729) concerns a hive of industrious bees which, when suddenly made virtuous, stop working and go and live quietly in a nearby tree. Its central argument is that the only way any society can progress is through vice, and that virtues are lies employed by the ruling elite to subdue the lower classes. Economic growth, stated Mandeville, stems only from the individual's ability to satisfy his greed. His ideas are often seen as the forerunners to the theories of Adam Smith in the 18th century.

See also: Adam Smith 160–63

JULIEN OFFRAY DE LA METTRIE
1709-1751

Julien Offray de la Mettrie was born in Brittany. He studied medicine and served as an army physician. The atheist sentiments expressed in a thesis he published in 1745, stating that emotions are the result of physical changes in the body, caused outrage, forcing him to flee from France to Holland. In 1747 he published *Man a Machine*, in which he expanded his materialist ideas and rejected Descartes' theory that the mind and body are separate. The book's reception caused him to flee again, this time to Berlin.

See also: Thomas Hobbes 112–15 ▪ René Descartes 116–23

NICOLAS DE CONDORCET
1743–1794

Nicolas, Marquis de Condorcet, was an early exponent of the French tradition of approaching moral and political issues from a mathematical perspective. His famous formula, known as Condorcet's Paradox, drew attention to a paradox in the voting system by showing that majority preferences become intransitive when there are more than three candidates. A liberal thinker, he advocated equal rights and free education for all, including women. He played a key role in the French Revolution, but was branded a traitor for opposing the execution of Louis XVI, and died in prison.

See also: René Descartes 116-23 ▪ Voltaire 146–47 ▪ Jean-Jacques Rousseau 154–59

JOSEPH DE MAISTRE
1753–1821

Born in the French region of Savoy, which was then part of the Kingdom of Sardinia, Joseph de Maistre was a lawyer and political philosopher. He was a ruling senator when the French revolutionary army invaded Savoy in 1792, and was forced to flee. He became a passionate counter-revolutionary. Mankind was inherently weak and sinful, he declared, and the dual powers of monarch and God were essential to social order. In *On the Pope* (1819), De Maistre argues that government should be in the hands of a single authority figure, ideally linked to religion, such as the pope.

See also: Edmund Burke 172–73

FRIEDRICH SCHELLING
1775–1854

Friedrich Schelling started out as a theologian but, inspired by the ideas of Immanuel Kant, he turned to philosophy. Born in southern Germany, he studied with Georg Hegel at Tübingen and taught at the universities of Jena, Munich, and Berlin. Schelling coined the term "absolute idealism" for his view of nature as an ongoing, evolutionary process driven by *Geist*, or spirit. He argued that all of nature, both mind and matter, is involved in one continuous organic process, and that purely mechanistic accounts of reality are inadequate. Human consciousness is nature become conscious, so that in the form of man, nature has arrived at a state of self-awareness.

See also: Benedictus Spinoza 126–29 ▪ Immanuel Kant 164–71 ▪ Johann Gottlieb Fichte 176 ▪ Georg Hegel 178–85

AUGUSTE COMTE
1798–1857

The French thinker Auguste Comte is noted for his theory of intellectual and social evolution, which divides human progress into three key stages. The earliest stage, the theological stage, represented by the medieval period in Europe, is characterized by belief in the supernatural. This gave way to the metaphysical stage, in which speculation on the nature of reality developed. Finally, there came the "positivist" age – which Comte saw as emerging at the time he was writing – with a genuinely scientific attitude, based solely on observable regularities. Comte believed this positivism would help to create a new social order, to redress the chaos generated by the French Revolution.

See also: John Stuart Mill 190–93 ▪ Karl Marx 196–203

RALPH WALDO EMERSON
1803–1882

Born in Boston, the American poet Ralph Waldo Emerson was also a noted philosopher. Inspired by the Romantic movement, he believed in the unity of nature, with every single particle of matter and each individual mind being a microcosm of the entire universe. Emerson was famous for his public lectures, which urged the rejection of social conformity and traditional authority. Emerson advocated personal integrity and self-reliance as the only moral imperatives, stressing that every human being has the power to shape his own destiny.

See also: Henry David Thoreau 204 ▪ William James 206–09 ▪ Friedrich Nietzsche 214–21

HENRY SIDGWICK
1838–1900

The English moral philosopher Henry Sidgwick was a fellow of Trinity College, Cambridge. In his key work *Methods of Ethics* (1874), he explored the problems of free will by examining intuitive principles of conduct. The pursuit of pleasure, he claimed, does not exclude altruism, or the providing of pleasure for others, since providing pleasure for others is itself a pleasure. A liberal philanthropist and a champion of women's rights to education, Sidgwick was instrumental in setting up Newnham, Cambridge's first college for female students.

See also: Jeremy Bentham 174 ▪ John Stuart Mill 190–93

FRANZ BRENTANO
1838–1917

Born in Prussia, the philosopher Franz Brentano is best known for establishing psychology as a discipline in its own right. Initially a priest, he was unable to reconcile himself with the concept of papal infallibility, and left the Church in 1873. Brentano believed that mental processes were not passive, but should be seen as intentional acts. His most highly regarded work is *Psychology from an Empirical Standpoint*. Its publication in 1874 led to him being offered a professorship at the University of Vienna, where he taught and inspired a host of illustrious students, including the founder of psychoanalysis, Sigmund Freud.

See also: Edmund Husserl 224–25

GOTTLOB FREGE
1848–1925

A professor of mathematics at Jena University, the German philosopher Gottlob Frege was a pioneer of the the analytic tradition in philosophy. His first major work *Begriffsschrift* (1879), meaning "conceptual notation", and *The Foundations of Arithmetic* (1884) effected a revolution in philosophical logic, allowing the discipline to develop rapidly. In *On Sense and Reference* (1892) he showed that sentences are meaningful for two reasons – for having a thing that they refer to, and a unique way in which that reference is made.

See also: Bertrand Russell 236–39 ▪ Ludwig Wittgenstein 246–51 ▪ Rudolf Carnap 257

ALFRED NORTH WHITEHEAD
1861–1947

An English mathematician, Alfred North Whitehead had a significant influence on ethics, metaphysics, and the philosophy of science. With his ex-pupil Bertrand Russell, he wrote the landmark study on mathematical logic, *Principia Mathematica* (1910–13). In 1924, at the age of 63, he accepted a chair in philosophy at Harvard, USA. There he developed what became known as process philosophy. This was based on his conviction that traditional philosophical categories were inadequate in dealing with the interactions between matter, space, and time, and that "the living organ or experience is the living body as a whole" and not just the brain.

See also: Bertrand Russell 236–39 ▪ Willard Van Orman Quine 278–79

NISHIDA KITARO
1870–1945

Japanese philosopher Nishida Kitaro studied Daoism and Confucianism at school and Western philosophy at Tokyo University. He went on to teach at Kyoto University, where he established Western philosophy as an object of serious study in Japan. Key to his thinking is the "logic of place", designed to overcome traditional Western oppositions between subject and object through the "pure experience" of Zen Buddhism, in which distinctions between knower and thing known, self and world, are lost.

See also: Laozi 24–25 ▪ Siddharta Gautama 30–33 ▪ Confucius 34–39 ▪ Hajime Tanabe 244–45

ERNST CASSIRER
1874-1945

Born in Bresslau, in what is now Poland, the German philosopher Ernst Cassirer lectured at Berlin University and then at Hamburg, where he had access to the vast collection of studies on tribal cultures and myths in the Warburg Library. These were to inform his major work *The Philosophy of Symbolic Forms* (1923–29), in which he incorporated mythical thinking into a philosophical system similar to Immanuel Kant's. In 1933, Cassirer fled Europe to escape the rise of Nazism, continuing his work in America, and later Sweden.

See also: Immanuel Kant 164–71 ▪ Martin Heidegger 252–55

GASTON BACHELARD
1884-1962

The French philosopher Gaston Bachelard studied physics before switching to philosophy. He taught at Dijon University, going on to become the first professor of history and philosophy of the sciences at the Sorbonne in Paris. His study of thought processes encompasses the symbolism of dreams and the phenomenology of imagination. He contested Auguste Comte's view that scientific advancement was continuous, claiming instead that science often moves through shifts in historical perspective allowing fresh interpretations of old concepts.

See also: Auguste Comte 335 ▪ Thomas Kuhn 293 ▪ Michel Foucault 302–03

ERNST BLOCH
c.1885–1977

A German Marxist philosopher, Ernst Bloch's work focuses on the possibility of a humanistic utopian world, free of exploitation and oppression. During World War I he took refuge from the conflict in Switzerland, and in 1933 fled the Nazis, ending up in the United States. Here he began his key work, *The Principle of Hope* (1947). After World War II, Bloch taught in Leipzig – but with the building of the Berlin Wall in 1961, he sought asylum in West Germany. Although he was an atheist, Bloch believed that religion's mystical vision of heaven on earth is attainable.

See also: Georg Hegel 178–85 ▪ Karl Marx 196–203

GILBERT RYLE
1900–1976

Born in Brighton on the south coast of England, Gilbert Ryle studied and taught at Oxford University. He believed that many problems in philosophy arise from the abuse of language. He showed that we often assume expressions that function in a similar way grammatically are members of the same logical category. Such "category mistakes", Ryle stated, are the cause of much philosophical confusion, so careful attention to the underlying function of ordinary language is the way to overcome philosophical problems.

See also: Thomas Hobbes 112–15 ▪ Ludwig Wittgenstein 246–51 ▪ Daniel Dennett 339

MICHAEL OAKESHOTT
1901–1990

Michael Oakeshott was a British political theorist and philosopher. He taught at Cambridge and Oxford universities, before becoming Professor of Political Science at the London School of Economics. Works such as *On Being Conservative* (1956) and *Rationalism in Politics and Other Essays* (1962) cemented his fame as a political theorist. He had an important influence on Conservative party politics in the late 20th century. However, since he frequently revised his opinions, his work defies categorization.

See also: Edmund Burke 172–73 ▪ Georg Hegel 178–85

AYN RAND
1905–1982

The writer and philosopher Ayn Rand was born in Russia, but moved to the United States in 1926. She was working as a screenwriter when her novel *The Fountainhead* (1943), the story of an ideal man, made her famous. She is the founder of Objectivism, which challenges the idea that man's moral duty is to live for others. Reality exists as an objective absolute and man's reasoning is his manner of perceiving it.

See also: Aristotle 56–63 ▪ Adam Smith 160–63

JOHN LANGSHAW AUSTIN
1911–1960

Educated at Oxford University, where he also taught, the British philosopher John Langshaw Austin was a leading figure in "ordinary language" or "Oxford" philosophy, which became fashionable in the 1950s. Austin argued that rigorous analysis of how language operates in ordinary everyday usage can lead to the discovery of the subtle linguistic distinctions needed to resolve profound philosophical problems. He is best known from his papers and lectures that were published after his death as *How to do Things with Words* (1962) and *Sense and Sensibilia* (1964).
See also: Bertrand Russell 236–39 ▪ Gilbert Ryle 337

DONALD DAVIDSON
1917–2003

The American philosopher Donald Davidson studied at Harvard and went on to a distinguished career teaching at various American universities. He was involved in several areas of philosophy, notably the philosophy of mind. He held a materialist position, stating that each token mental event was also a physical event, although he did not believe that the mental could be entirely reduced to, or explained in terms of, the physical. Davidson also made notable contributions to the philosophy of language, arguing that a language must have a finite number of elements and that its meaning is a product of these elements and rules of combination.
See also: Ludwig Wittgenstein 246–51 ▪ Willard Van Orman Quine 278–79

LOUIS ALTHUSSER
1918–1990

Born in Algeria, the French Marxist scholar Louis Althusser argued that there is a radical difference between Marx's early writings and the "scientific" period of Capital (*Das Kapital*). The early works of Marx reflect the times with their focus on Hegelian concepts such as alienation, whereas in the mature work, history is seen as having its own momentum, independent of the intentions and actions of human agents. Therefore Althusser's claim that we are determined by the structural conditions of society involves the controversial rejection of human autonomy, denying individual agency a role in history.
See also: Georg Hegel 178–85 ▪ Karl Marx 196–203 ▪ Michel Foucault 302–03 ▪ Slavoj Žižek 326

EDGAR MORIN
1921–

The French philosopher Edgar Morin was born in Paris, the son of Jewish immigrants from Greece. His positive view of the progress of Western civilization is tempered by what he perceives as the negative effects of technical and scientific advances. Progress may create wealth but also seems to bring with it a breakdown of responsibility and global awareness. Morin developed what became known as "complex thought" and coined the term "politics of civilization". His six-volume *Method* (1977–2004) is a compendium of his thoughts and ideas, offering a broad insight into the nature of human enquiry.
See also: Theodor Adorno 266–67 ▪ Jürgen Habermas 306–07

RENE GIRARD
1923–

The French philosopher and historian René Girard writes and teaches across a wide range of subjects, from economics to literary criticism. He is best known for his theory of mimetic desire. In *Deceit, Desire and the Novel* (1961), Girard uses ancient mythology and modern fiction to show that human desire, as distinct from animal appetite, is always aroused by the desire of another. His study of the origins of violence, *Violence and the Sacred* (1972), goes further by arguing that this imitated desire leads to conflict and violence. Religion, Girard states, originated with the process of victimization or sacrifice that was used to quell the violence.
See also: Michel Foucault 302–03

GILLES DELEUZE
1925–1995

Gilles Deleuze was born in Paris and spent most of his life there. He saw philosophy as a creative process for constructing concepts, rather than an attempt to discover and reflect reality. Much of his work was in the history of philosophy, yet his readings did not attempt to disclose the "true" Nietzsche, for example. Instead they rework the conceptual mechanisms of a philosopher's subject to produce new ideas, opening up new avenues of thought. Deleuze is also known for collaborations with psychoanalyst Félix Guattari – *Anti-Oedipus* (1972) and *What is Philosophy* (1991) – and for his commentaries on literature, film, and art.
See also: Henri Bergson 226–27 ▪ Michel Foucault 302–03

NIKLAS LUHMANN
1927–1998

Born in Lüneburg, Germany, Niklas Luhmann was captured by the Americans during World War II, when he was just 17. After the war he worked as a lawyer until, in 1962, he took a sabbatical to study sociology in America. He went on to become one of the most important and prolific social theorists of the 20th century. Luhmann developed a grand theory, to explain every element of social life, from complex well-established societies to the briefest of exchanges, lasting just seconds. In his most important work, *The Society of Society* (1997), he argues that communication is the only genuinely social phenomenon.
See also: Jürgen Habermas 306-07

MICHEL SERRES
1930–

The French author and philosopher Michel Serres studied mathematics before taking up philosophy. He is a professor at Stanford University in California and a member of the prestigious Académie Française. His lectures and books are presented in French, with an elegance and fluidity that is hard to translate. His post-humanist enquiries take the form of "maps", where the journeys themselves play an major role. He has been described as a "thinker for whom voyaging is invention", finding truths in the chaos, discord, and disorder revealed in the links between the sciences, arts, and contemporary culture.
See also: Roland Barthes 290–91 ▪ Jacques Derrida 308–13

DANIEL DENNETT
1942–

Born in Beirut, the American philosopher Daniel Dennett is an acclaimed expert on the nature of cognitive systems. Professor of Philosophy at Tufts University, Massachusetts, he is noted for his wide-ranging expertise in linguistics, artificial intelligence, neuroscience, and psychology. Using memorable and creative labels, such as "Joycean machine" for stream of consciousness, he argues that the source of free will and consciousness is the brain's computational circuitry, which tricks us into thinking we are more intelligent than we actually are.
See also: Gilbert Ryle 337 ▪ Willard Van Orman Quine 278–79 ▪ Michel Foucault 302–03

MARCEL GAUCHET
1946–

The French philosopher, historian, and sociologist Marcel Gauchet has written widely on democracy and the role of religion in the modern world. He is the editor of the intellectual French periodical *Le Débat* and a professor at the École des Hautes Etudes en Sciences Sociales (EHESS) in Paris. His key work, *The Disenchantment of the World: A Political History of Religion* (1985), explores the modern cult of individualism in the context of man's religious past. As religious belief declines across the Western world, Gauchet argues that elements of the sacred has been incorporated into human relationships and other social activities.
See also: Maurice Merleau-Ponty 274–75 ▪ Michel Foucault 302–03

MARTHA NUSSBAUM
1947–

Born in New York City, American philosopher Martha Nussbaum is the Ernst Freund Distinguished Service Professor of Law and Ethics at the University of Chicago. She has published numerous books and papers, mainly on ethics and political philosophy, where the rigour of her academic enquiry is always informed by a passionate liberalism. Her exploration of ancient Greek ethics, *The Fragility of Goodness* (1986), first brought her acclaim, but she is now equally well-known for her liberal views on feminism, as expressed in *Sex and Social Justice* (1999), which argues for radical change in gender and family relationships.
See also: Plato 50–55 ▪ Aristotle 56–63 ▪ John Rawls 294–95

ISABELLE STENGERS
1949–

Isabelle Stengers was born in Belgium and studied chemistry at the Free University of Brussels, where she is now Professor of Philosophy. She was awarded the grand prize for philosophy by the Académie Française in 1993. A distinguished thinker on science, Stengers has written extensively about modern scientific processes, with an focus on the use of science for social ends and its relationship to power and authority. Her books include *Power and Invention* (1997) and *The Invention of Modern Science* (2000), and *Order Out of Chaos* (1984) with the Nobel Prize-winning chemist Ilya Prigogine.
See also: Alfred North Whitehead 336 ▪ Edgar Morin 338

GLOSSARY

the Absolute Ultimate reality conceived of as an all-embracing, single principle. Some thinkers have identified this principle with God; others have believed in the Absolute but not in God; others have not believed in either. The philosopher most closely associated with the idea is Georg Hegel.

Aesthetics A branch of philosophy concerned with the principles of art and the notion of beauty.

Agent The doing self, as distinct from the knowing self; the self that decides or chooses or acts.

Analysis The search for a deeper understanding of something by taking it to pieces and looking at each part. The opposite approach is **synthesis**.

Analytic philosophy A view of philosophy that sees its aim as clarification – the clarification of concepts, statements, methods, **arguments**, and theories by carefully taking them apart.

Analytic statement A statement whose truth or falsehood can be established by **analysis** of the statement itself. The opposite is a **synthetic statement**.

Anthropomorphism The attribution of human characteristics to something that is not human; for instance to God or to the weather.

A posteriori Something that can be considered **valid** only by means of experience.

A priori Something known to be **valid** in advance of (or without need of) experience.

Argument A process of reasoning in **logic** that purports to show its conclusion to be true.

Category The broadest class or group into which things can be divided. Aristotle and Immanuel Kant both tried to provide a complete list of categories.

Concept A thought or idea; the meaning of a word or term.

Contingent May or may not be the case; things could be either way. The opposite is **necessary**.

Contradictory Two statements are contradictory if one must be true and the other false: they cannot both be true, nor can they both be false.

Contrary Two statements are contrary if they cannot both be true but may both be false.

Corroboration Evidence that lends support to a conclusion without necessarily proving it.

Cosmology The study of the whole universe, the cosmos.

Deduction Reasoning from the general to the particular – for instance, "If all men are mortal then Socrates, being a man, must be mortal." It is universally agreed that deduction is **valid**. The opposite process is called **induction**.

Determinism The view that nothing can happen other than what does happen, because every event is the **necessary** outcome of causes preceding it – which themselves were the necessary outcome of causes preceding them. The opposite is **indeterminism**.

Dialectic i) Skill in questioning or argument. ii) The idea that any assertion, whether in word or deed, evokes opposition, the two of which are reconciled in a **synthesis** that includes elements of both.

Dualism A view of something as made up of two **irreducible** parts, such as the idea of human beings as consisting of bodies and minds, the two being radically unlike.

Emotive Expressing emotion. In philosophy the term is often used in a derogatory way for utterances that pretend to be objective or impartial while in fact expressing emotional attitudes, as for example in "emotive definition".

Empirical knowledge Knowledge of the **empirical world**.

Empirical statement A statement about the **empirical world**; what is or could be experienced.

Empirical world The world as revealed to us by our actual or possible experience.

Empiricism The view that all knowledge of anything that actually exists must be derived from experience.

Epistemology The branch of philosophy concerned with what sort of thing, if anything, we can know; how we know it; and what knowledge is. In practice it is the dominant branch of philosophy.

Essence The essence of a thing is that which is distinctive about it and makes it what it is. For instance, the essence of a unicorn is that it is a horse with a single horn on its head. Unicorns do not exist of course – so essence does not imply existence. This distinction is important in philosophy.

Ethics A branch of philosophy that is concerned with questions about how we should live, and therefore about the nature of right and wrong, good and bad, ought and ought not, duty, and other such concepts.

Existentialism A philosophy that begins with the **contingent** existence of the individual human being and regards that as the primary enigma. It is from this starting point that philosophical understanding is pursued.

Fallacy A seriously wrong **argument**, or a false conclusion based on such an argument.

Falsifiability A statement, or set of statements, is falsifiable if it can be proved wrong by empirical testing. According to Karl Popper, falsifiability is what distinguishes science from non-science.

Humanism A philosophical approach based on the assumption that mankind is the most important thing that exists, and that there can be no knowledge of a supernatural world, if any such world exists.

Hypothesis A theory whose truth is assumed for the time being because it forms a useful starting point for further investigation, despite limited evidence to prove its **validity**.

Idealism The view that reality consists ultimately of something non-material, whether it be mind, the contents of mind, spirits, or one spirit. The opposite point of view is **materialism**.

Indeterminism The view that not all events are **necessary** outcomes of events that may have preceded them. The opposite is point of view is **determinism**.

Induction Reasoning from the particular to the general. An example would be "Socrates died, Plato died, Aristotle died, and each other individual man who was born more than 130 years ago has died. Therefore all men are mortal." Induction does not necessarily yield results that are true, so whether it is genuinely a logical process is disputed. The opposite process is called **deduction**.

Intuition Direct knowing, whether by sensory perception or by insight; a form of knowledge that makes no use of reasoning.

Irreducible An irreducible thing is one that cannot be brought to a simpler or reduced form.

Linguistic philosophy Also known as linguistic analysis. The view that philosophical problems arise from a muddled use of language, and are to be solved, or dissolved, by a careful **analysis** of the language in which they have been expressed.

Logic The branch of philosophy that makes a study of rational **argument** itself – its terms, concepts, rules, and methods.

Logical positivism The view that the only **empirical statements** that are meaningful are those that are **verifiable**.

Materialism The doctrine that all real existence is ultimately of something material. The opposite point of view is **idealism**.

Metaphilosophy The branch of philosophy that looks at the nature and methods of philosophy itself.

Metaphysics The branch of philosophy concerned with the ultimate nature of what exists. It questions the natural world "from outside", and its questions cannot be answered by science.

Methodology The study of methods of enquiry and **argument**.

Monism A view of something as formed by a single element; for example, the view that human beings do not consist of elements that are ultimately separable, like a body and a soul, but are of one single substance.

Mysticism Intuitive knowledge that transcends the natural world.

Naturalism The view that reality is explicable without reference to anything outside the natural world.

Necessary Must be the case. The opposite is **contingent**. Hume believed that necessary connections existed only in **logic**, not in the real world, a view that has been upheld by many philosophers since.

Necessary and sufficient conditions For X to be a husband it is a necessary condition for X to be married. However, this is not a sufficient condition – for what if X is female? A sufficient condition for X to be a husband is that X is both a man and married. One of the commonest forms of error in thinking is to mistake necessary conditions for sufficient conditions.

Non-contradictory Statements are considered non-contradictory if their **truth-values** are independent of one another.

Noumenon The unknowable reality behind what presents itself to human consciousness, the latter being known as **phenomenon**. A thing as it is in itself, independently of being experienced, is said to be the noumenon. "The noumenal" has therefore become a term for the ultimate nature of reality.

Numinous Anything regarded as mysterious and awesome, bearing intimations from outside the natural realm. Not to be confused with the noumenal; see **noumenon** above.

Ontology A branch of philosophy that asks what actually exists, as distinct from the nature of our knowledge of it, which is covered by the branch of **epistemology**. Ontology and epistemology taken together constitute the central tradition of philosophy.

Phenomenology An approach to philosophy which investigates objects of experience (known as **phenomena**) only to the extent that they manifest themselves in our consciousness, without making any assumptions about their nature as independent things.

Phenomenon An experience that is immediately present. If I look at an object, the object as experienced by me is a phenomenon. Immanuel Kant distinguished this from the object as it is in itself, independently of being experienced: this he called the **noumenon**.

Philosophy Literally, "the love of wisdom". The word is widely used for any sustained **rational** reflection about general principles that has the aim of achieving a deeper understanding. Philosophy provides training in the disciplined **analysis** and clarification of **arguments**, theories, methods, and utterances of all kinds, and the concepts of which they make use. Traditionally, its ultimate aim has been to attain a better understanding of the world, though in the 20th century a good deal of philosophy became devoted to attaining a better understanding of its own procedures.

Philosophy of religion The branch of philosophy that looks at human belief systems and the real or imaginary objects, such as gods, that form the basis for these beliefs.

Philosophy of science A branch of philosophy concerned with the nature of scientific knowledge and the practice of scientific endeavour.

Political philosophy The branch of philosophy that questions the nature and methods of the state and deals with such subjects as justice, law, social hierarchies, political power, and constitutions.

Postmodernism A viewpoint that holds a general distrust of theories, narratives, and ideologies that attempt to put all knowledge into a single framework.

Pragmatism A theory of truth. It holds that a statement is true if it does all the jobs required of it: accurately describes a situation; prompts us to anticipate experience correctly; fits in with already well-attested statements; and so on.

Premise The starting point of an **argument**. Any argument has to start from at least one premise, and therefore does not prove its own premises. A **valid** argument proves that its conclusions follow from its premises – but this is not the same as proving that its conclusions are true, which is something no argument can do.

Presupposition Something taken for granted but not expressed. All utterances have presuppositions, and these may be conscious or unconscious. If a presupposition is mistaken, an utterance based on it may also be mistaken, though the mistake may not evident in the utterance itself. The study of philosophy teaches us to become more aware of presuppositions.

Primary and secondary qualities John Locke divided the **properties** of a physical object into those that are possessed by the object independently of being experienced, such as its location, dimensions, velocity, mass, and so on (which he called primary qualities), and those that involve the interaction of an experiencing observer, such as the object's colour and taste (which he called secondary qualities).

Property In philosophy this word is commonly used to mean a characteristic; for example "fur or hair is a defining property of a mammal". See also **primary and secondary qualities**.

Rational Based on, or according to, the principles of reason or **logic**.

Proposition The content of a statement that confirms or denies whether something is the case, and is capable of being true or false.

Rationalism The view that we can gain knowledge of the world through the use of reason, without relying on sense-perception, which is regarded by rationalists as unreliable. The opposite view is known as **empiricism**.

Scepticism The view that it is impossible for us to know anything for certain.

Semantics The study of meanings in linguistic expressions.

Semiotics The study of signs and symbols, in particular their relationships with the things they are meant to signify.

Social contract An implicit agreement among members of a society to cooperate in order to achieve goals that benefit the whole group, sometimes at the expense of individuals within it.

Solipsism The view that only the existence of the self can be known.

Sophist Someone whose aim in **argument** is not to seek the truth but to win the argument. In ancient Greece, young men aspiring to public life were taught by sophists to learn the various methods of winning arguments.

Synthesis Seeking a deeper understanding of something by putting the pieces together. The opposite is **analysis**.

Synthetic statement A statement that has to be set against facts outside itself for its truth to be determined. The opposite is an **analytic statement**.

Teleology A study of ends or goals. A teleological explanation is one that explains something in terms of the ends that it serves.

Theology Enquiry into scholarly and intellectual questions concerning the nature of God. Philosophy, by contrast, does not assume the existence of God, though some philosophers have attempted to prove his existence.

Thing-in-itself Another term for a **noumenon**, from the German *Ding-an-sich*.

Transcendental Outside the world of sense experience. Someone who believes that **ethics** are transcendental believes that ethics have their source outside the **empirical world**. Thoroughgoing **empiricists** do not believe that anything transcendental exists, and nor did Friedrich Nietzsche or humanist **existentialists**.

Truth-value Either of two values, namely true or false, that can be applied to a statement.

Universal A concept of general application, like "red" or "woman". It has been disputed whether universals have an existence of their own. Does "redness" exist, or are there only individual red objects? In the Middle Ages, philosophers who believed that "redness" had a real existence were called "realists", while philosophers who maintained that it was no more than a word were called "nominalists".

Universalism The belief that we should apply to ourselves the same standards and values that we apply to others. Not to be confused with **universal**, above.

Utilitarianism A theory of politics and **ethics** that judges the morality of actions by their consequences, that regards the most desirable consequence of any action as the greatest good of the greatest number, and that defines "good" in terms of pleasure and the absence of pain.

Validity An **argument** is valid if its conclusion follows from its **premises**. This does not necessarily mean that the conclusion is true: it may be false if one of the premises is false, though the argument itself is still valid.

Verifiability A statement or set of statements can be verified if it can be proved to be true by looking at empirical evidence. **Logical positivists** believed that the only **empirical statements** that were meaningful were those that were verifiable. David Hume and Karl Popper pointed out that scientific laws were unverifiable.

World In philosophy the word "world" has been given a special sense, meaning "the whole of empirical reality", and may therefore also be equated with the totality of actual and possible experience. True **empiricists** believe that the world is all there is, but philosophers with different views believe that the world does not account for total reality. Such philosophers believe that there is a **transcendental** realm as well as an empirical realm, and they may believe that both are equally real.

INDEX

Numbers in **bold** refer to main entries, those in *italics* refer to the captions to illustrations.

M

N

O

ACKNOWLEDGMENTS

Dorling Kindersley would like to thank Debra Wolter and Nigel Ritchie for their editorial assistance, Vicky Short for her design assistance, and Jane Parker for providing the index and proofreading the book.

PICTURE CREDITS

The publisher would like to thank the following for their kind permission to reproduce their photographs:

(Key: a-above; b-below/bottom; c-centre; l-left; r-right; t-top)

23 Getty Images: Hulton Archive (tr). **25 Corbis:** Chan Yat Nin / Redlink (cl). **Getty Images:** Hulton Archive (bl). **27 Alamy Images:** Gianni Dagli Orti / The Art Archive (bl). **29 Getty Images:** M. Bertinetti / De Agostini Picture Library (br). **31 Alamy Images:** INTERFOTO (tr). **32 The Bridgeman Art Library:** Musée Guimet, Paris / Bonora (tl). **36 Getty Images:** Keren Su (bl). **38 Corbis:** Christian Kober / JAI (tr). **39 The Art Archive:** (br). **41 Corbis:** Visuals Unlimited (cra). **43 akg-images:** Wadsworth Atheneum (bl). **Getty Images:** G. Dagli Orti / De Agostini Picture Library (cr). **44 Corbis:** Bettmann (cr). **47 Corbis:** PoodlesRock (tr). **49 Corbis:** (br). **53 The Bridgeman Art Library:** Bibliothèque nationale, Paris / Archives Charmet (br). **55 The Bridgeman Art Library:** Pinacoteca Capitolina, Palazzo Conservatori, Rome / Alinari (tl). **Corbis:** Jon Hicks (bl). **59 Getty Images:** The Bridgeman Art Library (tl). **60 Corbis:** Elizabeth Whiting & Associates (tl). **63 akg-images:** British Library (tl). **Getty Images:** SuperStock (bl). **64 Réunion des Musées Nationaux Agence Photographique:** Hervé Lewandowski (bc). **65 Corbis:** Araldo de Luca (tr). **66 The Bridgeman Art Library:** Walters Art Museum, Baltimore, USA (cra). **73 Getty Images:** The Bridgeman Art Library (bl); SuperStock (tr). **75 The Bridgeman Art Library:** Bibliothèque municipale, Rouen / Giraudon (tr). **Getty Images:** Hulton Archive (bl). **77 Alamy Images:** Mary Evans Picture Library (tr). **78 Alamy Images:** Gianni Dagli Orti / The Art Archive (bl). **79 The Kobal Collection:** New Line Cinema (br). **81 Getty Images:** Hulton Archive (tr). **83 Corbis:** Bettmann (bl). **Photolibrary:** Dariush Zandi / GraphEast RM (cr). **85 Getty Images:** The Bridgeman Art Library (bl); Danita Delimont / Gallo Images (tr). **87 Alamy Images:** Gianni Dagli Orti / The Art Archive (tr). **Getty Images:** Bruno Morandi / The Image Bank (tl). **90 Getty Images:** Science & Society Picture Library (bl). **91 Alamy Images:** Gianni Dagli Orti / The Art Archive (tl). **92 Alamy Images:** Gianni Dagli Orti / The Art Archive (b). **94 Getty Images:** Chad Baker (bc). **95 NASA:** LAMBDA / WMAP Science Team (tr). **105 Corbis:** Massimo Listri (tl). **107 Corbis:** Bettmann (tr) (bl). **109 Alamy Images:** Gianni Dagli Orti / The Art Archive (bl). **Corbis:** Bettmann (tr). **111 akg-images:** (tl). **Corbis:** Bettmann (tr). **113 Corbis:** Bettmann (tr). **114 Science Photo Library:** David McCarthy. **115 Corbis:** Bettmann (br). **118 Getty Images:** Hulton Archive (cra). **120 akg-images:** Cameraphoto (tl). **122 Corbis:** Bettmann (bl). **123 Corbis:** Alberto Estevez / EPA (br). **125 Corbis:** Michael Nicholson (bl); Bill Varie (tr). **128 Alamy Images:** Gari Wyn Williams (tl). **Corbis:** Bettmann (bl). **129 Dorling Kindersley:** Natural History Museum, London (cr/flower on rock). **133 Corbis:** Bettmann (bl); LWA - Dann Tardif (tr). **135 Corbis:** Bettmann (tr). **136 Science Photo Library:** Matthew Hurst (tl). **137 Getty Images:** Science & Society Picture Library (tr). **139 Corbis:** Bettmann (tr). **147 Corbis:** Bettmann (bl). **Getty Images:** G. Dagli Orti / De Agostini Picture Library (tr). **150 Corbis:** Michael Nicholson (tr). **151 Corbis:** Ken Seet (bl). **152 Corbis:** Tomas del Amo - The Stock Connec / Science Faction (clb/tap). **153 Alamy Images:** Lebrecht Music & Arts Photo Library (tr). **157 The Bridgeman Art Library:** Detroit Institute of Arts, USA (bl). **Corbis:** Bettmann (tr). **158 Alamy Images:** V&A Images (bl). **159 Getty Images:** Peter Willi / SuperStock (br). **161 Corbis:** Hulton-Deutsch Collection (tr). **162 The Art Archive:** Museum of London (bl). **163 Corbis:** Karen Kasmauski (tr). **166 Dorling Kindersley:** Stephen Oliver (tr) (tl/tree in summer). **169 Getty Images:** Matheisl (tl/tree in winter). **170 Corbis:** Bettmann (bl). **171 Getty Images:** Hulton Archive (tr). **173 Corbis:** Bettmann (tr); Gianni Dagli Orti / The Art Archive (bc). **177 Getty Images:** David Sanger / The Image Bank (br). **180 The Bridgeman Art Library:** American Illustrators Gallery, NYC / www.asapworldwide.com (tr). **Corbis:** Bettmann (bl). **184 The Bridgeman Art Library:** Château de Versailles (bl). **185 The Bridgeman Art Library:** Germanisches Nationalmuseum, Nuremberg (Nuernberg) (br). **187 Getty Images:** Time Life Pictures / Mansell (tr). **188 akg-images:** British Library (bl). **189 The Bridgeman Art Library:** National Gallery, London (br). **191 Corbis:** Bettmann (tr). **192 Corbis:** Todd Gipstein (bl). **193 Corbis:** Bettmann (tc). **195 Corbis:** Bettmann (bl); Robbie Jack (tr). **198 Corbis:** Alfredo Dagli Orti / The Art Archive (tr). **200 Getty Images:** The Bridgeman Art Library (bl). **201 Alamy Images:** Gianni Dagli Orti / The Art Archive (br). **202 Alamy Images:** Gianni Dagli Orti / The Art Archive (tl). **203 The Bridgeman Art Library:** Private Collection (bl). **Corbis:** Bettmann (tr). **204 Alamy Images:** Dinodia Images / India Images (br). **208 akg-images:** (tl). **Corbis:** (bl). **209 Corbis:** Bettmann (bl). **217 Corbis:** Bettmann (bl); Kazuyoshi Nomachi (tr). **218 Corbis:** Bettmann (bl). **219 Corbis:** Bettmann (ca/Apollo); Jon Hicks (cra/saint). **220 Corbis:** The Gallery Collection (tl). **221 Getty Images:** Hulton Archive (b). **225 Getty Images:** Jeffrey Coolidge (bl); Imagno / Hulton Archive (tr). **227 Corbis:** Bettmann (bl). **Getty Images:** Richard Passmore (tr). **229 Corbis:** Bettmann (tr). **230 Getty Images:** G. Dagli Orti / De Agostini Picture Library (tr). **231 Corbis:** Philadelphia Museum of Art (tl). **232 Corbis:** Alan Schein Photography (bc). **235 Corbis:** Bettmann (bl); Hulton-Deutsch Collection (tr). **237 Getty Images:** MPI (tr). **238 Corbis:** Bettmann (clb). **239 The Advertising Archives. 241 Corbis:** The Gallery Collection (b). **243 Corbis:** Bettmann (tr). **TopFoto.co.uk:** FotoWare FotoStation (bl). **245 The Bridgeman Art**

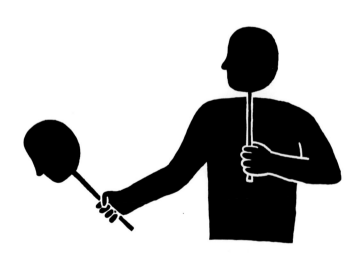